AN UNCOMMON CAPE

excelsior editions

AN IMPRINT OF STATE UNIVERSITY OF NEW YORK PRESS

an UNCOMMON *cape*

Researching the Histories and Mysteries of a Property

ELEANOR PHILLIPS BRACKBILL

cover photograph: Michael Torlen
painting, page i: Michael Torlen

Slightly different versions of chapters 2 and 6 were previously published in *The Hudson River Valley Review* and *The Westchester Historian*.

Published by
STATE UNIVERSITY OF NEW YORK PRESS, ALBANY

EXCELSIOR EDITIONS
is an imprint of State University of New York Press

Printed in the United States of America

For information, contact State University of New York Press, Albany, NY
www.sunypress.edu

Production and book design, Laurie Searl
Marketing, Fran Keneston

LIBRARY OF CONGRESS CATALOGING-IN-PUBLICATION DATA

Brackbill, Eleanor Phillips.
An uncommon cape : researching the histories and mysteries of a property / Eleanor Phillips Brackbill.
p. cm.
"Excelsior editions."
Includes bibliographical references and index.
ISBN 978-1-4384-4307-2 (hardcover : alk. paper) 1. Brackbill, Eleanor Phillips—Homes and haunts—New York (State)—Mamaroneck. 2. Cape Cod houses—New York (State)—Mamaroneck. 3. Mamaroneck (N.Y.)—History. 4. Mamaroneck (N.Y.)—Biography. I. Title.
F129.M17B73 2012
974.7'277—dc23

2011036270

10 9 8 7 6 5 4 3 2 1

To Michael and Liz,

who have shared our place and my journey

Contents

PART III
MYSTERIES OF THE LAND

Illustrations

Acknowledgments

Over the course of eight years spent researching and writing this book, many people aided and supported me. I am indebted to those who generously provided information or who facilitated the process of finding it: Terry Ariano, Somers Historical Society; Joan Berkowitz, Jablonski Berkowitz Conservation, Inc.; Heather Craane, Jay Heritage Center; Karen L. Frederick, Curator of Museum Collections, Greenwich Historical Society; Bill Gorman, New York State Archives; Jackie Graziano, Westchester County Archives; Eva Guggemos, Beinecke Rare Book and Manuscript Library, Yale University; Steven Haynes, Maine Granite Industry Historical Society; Margaret K. Hofer, Curator of Decorative Arts, New-York Historical Society; Joy Kestenbaum, Lauren Lazar, and Carrie Marten, Purchase College Library; Thomas Lannon and Lee Robinson, New York Public Library; Russell Lord, Metropolitan Museum of Art; Sarah Hermanson Meister, Katie Trainor, and Leslie Ureña, Museum of Modern Art; Gloria Pritts, Town of Mamaroneck Archives; and Jeffrey Williams, Westchester County Department of Planning. In addition, I would like to thank the following individuals and institutions: Susan Benton, Mamaroneck Public Library; Lynne Crowley, Larchmont Historical Society; Coi Drummond-Gehrig, Denver Public Library; Estate of Edward Steichen; Nancy Finlay and John Potter, Connecticut Historical Society; Todd Fix and Richard Wills, Royal Barry Wills Associates; Cynthia Gallaher, Neysa McMein Virtual Museum; Rory Glaeseman, *Journal News*; Pat Gordon and Vivian M. Santangelo, Meredith Corporation; Erica Green, Anne & Gordon Samstag Museum of Art, University of South Australia; Annika Keller and Tricia Smith, Art Resource; Library of Congress, Geography and Map Division and Prints and Photographs Division; Matthew Lutts, AP Images; Liz Mahoney, Environmental Data Resources; Carolyn B. Mandelker, Harrison Edwards Public Relations & Marketing; Arlene May, Sears Holdings Historical

Archives; Metropolitan Museum of Art; Kathleen Mylen-Coulombe, Yale University Art Gallery; Emma Rock; Caroline Robinson, Roton Point Association; Charles Seton, photographer; Town of Mamaroneck Assessor's Department; Westchester County Historical Society; Laurie Platt Winfrey, Carousel Research, Inc.; and Dallan C. Wordekemper, United States Postal Service.

Special thanks are due to Lori Friedli, head of adult reference, Mamaroneck Public Library, for help with some of the images and for asking, "Are you writing a book?" when I didn't yet know that I was, and to Thomas J. Schwarz, president, Purchase College, State University of New York, who responded warmly to an early presentation of the material and first recognized the value of including information on the research methodology.

Research involves a web, the linking of many threads in an ever-expanding network. The people who helped with the threads, giving me ideas or leads to other sources, include Jim Frank, Tom Panetiere, Richard Pieper, Marty Rennert, Ken Resen, Marj Simon, Simon D. Smith, Judy and Sol Tane, and Atiba Wilson. Several people kindly granted me access to their property: Kira and Brian Nickerson, Wendy Satin, and Mr. and Mrs. James Spindleman.

I am grateful to the many friends who gamely jumped into brainstorming with me as I wrestled with various hypotheses and who came up with numerous great ideas: Katherine Duncan Aimone and Steven Aimone; Don Ferencz; Scott Larson and Avis Larson, who purchased *McCall's* magazine on eBay for me; Charles Lyman, who assigned one of my mysteries to his materials lab class at Lehigh University and then helped me understand the results, and his student, Alexander Hollenbach, who spent two semesters at Lehigh University researching the date of the metal stakes; Page McBrier and Peter Morrison; Jon Pattengill; and members of the Neuberger Museum of Art volunteer research committee, who acted as a patient sounding board at moments throughout the project.

Many people provided advice and encouragement. Tracy Fitzpatrick, Lucy Hedrick, and Louisa V. North helped with guidance on the complexities of the publishing industry; Tom Foster and Dinah Seiver shared their experiences with publishing and copyright issues; and Beth Silver offered support and wise counsel in conjunction with another research and writing project unrelated to this book. Michael Lobel gave me encouragement on my writing as well as advice on publishing, and Patrice Giasson and Helaine Posner validated my editing skills. Patricia Bice and the Purchase College Professional Council invited me to present my research at an early stage, and many Purchase College and Neuberger Museum of Art colleagues responded positively to the presentation. Vicki Addesso, Beverley Brigandi, Michael Dick, Robert Funicello, Ann Ladd, Aline Libassi, Valerie Livingston, Tom Morck, Charles Phillips, Ginny Phillips, Marjatta Rautionmaa, and the docents of the Neuberger Museum of Art were interested cheerleaders. Debbie Allen and Steve Hoare of the Black Dome Press went out of their way to offer encouragement and suggestions after reviewing my book proposal. My editors at SUNY Press, James Peltz, Laurie D. Searl, and Timothy Loughman, guided the manuscript from acquisition to publication with amiability and aplomb.

I was fortunate to receive funds to support aspects of my research from Purchase College, State University of New York. Elizabeth G. Fuller and Katherine M. Hite, Westchester County Historical Society, and Chris Pryslopski, Hudson River Valley Institute at Marist College, decided to publish my articles, earlier versions of chapters two and six, in the *Westchester Historian* and the *Hudson River Valley Review* respectively, for which I am grateful. Richard Pieper and Simon D. Smith kindly allowed me to quote from their e-mails to me.

I would like to acknowledge my late parents for the dual gifts of appreciation for images and for history. My father was a serious photographer and my mother was passionate about history. On road trips he would take thousands of photographs to document our family vacations and she would stop regularly by the side of the road to read historic site markers, exclaiming, "Just think, it happened right here."

To my family I owe the most gratitude—to my daughter, Liz Blake, for always being encouraging, for helping with the maps, and for coming up with a key idea for chapter ten, and to my husband, Michael Torlen, for sharing the adventure of finding and living in our house, for being consistently supportive, even when he was writing his own book and pursuing other creative projects, for taking over more than his share of the domestic duties during the final few of months of manuscript preparation, and for assisting in many aspects of preparing this book, in particular, long hours spent working with me on the illustrations. Without his support the book would not have been written.

FIGURE 0.1 The house today. *(Photo by author.)*

Introduction

The day of the closing—that legal mumbo-jumbo moment of check signing and paper swapping when a property changes hands—I stood in the pouring rain outside the mortgage broker's office where the event was to take place. My husband had dropped me off to go park the car, and as I waited for the mystifying ritual to begin, I did my best to engage the seller in conversation. It was a minimal and strained exchange. I sensed that part of her did not want to sell the house and that she was not much interested in talking to me, but she did offer offhandedly, "It's a Sears house, or . . . something like that." The sale of her—but soon-to-be-our—house was upon us, the lawyers sat waiting, and there was no time to quiz her for more information. But I had heard all I needed to hear to embark on what became a quest to find out if what she had said was true.

Three weeks later, I began researching Sears houses, at first casually and then in earnest—on the Internet and in libraries. Sears, Roebuck mail-order, ready-to-assemble kit houses, manufactured from 1908 to 1940 and sent by rail car to their final destinations, had by this time acquired a certain cachet. I had been intrigued by them for a long time. My 1937 house both fit the time frame and was near a railroad line. Thrilled to think my house might be a Sears house, from the moment of that brief conversation I was determined to find proof that it was. But the Sears house notion was just the first of several mysterious bits of information in regard to the house and the property that I came upon in the course of the next year.

BUYING A PROPERTY

It was 2000 when my husband and I bought our parcel of land in the town of Mamaroneck in Westchester County, New York, and in so doing acquired a house in a

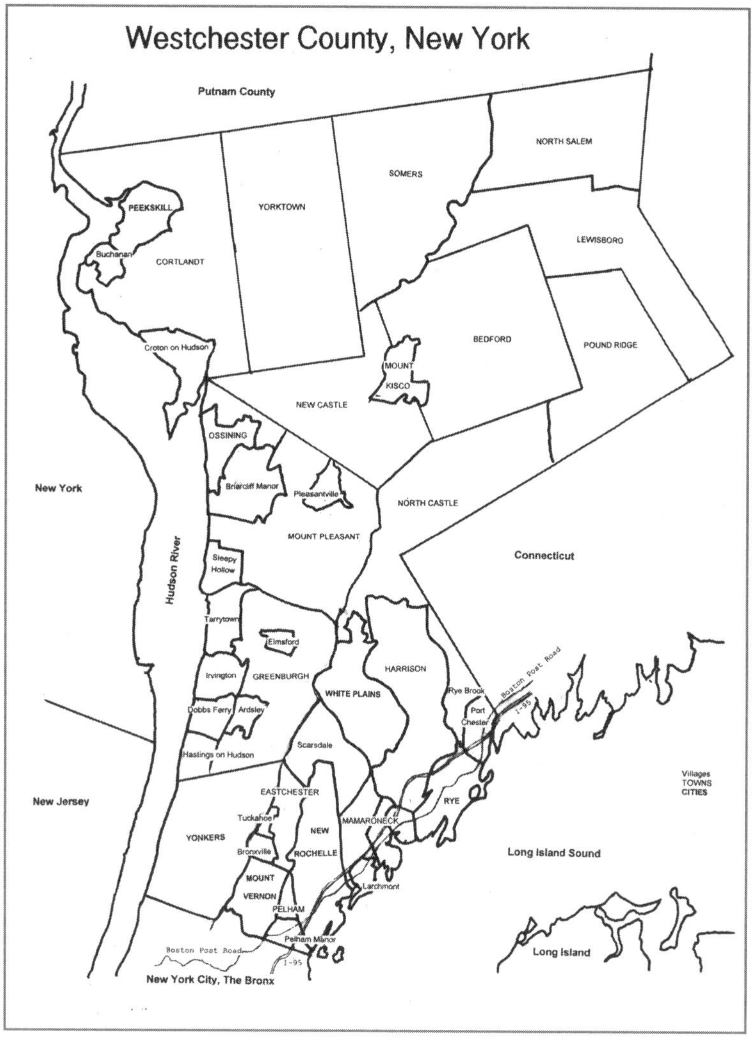

FIGURE 0.2 The cities, towns, and villages of Westchester County today with roads discussed in the book. *(Map by author.)*

process not unlike the one experienced by many—a right and a dream for Americans dating back three centuries. The ideology of land and home ownership has been part of the American social and political culture since colonial days. By the turn of the twenty-first century, the home ownership rate had reached nearly seventy percent, an all-time high, having grown from less than half the population in 1930.[1]

Much of the time such an acquisition results in something most ordinary, especially when one is talking about an average pre-World War II three-bedroom on a one-third-acre suburban lot like ours. At the least, buyers generally view such a place as shelter, as an investment, and perhaps as something that holds the promise of a future renovation or expansion. At best, it might be a bargain, a great location, something cozy and inviting, a place that acquires sentiment over time, or maybe a choice particularly suited to a family's needs. Only rarely is it extraordinarily beautiful or situated with a stunning view; even less often does it hold historic significance, architectural pedigree, or landmark status—rarely is there anything extraordinary about it. With our house we thought we had found something just right in terms of location and size and, indeed, to us it was cozy and inviting, but otherwise it seemed perfectly ordinary. Not only was it a typical suburban three-bedroom, but it was also a Cape Cod, possibly the most commonly found house in America.

The very ordinariness of this particular lot-and-house combination now stands in contrast to something more. In our case, and undoubtedly in that of many others, digging deeper would uncover some surprising things. Ever so gradually, peeling back layers of history, I have found that the house and the land it occupies are anything but ordinary. The remarkable adventure of discovering what makes the apparently commonplace special started the day we bought the property and expanded when more information came my way serendipitously, creating for me three mysteries to be investigated and changing my relationship to the house and the property forever.

THE MYSTERIES

Among the numerous documents we acquired at the closing was a letter from the village building inspector written in response to our lawyer's query about a certificate of occupancy. I noticed in the letter a reference to the house having had, at one time, a different address. How odd. I determined that the name of our street had not been changed, so why would the house have had another address? To find out, I went in search of the former address. Four blocks away, I found the answer. Although the street of the original address still exists, the house number does not. Where the house should be, according to the pattern of the house numbers, is a highway.

A few months later at a small social gathering hosted by our next-door neighbors, I had the opportunity to ask the former owner (I will call her Mrs. T———) about the second address. She seemed to be a woman of few words, but she confirmed what I had surmised—the house had been moved to make way for the interstate highway that blasted through the neighborhood in the 1950s. Where the house once stood is today a cloverleaf access ramp for Interstate 95. To her civil engineer husband the process of moving houses was a familiar one, and though she was horrified at the sight of her newly acquired house being moved up a steep hill on the back of a trucking rig, he thought nothing of it. Evidently, all went well. I now knew the reason for the former address, but still I was curious to know the details because house-moving in the suburbs of the twentieth century seemed to me an unusual occurrence.

At the same gathering I gained another piece of information, again from the previous owner. My husband and I had noticed several foot-long, rusted iron or steel stakes protruding at just above eye level from an

FIGURE 0.3 The rock viewed from the front yard of the house. *(Photo by author.)*

FIGURE 0.4 The rock and a five-foot ladder viewed from the back yard. *(Photo by author.)*

enormous rocky outcrop situated adjacent to the house. The density of the granite meant that someone had gone to great effort to insert the half-inch-thick cylindrical stakes into it. At roughly fifty by fifty feet and eight feet high with a flat horizontal surface of about twenty by forty feet, the outcrop is a remarkable feature of the property. Standing on the top, one is eye level with the roof of the house. When asked about the stakes, the reserved Mrs. T——— indicated they had been there in 1956 when she bought the property. "Someone a long time ago kept monkeys there, chained to the stakes," she stated flatly and without irony. That was all she knew. Was this some kind of suburban legend? I wanted to know more.

The next part of the story did not unfold until we had been in the house for nearly a year after our Labor Day weekend move. That first summer I ventured to the top of

FIGURE 0.5 Several foot-long stakes marked with white ties are embedded into the rock a little more than six feet from the ground. *(Photo by author.)*

the rock to show it to a visitor. The summer growth season had brought the trees into leaf—two towering maples, a Norway and a sugar, and a collection of smaller offspring in various stages of development. While gingerly picking our way through the thick accumulation of weeds poking out of every crevice, we discovered, under masses of entangled wisteria vines, what looked like steps—half a dozen huge granite boulders that had been chiseled into rectangular blocks and placed so as to fashion a staircase upon which one could mount the rock from the far side. By now we believed the stakes numbered nine, the others having been revealed when the undergrowth died back during the winter. Given all we could observe, it seemed that some specific human activity had taken place on or around the rock at some time in the past. Monkeys, iron stakes, and granite steps created strange enough images, but most intriguing were the words, "a long time ago." To an historian, such a concept is a frustration because of its vagueness. But more significantly, it is a lure. Just how long ago? It became something I had to figure out—what had taken place on that rock and when.

For some time these tantalizing questions and the other things I had learned about the property lingered in the back of my mind while I occupied my free time with settling into the house and working on the yard. One day as I was planting a perennial garden and struggling to get though the dense tangle of tree roots (with the belief that digging deep was the way to a healthy flower bed), I made an archaeological find—a flat, metal case, blackened and flecked with bits of a greenish patina, hinged to open like a book, and sized to fit in the palm of a small hand. The inside shows traces of gilding and blue paint, the bottom covered with a geometric pattern. Incised on the front in fine lines is a delicately rendered female figure, a dancing girl or nymph with arms extended, wearing diaphanous drapery and appearing to float in the air. Surrounding the figure is a shield-like form with curvilinear flourishes. Now I had unearthed what appeared to be tangible evidence that people had been on this site long ago and that even if the house was not very old, at least the property was.

FIGURE 0.6 The copper match safe dug up in 2001 in the house's back yard. It measures about two by one and three-quarter inches by one-quarter inch thick when closed. *(Photo by author.)*

Researching the origins and purpose of the case turned up a variety of answers. After first being told by one so-called expert that it dated from colonial times and once might have held a tiny book of verses or a woman's makeup such as rouge, I was a little disappointed to learn from a knowledgeable curator that it was probably a copper match safe, a container for matches used from the 1860s until the 1940s' invention of the lighter. She said the give-away for her was the roughly patterned bottom of the box, which appears to be a match-striking pad. Apparently, at the turn of the twentieth century every gentleman carried a match safe. Then another authority on antiques told me the form is more like a late Victorian-era or early twentieth-century matchbook case, a different category than the match safe. I have had to live with not knowing its age or original purpose, but finding it lit a fire, so to speak, in me. It led to thoughts about the past and the land where I had been digging.

LAYERS AND PLAYERS

I began to think of the land where we live as a "table" of contents, a surface, but one that holds much more than what meets the eye. I studied it closely to see what it might reveal, looking for the distinctive features of the site and its surroundings. The lot is not far from a small river, which flows into Long Island Sound and is dammed several hundred feet north of the house to form a reservoir. Nestled into the enclosing curve of one misshapen "leaf" of an interstate cloverleaf, eleven hundred feet south of the property, is the old Eleazor Gedney burial ground, an isolated chunk of land left intact by the highway's path. Civil engineers of the 1950s had altered the circular geometry ordinarily found in an exit ramp to accommodate the ancient gravesites.

Overall, the terrain of the area is rocky, the enormous outcrop next to the house the reason our lot is somewhat bigger than those nearby. Building on the rock or dynamiting it away would have undoubtedly cost a fortune; consequently, the rocky spot ended up an appendage to the nearest lot and became, in a sense, wasted land. And the rock provides a little boost to the already relatively high hilltop elevation—at that particular point one hundred feet above sea level, the highest point from the shoreline of Long Island Sound, roughly a mile to the southeast. The entire neighborhood of 180 houses rests on top of the remnants of an ancient mountain with our outcrop likely the summit. The real estate developer who subdivided the area in the 1920s claimed to have encountered eighteen feet of solid rock through which he had to drill to put in sewer lines.[2] And that rock substratum is plainly visible looming above one loop of the interstate cloverleaf where the removal of a slice of a hill made way for an exit ramp.

Given the added few vertical feet of the outcrop protruding above the topsoil on our property, it must have been something of a lookout spot, lofty enough to afford a view of the sound. A view of the sound would have been possible at a time when farming kept the area nearly treeless and without buildings. The outcrop itself is flat enough and large enough for activity to have taken place atop it. In summer when the numerous trees provide shade, we have chairs there and use it often as a seemingly remote and secluded woodland retreat. I wondered how else this speck of land might have been used in times past. What secrets does it hold? It became increasingly clear to me that much more had gone on here than the modest house and its quiet suburban cul-de-sac let on.

The land can tell us about much of what has happened in a given place. Every piece of property on this Earth has histories—geological, topographical, archaeological, geographical, architectural, demographic, political, economic, social, and cultural. The land has a recent past,

Examine Your Property

Investigate your property and your neighborhood to get a real sense of them by simply walking and observing. Take a tape measure and determine short distances as you walk and gauge drivable distances with your car's odometer. Study the geography, especially any features that are relatively unlikely to have been moved—natural ones such as streams, rivers, other bodies of water, and rock outcroppings, as well as manmade ones such as roads, cemeteries, stone fences and posts, old foundations, and ruins of any kind. In my neighborhood I noticed a place where the curb abruptly changes from Belgian rock to poured cement, an indication that part of the street was old and part was newer, probably post-World War II. Further research through maps confirmed that this was the case. Be cognizant of the elevation, hills, and valleys. Check the orientation of your property and house with a compass or a good map. Note any large plants that might have been there a very long time. Look at street signs and house numbers. Study contemporary maps and find and study old maps from various eras.

If you have reason to dig in your yard, take note of anything you dig up. I invited a metal detector enthusiast to scour my property with the hope he might unearth something remarkable. He did not, but keeping the numerous odd bits and pieces of things seemed like a good idea. You never know what else might turn up and what connections you might be able to make in the future. In the days before the existence of the town dump or municipal garbage collection, people would dispose of things they no longer could use by putting them in the privy. If you can locate the remains of one of those on your property, you will have an archaeologist's dream.

There are various ways to view a parcel of land. If you live near a body of water, find a boat and go out in it. Observe your neighborhood from the water vantage point. Imagine how people might have gained access to your area in the days before decent roads. What role might boats and water transport have played? View your property from an airplane, helicopter, or balloon if that's possible. If not, use Google Earth to survey your property from a bird's-eye perspective. With the ruler tool you can measure distances between everything you can see.

Examine the appearance of your building and those nearby. What styles are they? How old are they? Train your eye to pick up on key details. An interesting pattern I began to notice in many neighborhoods near mine is that every second or third house is an old one with newer ones stuck in between. Evidently people with large pieces of land in the early suburban developments subdivided them at various times, making way for newer houses to be built.

Keep returning to observe again and again. Each time you look, you're likely to see something new. As you collect data and make observations, always take notes and make sketches or photographs of anything you think you might want to refer to later. That way you are not always reinventing the wheel for yourself.

a long-ago past, a documented past, an undocumented past, and it even has an imagined past and one that never can be fully known. The land is a kind of palimpsest, a place that contains its history. According to the dictionary, a palimpsest is a "writing material (as a parchment or tablet) used one or more times after earlier writing has been erased" and "something having unusually diverse layers or aspects apparent beneath the surface."[3] Inhabitants "write on" or alter the land continuously, the land bearing the imprint, the evidence of humankind, both on and beneath its surface. The past is part of the present. And deeds in particular have a continuing impact on the land. Once property lines are established in a deed, they have a tendency to stay on the landscape in one form or another—a road, a stone wall, and a park boundary are but a few examples.

George Washington probably never slept on the property, situated twenty miles north of New York City just east of the Hudson Valley, but who did? I was certain that there must have been people living here before the woman from whom we bought the house. Who were they? What did they do for a living? What brought them to this exact spot? When did they arrive? What were their particular relationships to the land? Why did they leave? These questions, and others that emerged along the way, led me on a research odyssey to find answers.

The property began its association with humankind through the Native Americans who lived in this part of New York State until the 1700s. A European first laid claim to the area in 1661, as evidenced by a still-existing deed, which transferred the land from Wappaquewam, a *sakima* or leader of the indigenous Siwanoy people, to John Richbell, an English merchant. With that first deed, the land became a property—no longer just a piece of land, but real estate, a possession. Progressively, over decades, the property became part of ever-smaller farms, until developers made it into what we see today—

Databases

Databases are collections of data that have been selected and organized into a searchable format. Using them is a fast way to find targeted information. Part of what is sometimes called the invisible Web or deep Web, they are accessible only from within a website as opposed to through a search engine like Google, which searches the World Wide Web. Among the many types of information and documents typically found in databases are magazines, journals, patents, statistical data, newspapers, and all kinds of other publications. Access to some databases must be paid for, but libraries license research databases and make them available to their users without charge. Many of the ones produced by libraries, government agencies, and academic groups are free.

To research a topic, the words you enter (your keywords or search terms) are compared to all the words in the records being searched in order to find matches. Entering too many words will often result in too few, if any, results. Try entering fewer search terms. To avoid unnecessary work, it is a good idea to jot down your keywords as you go so you know what combinations you have already tried.

The claim that General or President Washington "slept here" has persisted for over two hundred years and attests to the enduring nature of the desire for such status. Using one of my favorite databases, *ProQuest Historical Newspapers Complete*—available on some public library websites without charge—with the keywords "Washington slept here" and "Washington AND slept" and a date range of 1985 through 2008, I was able to find more than a dozen headlines from the *New York Times* supporting the idea that association with the nation's first president affixes glory and special stature to a building or piece of property. Here is a sampling, most of them found through the search described:

George Washington Slept Here
(January 13, 1985)

Washington Slept Here and There and . . .
(February 17, 1985)

Washington Really Slept Here
(February 16, 1992)

George Washington's Troops Slept Here
(November 29, 1997)

George Washington, Among Others, Slept Here
(December 14, 2000)

Washington Slept Here . . . No, Over Here
(January 14, 2001)

Washington Slept Here. Ate Here, Too
(July 4, 2001)

Where Washington (And Slaves) Slept
(April 20, 2002)

Washington Slept Here. No, Really
(June 27, 2004)

Such a newspaper search in a full-text database such as *ProQuest Historical Newspapers Complete* finds not only headlines, but also words in the body of the article. For example, the search using the terms "Washington AND slept" also turned up an article titled "Landmarks of the Common Folk" (*New York Times*, October 25, 1990) about the urge to venerate and save the "unknown, the everyday and the ignored," because, the article stated, "these are definitely not places where George slept." This comment brought into focus for me the real value in using a searchable database: you can find the "unknown, the everyday and the ignored" because it searches every word, not just the title, allowing you to determine what is and what is not important.

There are a number of other useful databases for research in American history. *America: History and Life* offers in-depth coverage of North America from prehistory to the present. *American Memory* includes recordings, still and moving images, prints, and maps that document life in America. *American National Biography* contains biographic information on individuals as well as reliable bibliographies to aid further research. *Historical Statistics Complete* includes historical statistical data including demographics and economics. Databases of scholarly material include *JSTOR Arts and Sciences I-II*, *Academic Search Complete*, and *Project MUSE*. Although researching in databases requires an extra couple of steps beyond using a search engine such as Google, they are well worth the effort.

suburban streets lined with mostly quarter-acre lots where developers built, during the 1920s and the 1950s and '60s, single-family homes, a hiatus having been forced upon the process by the Great Depression and the Second World War. For the three and a half centuries for which the history can be traced, the land—which people have walked on, ridden across, farmed, mapped, and built upon—has borne witness as a kind of sentinel to all that has taken place upon it. The land itself is truly a figurative "table" of contents.

Aside from the first deed, recorded history in the precise area where the house stands dates back to the time Mamaroneck residents began keeping minutes at their town meetings in 1697, an early date by American standards, leading me to assume that much has happened there. It's not always possible to know who actually lived on a given parcel of land, but where records still exist, the owner can usually be found. And once you know an owner's name, there are other records to consult—birth, marriage, and death certificates, court records, wills, military service records, town meeting minutes, census records, and newspapers—the list goes on.

In the research associated with my property, I came across two well-known geographic place-names in the area—Heathcote and Gedney. Both Caleb Heathcote and several generations of Gedneys had owned large parcels of land in Westchester County at one time, including my property. Heathcote is the name of several roads and an elementary school in the county. And in this area, a neighborhood, the nearby cemetery, a park, a restaurant, a nursery, historic markers, at least six streets, and even my daughter's elementary school classmate bear the name Gedney. I thought it would be informative to find out who else once owned the land.

So I began my work searching deeds and studying property boundaries to find the names of the previous owners, while hoping I could solve the mysteries of the Sears house, the house's move, and the monkeys and the rock. As I pursued my inquiry, more questions developed, expanding the project. I have been surprised when what seemed at first like preposterously unfounded information proved to be rooted in fact. On balance, what I have discovered is that the ordinary often is extraordinary once you uncover the layers to see what lies beneath. And I continue to be astonished at how much information is to be found if you look for it. It is amazing just how strong is the human drive to document our lives and to record and save information—even in the years before the digital age, which has made saving information so much easier. I have realized that in signing a thirty-year mortgage, or even a lease, one ties oneself not only to the future, but also to the past. The story that follows is a kind of genealogy of a bit of land. The supporting documentation and the methods used to develop it serve as a model for researching and understanding any apparently ordinary property.

PART I

MYSTERIES OF THE HOUSE

one

Something Like a Sears House

Skyscrapers are Ready Cut. Why Not Your Home?[1]
—*Sears, Roebuck Catalog of Houses*, 1926

The previous owner's offhand comment to me at the closing on the purchase of the house had aroused my curiosity. "You know, it's a Sears house, or—oh, I can't remember—but it's something like that," she remarked. That immediately caught my attention. Sears, Roebuck and Co. mail-order, factory-produced houses began to receive attention as a historical phenomenon in the early 1980s in articles in the *Old-House Journal* and *Historic Preservation* and in the 1986 book *Houses by Mail: A Guide to Houses from Sears, Roebuck and Company*, which thoroughly examines and illustrates 447 models, nearly all the company's standard residential designs.[2] Interest grew and more articles appeared, with one 1985 national newspaper headline reading, "Mail-Order Homes Sears Sold in 1909–37 Are Suddenly Chic." Press coverage has continued in a steady stream.[3] Today real estate agencies even advertise houses with come-ons such as, "This 1930s original Sears built home will delight everyone. . . ."[4] and "Own your own piece of history! 1930s Sears & Roebuck home available for the first time. . . ." The latter, a bungalow called The Katonah in the Sears catalogues from 1917 to 1919, originally sold for $265 to $827 with no bath. It was on the market in 2004, presumably with a bath, for $925,000.[5] There was, and still is, strong interest in Sears houses.

Just what was my new house? I could see it was a Cape Cod, and Sears had produced many of them, but if it was a Sears, I was determined to confirm it with facts. Given my abiding interest in Sears mail-order houses, I already owned a copy of *Houses by Mail*. My initial awareness of them had come about during visits in the 1980s to see my college roommate and some relatives, living in different states a hundred miles apart. Struck by the similar feel of the doorknobs in the two houses, I also noticed they had mirror-image floor plans, even though the houses' exteriors bore no resemblance to each other whatsoever. Questioning the two families elicited responses suggesting the houses might be Sears houses—both families had heard rumors to that effect over the years. But I wanted to know more; consulting *Houses by Mail* confirmed that the rumors were true. I hoped the same simple research would tell me my new house was a Sears too.

FACTORY-BUILT HOUSES

Factory-made, mail-order houses developed out of a long-standing practice of prefabricating houses in a myriad of ways over several centuries. Explorers took knocked-down wooden houses on board ship from England to Canada in 1578; settlers of Cape Ann, Massachusetts, did the same in 1624. Prospectors in the 1849 California gold rush transported similar types of shelter and assembled them at the mining sites. Portable buildings were patented and manufactured in New York and Boston as early as 1861 and used by crews building the transcontinental railroad in the decade that followed. Throughout the 1800s, architects, builders, and lumber companies produced another precursor to factory-built housing—pattern books. At first offering skeletal plans only, just after the Civil War they began offering full-fledged architectural plans by mail.[6]

By 1870, houses produced in factories were being sold through catalogues in the United States. Initially spurred by the industrial revolution, a national railroad system, and the growth of balloon framing,[7] by the early 1900s the demand for factory-built housing had blossomed, partly the result of the passage of the Rural Free Delivery Act of 1896, which allowed catalogue selling to reach geographically isolated customers. Factory-built homes took the form of either sectional wood panels joined on site with bolts, or precut materials delivered by rail in a boxcar. The latter type, also known as ready-cut homes, made up the larger share of the industry. Shipped with detailed instructions, these houses were ready to be assembled on site by the owner or a local builder. Available styles followed fashion, changing over time. Research done in the early 1940s indicates that about one-quarter million of them were built in the preceding forty years.[8]

A number of mail-order house companies competed nationwide. The largest was Sears, Roebuck and Co. in Chicago, its Modern Homes division having been started in 1908. Others included Montgomery Ward, also in Chicago, Aladdin Homes and Lewis Manufacturing Company, both in Michigan, the Hodgson Company of Massachusetts, Bennett Homes of New York, and Pacific Ready-Cut Homes and Whiting-Mead Company of California. In 1928 the Gordon-Van Tine Company of Iowa produced one of the earliest Cape Cod types to be found in a mail-order catalogue for ready-cut houses.[9]

SEARS, ROEBUCK AND CO. MODERN HOMES

Given the popularity of Cape Cod-type houses in the late 1920s, it is not surprising that various companies included them among a number of other house types in their mail-order, ready-to-assemble house catalogues. Not until 1931, however, were Capes found in the catalogues of Sears, Roebuck and Co. From then until the last Sears house catalogue in 1940, there was at least one Cape Cod-type house in every annual issue but one, and most years there were several.[10] An enclosure in the 1939 catalogue announced, "'Nine new Sears Modern Homes, too late for publication in the catalog, . . . represent the latest thought in architectural design and planning, [and] we think you will find them especially interesting.'"[11] That year the catalogue included a total of eleven Capes, and of the nine

FIGURE I.1 The Attleboro in the 1934 Sears, Roebuck and Co. catalogue, *Modern Homes*, page 17. *(Photograph courtesy of the Sears Holdings Historical Archives.)*

THE ATTLEBORO ▲ ▲

▲ SIX ROOMS — BATH AND LAVATORY

MODERN HOME
No. 3384
ALREADY CUT AND FITTED
PRICE $1810^{00}

THIS type of Cape Cod home is one of the first designs built by the early New England settlers. Homes built over a hundred years ago grow old gracefully and still retain a certain warmth and beauty. It seems to have many friends in both urban and suburban areas. The Attleboro achieves distinction with its fine doorway, dormers, shuttered windows and correct architectural details. No "gingerbread" to get out of date. Outside walls are shown of Cedar shingles, but will look equally attractive with siding.

FIRST FLOOR PLAN

The first floor lavatory opening off the rear hall, in addition to complete second floor bath, adds greatly to the value. Closets for outer wraps handy to front and rear doors. Central hall with semi-open stairs, large living room, dining room and exceptional kitchen, complete the first floor plan. Double drainboard kitchen sink with built-in cabinets as shown by kitchen cabinets as shown are suggested at a slight additional cost.

SECOND FLOOR PLAN

Two large bedrooms and one smaller one, each with a good closet, open off the upstairs hall. Each bedroom is well lighted and contains good wall space. A hall closet for linens at the left of the bath is a real convenience. The bathroom plumbing "roughs in" directly over the kitchen which reduces installation cost. Three attractive "Aristocrat" plumbing fixtures as available in Specification 22B work out nicely in the bath. A built-in Venetian mirrored medicine case is part of the standard equipment furnished with this home.

The floor plan is 36 ft. wide by 26 ft. deep and will require a 60-foot lot on account of the 11 foot porch at the side. In case of a narrow lot, porch could be placed at the rear of the living room instead of at the side.

At the price quoted, we furnish all necessary material to build this six-room-and-bath home, consisting of lumber, lath, millwork, flooring, shingles, building paper, hardware, metal and painting material according to complete detail specifications.

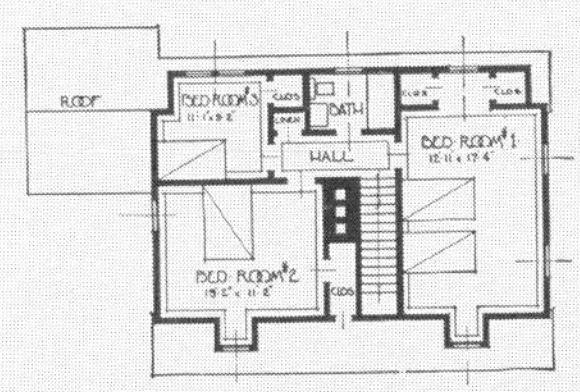

SECOND FLOOR PLAN

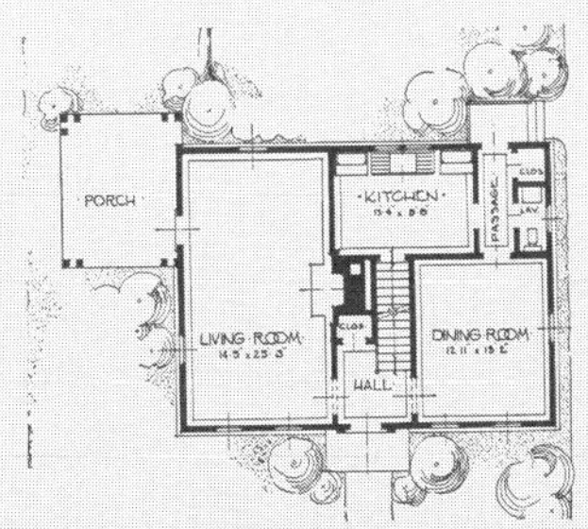

FIRST FLOOR PLAN

new houses announced in the insert, seven were Cape Cod types. Evidently Sears hoped to cash in on the latest fashions and economic trends in home building by offering so many Capes.

Sears houses came with everything—as many as 30,000 separate parts, including up to 750 pounds of nails, enough paint and varnish for four coats, a seventy-five-page bound book of instructions, and even the lock and key for the front door. Builders constructed an estimated 50,000 to 100,000 of them nationwide,[12] about two hundred in Westchester County, New York, alone. With Sears clearly featuring Capes in the mid- and late-1930s, I thought it perfectly possible that the former owner had been correct about my 1937 house. Its location near a railroad line was yet another characteristic it shared with many Sears mail-order houses. Unfortunately, though, the easy confirmation I had hoped for did not materialize. *Houses by Mail* included drawings and floor plans of seven Capes from the Sears catalogues of 1931 to 1937—The Gordon, The Stanford, The Cape Cod, The Portsmouth, The Concord, The Attleboro, and The Milford—but my house was not among them.

Perhaps my house had been somehow missed in *Houses by Mail,* so I sought out the actual Sears catalogues. They are hard to come by, some no longer in existence, but I checked the ones that have been reissued along with other books and journals where parts of the catalogues have been published, in order to match floor plans and façades with my house, but nothing added up. Though the company has no records of where all their houses ended up, the Sears Archives website does contain images of many of the houses. That, however, did not help either.[13] I even searched for physical evidence, one of the sure-fire ways to establish a house as a Sears. Equipped with a flashlight, I crawled around in the basement and attic looking for stamped numbers near the ends of exposed structural wood. I also checked for Sears markings on window and door hardware and on bathroom fixture faucets, some of the other clues one should look for. I was unable to find any physical verification.

"AUTHENTIC CAPE COD"

Still refusing to completely let go of the idea that my house was a Sears catalogue house in the absence of any proof to the contrary, I kept looking. It was the former owner's words, "something like," that spurred me on. Certain she had not fabricated or fantasized the whole thing, I sensed there was something there, some kernel of truth in what she had said, a link to something I was looking for.

So if all evidence indicated it was not a Sears, maybe it had been produced by one of the other mail-order companies. Knowing the houses had arrived by rail in boxcars and sometimes went up in a matter of days, I thought that such an event might have warranted local newspaper coverage. Armed with the knowledge that the house had been built in 1937, I went to the local library and began methodically turning the pages of enormous bound volumes of dusty, disintegrating newspapers from that year, standing because the pages were too big to do it sitting. It was slow going, to say the least.

Eventually, Eureka! I came upon an artist's rendering—clearly the image of my house—in a real estate section advertisement for a home construction business. Below the picture were the words "Authentic Cape Cod design—6 rooms, tile bath, attached garage." Fortunately, I continued looking. In the next issue, the same drawing appeared in an ad for the same builder, but this time, below the picture was the headline "A 'McCall's' Home-of-the-Month." The ad copy read: "We take pleasure in presenting this colorful home for your inspection. Chosen by McCall's Magazine for its livable room arrangement, it combines the quaintness and comfort of Cape Cod architecture with the newest trends in interior decoration and the best of

FIGURE I.2 A builder placed this ad in the weekly real estate section of a local newspaper for several weeks in the fall of 1937. *(Photograph courtesy of the* Journal News *and the Mamaroneck Public Library.)*

equipment."[14] The former owner's comment now began to make sense.

The newspaper discovery sent me racing to the New York Public Library, where I knew there were bound volumes of old magazines. I began working backward from the September 1937 date of the ads, and there, in the May 1937 issue, with Amelia Earhart on the cover (just weeks before her disappearance in an attempted round-the-world flight), was a photograph of a carbon copy of my own Cape Cod house, the *McCall's* "Home of the Month." Along with a photograph of the house were three alternative floor plans, the suggestion that the house could be expanded later by finishing the second floor, and the headline "The May

FIGURE I.3 Amelia Earhart on the cover of the May 1937 issue of *McCall's* magazine, purchased in 2005 on eBay. (Originally published in the May 1937 issue of *McCall's* magazine. *All Rights Reserved. ©Copyright 2009 Meredith Corporation. All Rights Reserved. Photo by author.)*

For you . . . and you . . . and you—a Cape Cod house whose rooms are elastic. Without changing the exterior, the first floor may have the three different arrangements shown below

THE MAY HOME OF THE MONTH

can be tailored to order

BY J. HAROLD HAWKINS

LORILLARD WISE, Architect

For everyone the upstairs is the same—two comfortable bedrooms with cross ventilation, clothes closets, linen closet and bath. And for everyone, an attached garage with doors at front or back, a shady open porch between the garden and the house

3 For you—if your family asks for two bedrooms and bath downstairs and you would like to finish the upstairs later—a complete home on one floor

2 For you—if you like rooms that are luxurious in size, with both bedrooms upstairs. There is a hall closet, too, and a convenient downstairs lavatory

1 For you—if you like a bedroom and bath downstairs and a homelike combination kitchen and dining room. The complete kitchen with a bay window added is shown on page 53

SEE IT YOURSELF. You are invited to visit the May, 1937, Home of the Month at the following addresses:

CALIFORNIA—Los Angeles—3676 Corinth Avenue

DELAWARE—Dover—Greenhill Road, Eastover Hills

NEW JERSEY—Teaneck—1103 Wilson Avenue

NEW YORK—Rye—Corner Park Avenue & Boston Post Road

TENNESSEE—Memphis—751 Mallory Ave., Longview Heights

1936 Homes of the Month are being built at these addresses:

OKLAHOMA—Tulsa—2140 East 31st Place, from the April, 1936, plan. At 2141 East 31st Place, from the August, 1936, plan.

MORE INFORMATION ABOUT THIS HOUSE—Directions for these plans, and for a one-story variation. Furnishing and planting plans. Send for HM-12—15c. Address The Modern Homemaker, McCall's, Dayton, O.

FIGURE 1.4 The May 1937 *McCall's* article, "The May Home of the Month." (Originally published in the May 1937 issue of *McCall's* magazine. *All Rights Reserved. ©Copyright 2009 Meredith Corporation. All Rights Reserved. Photo by author.*)

Home of the Month Can Be Tailored to Order."[15] A short article, "Cottage May Expand," in the *New York Times* on May 9, 1937, noted that the house appeared "pictorially in the current issue of *McCall's* magazine."[16] Though not actually my house, the one pictured in *McCall's* was a short distance away in Rye, a town adjacent to mine.

MCCALL'S "HOME OF THE MONTH"

The house began its rise to notable dwelling when architect Lorillard Wise teamed up with a local builder to create the "All American Model Home." Its prominent location in Rye on U.S. Route 1, a busy thoroughfare, assured that it would be seen by many.[17] By late 1936 at least eight houses based on the model had been completed or were under construction in the New York City metropolitan area. The builder had submitted photographs and plans of the model house to the *McCall's* "Home of the Month" series, the magazine selecting the house for its May 1937 issue. A second New York-area builder began advertising the same design in local newspapers, where I happened upon it, and in the *New York Times*. By 1938 at least twenty-five of them, including my house, and probably more, had been built across the country.

The *McCall's* "Home of the Month" series, which lasted nearly three years from 1936 to 1938, presented in a one- to two-page spread basic floor plans and photographs of houses submitted by architects or builders. Representatives from the National Association of Real Estate Boards and the magazine's architectural editor selected a house, based upon its "livability," for each monthly article in the series. Average, middle-class houses, only a few of them were large and grand enough to include servants' quarters.

In each segment of the series, *McCall's* invited interested readers to send fifteen cents (at a time when the magazine itself sold for ten cents) to the magazine's corporate headquarters to obtain additional information for any given "Home of the Month." In booklet form, the material included slightly larger and more detailed floor plans as well as elevations so that a local builder could be engaged to recreate the house. Finding the booklet for my house was a lengthy adventure leading me to a library at the University of Illinois, which may well have the only copy in existence. The simple publication—except for the cover, not even typeset—states, "The drawings and descriptions in this booklet are offered as practical suggestions for you to take to your local architect or realtor-builder and his architect . . . [who] will draw up working plans and specifications for your house, and will build your home for you." It characterizes the house as being unusually flexible, with a variety of possible room arrangements. The various choices allow for an extra-large kitchen or living room with bedrooms on the second floor or a combined living-dining room with two first-floor bedrooms. An article about the house in the *Washington Post* noted that it was "a home providing for later enlargement as its occupant's family grows."[18]

The booklet is specific in its recommendations. For example, the "Schedule for Room Color Schemes" suggests that the bathroom walls be dusty pink, the tile white, the floor brown, the shower curtain rosy red, and the towels brown and white. It also includes drawings for a one-story version of the house, and a detailed landscape plan for both a standard sixty-by-one-hundred-foot lot and a corner property, mentioning such details as a lilac bush and flowering vines on the porch posts.[19]

As part of each "Home of the Month" article, *McCall's* published the locations of houses built from the current featured plans as well as from previously published ones. The May 1937 issue lists street addresses where five examples of the featured Cape could be seen. The diversity of locations where people eventually built the house—including California, Connecticut, Delaware, Florida, Michigan, New Jersey, New York, Ohio, and Tennessee—attests to the popularity and the reach of the design.[20] Through historical newspaper research, information found in *McCall's* magazines of the 1930s, and simply looking as I drive around the area where I live, I have found twenty-five other *McCall's* May 1937 "Home of the Month" houses just like mine—spread out in twelve different towns in the New York City metropolitan area and in nine states across the country. Some have been slightly altered with front dormers or porticos added or shutters removed. Other examples probably exist but undoubtedly have been remodeled so as to be unrecognizable today. The majority of the sixteen I have seen in person, however, for the most part are unchanged.

During the run of the *McCall's* series, members of the Land Developers and Home Builders Division of the National Association of Real Estate Boards received a monthly publication, including photographs, architectural drawings, and landscaping designs similar to those contained in the booklet offered to readers. It stated that "any Realtor-Builder erecting this Home of the Month . . . will have his name and the address of his house published in that issue of *McCall's* which is on sale at the time his house is finished and open to the public. 2,600,000 copies of *McCall's* are sold every month."[21] That number was equivalent to one copy of the magazine for every forty-nine people or one for every eighteen households in the United States. *McCall's* magazine at the time had a very broad reach.

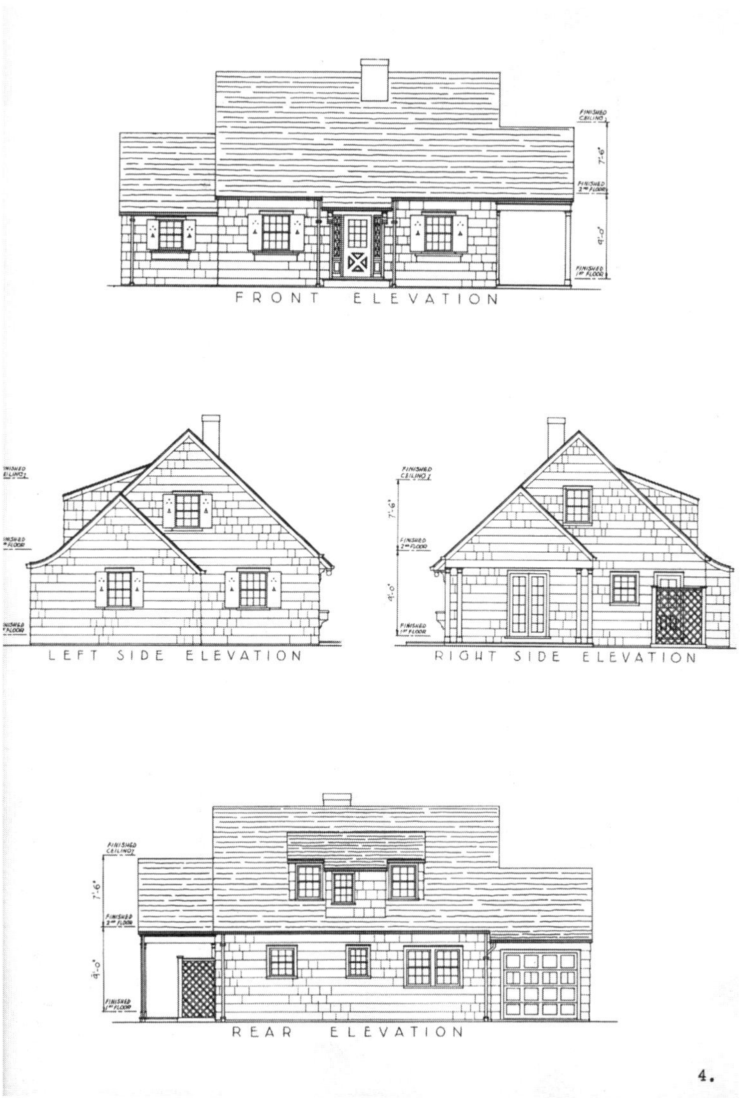

FIGURE 1.5 A page from the May 1937 "McCall's Home of the Month" booklet. (Originally published in a "send-away-for" booklet advertised in the May 1937 issue of *McCall's*® magazine. *All Rights Reserved. ©Copyright 2009 Meredith Corporation. All Rights Reserved. Photo by author.*)

MCCALL'S

The history of *McCall's* is worth noting in light of the "Home of the Month" series. *McCall's* began publication in the 1870s as a fashion sheet consisting of ten slim issues a year to promote the *McCall's* women's clothing sewing-pattern business. Gradually the magazine introduced other material—household-help ideas, fancywork sewing suggestions, fiction, jokes, editorials, and so on—until the 1890s when the editors asserted that it was no longer merely a fashion magazine, but included news and other items of interest to women. By 1900, each issue contained as many as seventy-two pages, partly due to increased advertising; by 1913, the total circulation had grown to 1.25 million. In 1917, *McCall's* increased its price to ten cents a copy. That change, along with the addition in the 1920s of famous and popular writers to its roster, raised the publication into a higher-class magazine category and helped to initiate what became its characteristic national coverage with nationwide appeal. In the 1930s *McCall's* became the first women's magazine to reach newsstand sales of over one million.

One of the publication's areas of expertise, beginning in 1934, was reader-interest research conducted through interviews. At the time, the magazine often referred to its national audience as "McCall Street" because the magazine's marketing staff had determined that the size of its readership would account for households located every twenty-five feet along both sides of a theoretical street running from Boston to San Diego.[22] According to Frank Luther Mott in his comprehensive history of American popular magazines, "What *McCall* editors were visualizing was a middle-class audience living on an American street in ordinary houses anywhere in the country"[23]—a street and house, it seems, like mine. It was just this "McCall Street" audience who would want the kind of homes represented in the *McCall's* "Home of the Month" feature.

A PEDIGREE OF A DIFFERENT SORT

I wondered how the family who built my house—we are the third owners—might have found the plans for it. Did they see it in *McCall's* and then decide to build? It is difficult to say for sure. The model house in Rye, pictured in the May 1937 issue, was already in existence by June 1936 and could have been seen just a short drive away from my neighborhood. A brief piece titled "Real Estate Notes" in the *New York Times* in June 1936 stated that houses based on the "All American Model Home" in Rye had sold in seven New York City area towns, including mine.[24] The family who built my house, however, did not buy the property for it until July 1936. Therefore, the house could have been constructed during the fall of 1936 before the magazine piece came out, or more likely, because of the February 1938 inspection date, in the summer and fall of 1937, just after the May *McCall's* appeared. It is impossible to know whether the choice of this particular house came about because of the nearby model house, as a result of the *McCall's* piece, or through some other means.

In any case, the comment by the former owner, "it's a Sears house," that had so captured my imagination proved to be inaccurate, but it contained a kernel of truth, one that led to the discovery of something equally remarkable, a pedigree of a different sort. Without doubt, as a Cape Cod type, my house is ordinary, a subject discussed at length in chapter three. At the same time, however, as a *McCall's* "Home of the Month," it is indeed noteworthy. And with one mystery concerning my house solved, I moved on to the next.

Newspapers

Consulting newspapers of the time period you are researching greatly enhances finding out about a particular topic at a given time and place and gleaning what contemporary public attitudes toward the issues surrounding it were. News articles, editorials, human interest stories, letters to the editor, and even advertisements all contribute to your understanding. *ProQuest Historical Newspapers Complete* contains the entire contents of a growing list of major newspapers including the *Atlanta Constitution, Boston Globe, Chicago Tribune, Detroit Free Press, Los Angeles Times, New York Times, Washington Post* and a number of others in PDF format dating back to various years as far back as the mid-1800s. The PDF format means you can read the pages just as they originally appeared, noting what made the front page and what was relegated to back pages. Searching these newspapers will give you information on both topics of national scope and topics relating to the broad geographic areas covered by them. Surprisingly, a large newspaper like the *New York Times* in the early years of the twentieth century listed by street address new houses that had recently been built, even in suburban communities, allowing for a search of exact locations. I was able to find several houses like mine because the search terms "McCall's Home of the Month" for 1937 yielded specific street addresses. Sometimes searching your own address or street name will turn up information.

A related database, *ProQuest National Newspapers,* includes the full text of several dozen important newspapers around the country from the last couple of decades. Included, among others, are newspapers from cities as geographically diverse as Denver, Houston, Minneapolis, New Orleans, Norfolk, Philadelphia, San Antonio, San Francisco, Seattle, St. Louis, and St. Petersburg. *Access Newspaper Archive* is a collection of newspapers from smaller cities around the country. *America's Historical Newspapers* includes newspapers from the eighteenth and nineteenth centuries. *Chronicling America* is a project of the Library of Congress containing selected newspapers from 1880 to 1922. And *Early American Newspapers, 1690–1922* is an ever-expanding database of newspapers representing all fifty states.

Specialized newspapers may be found through the *Archive of Americana,* a web-based collection of historical material at http://www.readex.com. The site provides links to collections of American ethnic newspapers including African-American newspapers, 1827–1998, U.S. Spanish language newspapers, 1808–1980, and more than two thousand other newspapers from all fifty states, along with additional primary source material.

Really small newspapers that cover topics of local interest can often be found in bound volumes or in microform in libraries. In all kinds of newspapers are obituaries, which are often useful and frequently indexed locally. Check libraries for such old indexes. Local newspapers will not necessarily be indexed (though increasingly will be searchable as they become digitized), but if you have a date or time period as a guide, you can always search page by page. With experience using a given publication, you learn useful time-saving shortcuts—for example, which day of the week real estate news was covered or where obituaries usually appeared.

Newspapers, of course, can be notably biased, so if the issue you are concerned with is at all controversial, reading the coverage in more than one newspaper is a good idea when possible. For example, coverage in New York newspapers of issues relating to the American Revolution varied markedly, depending on whether the editors sided with the British or with the Patriots. Nevertheless, newspapers offer an invaluable fresh and of-the-moment perspective difficult to find in any retrospective discussion.

two

The House Finds a Home

> The average small house weighs more than a quarter million pounds. It is not mobile, and once the final nail is driven your house is going to remain right where it is built for a long, long time. . . . Too much emphasis, therefore, can not be placed on the importance of care and caution in choosing the plot on which your house will stand as a monument to your judgment, good or bad.[1]
>
> —*House-of-the-Month Book of Small Houses*, 1946

The building inspector's letter I uncovered in the immense pile of papers documenting the purchase of my house had initially mystified me. It indicated that the house, during the first nineteen years of its existence, had had an entirely different address. A bit of deed research in the Westchester County Office of Land Records confirmed what Mrs. T———, the former owner, had indicated—the impending construction of the New England Thruway had required New York State to acquire the house's original lot through an eminent domain proceeding in 1955. The following year, she and her husband purchased the house at auction, moved it down the street, around the corner, and up a very steep hill. Fifteen of the immediate neighbors also had their property condemned and their houses relocated. In September 1956, a front-page photograph in a local newspaper showed three of the houses—including mine—separated from their foundations, poised on rollers, and ready for the move.[2] But the whole story of how my house came to be moved to a new piece of property four blocks away is a long and complex one.

Even now the six-lane highway that caused its relocation is only three hundred yards away, but just one tiny sliver of it is visible from the house because the adjacent rock outcropping serves as a screen. Moving traffic is audible only on summer nights when the windows are open and the wind blows from the south. Otherwise, the highway seems mercifully far away. It is, however, a part of my life whenever I leave the house on foot or by car.

The Daily Times

MONDAY, SEPTEMBER 10, 1956 — SERVING MAMARONECK AND LARCHMONT SINCE 1925

Egypt Proposes New To Break Suez Stale

PHONE CO. SEEKS NEW $1.5 MILLION COUNTY BUILDING

Greenburgh Gets Plea For Office Site To House Personnel

By WORTH A. JUDGE

FAIRVIEW—

A proposal of the New York Telephone Co. to build a $1.5 million office building on County Center Road, back of County Center, will be presented to the Greenburgh Town Board tonight.

Two applications will be made, one for lifting deed restrictions on the land, another for a rezoning of 20 per cent of the plot. The rezoning will be subject to a public hearing at a later date. Prior to the public hearing company representatives will meet with the Fulton Park Association to discuss details of the plan. This meeting has been scheduled for Sept. 17.

J. Robert Bleakley of the White Plains law firm of Bleakley, Platt, Gilchrist & Walker will make the presentation to the Town Board.

To House Management

According to Colby Kalloch, Westchester division manager of the New York Telephone Co., the proposed building would house management and clerical personnel of the division, now in several scattered locations.

The site is on County Center Road at Fulton Avenue, across the street from the First National Stores and Howard Johnson parking lots and a motel. Four-fifths of the lot is in a commerical zone, the remainder in

bon-monoxide chamber used at the shelter for disposal of animals. Photo was taken last December. It shows Mr. Lake with a crow found in Pleasantville after its wings had been clipped — Staff Photo by Ray Hoover

(Story on Page 9)

HOUSES are being moved in the North Barry Avenue section of Mamaroneck Village where some 16 residences, Huber's Winfield Hotel, and several stores must make way for the huge cloverleaf of the New England Thruway. Above, one home has left its foundation while work is underway to move the others — Staff Photo by Paul Byrne

Not Completed, Some Overcrowded

Ahead

May Put

FIGURE 2.1 The house in the distance, now mine, is ready to be moved in September 1956 along with others from the neighborhood. *(Photograph courtesy of the* Journal News *and the Mamaroneck Public Library.)*

Though the new superhighways of the 1950s would have offered residents travel conveniences and may have eased traffic congestion, they must have been a wrenching prospect both for the owner of my house and for others in the many towns nationwide divided by the coming of the first interstates. Ned Benton, publisher of the *Larchmont Gazette*, an online newspaper, asked in 2004, "Did Larchmont [a town adjacent to mine] and Mamaroneck take the wrong path in 1954 when the New England Thruway was being planned? Did we go along when we could have raised a ruckus?"[3] The fact is, public sentiment toward the building of highways through Westchester County has varied markedly over the course of the last eighty years.

When the Westchester County segment of the New England Thruway—officially designated the New England Section of the New York Thruway, but more commonly known simply as part of Interstate 95—was built between 1950 and 1958, hundreds of buildings had to be either destroyed or moved. As was the case with other highways constructed through metropolitan areas, it ripped through neighborhoods already well established. The massive highway-building program of New York State Council of Parks chairman and New York City construction coordinator Robert Moses displaced 250,000 people from their homes, most in New York City, from the 1920s to the 1960s.

Moses did not mince words when it came to the business of highway building, commenting in an interview with biographer Robert A. Caro that often there were "'people in the way,'"[4] and in a 1964 speech, "'When you operate in an overbuilt metropolis you have to hack

The Internet and the Web

The Internet, a network of interconnected computers around the world, offers a staggering amount of material for the researcher. It is a means for accessing information on the World Wide Web through a web browser such as Internet Explorer, Firefox, or Safari. An excellent glossary for definitions of Internet-related terms can be found at http://www.lib.berkeley.edu. Another website, http://www.findingdulcinea.com, explains key issues surrounding Internet usage.

When I first discovered that what is today an interstate highway near my house was some eighty years ago to have been a picturesque parkway I had never heard of, a quick search via the Internet turned up commentary by the publisher of a local online newspaper. He asked if our adjoining villages should have united in protest (as had recently been the case with opposition to a major retail business) and kept the super highway from cutting through our neighborhoods. His query—"Should we have raised a ruckus?"—led me to wonder about how the interstate had come to be and about 1950s public attitudes toward highway construction. Without that online article and the question it posed, my investigation of the parkway would not have materialized.

The Internet is great for getting fast answers. For example, the article in *Architectural Forum* about Cape Cod-type houses found everywhere across America used the image of the old Grand Army highway, now U.S. Route 6, to make the point: "If an architect from Mars were to take a cross country jaunt along the old Grand Army highway, now U.S. Route 6, . . . he would be struck by the persistence, throughout his journey, of [Cape Cod-type houses]."[1] I had no idea where Route 6 was or what its significance might be. Using the Google search engine, I immediately learned that at the time of the article's publication in 1949, U.S. Route 6 was the longest continuous U.S. route, extending 3,652 miles. Today it still traverses fourteen states and is the second-longest U.S. route. Its interesting history is detailed on the website of the Route 6 Tourist Association, http://www.route6tour.com. Getting an immediate answer enabled me to quickly get back to the *Architectural Forum* article with an enhanced understanding of its central idea.

Having access to catalogues of both local libraries and large libraries such as the Library of Congress or the New York Public Library through their websites is, of course, a boon to a researcher. Even if the full text of what is needed is not online in a database (and that is often the case with old sources), you can prepare your call slips with all the necessary information before your trip to the library so that your time actually spent there is very efficient.

Google and other organizations are now scanning copyright-free, out-of-print books into their servers, making the full text of many historical volumes available online that otherwise are difficult to find in libraries and sometimes nearly impossible to buy. As of early 2011, Google had scanned fifteen million books. For example, a detailed and lengthy history of Westchester County published in 1886 that has been extremely valuable to my research appeared online midway through my research after I had decided not to pay $150 for the reprint edition and made repeated trips to the local library to use its reference copy. Now I can call it up quickly on my home computer or download it. If you use something on an ongoing basis, it is important to keep checking online because you never know when something you need might appear there.

Internet communication allowed me to find on eBay and buy, for less than fifteen dollars, the issue of *McCall's* that featured my house's twin. Of course, the magazine is available to look at in large libraries, but owning the actual issue is much more fun than just having a photocopy of it. Finding the specific issue I wanted to buy would have been hugely more time-consuming without the Internet.

The World Wide Web via the Internet, on the other hand, as any schoolteacher will tell you, can yield information that is incomplete, misleading, or worse. For example, I would have thought that the Sears, Roebuck Archives website would contain complete information about the store's historic Modern Homes program, but it shows fewer than 120 of the nearly 450 house designs the company sold over the years. Finding the Stevenson and Jandl book *Houses by Mail* proved much more helpful. Had I stopped with the Web, I would have missed tremendous amounts of pertinent information. The lesson to be learned is, do not stop with an Internet search.

Although it is an understatement to say there is a lot out there on the Web, it is not everything, and what is there should be utilized with a bit of caution. Determining the credibility of the website is paramount. You have to be like a reporter and know your sources. Ask yourself who the author is, what that person's or organization's credentials and reputation are, what biases the site might reflect, and when it was last updated.

your way with a meat ax.'"[5] As vividly described by Caro, "[Robert Moses] tore out the hearts of a score of neighborhoods, communities the size of small cities themselves, communities that had been lively, friendly places to live, the vital part of the city that made New York a home to its people."[6]

Less densely populated than New York City, Westchester County nonetheless suffered the loss of hundreds of houses, apartment buildings, and businesses, destroyed or, in some cases, moved, as the construction of Interstate 95 progressed northeastward during the 1950s. The journey to that decade of interstate highway development, though, began more than 200 years ago.

A HISTORY OF HIGHWAYS

Highway building in the United States dates back prior to 1785, when stagecoaches had come into general use, requiring better roads. Because the states at the time had no funds to pay for highways, private companies built turnpikes and collected tolls. By the mid-1800s, however, railroads had taken over most long-distance travel, rendering the turnpikes no longer profitable. Without the private turnpike companies involved, roads deteriorated rapidly.

Toward the end of the 1800s, the phenomenal popularity of the bicycle focused attention on the inadequacy of existing roads, and in 1880 the League of American Wheelmen began promoting road improvement. The so-called Good Roads movement gained impetus with the coming of the gasoline-engine automobile, first introduced in 1893. That year the federal government established the Office of Road Inquiry, later the Bureau of Public Roads.[7] Then in 1916, with over 3.5 million motor vehicles in use, Congress passed the Federal Aid Road Act, also known as the Good Roads Act, establishing a federally funded highway program and representing the culmination of the Good Roads movement, a forty-year-long lobbying effort by various public and private entities.[8]

The rapid growth of suburbs between 1900 and 1920 and the increase in the number of automobile-owning families in the early 1920s[9] contributed to the development of a new concept in highway building—parkways. Although Calvert Vaux, Frederick Law Olmstead's collaborator in designing Manhattan's Central Park, first used the term "parkway" in 1868,[10] Westchester County actually pioneered the parkway-system concept in the twentieth century. Parkways came to be defined as ribbons of parkland containing roads, enabling the populace to travel easily by automobile to recreational parks, while allowing the vehicles' occupants to remain in aesthetically pleasing surroundings for the entire trip. By definition, parkways excluded commercial traffic and trucks. Having completed 160 miles of them by 1932,[11] Westchester County became the model for parkway development nationwide.

FIGURE 2.2 The Garth Woods section of the Bronx River Parkway in Yonkers, New York in 1925. The river can be seen to the left of the road. Historic American Engineering Record, Bronx River Parkway Reservation, HAER No. NY-327. *(Photograph courtesy of the Westchester County Archives.)*

WESTCHESTER'S FIRST PARKWAY

Westchester's first parkway, the Bronx River Parkway, developed from a need to clean up the Bronx River, by 1896 a virtual open sewer throughout its course in Westchester and New York City's northernmost borough, the Bronx. Public pressure to alleviate the situation had mounted, and in 1906, the state legislature created the Bronx Parkway Commission,[12] which recommended the building of a parkway reservation along the Bronx River. By 1912, both Westchester County and New York City had authorized the acquisition of land for the project.[13] The commission's annual report that year presented a grand vision for a comprehensive system of parks linked by parkways. It asked, "Who can pronounce too ambitious our forecast for the World's most magnificent outer park system!" It also described a parkway of the future along Long Island Sound on the eastern edge of Westchester County, an early hint of a highway that would eventually become the New England Thruway and the reason for my house's relocation.[14]

The planning and construction of the Bronx River Parkway proceeded from 1907 to 1923, with a brief hiatus during World War I.[15] At the official dedication in November 1925, in a letter read before a crowd gathered for the occasion,[16] Governor Alfred E. Smith noted that the parkway had set "a standard for all parkways in this country" and would be "of enormous benefit to the millions of people who seek fresh air and recreation and who may now travel from the city streets though a continuous narrow park into the open country."[17] A feature article in the *New York Times* described it as "magical," a "near-miracle," and a "long vista of sylvan charm." Accompanying the article were five artful, scenic photographs worthy of a book on romantic landscapes.[18] The new parkway even inspired a poem, also published in the *New York Times*, touting the parkway's beauty by comparing its vista to a Corot painting and asking if it might have been "planned by the hand of God."[19]

House & Garden magazine, with a nationwide circulation of over 130,000, featured the parkway in its July 1926 issue. The article praised the entire project as "a splendid example of what a well organized and ably administered commission can accomplish in the beautification of a large area. . . . The parkway tract, and the several others which will follow it . . . constitute a remarkable example of town betterment through the raising of real estate standards and the stimulation of community pride."[20] Illustrated with five photographs of the roadway and architectural drawings of two of the project's footbridges, the article extended to the reader an offer to send $1.00 for large-scale blueprints so that the charming, rustic bridges could be replicated elsewhere.[21] Even before the Bronx River Parkway's completion, its enormous success, both practical and aesthetic, was evident to all observers.

In the wake of this achievement, and pursuant to an act of the New York State Legislature, the Westchester County Board of Supervisors formed the Westchester

FIGURE 2.3 One of the original sixty footbridges built on the Bronx River Parkway Reservation, this one in Mount Vernon, New York. Historic American Engineering Record, Bronx River Parkway Reservation, HAER No. NY-327. *(Photograph courtesy of the Westchester County Archives.)*

County Park Commission, empowered to acquire land, borrow money, issue bonds, and manage and maintain parks and parkways—a broad authority for which there was ample public support.[22] The commission submitted a report to the board of supervisors in May 1923 recommending land purchases for four parks, as well as for two more north/southbound highways, the Hutchinson River Parkway and the Saw Mill River Parkway.[23] The park commission's work got off to a vigorous and impressive start.

In its 1924 annual report, the commission set forth the rationale for the development of a county park and parkway system. The key points included: the growth of suburbs made possible by improved transit; the development of the automobile, with a consequent demand for good roads; a growing interest in town and city planning; and the Bronx River Parkway, which had greatly influenced public sentiment in favor of additional parkways.[24] At the time, the commission believed that the projects it had authorized the previous year comprised a comprehensive park program. But after experiencing pressure from businesses and residents to relieve traffic congestion and fearing the rapid subdivision and development of land in the southern part of the county would leave little land available for public use,[25] the commission planned a dozen new park and parkway projects, the Pelham-Port Chester Parkway among them.

A PARKWAY NEVER BUILT—THE PELHAM-PORT CHESTER PARKWAY

Early in 1925, the park commission embarked on its plan to purchase 6,000 acres for new parks and forty-five miles of parkways. This included the Pelham-Port Chester Parkway, which would create a through route from New York City to Connecticut along Long Island Sound.[26] The county eventually built most of the parks

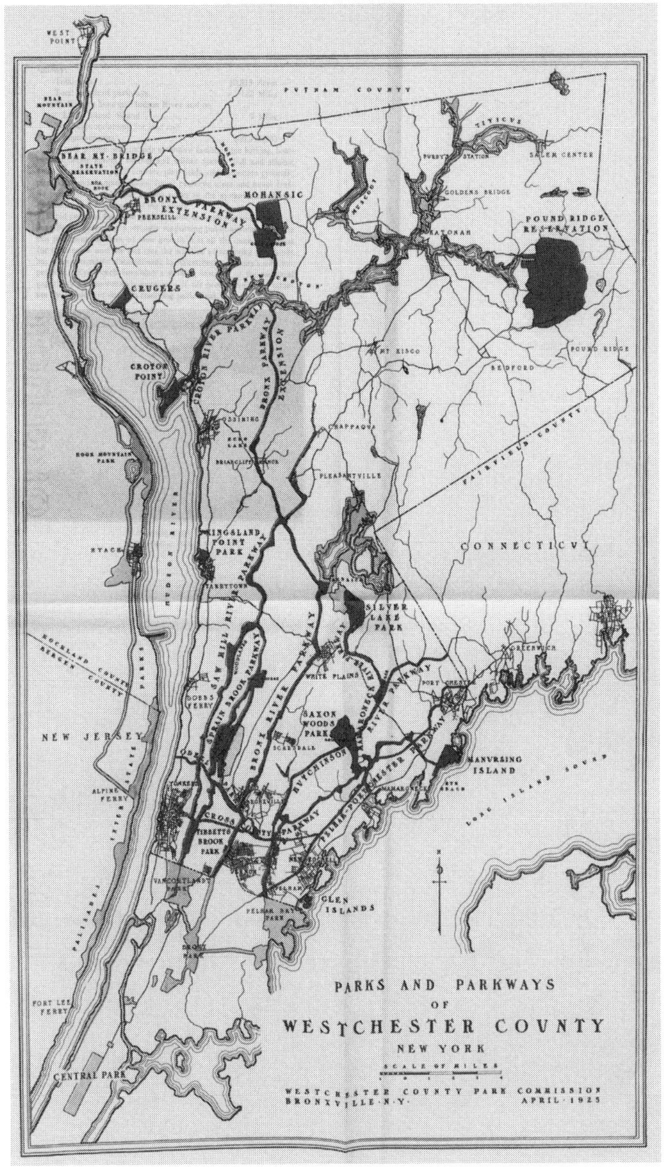

FIGURE 2.4 *Parks and Parkways of Westchester County, New York* showing six proposed parkways in 1925, among them the Pelham-Port Chester Parkway to the east, as well as the Bronx River Parkway, completed that year. *(Photograph courtesy of the Westchester County Archives.)*

and parkways proposed that year, but this is the story of one that was never built, a parkway plan with a long, convoluted, tortured, and politicized demise—and its subsequent gradual reincarnation.[27]

The thirteen-mile stretch of the Pelham-Port Chester Parkway was to traverse Pelham, New Rochelle, Larchmont, Mamaroneck, Rye, and Port Chester. It would parallel the New York, New Haven & Hartford Railroad and the Boston Post Road—one of the country's oldest thoroughfares, and long considered inadequate. Described in the park commission's 1925 annual report as "originally built in separate links from town to town, [the Boston Post Road] was constituted as one continuous road by act of the Legislature, in 1703, directing that 'one Public Common Highway be laid out and kept in repair from New York through that county and the county of Westchester four rods, English, wide, to be forever a Public Road to the Colony of Connecticut.'"[28] By the start of the twentieth century, it carried a large number of vehicles traveling between New York City and New England, as well as local traffic, increasing rapidly with the development of suburban real estate along the Long Island Sound. The park commission planned the Pelham-Port Chester Parkway to reduce the volume of traffic on the Boston Post Road.

Within months, the commission began buying land to create the parkway's right-of-way. Frequent acquisitions took place from early 1926 through 1927.[29] They were newsworthy enough to warrant coverage in the *New York Times* on a number of occasions during 1926.[30] By early 1928, however, the momentum seems to have slowed, causing various private and civic groups to lobby for construction to begin.[31]

Perhaps to assuage the citizenry, the commission had one underpass built in Larchmont. It carried Murray Avenue over the nonexistent parkway.[32] Completed by the spring of 1930,[33] the structure is still in evidence today beneath Murray Avenue, incorporated into a playground. Below two large stone arches where the parkway would have traversed, the asphalt surface displays a shuffleboard court and two large, concentric circles perhaps to be used as a tricycle-riding course. It is the only part of the Pelham-Port Chester Parkway ever actually built and today merely an unusual architectural feature to find in a playground.

THE BOSTON POST ROAD NEEDS RELIEF BUT OBSTACLES ABOUND

A front-page article in the *Daily Times* of Mamaroneck reported that during the 1926 Fourth of July holiday weekend, 1,400 cars per hour passed though the town along the Boston Post Road. It also noted that "at the traffic intersections not on the Post Road, traffic is reported to be normal."[34] Clearly, the traffic situation on this thoroughfare was an issue needing to be addressed. Park commission annual reports throughout the 1920s cited the urgent need for a highway along Long Island Sound, the same theme appearing in newspaper coverage for decades to follow. For example, the author of a 1937 article in the *New York Times* observed, "to relieve the Boston Post Road, now much overcrowded, the agitation has been renewed" to complete the parkway.[35] Thirteen years later, an editorial writer remarked on the ongoing pressure of traffic on the Boston Post Road: "Doubtless there is justification for a feeling that the incongruity of the Model T highway doing the job of a 1950 streamliner leaves Westchester atop a small volcano."[36] The commission continued to conduct studies and to produce engineering plans for the Pelham-Port Chester Parkway, but numerous obstacles hindered actual progress.

Impediments to the project's advancement fell into four categories: construction problems, increasing costs,

FIGURE 2.5 The unused parkway underpass is today a part of Memorial Park playground in Larchmont, New York. *(Photo by Michael Torlen.)*

World War II, and opposition from a variety of government, corporate, and private quarters. Construction and design challenges included the large number of required grade-separation bridges or underpasses, the proximity to the railroad line, and the projected pavement width of eighty feet, which, at the time, would have been the widest in Westchester County.[37] The original 1925 estimated cost for land acquisition of 250 acres was $1 million, a sum that turned out to be grossly insufficient.[38] Financing became increasingly difficult as the prices of real estate and construction inflated. As early as 1927, the commission stated its hesitancy to recommend expenditures large enough to begin construction.[39] After 1929 and the onset of the Depression, it adopted a very conservative fiscal policy.[40] In the next decade, due to the war emergency, New York State withheld funds on which Westchester depended for parkway repairs, causing the commission to indicate it might have to recommend closing the Bronx River Parkway.[41] If the government could not maintain existing highways, it was unlikely that it would allocate any funds to new highway construction.

Opposition to plans for building the Pelham-Port Chester Parkway took various forms. In 1926, three railroad companies with lines in Westchester lodged a formal protest over a park commission recommendation that the railroads pay one-half the cost of the construction of crossovers.[42] The following year, village authorities in Port Chester raised objections to the proposed path of the roadway, causing the park commission to agree it would not proceed on any planned route without village approval.[43] Late in 1929, the Larchmont Gardens Association and the League of Civic Associations of the Town of Mamaroneck protested the proposed use of the Pelham-Port Chester Parkway by commercial vehicles.[44] More strident opposition lay ahead as the entire vision for the highway along the sound began to change in the 1930s.

FROM PARKWAY TO THRUWAY—OUT OF COUNTY HANDS

The dream of a highway to connect New York City with New England and relieve pressure on the much-used Boston Post Road went through a conceptual transition from its inception as a parkway in 1925 to the groundbreaking of the New England Thruway in Westchester County in 1950. At the same time, the vision for possible funding sources for it changed as it first shifted from a county to a state undertaking, and eventually became part of a vast federal system.

An early hint that some believed New York State should take over the Pelham-Port Chester Parkway project appeared in 1929, just before the stock market crash. The *New York Times* reported: "Since the parkway is outlined on State highway maps and follows a State highway route, the county has taken the stand that the state must build the road."[45] Perhaps Westchester County leaders sought a more equitable distribution of state funds, given that in 1929, 70 percent of state funding allocated to the metropolitan region for parks and parkways was going to Robert Moses' projects in another rapidly developing suburban area, Nassau and Suffolk counties on Long Island.[46] In spite of a recommendation by the New York State Council of Parks that $1 million of state funds be allocated for construction of the Pelham-Port Chester Parkway in the 1933 budget year,[47] no aid was forthcoming.

The New York State Legislature soon created the Pelham-Port Chester Parkway Authority, which submitted a loan application to the Reconstruction Finance Corporation, created by Congress to aid self-supporting public works projects. Ultimately, the loan was denied.[48] In the view of the New York State Superintendent of Public Works in 1937, the Pelham-Port Chester Parkway topped a list of ten highways that the state most needed to build.[49] The same year, the chairman of the Westchester

County Budget Committee publicly insisted that the state undertake any new parkway development,[50] and other county officials resolved not to take on any major highway work at the expense of local taxpayers.[51] That the state should pay for the parkway's construction was a recurring theme in newspaper coverage from 1936 through 1938.

By December 1936, the ribbon of parkland once deemed exclusively for pleasure traffic—with the potential for becoming another "vista of sylvan charm"—had become the locus for a "freeway," defined in a *New York Times* article as a new type of highway "based on a right of way to which abutting property owners do not have access." The article bluntly asserted, "The Pelham-Port Chester Parkway will be a freeway," part of an extensive system of new highways around New York City recommended by the Regional Plan Association to ease traffic congestion.[52]

Envisioning a "truck toll route" that would be financed through a private authority created by the New York State Legislature, Robert Moses announced fourteen months later: "the railroad right-of-way and Westchester County's unused Pelham-Port Chester Parkway right-of-way alone would provide a possible route" for an express highway out of the city. The *Times* article reporting his announcement flatly stated, "The [Pelham-Port Chester] parkway project was abandoned because of the depression."[53] Now the parkway would become a truck and bus toll artery.

By 1938, federal aid became part of the funding-source expectation.[54] And by 1940—with a plan for a national interregional highway system in its infancy—a combination of state and federal aid was squarely part of the vision. World War II brought yet another identity for the Pelham-Port Chester Parkway—a federal defense highway. Creating such a highway meant that state and federal governments would take over building a mixed-traffic road on the Pelham-Port Chester Parkway right-of-way.[55] In fact, that is what happened.

THE 1920S AND 1930S—PUBLIC SENTIMENT PRO

Despite sporadic mild opposition, the public's attitude toward the building of the Pelham-Port Chester Parkway was generally positive in the 1920s and 1930s. Broad support for the development of parklands for conservation and recreation, appreciation of parkways such as the Bronx River Parkway as works of great beauty, and desire for ease of automobile travel all contributed to the early universal positive regard for parkway construction. According to Caro, although "almost all public works arouse some opposition," until the 1960s the majority of American voters "worshiped public works projects in and for themselves."[56]

Many people viewed parkways as economic growth stimulators. The *New York Times* quoted one real estate developer in October 1930: "Westchester is one of the few counties in and around New York that has already come out of the building slump into which the entire country was plunged in November of last year. . . . The chief increase of building activity has been on the Sound shore, in such villages as Rye, Harrison, Mamaroneck and Larchmont. This is largely due to the . . . impending construction of the Pelham-Port Chester Parkway. . . ."[57]

The real estate industry regarded the planned parkway as a residential sales asset. A newspaper article concerning a model home open for public viewing in conjunction with the New Rochelle Chamber of Commerce Better Home Show of 1935 touted the fact that the house "overlooks the Pelham-Port Chester Parkway" in "one of the choice residential sections."[58] Even before the Depression, an elaborate sales promotion brochure for the 1927 development of the neighborhood adjacent to where my house once stood included parkway proximity as a major selling point. The development, it stated, "is located in the hub of the new Westchester County Parkway System." Nearby was the Pelham-Port Chester Parkway—"more or less similar to the Bronx River Parkway, which is one of the wonders of Westchester County."[59] After acquiring the land for a subdivision, Harry Rich Mooney, developer of the nearly twelve acres that included my property, had his sales director write an article stating that he had generously deeded a portion of the property to the Westchester County Park Commission "at a nominal price, thereby showing his fine spirit toward the County, as well as securing for his development, or MAMARONECK KNOLLS, as it is called, an immediate link . . . [to] the parkway system."[60] These real estate perspectives indicate that many people viewed parkways favorably. People generally held parkways in high regard, but as the depressed economy of the 1930s slowed road construction and people newly installed in the suburbs began driving more, pressure to alleviate crowded roadways emerged as the single strongest driving force behind support for parkway construction.

THE 1940S—PUBLIC SENTIMENT CON

Although widespread support for highways persisted, in the early 1940s people began to raise questions about the wisdom of some aspects of their construction. For the Pelham-Port Chester Parkway, the parkway concept had since given way to the freeway concept, and more specifically to a defense highway concept. Though Westchester County residents who lived along the parkway route supported the war effort, they objected to the change in the road's purpose. Words like "betrayed," "revolt," and "protest" began to appear in the press. The Town of Mamaroneck supervisor contended that Westchester residents felt betrayed because the property originally had been purchased to create a pleasure car route, a parkway, not a commercial truck highway. He also asserted that Robert Moses wanted to create feeder highways for New York City rather than help Westchester solve its traffic problems and that building the road would decrease property values significantly.[61]

The *New York Times* called the reaction of the Westchester County Board of Supervisors to the Pelham-Port Chester Parkway plans "a revolt against having expensive parkway plans made public and forced upon them without prior submission for revision." One town supervisor, claiming he did not have access to information, declared, "'People with life savings invested in homes'" have suddenly learned that a major highway would soon "'shoot past them.'"[62] Signaling the development of a grassroots movement against Moses' "mixed-traffic" plans for the Pelham-Port Chester Parkway, the Larchmont Gardens Association held a mass meeting to rally for a parkway limited to pleasure cars.[63] The objections seemed to quiet during the war, only to be revived as the war's end approached and plans for road construction resurfaced.

Once again, the issue among protesters was truck traffic and the resulting loss of property values. A number of civic organizations, as well as several individuals, submitted written protests to the county board of supervisors.[64] One citizen filed a lawsuit in federal court to prevent the county from turning over the parkway land to the state because property use for the Thruway would lower property values and increase taxes for Westchester residents.[65] As construction moved across the state line into Connecticut, residents there also began to raise objections. A Westport citizen cited Port Chester as "an example of a town 'well-nigh ruined' by main highways and inter-connecting roads."[66] Throughout the 1940s, those living near the parkway right-of-way continued to object sporadically to the prospect of its use for mixed traffic.

A few astute observers recognized that in their fury to alleviate traffic conditions, government officials had overlooked the drawbacks to massive road building, particularly when done without adequate planning. Lewis Mumford, a vocal advocate of urban planning and a long-time critic of New York City development, commented in a 1946 interview, "'A large part of the money we are spending on highways right now is wasted because we don't know whether we want people where the highways are going. But highways are an impressive, flashy thing to build.'"[67]

Expressing the opposing point of view, Robert Moses wrote dramatically (and for many, persuasively) of his highways: "'Our new arteries will give us a better city, more accessible, less congested, more comfortable and convenient for living and working than it was before, and, as an important incident, we shall have the finest collection of land bridges, intersections, clover leaves, chicken guts, ever conceived, since Daedalus built the labyrinth for Minos of Crete, 'a mighty maze,' as the poet said, 'but not without a plan.'"[68] Those against the "impressive, flashy" highways being planned and built everywhere were in the minority. Despite the recurring objections from a few average citizens and outspoken critics like Mumford, a majority of the public continued to support highway building throughout the 1940s and into the 1950s, as did public officials, both within the county and at the state and federal levels.

NEW ENGLAND THRUWAY GROUNDBREAKING

In 1943, Westchester County had pledged to make a gift after the war of the Pelham-Port Chester Parkway right-of-way to New York State for construction of a mixed-traffic express highway.[69] Soon after, Robert Moses disclosed that the federal and state governments had finally granted modest appropriations to study the project, and highway officials from New York and Connecticut announced they would meet to discuss the post-war improvement of the Boston Post Road.[70] By the summer of 1944, the press began referring to the planned highway as the New England Thruway.[71] The same year, the Federal Aid Highway Act of 1944 laid the groundwork for the Interstate Highway System,[72] today the Dwight D. Eisenhower System of Interstate and Defense Highways,[73] of which the New England Thruway was destined to become a part.

In September 1949, construction began on the Bronx segment of the New England Thruway, while the Westchester portion remained in the planning and contract-bidding stages.[74] With many Westchester County residents becoming impatient over the delays and uncertainty, the county board of supervisors began waging an all-out campaign to commence construction and thereby relieve traffic on the Boston Post Road, reputedly the second most heavily traveled road in the U.S.[75] At last, by mid-1950 workers had broken ground in New Rochelle,[76] and the New England Thruway finally began its slow northward advance through the county. Westchester officially handed over the thirteen-mile-long property to New York State in February 1952,[77] completing the transition from parkway to Thruway and from county control to state and federal control.

THE 1950S—THE GREATER GOOD, RESIGNATION, AND ACCEPTANCE

By the time construction on the New England Thruway and the New York-Buffalo Thruway (later known as the Major Deegan Expressway, a northbound highway through the center of the county) began in earnest, what opposition remained had diminished to resigned sadness in those directly affected. The *New York Times* reported in 1953: "Residents of this city [New Rochelle] and Yonkers, two of the communities hardest hit by the state's new Thruway construction, shook their heads disconsolately today as they told of dislocations in business and social life caused by the loss of shops, offices, factories, homes, churches, parks and local streets in the paths of the Thruways. . . . Besides cutting broad swaths through old business areas of New Rochelle and Yonkers, with a loss of 450 structures, the Thruways will cause scattered business dislocations and home demolitions elsewhere."[78]

Two years later, the same reporter wrote an article titled "Thruway to Cut a Painful Gash Across Heart of New Rochelle." He cited 300 homes, churches, and commercial buildings scheduled for demolition and 260 graves from two cemeteries slated for relocation,[79] failing to mention, however, the caves beneath the blasting site where Native Americans had once buried their dead.[80] In the face of what the New Rochelle City Affairs Committee deemed the "'catastrophic'" effect of the construction and another claim that the city was "being 'needlessly blown to pieces,'" the mayor forecast a future renaissance in downtown business, declaring that despite the challenges, the Thruway was essential to alleviate the "daily traffic load of 25,000 pleasure cars and gargantuan interstate trucks" on the Boston Post Road.[81] Whether or not his prediction about a downtown business renaissance was accurate is debatable, but his comments are representative of the attitudes of many during the mid-1950s.

As construction moved northeastward toward Connecticut, New York State announced various design changes instigating intermittent protest. In 1954, upon learning of plans to construct a cloverleaf interchange that would create eight separate sidewalk crossings near an elementary school, the Mamaroneck Board of Education voted to formally protest.[82] Eight school-related organizations and the village board added their official disapproval. Devaluation of nearby property was obviously a concern, but typical of the objections was the one from the Mamaroneck Heights Association, a group representing my house's neighborhood: "While recognizing the 'thruway proper' as a major step in the progress of transportation for the eastern seaboard, the association based its request 'primarily upon the potential hazard to elementary school children.'"[83] By January 1955, community members had submitted to the Thruway Authority at least six alternative designs to reduce the number of crossings. Indeed, it seems the effort to alter the highway entrance and exit plans near the school was partially successful. Today, the cloverleaf has just five crossings along Mamaroneck Avenue, instead of the originally planned eight. Among the changes residents could not stop, though, were the two cloverleaf loops that plowed directly through the spot where my house once stood, necessitating its removal.[84]

FIGURE 2.6 An Interstate 95 entrance ramp where the house once stood in the area near the car. *(Photo by Michael Torlen.)*

Although residents directly affected by major highway construction continued asserting their will to try to control certain small design aspects, by this time they had acquiesced to the disruptions and property loss. Even people inconvenienced by the work on a daily basis accepted, for the most part, the necessity of progress. After the construction process injured four people and, in a separate incident, a forty-seven-pound rock flew one thousand feet into a vacant house—the results of dynamite blasting to clear rock ledges for the Thruway's roadbed—Mamaroneck village officials and contractors met to plan an alternative blasting method. Required to evacuate their houses before scheduled detonations—sometimes even in the middle of meal preparations—residents also endured the constant dust, dirt, and noise of drilling. One man living directly behind the blast site pointed out numerous cracks in his house to a newspaper reporter and then stated that no matter what the compensation was, his house would never be the same. Nevertheless, he acknowledged that he recognized that such roads must be constructed. The article noted that the man's daughter "struck a new note when she declared that she did not feel that 'they have any right to subject people to such indignities.'" Her perspective seems to have been the exception rather than the rule.[85]

THE MOHICAN PATH OPENS

The New England Thruway, a part of Interstate 95, officially opened on October 18, 1958, much of its length following the Pelham-Port Chester Parkway right-of-way. Newspaper coverage noted that despite its name, the fifteen-mile, six-lane superhighway did not actually go through any part of New England, but connected high-

FIGURE 2.7 A Mamaroneck family evacuates their house before a dynamite detonation for the construction of Interstate 95 in 1956. *(Photograph courtesy of the* Journal News *and the Mamaroneck Public Library.)*

ways in New York City's Bronx with the Connecticut Turnpike. Governors Averell Harriman of New York and Abraham Ribicoff of Connecticut presided over a ceremony held at the border between the two states. Included in a *New York Times* article that autumn was a highlighted inset informing readers: "The New York Legislature decided at its latest session to bestow upon" the New England Section of the New York Thruway the "inspiring historic" name The Mohican Path, in honor of the region's first residents,[86] an unthinking gesture given the Native American burial sites that had been disregarded during the blasting for the highway's construction. For whatever reason, the designation has not stuck. I could find no one today who knows the highway as The Mohican Path.

"WE" 50 YEARS AGO AND "WE" TODAY

Considering Ned Benton's questions—"Did Larchmont and Mamaroneck take the wrong path in 1954 when the New England Thruway was being planned? Did we go along when we could have raised a ruckus?"—it seems that we did raise a ruckus at times, but not enough of one to greatly alter the course of events. Moreover, and perhaps more significantly, the "we" of the 1950s was different from the "we" of today. Not only did public attitudes toward the building of highways change in the thirty years from the conception of the Pelham-Port Chester Parkway to the realization of the New England Thruway, but they also have changed in the fifty years since those first interstates tore through established communities all over the United States. Broadly speaking, throughout most of the twentieth century the public's attitudes toward highway construction were shaped by government policies and subsidies that favored the development of an automobile-based transportation system and the roads it required over mass transit.[87]

No area of this country, particularly in the 1950s, was immune to these pressures and to the "march of progress" and its concomitant disruption. State and federal governments were building highways everywhere, and the public generally was pleased about it. In the 1950s, Westchester County citizens, like their counterparts elsewhere, came to embrace the concepts of the greater good and progress in the modern world. Pointing to the experience of modernity and how it produced an atmosphere in the mid-twentieth century that repeatedly sacrificed the past and present to make way for the future, Marshall Berman in *All That Is Solid Melts into Air* observed: "The developers and devotees of the expressway world [the modern environment that emerged after World War II] presented it as the only possible modern world: to oppose them and their works was to oppose modernity itself, to fight history and progress, to be a Luddite, an escapist, afraid of life and adventure and change and growth. This strategy was effective because, in fact, the vast majority of modern men and women do not want to resist modernity: they feel its excitement and believe in its promise, even when they find themselves in its way."[88]

MOVING HOUSES

The moving of houses simply came with the territory of building major highways in the mid-twentieth century, yet still I wondered about the relocation of my own house. I found a photograph of it in its original location in the town's tax assessor's office. In a tiny black and white image stapled to a building inspector's report, the house looks just as it does today except for its setting on a sloping street and a side porch, now enclosed and a part of the living room.

Unable to ascertain what the original owner of the house thought about losing her property in an eminent domain proceeding, I imagined that surely she would

FIGURE 2.8 The house as it appears in the town's tax assessor's records in its original location in 1938 and in its current location in 1957. *(Courtesy of the Town of Mamaroneck Assessor's Department. Photo by author.)*

Think Local

Small organizations often do not have the resources to digitize materials and put information online, so going to their facilities in person is a necessity. Local town archives and historical societies may have files that you can peruse. These sorts of resources tend not to be fully indexed, so sometimes the only way to see what is in them is to look item by item. My town's archives had a collection of maps of the area dating back to the 1700s. This resource was invaluable for understanding the changes that had taken place on my property over the years.

Leafing through a historical society file, I ran across a 1961 photo spread clipped from a local newspaper on remnants of Native American culture in my area. One image shows a few large rocks set in a grassy area. The caption notes that the rocks were located on my block-long street and read, "The center photo shows Indian-placed rocks in a semi-circle. This was where the Indian Council met. . . . The chief sat on the largest of the stones in the semi-circle."[1] This bit of information broadened my view of what constitutes the history of a place—recorded history and history before records were kept. I also learned by asking neighbors that this rock circle had been partly in my backyard and partly in the backyard of the house next door in the years before the owners installed an in-ground swimming pool. (See chapter 10.)

Check with local officials. Ask them about offices with records in regard to property. Villages, towns, cities, counties, and other government entities keep different kinds of records, many of them open to the public. In the tax assessor's office for my town, I found on the tax card for my property two small photographs of my house, one from 1938, at the time of its first inspection in its original location, and one from 1957, after it had been moved. Various governmental bodies maintain minutes of meetings and generate commission reports concerning a variety of ongoing and special projects. I found a wealth of material on the building of the parkways in my county in commission reports produced over a period of more than a decade. Now housed in the county archives, the documents are catalogued and accessible to the public.

County government offices are most often the repositories for deeds that record property transfers. Court records for proceedings regarding mortgage defaults and nonpayment of property taxes are often found in the courthouse. Local libraries frequently have special collections that pertain to local history. Churches may maintain useful records, particularly in regard to baptisms, marriages, and burials. Reading tombstones in local cemeteries can be helpful too. In sum, always check for what is in your own backyard.

have enjoyed the handsome parkway (with no roadway to mar its beauty) adjacent to her property when she bought it in 1936. Given all the local publicity surrounding parkways throughout the 1930s, she would have known that the proposed roadway in that parkway was evolving into another kind of highway, one difficult to visualize at the time. Might she have envisioned her property overlooking a swath of green with two lanes of cars cruising at forty miles an hour, rather than the broad slash of gray concrete with huge eighteen-wheelers speeding along at seventy, tires droning—what the highway presents today? A parkway sits in the land; even the people on it feel like they are riding through nature. The Thruway, on the other hand, overpowers nature and leaves one with the sense of nature scarred.

Having had the house built in 1937, the owner received a Notice of Appropriation, dated April 25, 1955, stating that the Superintendent of Public Works deemed it necessary to acquire her property on behalf of The People of the State of New York for purposes connected with the construction of the New York Thruway, New England Section. Once in the possession of the state, the house sold at auction before being moved by the new owners. In less than two decades the house went from being in a choice location, overlooking the Pelham-Port Chester Parkway in 1936, when people viewed being in such a location as an asset, to being directly in the path of a vastly expanded future highway and its cloverleaf in 1955.

The moving of houses seems to have been much more common during the 1950s than it is today. With highways being built everywhere, many owners chose to move rather than demolish. An article in *Westchester Life* shows five houses in 1952 in various locations around the New York metropolitan area being moved, including a row house—without the rest of the row. House moving, it seems, was a lucrative business. One man, for a mere $50, bought at auction a dwelling condemned to make way for a highway project, moved it to a newly purchased lot, placed it on a new foundation, and landscaped the lot, all for $10,000. He turned around and sold it shortly thereafter for $15,000.[89] Even whole towns have been moved to make way for public works such as reservoirs. And it happens that Cape Cod-type houses were frequently moved during the seventeenth and eighteenth centuries. If a Cape's original site proved to be too much battered by storms or if the winds of business shifted, the owner simply moved it. Its squat shape and sturdy design made it particularly suited to being "hoisted over the dunes or floated across the bay" to a more promising location.[90]

My house, which everyone refers to as a "Cape Cod," now seemed to share something with its ancestors. But what exactly is a "Cape Cod" house in New York? With the explanation for the former address of my *McCall's* "Home of the Month" thoroughly understood, I now began to wonder about the house's design and its New England coastal designation.

three

The Cape Cod House: Why So Common, Why So Popular?

> "The Cape Cod Cottage" is one of those pleasant alliterations which springs readily to the lips of real estate salesmen when they are describing a small, trim, story-and-a-half house. It is a phrase which has endured some rather loose handling.[1]
>
> —Samuel Chamberlain, "The Real Cape Cod," *House Beautiful*, 1937

Real estate agents tend to generalize and categorize. How else to make sense of the wide variety of houses they sell? My husband and I saw houses in at least eight categories during our search for a house, most of them common in the Northeast—farmhouses, Victorians, colonials, Tudors, ranches, split-levels, and contemporaries—yet based on our agent's lingo, the great majority seemed to be Capes, including the one we eventually bought. Why was every second house we looked at a Cape? Many of the so-called Capes bore little resemblance to each other. I was confused. Just what is a Cape? Why are there so many of them and what do they have to do with Cape Cod? Even though I had spent five years living in Massachusetts and had undoubtedly seen many Cape Cod-type houses, nothing about them stood out to me. Perhaps my failure to see them was precisely because they are so common. The Cape we found seemed attractive and fit our needs in terms of layout, size, and price, but was basically ordinary. Little did I know, until I began doing some research and carefully looking at houses around me, just how ordinary, but also exceptional, the Cape Cod-type house really is.

My research quickly took me to a lengthy two-part 1949 article in *Architectural Forum* titled "The Cape Cod Cottage." The unidentified author observed, "If an architect from Mars were to take a cross-country jaunt along the old Grand Army highway, now U.S. Route 6, starting in lush, semi-tropical California and ending on the sandy, windswept hook of Cape Cod, . . . he would be struck by the persistence, throughout his journey, of one particular building type . . . and . . . would see, over and over again a small, white box-like house with a pitched roof and shuttered windows, . . . twentieth century America's most popular house design, . . . the Cape Cod Cottage."[2] At the time of the article's publication, Route 6 was the longest continuous U.S. route, extending 3,652 miles. The image of a trip on U.S. Route 6, traversing the entire country where one would see Capes over and over again, is oddly reminiscent of the "McCall Street" notion of a theoretical cross-country street. With a house every twenty-five feet (an unlikely prospect), it nonetheless represented the scope of the *McCall's* magazine readership—a kind of 1930s version of Middle America.

It was in the 1930s that the Cape, finding its way into nearly every county nationwide, developed into what *Architectural Forum* deemed "almost a national institution."[3] By 1940, the results of a questionnaire sent to building suppliers across the country revealed that "prospective small-house owners preponderantly prefer the Cape Cod Colonial" house.[4] Even as recently as the early 1980s, Stanley Schuler, in his thorough examination of Cape Cod-type houses, subtitled his book "America's Most Popular Home."[5] From the historic, restored, colonial-era Cape Cod cottages of New England, to the pre-World War II revival Cape, to the hundreds of thousands of postwar revival Capes, many of them found in tract-housing developments, the Cape Cod is a house still found everywhere in the United States. How did this happen?

ORIGINS

The Cape Cod house had its origins in the fisherman's cottage of New England's early English settlers. Built between the mid-1600s and about 1840, it was a simple, pragmatic, one-story design, its architectural elements shaped by climate, topography, and the resources at hand. The steeply pitched, side-gabled roof releases snow readily and was what the English knew—their thatched roofs had been designed to shed water. Built low to the ground with eaves projecting but a few inches in order to withstand high winds, the Cape's primary design rule was "'a short hoist and a long peak.'"[6]

A rectangular box with a nearly square floor plan, the Cape generally appeared in one of three sizes—known as a half-house, a three-quarters house, and a full house. The latter ranged from thirty-four to forty feet wide and twenty-eight to thirty-four feet deep, and had two small-paned windows on each side of a central entrance. The frame construction supported shingles; in later years, New Englanders often applied painted clapboarding to the façades only, as they considered this treatment on the sides and back ostentatious. (Even today, an eighteenth-century house we stay in each summer in Maine has clapboard painted salt hay yellow on the two sides visible from the road and bare, weathered gray shingle on the other two.) Added to the harsh environment and the meager available resources were the strict mores of the New England Puritan church, resulting in the Cape's austere appearance.[7]

The interior's absence of ornamentation and its simple plan echoed the sober appearance of the exterior. In a full Cape, there were normally two rooms at the front with a large keeping room or kitchen and small pantry across the rear and a large attic for sleeping or storage upstairs under the tall gable. Situated opposite the entrance, a chimney of mammoth proportions accommodated two or more fireplaces, a necessity for distributing warmth in a cold climate.

Nineteenth-century New England writers recognized the Cape's distinctive character and handsome practicality. Credit belongs to Reverend Dr. Timothy Dwight, from

Magazines

Like newspapers, magazines tell us much about a time period, particularly in regard to popular culture. Compared to newspapers, magazines historically have tended to be more relaxed in pace, somewhat more literary in tone, and retrospective rather than timely. Before the late nineteenth century, they had been for the affluent alone, but when printing methods developed, allowing the price to become more affordable, they began to reach the middle class as well.

The end of the nineteenth century brought a flurry of new magazines, available at newsstands and by subscription through the postal service. Eleven thousand magazines were published in the United States from 1885 to 1905, with some folding and others merging with similar publications. During that period, the number of periodicals published at a given time nearly doubled, reaching six thousand in 1905.[1]

Reader's Guide Retrospective is a database index of subjects in much of the popular press beginning with this burgeoning of magazines in America. Through it you can search for citations of articles that chronicle major events as well as the daily lives of Americans from 1890 to 1982. *American Periodicals Series* is a database of digitized images of the pages of over eleven hundred magazines published between 1741 and 1900.

For magazines older than 1890 that are not in a database, seeing what is in them requires using indexes, where they exist, or leafing through them page by page in a library's bound volumes or in microform. While turning the pages of old magazines may seem like a tedious and primitive way to do research, do not underestimate the value of this kind of browsing. With a topic such as the popularity of the Cape Cod type house, for example, gauging the pulse of the times through skimming every page of popular magazines was invaluable.

Frank Luther Mott's five-volume *A History of American Magazines*, which covers the years 1741 to 1930, offers summaries of the content, readership, circulation, and years of publication of hundreds of magazines. Organized by time period and broad subject area such as agriculture, construction, economics, geographic region, politics, and transportation, the book discusses magazines that address each subject. At the end of each volume are a few dozen detailed sketches of what Mott considered to be the most important magazines of the time. Mott is a perfect starting point for magazines not full-text digitized in databases.

Advertising supports magazines, and ads, like the articles and editorials, communicate much about a culture and an era. Check the back pages of bound volumes of old magazines. Sometimes the advertising sections from the back of each issue have been removed and are bound together with the covers and placed at the end of the volumes.

The entire range of magazines and journals—from the general and popular to the more specialized—is useful for creating a context. Magazines are conveyors of information and not only reflect the culture at any given time, but also interpret it.

FIGURE 3.1 Jonathan Collins House, South Pamet Road, Truro, Barnstable County, Massachusetts. Built in the 1800s. *(Photograph courtesy of the Library of Congress, Prints and Photographs Division, Historic American Buildings Survey, HABS MASS, 1-TRU,8-1.)*

1795 to 1817 the eighth president of Yale College, for first using the term Cape Cod to describe the houses he found on a trip to Massachusetts in 1800.[8] Addressing an imaginary Englishman in letters published in 1822 in *Travels in New-England and New-York*, he described the modest houses of Cape Cod as exhibiting "a tidy, neat aspect in themselves, and in their appendages; and furnish[ing] proofs of comfortable living."[9]

Henry David Thoreau made four trips to Cape Cod between 1849 and 1857. In 1855, *Putnam's Monthly* published his three articles about the geography, history, and culture of the Cape, the material issued posthumously in book form in 1865. Thoreau described the houses he found there as "sober-looking . . . low and broad. . . . Generally, the old-fashioned and unpainted houses on the Cape looked more comfortable, as well as picturesque, than the modern and more pretending ones, which were less in harmony with the scenery, and less firmly planted."[10]

No one knows whether the Cape Cod house actually originated on Cape Cod; it may have started in other areas of New England.[11] As a type, though, it spread throughout New England and beyond and persisted into the mid-1800s, succumbing to Victorian-era styles, only to be revived eighty years later as a part of the colonial revival in American architecture. Whatever its origins, the Cape Cod house has proved to be enduring and widely imitated—popular, ubiquitous, and hence, seemingly ordinary.

THE COLONIAL REVIVAL IN ARCHITECTURE

The twentieth-century Cape Cod house was one of several types of colonial revival homes built initially along the Atlantic coast that drew inspiration from seventeenth- and eighteen-century English and Dutch houses. Observers in the late 1800s and early 1900s used the term "colonial" to refer to a large number of architectural types, all associated with "'ancestral security' and 'roots.'"[12] For example, one writer observed in *House Beautiful* in 1897 that colonial architecture, becoming more appreciated, was still the only distinctively American style—"simple, dignified . . . pure and simple . . . for honest folk."[13] Six years later, another, writing in *House & Garden*, offered an appreciation of the classic Cape: "All along the New England shore are small houses, remnants of the earlier settlement, which . . . [show] quiet charm, and refinement of mass and detail, . . . value of restraint, the true meaning of proportion in its broad sense." The author went on to recommend that a collection of documentary drawings and photographs be made lest the charming buildings be forgotten.[14] The six-month-long 1876 Philadelphia Centennial Exposition, celebrating the one hundredth anniversary of the signing of the Declaration of Independence, was an impetus to this renewed attention to the country's heritage, particularly the American colonial era. It also stimulated the search for a national identity and the development of the colonial revival in new architecture.

Although the specific Cape Cod type would emerge as a favored housing model somewhat later, by the early twentieth century, several other colonial-revival architectural types were becoming a major part of domestic architecture. Speaking in 1913 of colonial housing types in general, well-known architect Aymar Embury II commented on their compatibility with modern requirements and value as prototypes, appreciated by architects and the public alike: "the . . . sympathy with New England Colonial work . . . becoming so general that at times we almost feel as if the Victorian era had never existed, and the Colonial tradition had persisted unbroken."[15] By 1918 at least one example of a Cape Cod-type house had appeared—in the architectural plans for an employee housing development for the Connecticut Mills Company in Danielson, Connecticut. Along with an apartment house and a "unity" group—a school, a recreation center, churches, and stores—were one- and two-family cottages. Among the several designs for single-family residences was a five-room Cape Cod-type house, several examples of which are still in existence today.[16] Most architects and observers at the time, though, seemed only to recognize the mere possibility of small New England colonial houses, such as Capes, as modern prototypes.

For example, a 1919 article on colonial architecture and the restoration work of architect Dwight James Baum noted that the work of the colonists had stood the test of time and, as a fundamentally American expression, was an appropriate source for domestic architecture of the twentieth century.[17] In writing about the old houses of Plymouth, Massachusetts, Baum himself noted two years later that much had been published on "important" architecture of the colonial period, but the simpler buildings had been neglected. Adaptable as prototypes for a typical American architecture, these small houses were "devoid of all affectation . . . and beautiful in their sturdy proportions, outlines, and relations of ground-line to sky-line and chimney silhouettes."[18]

Commenting in 1922 on Puritan architecture as "essentially American" with "simplicity, dignity, virility," another critic wrote of the moment being right for its revival.[19] Observers lauded colonial traditions in architecture for their associations with American heritage and found the dignity and beautiful proportions of the houses of the earliest New England settlers worthy of a revival. In the effort among architects during the 1920s to create a specifically American domestic architecture, the small colonial house began to be viewed as an appropriate prototype.

THE CAPE BEFORE THE CRASH

One of the first places that specific interest in historical Cape Cod cottages (as opposed to colonial houses in general) seems to have developed in a sustained way was in the White Pine Bureau's *White Pine Series of Architectural Monographs*. Created by an association of white pine timber producers in 1914 and directed primarily toward architects, the bimonthly publication promoted the structural uses of white pine in an effort to correct the perception that the white pine tree was no longer plentiful in the United States. Each issue, amply illustrated, examined outstanding examples of early American buildings made of white pine. In at least eight of the issues from 1917 to 1933—with four of them published before 1921—were photographs and, in some cases, measured drawings, of Cape Cod cottages in Maine, Massachusetts, Connecticut, and New York. Conceived as a promotional brochure during its first ten years, its distribution free of charge to five thousand architects across the country ensured its wide reach within the building industry.[20]

Photographs of Cape Cod-type houses also appeared in publications for a more general audience in the 1920s and early 1930s. Wallace Nutting published a series of picture books, beginning with his 1923 *Massachusetts Beautiful*, which included several Capes situated in pastoral surroundings.[21] Knowlton Mixer included historic Cape Cod-type cottages in his 1927 *Old Houses of New England*.[22] The first book focusing on the historic architecture of Cape Cod itself, *Colonial Architecture of Cape Cod, Nantucket and Martha's Vineyard* of 1932, included photographs of more than twenty Cape Cod-type houses. Its author, architect Alfred Easton Poor, noted in the foreword that his measured drawings and photographs would inspire those building small houses and those who feel the Cape Cod house is distinctively American.[23] Architectural plan books of the time also included Cape-type designs. For example, the J. D. Loizeaux Lumber Company of New Jersey included among its 170 designs in its 1927 plan book an entry labeled "The Cape Cod."[24]

Advertisements, too, included Cape Cod-type houses, as seen in a drawing in a 1922 issue of *Good Housekeeping*. In the ad, Lowe Brothers Company, with factories up and down the East Coast and in the Midwest, promoted their product line of paints and varnishes through the story of two women who had renovated their "homey" one-hundred-year-old house in Provincetown at the tip of Cape Cod.[25]

From the mid-1920s through the early 1930s, articles in both popular and professional periodicals examined

Cape Cod houses from various perspectives. Stories of restorations, historically sensitive renovations, and re-creations appeared widely, one author noting in 1930 that in the previous six to seven years people had come to view old houses more sympathetically, with scores of old Cape Cod cottages having recently undergone proper restorations.[26] A 1926 article in *Architectural Forum* declared that colonial bungalows, defined as small houses with most of the main rooms on the first floor, "can feel at home in any part of the United States, for it is the style that is best suited to the average American temperament."[27] "A Cape Type of House," a 1927 pamphlet, pointed to a nationwide awakening of interest among architects and homebuilders in "the Cape Cod type house. Even in far-away Texas they are putting up what they fondly believe to be examples of this kind of dwelling."[28] The author recognized that the Cape's beauty lay in its proportions, simplicity, and moderation in ornamentation.[29] What had begun in the 1890s as a heritage-inspired interest in large homes of the colonial type had, by the 1920s, spread to small, modest ones.

Popular magazines of the 1920s began publishing articles with a decidedly romantic and nostalgic tone, demonstrating both a general admiration for and a willingness to replicate the architecture of Cape Cod houses. "Cape Cod: Where Houses Were Built to Suit the Land" included photographs and a painting of several "honest little houses" of the Cape Cod type that "crop out as naturally from the soil as do the gray boulders of glacial rock."[30] The same issue of *House Beautiful* included a sketch and plans for a prize-winning Cape Cod house, the jury commenting on its "restfulness of outline."[31] Even professional journals included articles with a similar tone. One recommended to architects seeking simplicity in architecture "an astounding wealth of sketchable material . . . [and] simple white cottages of pleasing proportion" in Provincetown on Cape Cod.[32]

House Beautiful in 1923 presented a story on expanding a Cape Cod cottage for the occupant who yearns for the coziness a small house can offer.[33] Another story that year discussed building a typical Cape Cod cottage for summer use in Massachusetts, its exterior an exact replica of an eighteenth-century house, but its interior altered by the architect to suit more contemporary needs. After detailed descriptions of the house and landscaping, the author declared, "Whosoe'er can picture these things knows in his heart the changing magic of a New England summer."[34] The Cape Cod cottage even inspired a romantic poem, "Cape Cod Cottage," published by *McCall's* in 1930. After eight lines describing a Cape in a seaside setting, a place of "beauty and happiness," the poem's concluding words reference the house as "a sheltered hope."[35] It seems that here the Cape embodies a longing for security that would soon be a widespread sentiment during the early years of the Great Depression. Considering the language used to describe them, Capes seemed to be clearly striking an emotional chord with Americans.

Both professional architecture journals and popular magazines of the time addressed another consideration—the pragmatic demand for small houses. *Architectural Forum* in March 1926 included articles titled "Importance of Good Architecture in the Small House" and "'Bungalows' in the Colonial Style."[36] In 1927 *House Beautiful* offered stock plans for a Cape by architect Charles S. Keefe, who soon would be known for replicating Cape Cod cottages. The author noted the increasing popularity of colonial cottages of this general type;[37] indeed, in *House & Garden* alone, over the next three years there were at least another three articles on Cape Cod-type houses.[38] By the early 1930s periodicals regularly published articles on Cape Cod type houses, both reflecting and creating a demand for Capes.[39] And, as it happens, by fall 1927 a developer had built a house, described in sales literature as a "charming home imported [in this case, figuratively] from the shores of Cape Cod," on the same block where my Cape would end up three decades later.[40]

THE CAPE AND THE GREAT DEPRESSION

The Great Depression brought about a shift in attitude in regard to the Cape Cod-type house. The trickle of Capes being built through the 1920s grew and finally became a substantial part of the colonial revival movement in the 1930s, when economic necessity increased the demand for small, modest houses. The colonial Cape offered a point of departure that fit comfortably within this imperative. When the housing market began to rebound a few years after the 1929 stock market crash, a modest, streamlined, one- or one-and-a-half-story choice was more in keeping with the depressed economic times than the larger houses built in the early years of the twentieth century.

Not surprisingly, the emphasis in contemporary magazines now was on economics and practicality. An architect wrote in *House Beautiful* in 1931 in an article titled "Effective Economies in Building a House" that a small, story-and-a-half colonial was affordable because of its simple roof and straightforward plan. Two of the three houses discussed in the article were Capes.[41] The same year, *House & Garden* presented an article on "houses that grow" along with the needs and resources of the owner, highlighting the flexibility and adaptability of the Cape's plan. In February 1932, *House Beautiful* titled an article on the design and building of a Cape, "For Less Than Nine Thousand Dollars."[42] Later in the 1930s, "Portfolio of 16 Small Colonial Houses" in *American Home* featured small colonial houses, four of which were Capes located in four different states—Connecticut, Massachusetts, Illinois, and New Jersey.[43] A survey of magazines of the 1930s demonstrates the increasing visibility and popularity of the Cape as modest houses came to be valued in a tight economy.

Professional journals, too, included articles reflecting the economic times, and Cape Cod-type houses were well represented. In 1934, *Architectural Forum* displayed two prize-winning Capes in Virginia and New York as part of its annual event, the Better Homes in America Small House Competition. In its fourth year, the competition had been developed for three purposes: to find the best in small-house architecture, to encourage architects to design small houses, and to bring to the attention of the American people the highest standards in small-house architecture.[44] By the mid-1930s an architect looking for ideas to capitalize on the economic necessities brought about by the Depression would have found ample source material on the Cape Cod-type house in professional journals as well as in books and popular magazines.

Another influence on the growing popularity of the Cape Cod house was the National Housing Act. Signed into law on June 27, 1934, it created the Federal Housing Administration (FHA), an agency that underwrote bank loans for construction costs, insured owner mortgages of up to 80 percent of the FHA-appraised value, and established standards of cost, structure, and style for small-house design. From its beginning, the FHA regularly produced bulletins recommending the construction of Cape Cod-type houses.[45] The agency found the Cape to be the perfect prototype because it was economical to build, with a simple plan, unbroken roofline, little detail, and extra space for future expansion in the attic under the gabled roof. Average people wanting to own a home and looking for financing would have been drawn to an FHA-approved design as a way to ensure getting the necessary funds.[46]

FHA pamphlets and brochures of 1935 and 1936 promoted home ownership made "safe, economical, convenient" and explained that its insured mortgages could be paid off in rent-like payments over as long as twenty years.[47] A more detailed booklet, printed in November 1935, "How to Have the Home You Want," included photographs of nine houses, four of which were Capes, and explained that the primary purpose of the National Housing Act was to provide better homes for the American people.[48] Pocket-sized pamphlets aimed at the average citizen included "If You Want a Better Home," "How You Can Build, Buy, or Refinance Your Home," and "How to Own a Better Home." The Cape was the centerpiece home in these pamphlets, which included coupons for the reader to use in requesting more detailed information. The FHA in several ways, both direct and indirect, promoted the Cape Cod house. In general, by the late 1930s people recognized the compatibility of the Cape Cod-type house with the small-house requirements of the Depression era. "The Minimum Home" in *Ladies Home Journal* in 1937 summed it up nicely in noting, "The Cape Cod tradition in architecture is extremely sympathetic to the design of the small house."[49]

QUALITY AND AUTHENTICITY

As the Cape Cod house became accepted as a traditional and practical single-family housing choice for moderate-income people during a time of economic hardship, discussions on quality and authenticity in architectural design surfaced as well. Henry C. Kittredge, in a review of Poor's *Colonial Architecture of Cape Cod, Nantucket and Martha's Vineyard,* recommended that builders utilize such books of photographs of houses on Cape Cod to avoid creating the more nondescript bungalows that had become the fashion.[50]

Author and photographer Samuel Chamberlain in a 1937 issue of *House Beautiful* promoted the virtues of authenticity in Cape Cod-type house design. Citing "loose handling" of the subject by real estate salesmen, he argued that "true" Cape Cod cottages are "genuine, honest and sedate. They have no need to assert themselves like newcomers anxious to impress, for they have been a part of the American scene for centuries." For Chamberlain, adhering to the model of the originals meant building a large central chimney of ample proportions, small-paned windows, and a roof with low eaves, and finishing the structure with white trim, shingles, and no ornament. Properly designed, with its sturdy, simple lines and small size, a Cape, he believed, could offer its occupant a sense of restfulness.[51]

Chamberlain managed to further promote the Cape Cod type by producing in the mid-1930s a number of handsome picture books including *Cape Cod in the Sun, Open House in New England*, and *A Small House in the Sun: The Visage of Rural New England*, each with a number of photographs of Cape Cod-type houses.[52] During the Great Depression, in addition to its practical aspects, the Cape seemed to offer a pleasing and tangible reminder of a stable past to counterbalance the economic precariousness of the present.

Though many architects designed Cape Cod-type houses beginning in the late 1920s and especially in the 1930s, one in particular popularized them.[53] Early in his career, Royal Barry Wills of Boston altered and restored an old Cape Cod-type house; *American Architect* published a photograph of his work in March 1929.[54] Three years later he won the gold medal in the 1932 Better Homes in America small-house architecture competition with an entry the *Boston American* said embodied the "spirit of old Cape Cod."[55] Wills continued to work from the historical Cape Cod cottage prototype, largely adhering to the exterior proportions of the originals while promoting his designs in drawings and floor plans in newspaper articles in the mid-1930s as well as in a series of books in the 1940s.[56] The author of the anonymous 1949 *Architectural Forum* article noted, as have many others since, that Royal

FIGURE 3.2 Royal Barry Wills. Jacob Shore House, Providence, Rhode Island. 1941. *(Photograph courtesy of Richard Wills, Royal Barry Wills Associates.)*

Barry Wills was the rare twentieth-century architect who "managed to copy the original Cape Cod Cottage without ruining it" and that he did so while satisfying modern living requirements.[57]

THE CAPE AFTER WORLD WAR II

The practical aspects of building the Cape Cod-type house found another impetus when the housing shortage on the heels of World War II spurred the federal government to encourage the construction of large-scale suburban housing projects for returning, low-income veterans and their young families, through amendments to the 1934 National Housing Act. Funded by mortgages backed by the GI Bill and the FHA, the basic Cape Cod house, both economical to build and affordable to own, was a perfect fit.[58] Additionally, people at the time, eager for peace and a return to normalcy, may have been drawn to the Cape's aura of security and nostalgia to which Chamberlain had alluded in 1937.

One well-known example of a suburban, single-family tract-housing development is Levittown on New York's Long Island. The initial phase of building what eventually would be sixteen thousand houses included six thousand Cape Cods completed by the end of 1948. The monotonous uniformity of the Levittown tract houses provoked much criticism. Humorists made fun of "replicated Cape Cods" and denounced them for their homogeneity.[59] Particularly after World War II and in mass-produced developments such as Levittown, builders altered the proportions, rendering the houses awkward in appearance and adding more weight to Chamberlain's prewar observations on form, proportion, and authenticity. Observers frequently went so far as to claim that, in many instances, architects and builders had ruined the Cape Cod type.

A comparison of original Capes with many of their twentieth-century revivals, particularly post-World War II examples, reveals a number of differences. The twentieth-century Capes often include an entry accentuated with sidelights or pediment, dormers in front or shed dormers in back, larger windows and windowpanes, a smaller chimney, higher ceilings, and a garage. The horizontal lower edge of the roof tends to be at a distance from the windows rather than directly above the lintels. With a reduction in overall width and depth, the increased height resulted in what many say are proportions less pleasing than those of the originals. Fortunately, Wills in the 1930s (and some other architects in the 1960s) saw the error of their predecessors' ways and began to adhere more closely to the Cape's original proportions.[60]

FIGURE 3.3 Aerial photograph of a portion of Levittown, New York, in 1948, shortly after the suburb was completed on Long Island farmland. *(© 1948 The Associated Press.)*

Perhaps that realization brings us full circle to the happy accident that is the Cape Cod house. Stanley Schuler, author of the 1982 *The Cape Cod House: America's Most Popular Home* and the architecture and building editor for *House Beautiful* in the late 1930s and early 1940s, when modern Capes were in their prewar heyday, admired the early Cape's subtleties of mass and proportion, sometimes difficult for people to see. He remarked that he often wondered how ordinary, uneducated people of the seventeenth and eighteenth centuries could have created such masterpieces when most people of his own time could not even copy a Cape correctly, adding that he had never found an explanation.[61] Or, as another author put it in *House & Garden* in 1903, the "value of restraint, the true meaning of proportion in its broad sense . . . actuated, perhaps unconsciously, the early builders of these modest farmhouses. If they built without knowledge, they must have been gifted with happy instinct."[62]

AND SO THE CAPE CONTINUES

Regardless of how the Cape Cod house came to be, multiple factors account for the general public's continuing broad appreciation of it. As the 1949 *Architectural Forum* article put it: "Seldom has one house design achieved such universal popularity with builders and home owners alike."[63] With hindsight, it is evident that the author of a short piece in the November 1929 *Popular Mechanics* was especially prescient in succinctly summarizing the key reasons for what would become the Cape's enduring popularity. In the discussion of the featured house, "patterned after [a] Cape Cod colonial," the author noted that it is "the outgrowth of simple, honest housing requirements of our forefathers," is "economical to build," and has "good proportions."[64] Others since then have sought to find the reasons for the Cape's popularity, and the results have been much the same.

Issues surrounding the country's heritage, nationalism, historical consciousness, and nostalgia—all a part of the colonial revival in architecture—explain a major aspect of the Cape's popularity. Ethel B. Power, writing about all types of colonial revival housing in 1935, observed of the colonial house in general that "our traditions are rooted in it" and its appeal derived from sentiment.[65] Of the nine colonial houses presented in sketches accompanying her article, three are Capes.

The practical and cost-effective aspects of the Cape loom large in accounting for its popularity. According to *Popular Mechanics* in 1929, it was the Cape's simple plan and absence of ornament that made it economical to build. Power agreed when she noted that a Cape was inexpensive due to its unbroken roof line and straightforward plan.[66] *Architectural Forum* called it flexible, "practical and thrifty," and using stock parts, the "cheapest cubage that can possibly be put together."[67]

Another note that recurs in the discussions is the assumption of an ethical stance. *Popular Mechanics* called the Cape "honest,"[68] as did an earlier writer in *House Beautiful* in 1926;[69] Power referred to its "sincerity . . . dignity and directness."[70] David Gebhard, whose thorough examination of the colonial revival building types' enduring nature, noted that the small, unpretentious houses of the 1930s became a symbol of modesty and reserve during the Depression when such ideals were valued.[71]

Lastly, aesthetics plays a role. Most observers from the early nineteenth century to the present have commented on the Cape's good proportions, pleasing and graceful mass, and simplicity of line, particularly in its original form.

It is the Cape's exceptional combination of practicality, nostalgia, and beauty that accounts for its persistence. Ethel Power made this observation and predicted that colonial types of houses would stay popular for a long time to come. The anonymous author of the *Popular Mechanics* article also predicted the Cape Cod type would last, being "a style as liquid in public approval as a Liberty bond at a bank."[72] And how right they both were.

Indeed, the Cape continues to be with us. When its popularity began to grow in the 1930s, the weak economy limited housing construction. After the war, the industry flourished. Hence, most twentieth-century Capes were built after 1945 and are still in existence. And they continue to be constructed. A quick Internet search using the search terms "Cape Cod house plans" yields over two hundred thousand results. The *New York Times* Sunday real estate section listing of regional suburban home sales seems to average about 15 percent Cape Cods in the lower price ranges. Of course, real estate agents deem just about any house a "Cape" as long as it has one and one-half stories and a vaguely Cape-like form, regardless of whether it is clad in clapboards, stone, stucco, or brick. That, it turns out, is the explanation for our real estate agent's frequent "Cape" offerings.

Nevertheless, Cape Cod-type houses largely based on historical prototypes—what Samuel Chamberlain would have deemed "true" Cape Cod cottages—are still to be found everywhere, particularly in the Northeast and mid-Atlantic regions. As recently as 1980, the Aladdin Company placed a classic Cape Cod on the cover of its mail-order house catalogue.[73] *Country Living* magazine chose a Cape cottage as its "House of the Year" for 1989 and described it as a new home with the look and charm of an eighteenth-century original.[74] Popular magazines in the last twenty years have featured classic Cape Cod-type houses regularly, sometimes as a house with historic associations, sometimes as the residence of a famous person, and often simply as a smart choice for today's homeowner.[75]

At this point, through my research, I had learned a great deal about Cape Cod-type houses and just how ubiquitous and ordinary they are. I also learned how my house fits into the history of the Cape Cod house revival. Its design adheres to many aspects of the original Capes, features not often found in the many slightly later, post-World War II examples. For example, it has a central chimney of fairly ample proportions, a steeply pitched roof, an entrance with sidelights, accented with amethyst-tinted glass (a hallmark of original Capes), and an overall ground plan with proportions similar to those of the original Capes. It fit perfectly with 1930s building trends across the country. It is a prewar Cape Cod revival type and is one of the earlier and more authentic, thoughtful examples of a very popular style, an example that garnered notice in the national press as a *McCall's* "Home of the Month."

Now that I understood the origins of my house's design and how it came to be where it is, I wondered what other buildings might have been on my property at one time and, more significantly, who their occupants were. What did they do for a living? How did they come to this particular place? What was their relationship to the land?

PART II

THIRTY-TWO OWNERS IN 350 YEARS: A FOCUS ON FOUR

THE OWNERS

Beginning with Native American Wappaquewam, the first party in a series of deed transactions, the owners of my property have included a broad range of people from the lord of a manor to several who farmed the land to real estate speculators and developers to suburban homeowners like me—thirty-two owners in all.

More specifically, the owners of this one-third of an acre have included a Native American *sakima*; an English merchant; the mayor of New York City, who was simultaneously the mayor of the town of Westchester, a judge, and a missionary; a shipwright; a carpenter; the town's clerk, assessor, and recorder; the town's overseer of highways and "fence and damage viewer," also a Tory during the American Revolution; two slave owners; a lieutenant who fought for the British in the Seven Years' War (French and Indian War) and then became the captain of a regiment of Westchester County minutemen during the American Revolution; a New York City distiller; a New York City grocer; a Masonic Lodge trustee, who was also an elections inspector and the town auditor; the Mutual Life Insurance Company of New York; a banker; a refrigeration engineer and inventor; two real estate development companies; a plumbing supply business owner; a civil engineer; and, most recently, an artist and a historian. The stories uncovered are those of people, some quite ordinary and others less so, across four centuries, who shared one thing—possession of one particular plot of land. Here are four of the former owners considered within the context of the time in American history in which they lived.

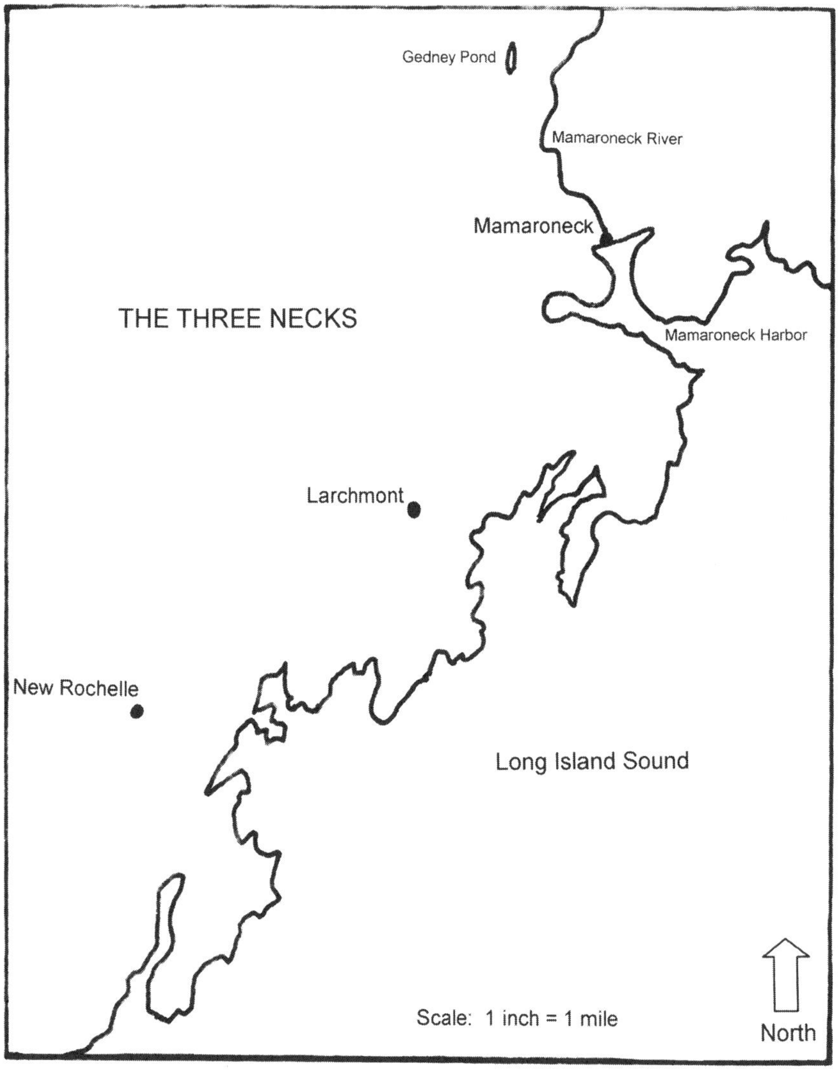

FIGURE 4.1 The three necks of land along Long Island Sound that made up John Richbell's 1661 purchase from Wappaquewam and other Siwanoys. *(Map by author.)*

four

Wappaquewam: Siwanoy Sakima

Both you & the English are White. We live in a Country between, therefore the Land does not belong either to one or the other; but the GREAT BEING above allow'd it to be a Place of residence for us.[1]

—Tanacharison, Native American leader, to George Washington, 1753

While reading about the history of Mamaroneck in a book published in 1886, I stumbled upon the name *Wappaquewam*. This person seemed to be the owner of a piece of land and had signed a 1661 document labeled "Indian Deed to John Richbell." The deed, as it appears in the book, describes the property as "three Necks of Land, the Eastermost called Mammaranock neck" along Long Island Sound, and says something about the property extending "Twenty miles Northward."[2] My property, just over one mile due north of the easternmost neck or peninsula described, would have been included in this great tract of land.

So Wappaquewam owned it then, or at least the Englishmen who wrote the deed deemed it so, and my husband and I own it now. I wanted to know who else it had belonged to. To find out, I traced the chain of deed transactions back through three and a half centuries, a process that once completed, confirmed what I had suspected. There had been numerous other owners, more than thirty, and the deeds, starting with ours (each one linked to the one before and the one after), led back to Wappaquewam.

Yet a closer reading of that first deed from the time of early European contact with the Native Americans revealed something more. Although John Richbell purchased the coastal land comprising the three necks, when it came to the larger part of the tract running "twenty miles Northward from the marked Trees of the Necks," the words of the deed merely granted him the right to "freely feed cattle, or cutt Timber."[3] What exactly did that mean? Who was John Richbell? What were the circumstances of his acquisition of this parcel of land? Who was Wappaquewam, and what was he thinking in 1661 when he sold his ancestral land? Assuming he was part of a community, what happened to that community? As far as I knew, there were few, if any, Indians of North American origins living in my town in the twenty-first century.

Thinking the version of the deed in the book might be incomplete, I sought out the original. What I found, I am told, is as original as one can get. The original "original," undoubtedly on parchment, no longer exists, but what does is part of a collection of early deeds and other land records, hand-copied, indexed, and bound into volumes during the late seventeenth and eighteenth centuries and now available to the public on microfilm in the New York State Archives. Recorded on March 13, 1666, the September 23, 1661 deed states:

> That I Wappaquewam Right owner & Proprietor of part of this Land, doe by order of my brother who is another Proprietor & by consent of the other Indyans doe this day, sell, lett & make over from mee my heyres & assignes for ever, unto John Richbell of Oyster Bay his heyres & assignes for ever three Necks of Land, The Eastermost is called Mammaranock Neck, and the westermost is bounded with Mr. Pell's purchase . . . with all the Meadows Rivers and Islands thereunto belonging, Also the sd. Richbell or his Assignes may freely feed cattle or cutt Timber twenty miles Northward from the marked Trees of the Necks; ffor & in consideracon the sd. Richbell is to give or deliver unto the aforenamed Wappaquewam the Goods here under mentioned, the one halfe about a moneth after the date hereof, & the other halfe the next Spring following, . . . I Wappaquewam doe acknowledge to have recd. two shirts & ten shillings in wampom, the day & date above written.

Changing Language, Changing Attitudes

Be cognizant of using stereotyping language when speaking or writing about times past or choosing language that might be culturally insensitive in today's world. Especially when working from historical sources, remember that times change. There are obvious examples of cultural insensitivity such as in the derogatory words of the Dutch clergyman Jonas Michaëlius, who wrote in 1628 describing the Native Americans he encountered in the New World: "I find them entirely savage and wild, strangers to all decency, yea, uncivil and stupid as garden poles, proficient in all wickedness and godlessness; devilish men, who serve nobody but the Devil."[1]

However, there are more subtle examples, such as one that appeared in 1956 in the *Westchester Historian*, a respected, award-winning, local history journal. The author of "The Waldorf Mill and the Legend of the White Deer" described the Native Americans of Westchester County as "simple children of the forest."[2] Such a gentle description probably would have been perfectly acceptable to many in the nineteenth century and during much of the twentieth, but in the twenty-first it would not be. History is not static, it is ever-changing.

Another concept that has undergone change in the last several decades is that of 'discovery,' as in Columbus "discovered America." A preferred concept is 'contact.' It offers a neutral way to describe the moment when Europeans first came to the Americas. Other neutral ways of describing the moment are ones of exchange and of cultures meeting. The implication imbedded in the concept of European 'discovery' is that there was no history for the people who lived in the Americas until Europeans arrived and began to create a written historical record. The differences between the cultures were enormous, of course, and laid the groundwork for misunderstandings and clashes in the future.

Usage of the terms *Indian* and *Native American* can be difficult to sort out. Charles C. Mann in his book *1491: New Revelations of the Americas Before Columbus*, concisely explains his use of the term *Indian.* He points out that while the term can be considered historically improper, a misnomer, it has persisted ever since Christopher Columbus, believing he was in Asia, called the indigenous people he encountered on the Central American island of San Salvador *los Indios*. Mann's approach is to use the terms Indian and Native American interchangeably, but when possible, to call people by the names they use themselves. In his experience, the "overwhelming majority of the indigenous peoples" he has "met in both North and South America describe themselves as Indians." Mann also notes that he uses *Indian* as the equivalent of *European*, rather than as a racial designation.[3] Other writers use the term of the specific group or tribe, such as *Siwanoy* or *Delaware,* when possible, rather than the more generic *Indian.*

Word choices are important for they carry powerful messages and implications. Some cognitive psychologists would argue that language represents thought and, to an extent, even controls thought and action. Sensitivity in the choice of words supports the efforts in our own time toward inclusiveness and acceptance of diversity.

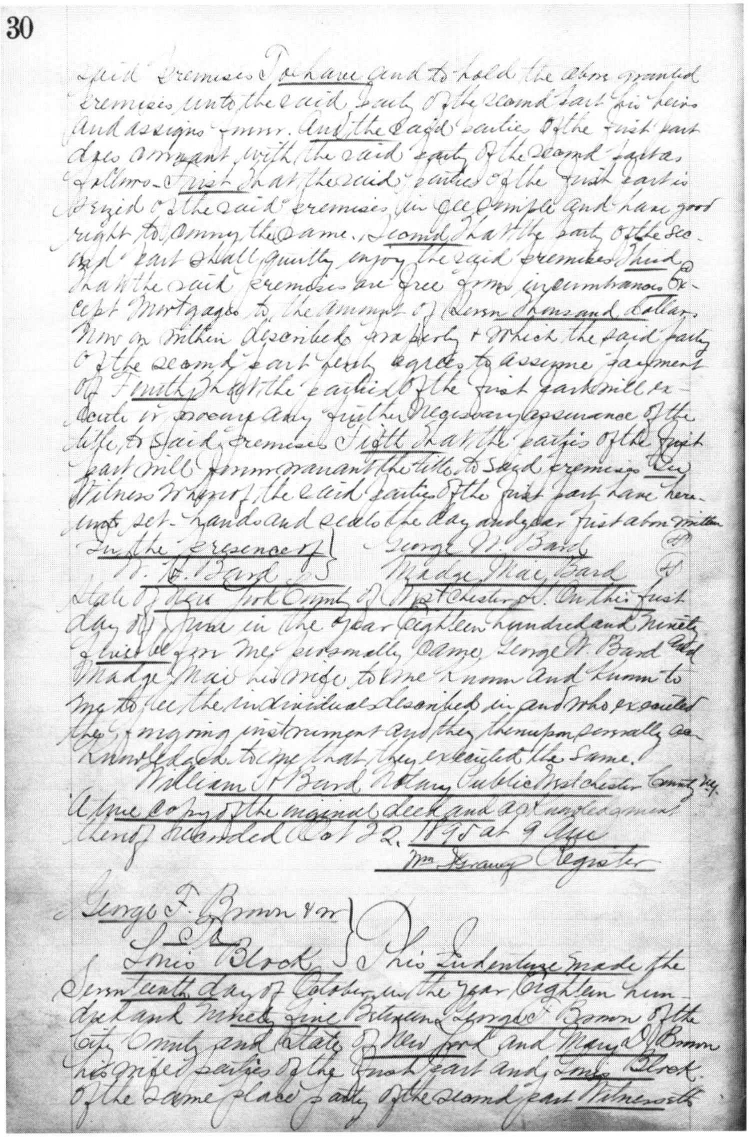

FIGURE 4.2 Sample page from a three-page, handwritten 1895 deed to the property. *(Photograph courtesy of the Westchester County Archives.)*

The Deed Chain

A deed is a contract that transfers the title of ownership of real property (immovable property) from one owner to another. Written records of land ownership go back further than most other records in the United States. The owner can be an individual, more than one person, a corporation, or a government entity such as a village or town. Deeds are usually kept by county offices. Some counties post their deed records online, some have them on internal computers accessible in a county office, and still others (depending on the time period of the deed) keep them in bound volumes on shelves. Regardless of the system, they are most often indexed alphabetically by owner surname. The index will show the names of the grantor and grantee (seller and buyer) and the numbers of the file book and page where the deed may be found.

Deeds are a matter of public record and thus are open to anyone. In the case of my property, the records are kept by the Land Records Division of the county clerk's office. Historical ones were until recently housed there in huge bound volumes (libers), now in the county archives. The scanned pages from the libers are online at computers in the county office and available remotely for a subscription fee. In addition to the names of the parties involved, deeds include other useful information such as the property's exact location and boundaries, the price paid for the property, the date of the transaction, and whether a mortgage was involved.

Normally, a given piece of property was at one time part of a much larger plot, so the best way to find past owners is to start with the current owner and work backward. If you know the name of the current owner, you can find the name of the seller, who then becomes the buyer in the previous transaction. Each buyer/seller pair is a link in a chain of events, each one tied to the one before and the one after in a series of deeds.

Sometimes the deed chain is broken by another type of property transfer, such as in a will, or in an auction sale by the administrator of a deceased person's estate. A judge's name can be listed as the grantor in cases where the property has been taken over by a local municipality, often for nonpayment of property taxes, or by a bank for a default on a mortgage. In these cases, other legal records, such as wills found in probate court records, have to be consulted in order to find the next link in the chain.

From the 1600s through the 1800s, deeds were written longhand by someone with an elegant hand, often in a particular locality by the same person over a period of years. The elegant hand, however, is not always legible, at least to modern eyes. The challenge of reading such deeds is considerable, though not insurmountable. After enough time spent reading a given handwriting, you become accustomed to its idiosyncrasies. In my area of New York, during the latter years of the Great Depression, people hired by the Works Progress Administration

(WPA) were put to work typing a number of the longhand deeds from early years. Unfortunately, they never finished the job. The deeds from about 1853 to 1896 are still in longhand.

Details in deeds are clues to the historical moment. For example, in the eighteenth century, women in Westchester County who signed deeds often did so with their marks, whereas their husbands most often signed their names, indicating that women were more likely to be illiterate. Familial relationships become clear in deeds through frequent references by name to wives, sons, and occasionally daughters. Deeds often refer to occupations—for example, in deeds of the eighteenth century I found reference to yeomen (farmers), carpenters, and shipwrights. Nineteenth-century deeds mention distiller and grocer as the occupation of the buyers, an indication of changing times. Deeds sometimes describe the locations of certain buildings and other alterations to the land. Caleb Heathcote's sawmill is more or less locatable from deed descriptions; deeds also reference a house, a barn, an orchard, fencings, and easements.[1] And one of Heathcote's confirming deeds for the purchase of land included the signatures of eight Native Americans, three of them women.[2] As both men and women in their culture had rights to land, leaders of an entire kinship group might sign a deed for the transfer of land, signaling agreement on the action.[3]

A deed to my property from 1793 discusses the family burial ground and specifies that the new owner "shall not breack the ground nor till the land containing the Graves of deceased persons already buried in the Buring ground in said farm for planting soweing or reaising Grain in said Buring Ground."[4] The burial ground had never been mentioned in the several deeds through which the property passed among Gedney family members. It seems that only when it passed out of the family was it necessary to create this restriction. The fact that the property previously had been transferred by will is mentioned in one deed. Without this information, I would not have known for sure how the property had passed from father to son. Sometimes there was a deed and actual money (token amounts or more) exchanged between father and son, and other times it passed by will.[5] And through a document in the deed libers (though not part of an actual deed), I learned that Eliezer Gedney, the first Gedney to own the property, recorded with the clerk of courts on April 5, 1725, some twenty-five years after his arrival, that "his creatures ear mark" was "a crop in each ear & a slit in each ear."[6] All of these details proved to be fodder for further research. If read carefully, a deed is much more than a dry legal document.

Twenty two Coats.
one hundred fathom of Wampom.
Twelve shirts,
Ten paire of Stockings.
Twenty hands of powder.
Twelve barrs of Lead,
Two firelockes
ffifteene Hoes.
ffifteene Hatchets.
Three Kettles.[4]

In addition to the deed, there were other discoveries that energized my thoughts about the earliest inhabitants of the property. I learned, for example, that two decades before Wappaquewam signed John Richbell's deed, the same general territory was said to have been purchased by Dutch settlers from some Native Americans, though no record of such a transaction exists today.[5] Even the name Mamaroneck has Native American roots. There is more than one story offered for its origins, but the most vivid, poetic, and oft-repeated one is this: in the language of the first residents, Mamaroneck means "the place where the fresh water falls in to the salt."[6] At the point where the Mamaroneck River empties into Long Island Sound, near the town's center, there once was a rocky reef, high enough to prevent the salt water of the sound from flowing back into the river at high tide. This unusual natural occurrence warranted a descriptive name, one that Europeans adopted and has persisted.[7] The variety of spellings I have found in seventeenth- and early eighteenth-century documents—Mamaranet, Mamaranock, Mamarinek, Mamaronack, Mamaronocke, Mammaranock, Mammarinikes, Mamorenack, Mamorinack, Marinac, Marramack, Merrimack, Merrinack, Merrinak, Momoreanoke, Momoronock—probably represents European efforts to express the sounds of the Indians' language.

Metes and Bounds

The metes-and-bounds system of defining a property's boundaries in a deed deserves special attention. Imported from England, it has been used for centuries. An understanding of it is essential if you are working on properties in the states that use metes and bounds—those that were the thirteen colonies and their derivatives, Maine, Vermont, West Virginia, Kentucky, and Tennessee. (The other states, with the exception of Texas and Hawaii, consist of land that was initially controlled by the United States government and use a survey system based on geographic meridians.) The metes-and-bounds system uses physical features of the land, both natural and manmade, to define lines and points along the perimeter of the property. Descriptions read as narratives and follow the boundary around and back to the starting point. *Metes* is used for straight lines that connect two points; *bounds* refers to a path that might follow a meandering line marked by a river, a stone wall, or an adjoining property.

The very earliest deeds that I read in connection with my property research used a less specific way of describing a parcel of land. The description section of one deed from 1697 reads simply "all that parcel or neck of land . . . called the East Neck and to begine at the westward part thereof at a certaine creeke lyeing being and adjacent by & betweene the neck of land comonly called the Great Neck, and the said East Neck, and soe to runn eastward as farr as Momorronek River including therein betwixt the said two lines, all the lands as well north into the woods above Westchester Path [Boston Post Road or U. S. Route 1] twenty miles as the lands below the Path southward to the sound."[1] You get the picture.

By at least 1716 the colonists in New York seem to have been using metes-and-bounds descriptions. One deed describes an eighty-acre plot thus: "Beginning at a red oak tree which is a corner bound of a lott of land number eight, thence running a northwest course thirty five degrees, northerly by markt trees till it meet with Mamaroneck River one hundred & thirty two rods [2178 feet], then running down ye sd. River till it meet with a red oak tree standing by ye sd. River markt on two sides, thence down ye river till it meets with a Shake bark walnut tree being ye eastermost corner of land bought by sd. Eliezer Gedney of William Penior, thence to ye red oak tree first mentioned."[2] The "northwest course thirty-five degrees, northerly" means the line runs northwest at a thirty-five degree angle from due north. A compass comes in handy here when tracing the descriptions of property boundaries.

In addition to using markers such as a "red oak tree" or "hilly ground," metes-and-bounds descriptions sometimes include "a heap of stones," "a stake with stones about it," "a stump," "a house," or "the saw mill." Natural or man-made, these types of markers, so frequently used, rarely last a long time, and even a stream might change course through erosion, so the job of figuring out the property boundaries becomes especially challenging. In my part of the country and in many other areas, "a stone wall" is often cited as a marker or a boundary. Unlike the trees, stumps, and saw mills, at least some of them still exist.

Another bit of information came my way as I searched the files of a local historical society—an image clipped from a 1961 newspaper showing a cluster of large rocks in a field. The caption states that the photograph had been taken on my block-long street and shows "Indian-placed rocks in a semi-circle. This was where the Indian Council met."[8] This information reinforced what my next-door neighbor had told me. When he bought his house in 1971, the rock arrangement shown in the photograph filled his backyard, spilling over a little into mine. Although the terrain of the immediate vicinity is rocky with outcroppings everywhere, some of the rocks in the photograph appear as if they had been deliberately placed. The neighbor found himself in a quandary about how to preserve the rocks—something of historical significance to him. After some deliberation, he opted for installing a swimming pool over preservation, and all but one of the rocks had to go. Unfortunately, the backhoe broke the sole remaining one he had hoped to save, leaving a granite chunk less than half its original size. Today, a solitary remnant of times past, it rests all but hidden in the flowerbed that borders the pool.

Then there was the story of the archaeologists' visit. The one time (other than at the closing on the purchase of my property) that I talked to the most recent former owner, she told me that many years earlier, a group of archaeologists had come knocking on her door. They believed that the enormous outcropping in one corner of the property was a spot where Native Americans would have been likely to gather long ago. She granted them permission to investigate. They climbed the rock, looked around, and left. That was all she knew. Given the nearby river, navigable by canoe, the outcropping's elevation, affording a view of Long Island Sound just over a mile away, and the natural human tendency to seek naturally defensible spots, it seemed plausible. Later, as I explored the rock, I found in the crevices clam shells and what I thought might be obsidian arrowheads. Upon further examination and research, however, I thought it unlikely that Native Americans had left the shells there and that the shiny black stones really were arrowheads. But somehow, at that moment, it seemed not to matter. All these findings, except for the deed, stayed squarely in the realm of unverifiable information and conjecture, but they fed my imagination and curiosity nonetheless.

THE SIWANOYS AND THE LENAPES

Although to scholars the political alignments of and the proper terms for the Native American groups who once lived along the shore northwest of Long Island Sound remain uncertain, according to reports by Europeans as early as 1619, it was the Siwanoys who lived there.[9] Wappaquewam was undoubtedly one of them. These Eastern Woodland Indians were among the many bands that comprised the Lenapes, a branch of what are now called the Delaware Indians, whose territory included southeastern New York along the lower Hudson River and east along Long Island Sound into southwestern Connecticut and western Long Island, as well as New Jersey and eastern Pennsylvania. *Lenapehoking* or "The Land of the People" is a term used by some scholars to describe this area. Each band in Lenapehoking had separate political and geographical identities; however, those living north of the Delaware Water Gap shared a common tongue, Munsee, one of the Algonquian family of languages.[10]

At the time Europeans first arrived in Lenapehoking in the 1500s, the Siwanoys hunted deer, elk, black bear, raccoons, turkeys, and geese, with bows and arrows, utilizing all parts of the animal. They fished with large nets, collected shellfish, and gathered berries, roots, chestnuts, acorns, and other nuts. Using hoes made of stone or bone for cultivation, they probably supplemented their diet with corn, squash, and beans.[11] Food preparation methods included boiling in earthenware pots, roasting in hot ashes, and drying items to be stored for use in leaner times.

The Siwanoys probably migrated seasonally, in spring and summer going "to salt" to live near the sound where they could harvest clams and oysters, and in fall and winter moving a distance of about a fifteen-minute walk inland to be near various food sources, firewood, and shelter from coastal wind. They would have gone long distances to engage in exchange with other bands via creeks, rivers, and the sound, traveling in bark canoes as well as in dugout canoes made of logs burned with hot stones and then shaped by scraping away the charred areas.[12]

Clothing varied, depending on the season. In warm weather, men wore leather breechcloths fastened around the waist with a belt, and women wore wrap-around skirts of animal skins, decorated with paint, porcupine quills, or beads. In winter they added cloaks, leggings, and moccasins made of various animal skins. Body paint in red, black, blue, and yellow pigments was widely used, particularly for special occasions, and some men tattooed various body areas. Both men and women made their hair shiny with bear fat.[13]

The Siwanoy band, like other Lenapes, most likely lived on sparsely distributed, small farmsteads in longhouses, with as few as five people per square mile.[14] Dutch clergyman Jasper Danckaerts, visiting the New World in 1679 with plans to establish a colony, described in a journal entry a visit to a Lenape longhouse in what is now Brooklyn, offering a glimpse into Native American housing and domestic life at the time.

> We went from thence to her habitation, where we found the whole troop together, consisting of seven or eight families, and twenty or twenty-two persons, I should think. Their house was low and long, about sixty feet long and fourteen or fifteen

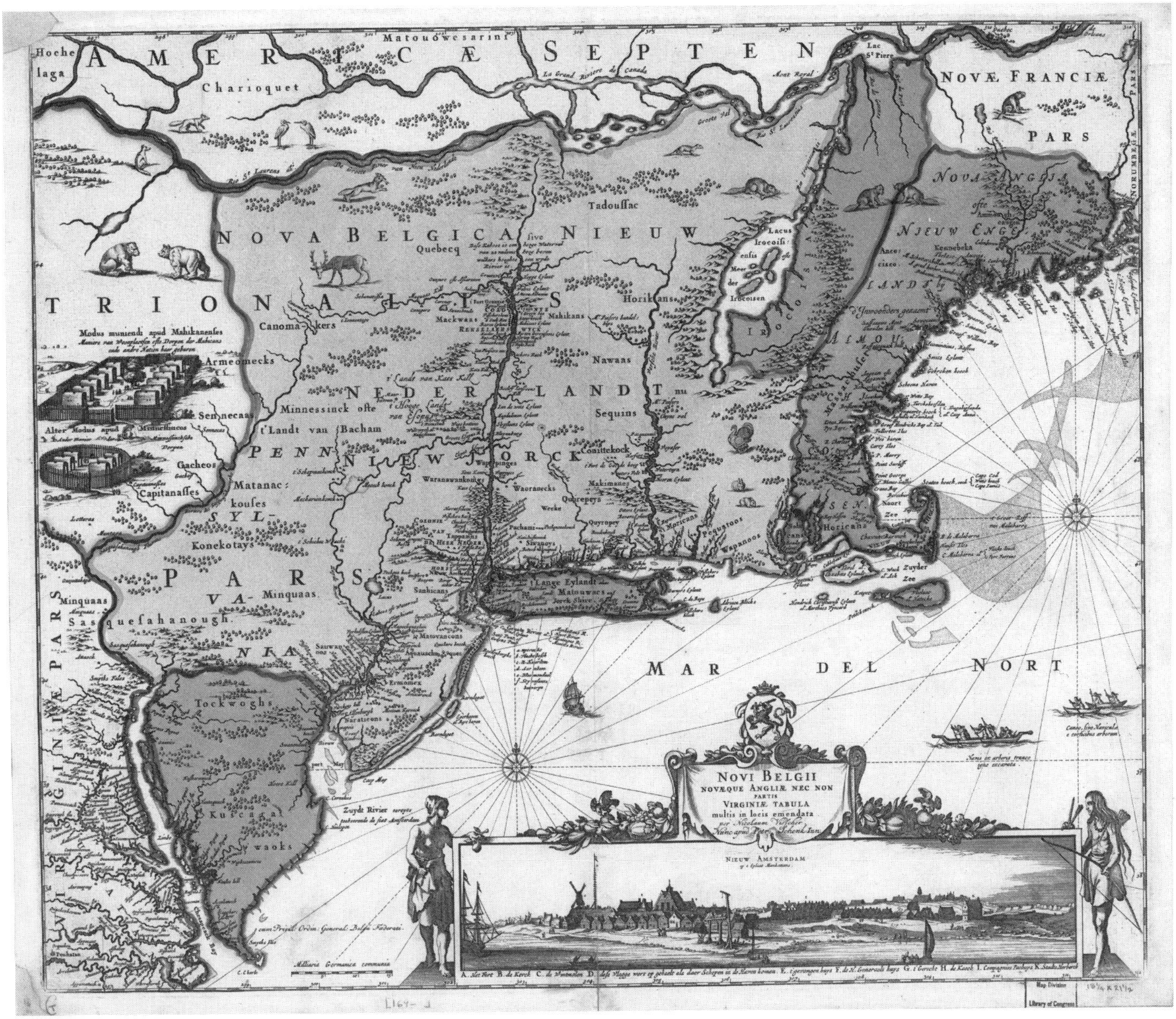

FIGURE 4.3 Nicolaes Visscher. *Novi Belgii Novæque Angliæ*. . . . 46 x 55 cm. Hand colored. [Amsterdam?, 1685]. A copy with modifications of the 1651 Jan Jansson map. Just above Long Island near the center of the map can be seen the word *Siwanoys*, among the many Native American peoples named. *(Photograph courtesy of the Library of Congress, Geography and Map Division.)*

> feet wide. The bottom was earth, the sides and roof were made of reed and the bark of chestnut trees; the posts, or columns, were limbs of trees stuck in the ground, and all fastened together. The top, or ridge of the roof was open about half a foot wide, from one end to the other, in order to let the smoke escape, in place of a chimney. . . . They build their fire in the middle of the floor, according to the number of families which live in it, so that from one end to the other each of them boils its own pot, and eats when it likes, not only the families by themselves, but each Indian alone, according as he is hungry, at all hours, morning, noon and night. By each fire are the cooking utensils, consisting of a pot, a bowl, or calabash, and a spoon also made of a calabash. . . . Their other household articles consists [*sic*] of a calabash of water, out of which they drink, a small basket in which to carry and keep their maize and small beans, and a knife. . . . All who live in one house are generally of one stock or descent, as father and mother with their offspring. . . . Their bread is maize, pounded in a block by a stone, but not fine. This is mixed with water, and made into a cake, which they bake under hot ashes.[15]

Archaeological evidence confirms that the northern Lenapes lived in oval longhouses sited alone or in small groups of two or three houses rather than in large clusters or within fortified stockades, indicating that in the time before contact with Europeans, they probably did not fear being attacked.[16]

CONTACT

It is not possible to know with certainty what expectations Wappaquewam might have had of the Englishman who wanted to buy the land of his people. Europeans and Native Americans responded to "the other" from the perspective of their own cultural contexts, their own experience and expectations.[17] At the time of their earliest contact with Europeans, Native Americans had lived in Lenapehoking for at least ten thousand years and probably several thousand years longer. Today, what we know about them as a whole, and by inference about Wappaquewam, derives from several sources: the often-biased observations of European explorers, traders, and early settlers; contemporary documents, such as deeds, written by Europeans; oral traditions of the native peoples; and sparse archaeological excavation evidence.

There are no written accounts from the sixteenth- and seventeenth-century North American indigenous point of view, but a number of Europeans recorded their observations and attitudes during the early years of European-Indian contact. The first known European visitors to Lenapehoking were Italian explorer Giovanni da Verrazzano and his crew, who entered New York Bay in 1524. Though the records they left are minimal, their encounters with Native American groups apparently were peaceful. The following year, however, Estevão Gomes, a Portuguese commissioned by the king of Spain to explore the eastern coast of North America, returned to Spain with fifty-eight enslaved Indians.[18] To the extent that word travels, his actions undoubtedly contributed to the Lenapes' mistrust of those who came later. Whalers, fishermen, and fur traders continued to visit the area over the course of the next century, but the only surviving reports are sketchy.

The seventeenth century brought increased contact. Henry Hudson, an Englishman engaged by the Dutch East India Company to find a shorter passage to Asia, entered New York Bay in September 1609 on his third voyage to the New World. Not only did the Native Americans display no fear of the visitors, they also seemed prepared to trade, suggesting they had had previous experience bartering with Europeans.[19] According to a report writ-

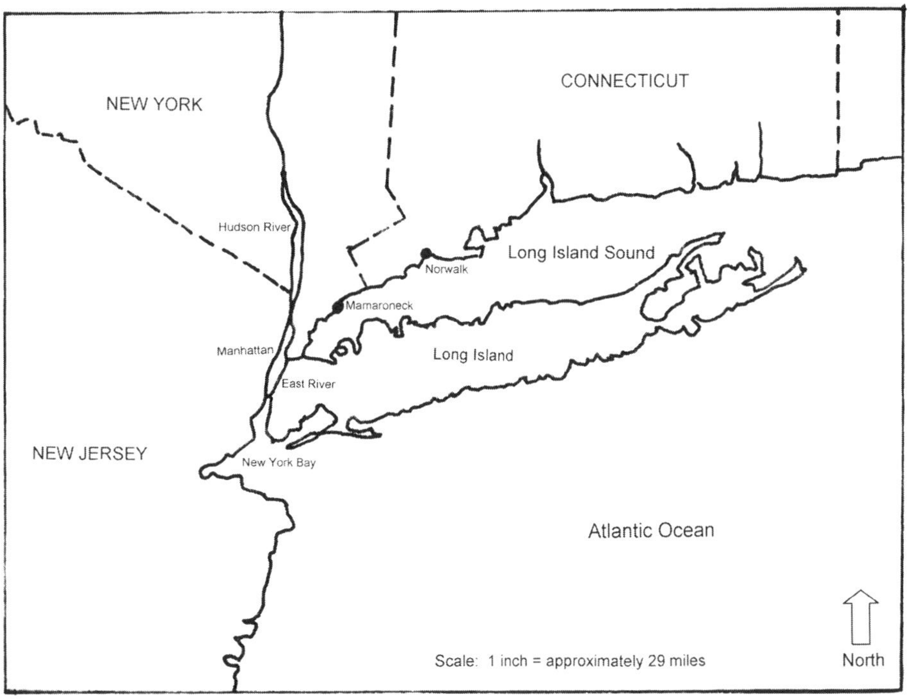

FIGURE 4.4 The New York City tri-state region. *(Map by author.)*

ten by Hudson's first mate during their first days in the bay, his crew detained two members of a group of Native Americans who had come on board their ship. Though the detainees escaped by jumping overboard, they and their companions were understandably angry and spread the word of their ill treatment. Hudson then traveled north up the river that today bears his name to what is now Albany, finding numerous groups of Native Americans along the way, the majority of them friendly and welcoming, eager to bestow gifts and to trade assorted small items. Upon Hudson's return downriver three weeks later, however, the aggrieved Indians he had earlier offended attacked his ship with bows and arrows. Using muskets, Hudson's men killed several of them in retaliation. The Indians continued their attacks further south, and Hudson's crew shot and killed several more of them.[20]

From 1611 to 1614 at least fourteen more Dutch ships sailed into the Hudson River to trade for fur with the Indians.[21] Fire destroyed one of the ships, the *Tiger*, while anchored at Manhattan Island. No doubt with the help of the Native Americans living in the area, Captain Adriaen Block and his crew built another, the *Restless*, in which they traveled around the tip of Manhattan, up the East River, and out into Long Island Sound, the first Europeans to explore these waters. Block reported that the Siwanoys lived as far west as Hell Gate, a treacherous spot in the East River near the northern tip of Manhattan where tide-driven currents converge with the waters of Long Island Sound, and as far east as Norwalk, Connecticut—a stretch of eight leagues or roughly twenty-eight miles. Based on his reports and those of other explorers and traders, the Dutch States-General claimed a trade monopoly as well as a large territory, naming it New Netherland.[22] The Dutch West India Company, formed in 1621, established major trading stations in the region, one at New Amsterdam, eventually New York City, and the other at Fort Orange, later Albany. By 1626 the West India Company, in effect the governing body of the colony, reported that it had acquired "two ships destined for the trade and settlement of the Colony in New Netherland."[23]

Later in the seventeenth century, as more Europeans came to New Netherland with plans to settle there, detailed observations and distinct viewpoints emerged. In regard to the Indians of the region, Reverend Jonas Michaëlius, a Dutch clergyman, wrote in 1628:

> As to the natives of this country, I find them entirely savage and wild, strangers to all decency, yea, uncivil and stupid as garden poles, proficient in all wickedness and godlessness; devilish men, who serve nobody but the Devil. . . . They are as thievish and treacherous as they are tall; and in cruelty they are altogether inhuman, more than barbarous. . . . How these people can best be led to the true knowledge of God and of the Mediator Christ, is hard to say. . . . If we speak to them of God, it appears to them like a dream . . . ; and as the people listen, some will begin to mutter and shake their heads as if it were a silly fable; and others, in order to express regard and friendship for such a proposition, will say *Orith* (That is good). Now, by what means are we to lead this people to salvation . . . ?[24]

Some observers were even more venomous in their reportage. Johan Printz, the governor of New Sweden in the southern part of Lenapehoking from 1643 to 1653, wrote contemptuously in 1644 in reference to the Lenapes and the Delaware River, "Nothing would be better than a couple of hundred soldiers should be sent here and kept here until we broke the necks of all of them in the river. . . . With the help of God not a single savage would be allowed to live in this river."[25]

Others were thoughtful, measured, and positive, even admiring, in their observations. William Penn described the Lenapes he knew in Pennsylvania in 1683 as "generally tall, streight, well-built, and of singular Proportion; they tread strong and clever, and mostly walk with a lofty Chin."[26] Hoping to acquire land, Adriaen van der Donck came to New Netherland in 1641 as a legal officer for Rensselaerswyck, the Dutch patroonship (a land estate granted by the colonial Dutch government) where Albany is today; he later purchased much of what is now the Bronx. In a book published in 1655 he comprehensively described New Netherland and the Native Americans living there with the goal of promoting trade and settlement in the colony. Of their appearance and attributes, he wrote:

> Both men and women are equal to the average and well-proportioned sort here in the Netherlands. In height, . . . weight and girth, they vary as elsewhere. . . . Their limbs are nimble and supple, and they can run strenuously with striking stamina, carrying big and heavy packs with them. . . . Congenital defects and deformities are very seldom seen. . . . One finds no fools, madmen, maniacs, or lunatics among them. . . .
>
> . . . It is true that at first sight they appear somewhat strange to our people, because color, speech, and dress are so different, but for those who associate with them frequently the strangeness soon passes. . . .
>
> . . . Cold, heat, hunger, and thirst they bear remarkably well, and they disregard hardship. . . .
>
> From the youngest age they swim like ducklings.[27]

Van der Donck, compared to many of his European contemporaries, proved to be unusually sensitive to the ways of the indigenous peoples of the region—both the Lenapes and other groups living further north—visiting their homes, learning some of their languages, observing and meticulously recording their rituals and customs, immersing himself in their cultures.[28]

TRADE AND GOVERNANCE

In the years before Wappaquewam and his people decided to sell their land, before European settlers came to the Americas, trade was the primary reason for close contact between Native Americans and Europeans. When the latter first arrived in Lenapehoking, animal skins held no prestige for the Indians and had no value as an exchange medium. They used skins as clothing, as covers for sleeping, as bags to contain things, and sometimes as shelter. To Europeans, on the other hand, fur had been since medieval times a status symbol, used as luxurious trim and for warmth in mittens and muffs. So great was the demand that even by the sixteenth century many animal species had become extinct in Europe. The desire for beavers, in particular, was intense due to the immensely popular felt hat, made by matting and compressing the soft underfur of the beaver pelt.

Each side in the trade dyad found the customs and values of the other baffling. To the Indians, the Europeans' insatiable appetite for animal pelts was incomprehensible. In the words of one Native American speaking to a French Jesuit missionary in 1634 while displaying a beautiful knife, "'The English have no sense; they give us twenty knives like this for one Beaver skin.'"[29] Gradually the Indians came to want what they could obtain in exchange for animal pelts—iron axes, hoes, knives, fishhooks, kettles, clothing, thimbles, needles, thread, fabric, jewelry, mirrors, glass beads, clay pipes, rum, beer, and guns with powder and lead. Acquiring these items would change their lives forever.[30]

Wappaquewam's deed to John Richbell listed "one hundred fathom of Wampom" among the items he was to receive for the land he was selling. Wampum, central to many types of exchange, including the fur trade, was a Native American form of currency fashioned from shells and used during the colonial period. A fathom is equal to six feet, so this entry on the list described six hundred feet of shell beads, pierced and strung. Though not made extensively by the Lenapes in Westchester County, these small beads were nonetheless the main medium of exchange between Europeans and Indians in the region in the seventeenth and eighteenth centuries. In a complicated system, different colors had different monetary equivalents, and there were corresponding values in various European currencies. When Europeans tried manufacturing wampum, the Indians refused to accept it, regarding it as counterfeit.[31]

Providing various Lenape bands a means for trade, the exchange of ideas, and marriage partners was a network of paths crisscrossing the region and connecting settlements and trading stations. After Europeans arrived, the paths facilitated the development of the fur trade and then later became the postal routes of colonial times and eventually some of the main highways of the twentieth century. Cutting right through the property that Wappaquewam sold to John Richbell was one of the most traveled paths, what historians have called the Westchester Path and "Sachkerah" or Shore Path. A segment of the "post-road" from New York to Boston, the path was part of the first major mail delivery route on the North American continent, established in 1673 by proclamation of colonial Governor Francis Lovelace.[32] As a postal route on a map, it was first represented on British cartographer Herman Moll's celebrated 1715 "Beaver Map," so designated because of the hard-working beavers represented in the inset.[33]

Paralleling the shore of Long Island Sound from New York City through Westchester County and Connecticut

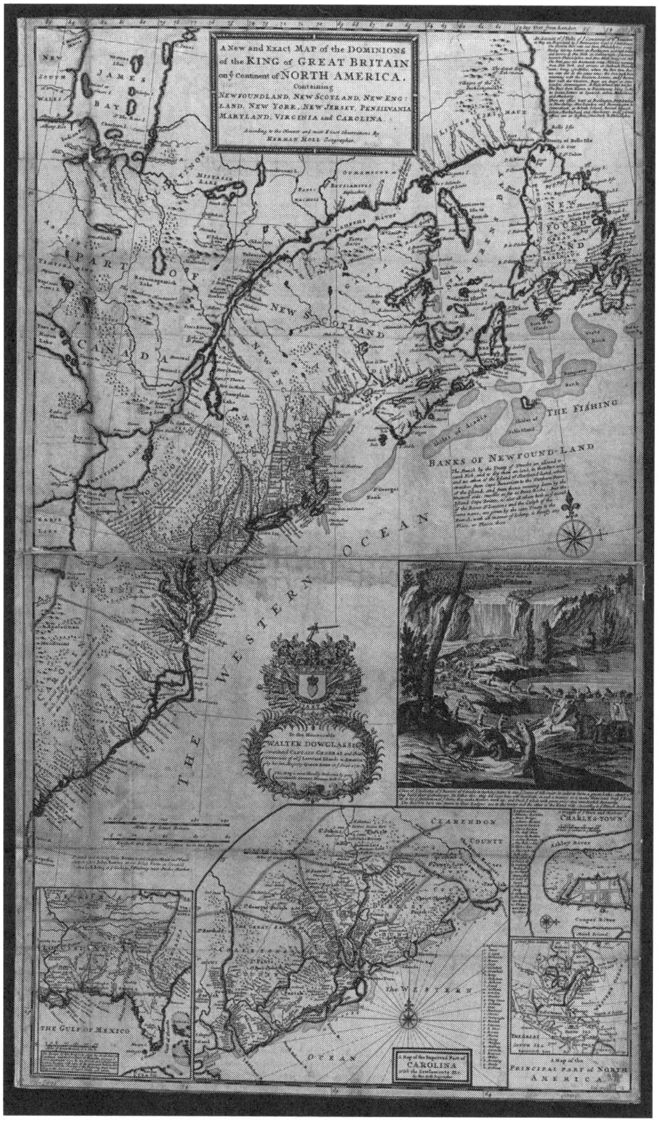

FIGURE 4.5 Herman Moll. *A New and Exact Map of the Dominions of the King of Great Britain on ye Continent of North America. . . .* 101 x 60 cm. Hand colored. [London] 1715 [i.e. 1731]. Commonly known as the "Beaver Map." *(Photograph courtesy of the Library of Congress, Geography and Map Division.)*

and then turning northeast to Boston, in its earliest years the path was but a densely wooded trail, known in colonial times as The King's Highway.[34] Sarah Kemble Knight, as an adventuresome thirty-eight-year-old, accompanied the postriders on horseback from Boston to New York and back in 1704–05. In her journal she observed, "Here We found great difficulty in Travailing, the way being very narrow, and on each side the Trees and bushes gave us very unpleasent welcomes wth their Branches and bow's, wch wee could not avoid. . . ."[35] The path in Westchester County eventually developed into a stagecoach route in 1772 and later the Boston Post Road and a segment of U.S. Route 1. Today locals still refer to it as "the Post Road."

The societies of the Siwanoys and other bands tended to be egalitarian with decision-making achieved through dialogue, persuasion, and consensus. As Van der Donck observed in 1655, "Social differences among the Indians are not nearly as great and obvious as among us. They say frankly they are unable to understand why one person is so much higher placed than another, as they are in our estimation."[36] Trade, however, called for a spokesperson to represent the group, so when Native American groups needed to negotiate a business transaction, they would agree upon a *sakima,* a term derived from the Dutch word *saeckemaecker* meaning "one who makes things [happen]" or "trade maker."[37] The sakima (or *sachem* in English documents) could be male or female and gained power through kinship or force, but had no more material goods or other advantages because of his or her position than other members of the group. As is noted in an official document sent back to the Netherlands in 1647 during the colonial governorship of Willem Kieft: "They dwell together in tribes, mostly of one consanguinity, over which commands a chief who is general and is generally called *Sackema,* possessing not much authority and little advantage. . . ."[38]

The egalitarian nature of Siwanoy culture is also evident in documents concerning property transactions. A power of attorney written for one 1661 land sale in

Westchester County went so far as to name five sakimas and "all Ingines living up Hudsons River and elsewhere in America" as having given full power to their representative to sell a tract of land, implying that all Indians across the continent needed to be included in the consent to the transaction.[39] Richbell's deed states that the sale is "by Consent of the other Indyans." It seems Wappaquewam's people appointed him sakima to represent them in the negotiations leading up to the writing of the deed and the sale of their homeland to the Englishman who landed on their shores in 1661.

JOHN RICHBELL AND THE DEED

John Richbell, who acquired my property (and a vast area surrounding it) from Wappaquewam and his people, was a well-connected English merchant trading with America through Barbados and New England. While in Barbados in September 1657, he entered into a partnership with two of his countrymen to purchase land in New Netherland.[40] Although the partnership agreement never directly mentions the business of trade and I have not found any information as to how the business fared, their collective goal was probably to establish a North American site from which to carry on trade activities not permitted under the restrictive English navigation laws. The peninsulas and coves of Long Island Sound's deeply-cut coastline lent themselves to covert activities such as smuggling seaborne merchandise as well as captives to be sold as enslaved workers.

Richbell settled first on Long Island, where in 1659 he made a business agreement with Taccaponsha, "Cheife Sackemack and Proprietor" of a portion of the south shore of Long Island, to purchase for six pounds every whale that "is, shall or may be, Cast up or driven on Shoare within any part" of his land. Richbell further agreed to give "the Indian that brings word of the Casting up of any whale or Whales . . . one paire of Shooes, or a Shirt, or nine Shillings of Wampome. . . ."[41] Buying property at Oyster Bay the following year,[42] he presumably had begun the process of becoming familiar with the entire region. With a set of instructions from his Barbados partners as his guide, he traveled across Long Island Sound and located a spot on the shore that precisely fit its terms. The instructions directed Richbell, upon his safe arrival, to

> Informe yourselfe fully by sober understanding men of that parte of land which lyeth betwixt Connecticott and the Dutch Collony and of the sea coast belonging to the same and the islands that lye bettwixt Long Island and that Maine, viz.: within what Government it is, and of what kinde that Government is whether very strict or remisse, who the cheife Magistrates are, on what termes ye Indians stand with them, and what bounds the Dutch pretend to. And being satisfyed in these particulars, (viz.) that you may with security settle there and without offence to any. Then our advice is that you endeavor to buy some small Plantation that is already settled and hath an house and some quantity of ground cleared and which lyeth so as you may enlarge into the woods at pleasure in each, be sure not to fayle of these accommodations.
>
> 1. That it be near some navigable Ryver, or at least some safe Port or harbor, ...
> 2. That it be well watered by some Running Streame. . . .
> 3. That it be well wooded which I thinke you can hardly misse of. That it be on healthy high ground, not bogs or fens. . . .[43]

The agreement further stipulates that Richbell should carefully research the title to the land so as to "have all pretenders satisfied before you purchase." After taking care of that, he should plant "corne, pease, beanes and other provisions . . . increasing your orchards and gardens, your pastures and inclosures; and for ye familyes employment in the Long winter be sure . . . to put an acre or Two of hempseed into the ground, of which you may . . . make a quantity of canvass and cordage for your own use." He also was to advise his partners on how his affairs progressed "for the life of our businesse will consist in the nimble, quiet and full correspondence with us."[44] Richbell could hardly have found a more perfect parcel of land to fulfill the terms of his agreement. Situated on the coast between the English colony of Connecticut and the heart of the Dutch colony of New Netherland, it included a river, running streams, and few low-lying areas. Though the property lacked a house, there were nearby Dutch and English settlements and plenty of woodlands in which to expand the operation.

Most seventeenth-century settlers recognized what they considered to be the Indians' "natural rights" to the land. An established principle at the time, before applying for title to land, a settler had to gain permission from the provincial government to acquire it and then prove he had purchased the land from the indigenous residents and paid them for it. Not until 1823 did the U.S. Supreme Court rule that Native Americans could sell land only to the U.S. government and not to private citizens.[45] Dutch and English colonists wrote numerous deeds signed by Native Americans in the 1600s, as in the now legendary sale of Manhattan Island by Indians to Dutch settlers in 1626. The first land sale in Westchester County was in 1639, and together these transactions initiated a new era. Now Europeans sought not only fish and furs, but also land.

Once John Richbell had made his agreement with Wappaquewam, he applied for a "ground brief," a permit to extinguish the Siwanoys' title, and then a "transport," a document that would make the conveyance of land legal in the eyes of the Dutch colonial government. Director-General Peter Stuyvesant eventually signed the papers confirming Richbell's title, but not before substantial controversy and litigation had taken place.[46]

FIGURE 4.6 Warren Chase Merritt. *John Richbell and Wappaquewam Negotiate the Sale of the Land in 1661.* 1936. Mural. Mamaroneck Public Library. *(Photograph courtesy of the Mamaroneck Public Library, Mamaroneck, New York. Photo by Charles Seton.)*

A PLAYER, NOT A PAWN

Wappaquewam was again a player in property matters as John Richbell found himself involved in litigation, a common and an acceptable way to resolve conflict in the seventeenth century. Richbell's legal challenge came in the form of another Englishman, Thomas Revell, who claimed to have bought most of the same property from Wappaquewam and his brother, Mathetuson, at about the same time that Richbell had made his purchase. To defend their respective claims to the colonial authorities, Richbell and his adversary gathered a number of depositions. In them, as well as in the deeds and powers of attorney, Wappaquewam's name appears a total of thirty-three times. One document refers to him as Captain, a designation of general respect at the time. The details of the statements are revealing and serve to humanize Wappaquewam, allowing him to emerge as a historical character, actively engaged in his own destiny, a player rather than a pawn.

Among the deponents were two interpreters whom Richbell had engaged to assist him in his negotiations with Wappaquewam. They affirmed that they had been present at the signing of the deed, which took place at the junction of the Mamaroneck River and the sound. They also agreed that Mathetuson, Wappaquewam's brother who had been present at the signing, "seemed to bee much disturbed in his Mind" upon hearing that a contract for the sale of the land had been made with a second European.[47] Another witness, William Joanes, stated that some months after the deed-signing, Richbell and the two interpreters constructed a shed on the property for protection from the elements. As the three waited in it for Wappaquewam to come to collect some of his pay for the land sale, Richbell sent Joanes to find food. While on his mission, he heard that Thomas Revell had taken steps to buy the land. When Richbell learned of this, he and the interpreters set out to warn Revell not to make the purchase; on their way they encountered Wappaquewam. One interpreter spotted Wappaquewam attempting to slip away and asked him if he was "ashamed" of what he was doing in selling the same property to a second buyer.[48]

Whether Wappaquewam's altered course was the result of his desire to cut a better deal or his frustration at not having been fully paid is unclear. According to one deponent, Wappaquewam had admitted to having been persuaded by other Indians to sell the land to Revell because Revell "would give a great deale more" for it.[49] More than one witness attested to the fact that Wappaquewam offered to return to Richbell the goods he had been given in the exchange in order to nullify the contract. But Richbell refused to accept them, maintaining that "according to bargaine hee would have the land & pay him (the sd. Indyan) his pay"—in other words, a deal is a deal.[50] Most of the deponents noted, however, that Richbell still owed Wappaquewam some goods for the land. An undated account of "ye purchase at Momoronock by Mr. Richbell & Mr. Revell" states that "Wappaqueem saith that Mr. Richbell was ye first that spake to him about ye purchase of ye said lands . . . , that Mr. Richbell came & viewed & agreed for ye Land but not bringing his goods tyme enough he sold it to Mr. Revell."[51]

The court finally settled the issue, aided by a statement obtained in 1666 from Wappaquewam, who affirmed that he had sold "to Mr. John Richbell of Oyster Bay, to him and his Heires forever, the . . . three Necks of Land, together with all other Privileges thereunto belonging, Six weeks before I sold it to Mr. Thos. Revell."[52] The court found in Richbell's favor in 1668 and ordered Revell's estate to pay him fifty pounds "for damages sustained by this dilatory and vexatious suit together with costs."[53] Had Wappaquewam been able to undo his first sale in order to sell the land to Revell, might the long-term result for him and the other Siwanoys have been much different? Probably not.

DEED DISTORTION

The colony changed hands in 1664 when Charles II of England gave to his brother James, later King James II, an enormous tract of North American land that included New Netherland and then sent ships to Manhattan demanding that the Dutch surrender. Because the colony had become financially unprofitable for the Dutch and was in no position to resist, the Dutch decided to cede New Netherland to the English, signing a treaty on September 9, 1664. With the colony now in English hands and renamed New York, Richbell had to request a patent from the British Crown. He did so, and Governor Francis Lovelace signed it in 1668. It included a clause, common to royal patents, requiring Richbell to pay an annual quit-rent—for Richbell the quit-rent was ". . . the vallue of Eight Bushells of Winter Wheate, . . . if demanded unto his Royall Highness and his Heyrs. . . ."[54]

The 1668 English patent, however, contained something new—wording not seen before in the property's boundary description. This time it reads, "to ye South ye Sound and running Northward from ye marked Trees upon ye said Necks Twenty Miles into ye woods which said Parcell or Tract of Land hath been heretofore lawfully Purchased of ye Indyan Proprietors by John Richbell of Momoronock Govt. in whose Possession now it is. . . ."[55] Now the property actually extended twenty miles into the woods, an alteration of the original deed's provision, which only granted Richbell permission to "freely feed cattle or cutt Timber twenty miles Northward from the marked Trees of the Necks."

Deeds of the time routinely contained ambiguity in the descriptions of boundaries. In the earliest days of colonial settlement there was plenty of land to go around so precise descriptions were unnecessary. With the passage of time and a growing population, however, there were more disputes. Properties overlapped each other, and people sold parcels of land more than once, sometimes inadvertently. In the case of the Wappaquewam-to-Richbell deed, however, the change in language seems to have been deliberate. At the time, the boundaries of a property could be whatever an aggressive owner managed to make them. Thus, without the benefit of sanction from Wappaquewam and the other indigenous proprietors, Richbell now, after just seven years, owned a tract of land more than twenty times the size of the original purchase. He had twisted the language to his advantage.

Richbell, in addition to probably intending to engage in smuggling on his new property, was a bit of a scoundrel or at the least, on one occasion, ran seriously afoul of the law. Though by 1670 he had settled three outstanding debts for which he had been taken to court,[56] the following year Governor Lovelace issued a warrant for his arrest to the sheriff of New York City "'in his majesties name to authorize and impower you to seize upon ye person of John Richbell of Mamaroneck, in what place soever he shall be found within this government, he being a prisoner under arrest for debt in this city, from which place he hath absented himself contrary to his engagement and that you cause him to be brought back hither to answer ye several suites of his creditors, and to abide the judgment of court therein according to law. . . .'"[57] By contrast, in 1668 he had served as a juror in a murder trial[58] and as a court-appointed commissioner to settle a land dispute.[59] The following year he became an inventory appraiser for the extensive estate of Thomas Pell, a large landholder in a nearby town.[60] Regardless of John Richbell's varying reputation as a scofflaw or as an upstanding citizen, there is evidence that the Siwanoys were not satisfied with what had occurred after the sale of their land. Some thirty years later, their leaders would challenge in court the size and terms of Richbell's original purchase.

CONCEPTS OF OWNERSHIP

A discussion of the contrast between the European concept of land ownership and that of the Native Americans enhances the understanding of property transfers in the seventeenth and eighteenth centuries. Europeans had come from an overpopulated place where land was at a premium and land ownership was something for the wealthy few. Someone owned every parcel of land, and as a commodity or real estate, it could be exploited for individual gain and bought and sold. For European settlers in the New World, acquiring and "improving" land was the primary way to amass wealth.

Native Americans, on the other hand, moved regularly in order to take advantage of the land's seasonal resources. Their concept of land possession was based on use. What they owned was not the land per se but rather what was on the land and of the land.[61] As Adriaen van der Donck wrote in the 1650s, for the Indians of the Hudson Valley, the "wind, stream, bush, field, sea, beach, and riverside are open and free to everyone of every nation with which the Indians are not embroiled in open conflict. All those are free to enjoy and move about such places as though they were born there."[62] In the late 1700s, an English Moravian missionary living among the Native Americans of the Ohio Valley—some of them probably descendants of the Siwanoys who had migrated there—observed that they believed that the Great Spirit "made the earth and all that it contains for the common good of mankind; when he stocked the country that he gave them with plenty of game, it was not for the benefit of a few, but of all. . . . Whatever liveth on the land, whatsoever groweth out of the earth, and all that is in the rivers and waters flowing through the same, was given jointly to all, and every one is entitled to his share."[63] Europeans of the time frequently remarked upon the Indians' tendency to share all material goods with others.

For the Siwanoys of the early seventeenth century, like other Eastern Woodland Indians, there were no concepts of private property and title. They historically had not used fences and had no notion of trespass. Even if they could have read Dutch or English, they might have found the legal jargon that characterizes deeds perplexing. Viewing the land as something to be inhabited and utilized, they believed that if it was not being occupied and used by one group, then it could be occupied and used by others. Likewise, once vacated, it could be "sold" again to another. In "selling" a piece of land, they often took for granted that they retained the right to use it later and at times assumed they would share the land with the "buyer," perhaps simultaneously entering into a defensive alliance.[64]

Exactly why Wappaquewam chose to sell the property is unknown, but it is possible to make an imaginative and informed guess as to the reasons. Scholars have advanced a number of theories on why Native Americans of the Northeast sold their lands relatively cheaply to European settlers in the 1600s. Hypotheses range from naive gestures of friendship on the part of Native Americans, to their inability to understand the transactions, to land as purely an article of commerce, the sale of which was a way to make ends meet or to clear up debt.

Given that Wappaquewam had probably lived through the intense violence of the 1640s between Dutch settlers and Native Americans, which spilled from Manhattan into Westchester County, it is unlikely that his sale was an innocent, magnanimous gift. By 1661 he surely would have been aware of land sales that had taken place in the previous two decades, including the large parcel adjacent to his that other Native Americans had sold to Englishman Thomas Pell seven years earlier, so it is doubtful he was ignorant of the European view of land ownership. The sale might have been an act of expediency to relieve his people of accumulated debt, a solution to a problem brought on by changed circumstances. In 1655 Van der Donck reported that in New Netherland hunters took an average of eighty thousand beavers in a single year.[65] As they depleted the animal resources, the fur trade began to collapse. This development, coupled with the fact that the business of trapping was seasonal, forced some Indians to depend on credit in order to survive. As their debts increased, they turned to the selling of land to satisfy their European creditors.[66] This practice may explain the Siwanoy band's choice to sell land to John Richbell.

Wappaquewam's apparent attempt to sell the land twice may have stemmed from differing concepts of land rights. When it came to the transfer of land, as William Cronon has observed, Native Americans, at least in the early years of contact, believed they were selling one thing and the English thought they were buying something else. This situation could result in a group of Indians conveying what they regarded as the right to use a piece of land to more than one European simultaneously.[67] On the other hand, Wappaquewam's actions may have been an indication of a conscious, calculated move to strike a better deal for himself and his people. Given his choices, Wappaquewam may have been manipulating the situation to his own advantage, doing what was practical—a form of adaptive behavior. The Siwanoys by this time probably had learned how to manage the European presence in the best way possible.

Whether Wappaquewam understood the agreement with Richbell to be a "sale" in the European sense of the term or a kind of lease granting occupancy and usage is unknown. Either way, not only were the Dutch and the English settlers actually taking possession of the land of the original inhabitants, with all their related concepts of ownership and trespass, but they were also altering the landscape more dramatically and extensively than had the Native Americans before them, clearing large swaths of its forests in order to cultivate crops and graze cattle. The land and what it gave the Siwanoys was the one known entity they had lived with and could count on, and in little more than fifty years, it and the resources it offered them were no longer theirs to use. Their decision to sell would have marked merely the beginning of the troubles that lay ahead for Wappaquewam and his people.

DISPOSSESSION AND DEPOPULATION

One historian concluded his 1886 discussion on the Native Americans of Westchester County by observing, "The Indians vanished from Westchester as noiselessly as the morning mists disappear before the advancing day. . . . They left behind them so few material evidences of their existence here that we find them only by accident or by careful search. But many of the names applied by them to mountains, streams and localities have been fortunately retained. . . ."[68] It is true that relatively little archaeological evidence of the Siwanoys has been found and many of the Westchester County place names they used have been retained. And with the passage of two hundred years, it may have seemed with hindsight in the late nineteenth century that they went "noiselessly," but if that is the case, they did so with considerable pain. The magnitude of their difficulties and displacement is staggering.

Hostility among the Lenapes toward the European visitors had been engendered by incidents such as Henry Hudson's crew members' savage retaliation in the early 1600s. Because Native Americans had no written language, they committed to memory events of great import, such as Hudson's actions, and passed them down orally from generation to generation so that resentment could linger for decades. Even so, the Lenape peoples are known to have helped the settlers at times,[69] but as more and more Europeans occupied the Indians' territories, conflicts increasingly arose.

A series of culture clashes escalated into what became known as Kieft's War, which raged in and around Manhattan from 1643 to 1645. Most residents of New Netherland wished to proceed slowly with settlement and the conflicts it caused and address individual transgressions on a case-by-case basis; however, the open antagonism toward Indians of the ruthless Dutch Director-General Willem Kieft exacerbated the situation. In three years of intense clashes between European settlers and Native Americans, it is said that anywhere from five hundred to sixteen hundred Native Americans died.[70] Though centered on Manhattan, the conflict migrated into Westchester County and included one notorious incident. Anne Hutchinson, seeking religious freedom in the tolerant New Netherland, had recently relocated from the Massachusetts Bay Colony via Rhode Island to the southern part of the county. She, six of her children, and nine others were massacred by a band of Siwanoys.

Some among the leaders of New Netherland recognized the tragic results of the war for both the Europeans and the Native Americans. In 1644 a group of elected Dutch representatives known as the Eight Men wrote to the directors of the West India Company in the Netherlands, asking for help with a "most unfortunate plight. . . . Our fields lie fallow and waste; our dwellings and other buildings are burnt; not a handful can be planted or sown this fall on all the abandoned places. . . . All these are now laid in ashes through a foolish hankering after war; for it is known to all right thinking men here, that these Indians have lived as lambs among us until a few years ago, injuring no one, affording every assistance to our nation."[71] The characterization of the Indians "as lambs" here may be an example of the myth of the Noble Savage at work. Nonetheless, it probably is indicative to some extent of the experience and perceptions of these Dutch colonists. In response to the demands of the Eight Men that Director-General Kieft be replaced, the West India Company recalled him and appointed Peter Stuyvesant in his place, but the damage had been done. The Siwanoys and other bands in Westchester County had already begun retreating further north in New York and west into New Jersey.

Besides ongoing conflict and all-out slaughter, there were other difficulties for the Siwanoys and the Lenape peoples as a whole, more subtle but nonetheless devastating. Trade opportunities that had developed with the coming of European traders in the 1500s quickly diminished for several reasons. Already at a disadvantage when it came to obtaining animal skins because they lived in a relatively warm climate where fur of available animals was less thick and therefore of less value than that obtained further north, the Lenapes were at times prevented from trapping by more powerful, better organized tribes to the north. The once-abundant animal stock diminished, a result of guns acquired from European traders that enabled Indians to kill increasing numbers of animals, particularly beavers.[72] In 1644 Governor Printz of New Sweden said of the Lenapes, "We have no beaver trade with them but only the maize trade. They are a lot of poor rascals."[73]

In addition, as Dutch and English settlers cleared the land for cultivation, they depleted the forests where Indians obtained much of their food, their firewood, and their materials for shelter. In order to preserve the hunting and gathering aspects of their economic systems, Eastern Woodland Indians found it necessary to put great expanses of woodlands between themselves and the agricultural and livestock pursuits of the colonists, beginning a pattern of migration and land alienation.[74] Also, Europeans preferred to conduct trade with a single individual representative rather than with a group, but this was antithetical to the Indians' egalitarian social organizations. Thus, with the means of their livelihood destroyed and their community structures altered, the social order the Native Americans had lived with for centuries began to unravel.

Of all the changes brought to the New World by Europeans, infectious diseases may have taken the most immediate and devastating toll on Native Americans. Adriaen van der Donck estimated the affects of small pox when he wrote in the 1650s that "the Indians tell us that . . . after the arrival of the Christians, . . . their numbers have dwindled owing to smallpox and other causes to the extent that there is now barely one for every ten."[75] A 1633 epidemic was the first time the Siwanoys and other Eastern Woodland Indians encountered smallpox, an event remarked upon by most contemporary observers. Though population data for the Siwanoys and other Lenape peoples is lacking, recent research utilizing mathematical models with the methods of archaeology and history concludes that the population of Native American groups in the Northeast as a whole declined markedly from the time of contact with Europeans to the beginning of the nineteenth century, with estimates ranging from a 73 to a 95 percent decline.[76]

The ethnocentrism and arrogance of one Englishman who surveyed the situation on Long Island shortly after the English took over New Netherland from the Dutch is appalling. Daniel Denton, having spent two decades in the New World, wrote in 1670 in a promotional piece designed to attract English settlers:

> To say something of the Indians, there is now but few upon the Island, and those few no ways hurtful but rather serviceable to the English, and it is to be admired, how strangely they have decreast by the Hand of God, since the English first setling of those parts; for since my time, where there were six towns, they are reduced to two small Villages, and it hath been generally observed, that where the English come to settle, a Divine Hand makes way for them, by removing or cutting off the Indians, either by Wars one with the other, or by some raging mortal Disease.[77]

Regardless of the involvement of the hand of God and the prevailing attitude of religious determinism, by the late 1600s, disease had nearly destroyed the indigenous population of southern New York.

Nonetheless, as late as 1699, the Siwanoys were still a small presence in Mamaroneck, though contemporary documents do not mention Wappaquewam. In a petition to the governor of the colony, they finally made the claim that they had never received what had been promised to them for the sale of their land to John Richbell, by then deceased. They also maintained that Richbell's heirs had more property than Richbell actually had purchased. Three Siwanoys presented the petition to the Executive Council of the Province of New York on August 2, 1699, asking for "'redress and relief in the promises'" and for Richbell's heirs to "'be ordered to satisfy your Petitioners and that they may have no more land than was actually sold unto them.'"[78] According to a nineteenth-century historian who presumably saw the petition as it appeared in the colony's Executive Council's minutes, no longer in existence for this date, there is no further mention of the matter, leading one to believe that the Council took no action on it.[79] Perhaps it was in response to this petition that Caleb Heathcote, who in 1697 had purchased the part of Richbell's lands that encompasses my property, paid seven Siwanoy representatives for land in the area, as did another purchaser of Richbell property in 1701. These actions are indications that, though the properties had previously been "sold," the Siwanoys had not yet completely relinquished their claims to Mamaroneck lands.[80]

Many of the Siwanoys and other Lenapes who had survived the epidemics of the 1600s continued migrating in the early 1700s, sustaining the spiral of dispossession. In 1710, according to church records, a few Siwanoys still attended an Anglican church in the southern part of Westchester County.[81] At about the same time, the Reverend George Muirson, rector of the Anglican church in Rye, a town just northeast of Mamaroneck, wrote to the Secretary of the Society for the Propagation of the Gospel in England, "As to the Indians, the natives of the country, they are a decaying people. We have not now in all this parish twenty families; whereas, not many years ago, there were Several hundreds. I have frequently conversed with Some of them, and been at their great meetings of *powowing*, as they call it."[82] Around 1719, one of his successors wrote to the Society that there were but four or five Indian families living in the parish and that they moved frequently, as often as every month or six weeks, implying that they were landless and probably homeless.

According to Charles W. Baird, a nineteenth-century rector of the Rye parish and local historian, little more was heard of the Indians in Rye, "except as slaves," after about 1720.[83] Even several decades earlier, the Court of Assizes for New York, the colony's high court to hear major civil suits and criminal cases, had ordered that "noe Negro or Indian Slaves" were to absent themselves from their masters' houses or plantations on the Sabbath without their masters' written consent, indicating that some Native Americans had already become enslaved by 1682.[84] Well into the next century, a 1755 slave census listing forty-eight enslaved people in Mamaroneck and Scarsdale began with the words, "A List of the Indian Negro and Malatto Slaves Within and Belonging to the Township of Mamaroneck and Mannor of Scarsdale."[85] It is clear that some Siwanoys came to be included in the population of enslaved people.

The irreversible Native American population loss continued. By 1782 there was just a single small Siwanoy settlement still in existence at Bear Swamp Road in today's Bronx.[86] When the population of a Native American village reached dangerously low numbers, the remaining residents would seek refuge with linguistically similar bands with larger populations and become integrated into the new group. Often they would migrate a great distance. Some Siwanoys, like many members of other bands, probably became part of larger Native American groups. For a myriad of reasons, by the 1800s the Siwanoy people as a people no longer existed.

Today, a legend and a related story about the Siwanoys endure. More than fifty years ago *The Westchester Historian*, a local history journal, published a paper written sometime after 1866 by an unidentified author and found among the records of an old Westchester County family. It tells the "Legend of the White Deer." North of my property up the Mamaroneck River a mile or two is a six-stepped falls, the site of an old gristmill and sawmill and now in someone's backyard. It is said that at the full moon every May, a "great white deer would visit the falls, and standing in the middle of the water, take a long drink, and if anyone was lucky enough to see him they would have good fortune and success for a year." Perhaps what they saw were simply reflections in the water from the moon shining at a certain angle, but Indians "from the farthest point on Long Island to the Great Lakes . . . flocked to see the Great White Deer" each year.[87] The spot gained much importance, and Native American families sent their young boys there to learn how to behave like men and to shoot, which explains why many farmers reported finding arrowheads nearby. For years after the Siwanoys ceased to live in the area year-round, some would come annually to spend a month at the falls. By 1805 just one member of the group came. Known as Indian Dan, he returned for a couple of months each year until about 1866, making baskets in a little home he would build for himself beneath the oak trees.[88]

The literature refers to Siwanoys (who by the 1800s had migrated into New Jersey and Pennsylvania and melded with other Lenapes) as Munsees if they lived north of the Delaware River and as Delawares if they lived in the southern parts of Lenapehoking. No longer Siwanoys as a people, they endured additional tragic and horrific disruptions. The gradual diaspora continued westward into the Ohio

Valley in the early nineteenth century until the U.S. Office of Indian Affairs intervened and forced the remaining bands to vacate Ohio and Indiana by 1821, granting them reservation land further north and west. Perhaps some of the descendants of Wappaquewam—assuming he had them and they survived—are living in Oklahoma, Wisconsin, or Ontario, Canada, where Lenapes have settled and today work to reclaim their language and their heritage.[89]

five

Caleb Heathcote: Manor Lord

It is not only large in extent, and the land very good, but near the city. So, consequently, it will in time be a great settlement.[1]

—Caleb Heathcote to the secretary of the Society for the Propagation of the Gospel, 1705

I know no man understands ye Province or ye People better, or is more capable of doing her Majestie reall service. He is an honest man.[2]

—Lewis Morris, writing of Caleb Heathcote to the Secretary of State in London, 1708

As Wappaquewam and other Siwanoys vacated Westchester County, increasing numbers of Europeans from various countries settled there. One of them was Englishman Caleb Heathcote (1666–1720), who four years after his arrival acquired a large tract of land from John Richbell's widow. A historical figure of some note locally with a school in a nearby town and several roads in the area named after him, Heathcote was familiar enough to me that his name leapt off the grantee index page when I unexpectedly ran across it in my deed research. But Heathcote Road and Heathcote School are several miles from my house. Could he have owned that land and my land and all that lies in between? How Heathcote came to be a truly major landholder and the lord of a manor in Westchester County is a story that began with his birth into a distinguished, landed family in Chesterfield, Derbyshire, in 1666, the same year John Richbell gained official title to the Westchester property under British law. As the sixth of seven sons, Caleb Heathcote would have had little chance of inheriting real property in his home country, which may explain his ambitions in the realm of land acquisition.

He arrived on the island of Manhattan in 1692 at the age of twenty-six, two years after the death of his father, the mayor of the city of Chesterfield. On his father's tombstone, Caleb and his six brothers had placed the inscription, "he had the particular blessing to see all [seven of his surviving sons become] Merchant adventurers, either in England or in foreign parts."[3] With a considerable inheritance from his father and the connections of his five older brothers, already established in foreign trade in New York and elsewhere, merchant-adventurer Caleb Heathcote soon gained the status of a freeman in the colony and thus could begin work as a correspondent for large London traders. He also entered into the business of obtaining military contracts to equip soldiers and to supply stocks of gifts for Native Americans,[4] quickly establishing himself as a successful merchant in the growing city.

New York at the time was still half Dutch, but very diverse, a haven for adventurers and refugees. The English were the second largest group; others included Protestant Flemings and Frenchmen, Iberian Jews, Danes, Norwegians, Swedes, Irishmen, Germans, Poles, Bohemians, free and enslaved people of African origins, and a shrinking number of Native Americans. In this polyglot, energetic, and growing province, Governor Fletcher soon appointed Heathcote a member of his council, a powerful body of twelve who passed laws, advised the governor, and sat with him as a tribunal to consider important judicial cases. Heathcote's meteoric rise was a consequence of his being among the extremely small number of immigrants to America who arrived with both money and good credit. As a member of the governor's council, he was expected to lend money to the province when revenues or appropriations were late or fell short. With his appointment came the designation *the Honorable,*[5] and although councilors served without pay, they received compensation beyond the honorific title in the form of large land grants for themselves and their families and friends.[6]

Heathcote began to acquire land in Westchester County in 1696, but the way had been paved for his connection to the county four years earlier by his commission as chief officer of the Westchester militia, affording him the title *Colonel,* one he retained for the rest of his life. Perhaps to reestablish order in the militia, an organization with a reputation for unrest and rebelliousness, the governor also granted Heathcote a commission as judge advocate, empowering him to conduct court-martials. In addition, as a member of the governor's council, he was a judge in the Court of Sessions, through which he heard criminal cases, and in 1693 the governor appointed him first judge of the Court of Common Pleas with jurisdiction over civil cases. Some years later, as judge of the Prerogative Court, he could probate wills and grant marriage licenses.[7]

One of his first judicial actions was to establish "Wolufe Pitts" to receive wolves, which had become a menace to livestock. Upon receipt of the slain animal's head, the constable was to "Cutt of[f] the Eares of[f] of from the said wolufes head and Naile it Up in some Conven[ien]tt Publick place." The captor would be paid twelve shillings, although Native Americans who performed the same task would receive just ten shillings.[8] In sum, Heathcote had authority over civil, criminal, and military judicial matters in Westchester County, all by age twenty-seven and within less than two years of his arrival in the province.

In 1696 Heathcote became the first mayor of the town of Westchester in the southern part of the county, a position he held until his death. In establishing the town's charter, he managed to include several remarkable provisions. The town would have its own representative in the provincial assembly, a privilege no other town but Schenectady had.[9] He also stipulated that the mayor be elected—at a time when even the cities of New York and Albany had mayors appointed by the colony's governor. Even more noteworthy was the provision that the right to vote in the mayoral elections was not limited to freeholders with property of a certain value, making the town of Westchester possibly the first place in the world to have the benefit of universal free male suffrage.[10] To his extensive judicial and military authority in the county, Heathcote had added executive powers.

FIGURE 5.1 Caleb Heathcote (1666–1720/21). *(Reprinted from Scharf, History of Westchester County, 1886, vol. 1, opp. p. 152. Photo by author.)*

LORD OF THE MANOR

John Richbell, the first European owner of my property, had conveyed the East Neck of his land, one of the three peninsulas of land described in his deed, to his mother-in-law in 1668 as repayment for a debt. She, in turn, immediately gave it to her daughter, Anne Richbell, John's wife. Three decades later, widow Anne sold the land to Caleb Heathcote, who recently had enhanced his connections among New York's elite by marrying Martha Smith, daughter of the chief justice of the province and one of its wealthiest men. The Heathcotes built a spacious two-story brick house as their residence, soon known as Heathcote Hill, facing the Westchester Path and overlooking Mamaroneck Harbor. Heathcote was now one of New York City's first commuters with a commuting distance of about twenty-two miles. He also built the necessary outbuildings to run a farm, quarters for ten enslaved workers and other servants, and several mills.[11] On the nearby Mamaroneck River where it flowed under the Westchester Path, he built a gristmill, a particularly vital amenity to a community. Not having access to one meant grinding grain into meal or flour with a mortar and pestle.[12] Communities valued the mill and granted special privileges to its owner, often looked upon as a leader, as Heathcote undoubtedly was by now.

To be prudent, as part of the process of buying Anne Richbell's land, Heathcote secured from her permission to purchase from the Siwanoys the same lands that had been included in her husband's purchase. A new generation of Siwanoys was in charge now, with Wappaquewam no longer in the picture, but they still maintained a claim to the land.[13] At the time, it was not unusual for Europeans to obtain confirmatory indentures or second deeds to ensure the cooperation of the Native Americans. In light of the claim that several Siwanoys had made against the Richbell property in 1699, Heathcote wisely adhered to his practice of negotiating with Indian proprietors and acquiring indentures for which he paid them sums of money. Following his purchase of the Richbell land, he drew up two indentures with seven Siwanoy representatives to secure the tract in 1701.[14] By reducing the possibility of further claims against the property, this process served as a kind of insurance policy.

Heathcote also formed a land-buying syndicate of about a dozen men and with them acquired additional land in the county north of the Richbell parcel. Between 1696 and 1702 the group secured at least four Indian indentures for 70,000 acres, known as the three Great Patents. Heathcote's share was over 12,000 acres of "improvable land."[15] On March 21, 1701/02[16] the governor signed documents consolidating all of Heathcote's properties and creating for him the Lordship and Manor of Scarsdale, the last one to be granted in Westchester County by the British Crown. Scarsdale was the name of Heathcote's father's estate in England, and establishing a provincial equivalent enabled him to follow in the footsteps of his English landed-gentry forebears, who placed a high value on the vast country estate. Most of this property was the land that Richbell had bought from Wappaquewam forty years before. One of six manors in Westchester County and one of sixteen in the State of New York,[17] today it comprises the towns of Mamaroneck (except for a few small parcels), Scarsdale, White Plains, and parts of Harrison and North Castle.[18] Heathcote's quit-rent to the Crown was "*five pounds* current money of New Yorke," due annually on Christmas day.[19]

Manors in America were a remnant of medieval English feudalism, which required a local area to be supervised in the interest of the Crown. Governmental in nature, the privileges of a colonial manor grant could be bestowed upon those who already owned land. The lord of the manor held court on his property to consider land-related issues such as metes-and-bounds conflicts and trespass, as well as other misdemeanors and crimes. Caleb Heathcote, of course, was already judge and jury over most local matters, so his becoming lord of the manor probably made little difference to the 150 people who, at the beginning of the eighteenth century, lived within the newly-created Manor of Scarsdale.[20]

Among the many responsibilities of a manor owner were operating not only gristmills, but also sawmills for the residents' use. Heathcote built one of his mills, used for both grinding grains and sawing wood, next to the falls where the "Legend of the White Deer" originated.[21] Other duties included surveying tenants' leased properties and supplying livestock for their farms. As lord of the manor, he also was expected to provide a teacher for the school, a physician, a clergyman, a boat builder, and other skilled laborers. Heathcote must have earned the trust and respect of his tenants because they came to him for advice on their most private concerns, such as settling family disputes and drawing up wills.[22]

THE MAYOR AND MORE

In 1711 the governor appointed Caleb Heathcote mayor of the City of New York, a post he held simultaneously with his mayoral duties in the town of Westchester. He served three one-year terms in the city whose population had grown to 6,000 at the same time that his brother, Sir Gilbert Heathcote, was Lord Mayor of London. As mayor of New York, Heathcote's tasks were varied and included appointing the keeper of the pound, the public whipper, the scavengers of the streets, and the bellman. He and his council regulated the size and quality of bread loaves and set their prices quarterly. Among the laws he enforced were prohibitions against driving carts in the public sewers, firing guns in the streets, and removing turf from the common. During Heathcote's term, the courts began to grant money to cover expenses incurred by witnesses who traveled great distances to testify and to provide counsel for people lacking the resources to pay for professional defense. His administration was also responsible for a number of public works projects, such as planting rows of shade trees and grading the main artery, Broadway, from the southern tip of Manhattan as far north as the common, today's City Hall Park, a distance of about one mile.[23]

Heathcote's biographer, writing in 1926, informs his reader that among his accomplishments was the designation of a more convenient location for the slave market. By this time, the City of New York included a large number of enslaved Africans among its inhabitants, about one-sixth of the population. Heathcote was in office during the revolt of 1712, when a group of enslaved residents conspired to seize the city. The government thwarted their plans but not before at least nine citizens were killed. The perpetrators escaped, the authorities later capturing and trying them in court. In the words of Governor Robert Hunter, "In that court were twenty seven condemned whereof twenty one were executed. . . . Some were burnt others hanged, one broke on the wheele, and one hung a live in chains in the town, so that there has been the most exemplary punishment inflicted that could be possibly thought of. . . ."[24] According to the minutes of the Common Council, Heathcote had ordered the sheriff to be paid "the sum of thirty Six pounds & ten pence" for iron work, gibbet, carting, firewood, laborers, and other expenses "for the Execution of several Negro slaves for Murders by them Committed in April last."[25] Said to have been capable and vigorous, his administration was at times, by twenty-first-century standards, cruel and inhumane.

In 1715, at the conclusion of Heathcote's third mayoral term, the governor appointed him surveyor-general of customs for the northern department of North America, a job that involved the supervision of New York Harbor's inbound and outbound traffic. Heathcote's concerns had grown beyond the city and the county to the continent. Developing a particular interest in naval stores, the materials needed for the British Crown's navy and shipping industry, he recognized that North America had all the necessary resources—forests with timber suitable for masts, hemp for rigging, flax for sails, as well as tar, pitch, and rosin—materials that England lacked and had been importing from Russia and Scandinavia. For more than a dozen years, Heathcote wrote letters to the home government in England, setting forth schemes for supplying the navy more economically by using American material resources and colonial militiamen as laborers.[26]

Heathcote suggested that his naval stores and shipbuilding plans also be tied to the larger matters of taxation and defense, with the American colonies uniting and arming themselves collectively against both French and Indian threats.[27] In a 1715 letter to Governor Hunter he wrote, "I do humbly beg leave to offer your Excellency my opinion . . . whether it would not be very proper . . . for your Excellency to desire a meeting or congresse at some convenient place, of all or as many of the Governours on this Continent as can with conveniency come & attend it."[28] To Lord Townshend, the British Secretary of State, he wrote the same month, "North America must immediately arm itself, unite & be very vigorous, or the whole will be in danger." He concluded the letter with, "I have since . . . recd the Governours answer to my letter, who tells me that the Governours can't meet or hold a congresse without expresse orders from the King."[29] The authorities in England rejected all of his proposals.

Although one might consider Heathcote ahead of his time in favoring a plan for taxing the entire continent to support the defense of the colonies as a unified whole, his ideas for joining the colonies had nothing to do with independence. A strong supporter of the empire, he directed his patriotism toward advancing British interests around the world[30] and subscribed to the notion that the

Primary Sources

A primary source is a document created during the time being considered and is usually authored by someone with direct personal knowledge of the topic. The importance of seeking out primary documents in lieu of relying solely upon and trusting secondary sources, which are written later, is made clear through two examples. Harry Hansen in his *Scarsdale: From Colonial Manor to Modern Community* of 1954 offers a useful, succinct summary of Caleb Heathcote's life story and its part in the history of the town of Scarsdale, New York, today a suburb in Westchester County. However, in his discussion of the 1712 slave revolt, which took place in New York City during Heathcote's mayoral administration, he states, "It is not clear what part Colonel Heathcote played, but there is a sinister record that about this time he was paid £36-0-10 for irons, cartage, labor, gibbets and finished firewood."[1] By checking an original source, Heathcote's role becomes perfectly clear. As the mayor of the City of New York, he had ordered the sheriff to be paid "the sum of thirty Six pounds & ten pence" for iron work, gibbet, carting, firewood, laborers, and other expenses "for the Execution of several Negro slaves for Murders by them Committed in April last."[2] These words from the published minutes of the meetings of the Common Council, lacking the veneer of judgment that comes with a twentieth-century perspective, reveal in no uncertain terms what transpired.

Even Dixon Ryan Fox's thoroughly documented 1926 biography of Heathcote fails to fully flesh out the story. His account of the slave revolt and Heathcote's role in it is a mere half paragraph in a nearly three-hundred-page book. The other part of that paragraph lists Heathcote's admirable public works projects and then states, "As one reads the record the impression grows that the administration was energetic and efficient. The item that a more convenient place was designated for hiring and selling Indian and negro slaves recalls the first negro plot, which took place during Heathcote's terms."[3] In his brief description of the "negro plot" that follows, he never mentions the part of the event described in June 1712 by the provincial governor in his periodic report to the Lords of Trade in London: "In that court were twenty seven condemned whereof twenty one were executed. . . . Some were burnt others hanged, one broke on the wheele, and one hung a live in chains. . . ."[4] In this case, an omission of significant information in a secondary source distorts the reality of what happened.

purpose of a colony was to support the home country. Lewis Morris, a colleague and lord of Morrisania, another of the Westchester County manors, wrote of Heathcote in 1707/08 to the Secretary of State in London, "he will be a man to ye generall sattisfaction of ye people. . . . I know no man understands ye Province or People better, or is more capable of doeing her Majestie reall service. . . ."[31] Heathcote's primary loyalties were to the British Crown.

Heathcote's role as public servant has been memorialized through public art. For example, a lineup of eight over-life-sized sculptures depicting eighteenth- and nineteenth-century City of New York mayors by Franco-American sculptor Philip Martiny graces the cornice line above the fifth floor of the main façade of Manhattan's Surrogate's Court, completed in 1911 and a National Historic Landmark since 1977. The artist represented

FIGURE 5.2 Warren Chase Merritt. *Caleb Heathcote Installed as Mayor of New York, 1711.* 1936. Mural. Mamaroneck Public Library. *(Photograph courtesy of the Mamaroneck Public Library, Mamaroneck, New York. Photo by Michael Torlen.)*

Heathcote wearing a judicial robe and a wig of flowing curls. Originally the Hall of Records, the building today houses not only the Surrogate's Court, which handles wills and estates, but also the city's archives. Closer to Heathcote's home is a New Deal-era mural prominently displayed in the Mamaroneck Public Library, depicting him at his 1711 mayoral installation in recognition of his service to the nearby metropolis.[32]

THE MISSIONARY

Caleb Heathcote, merchant, magistrate, mayor, and manor lord, was also called to be a missionary. It was his belief that only the Church of England could make "proper English Christians or proper English subjects."[33] Arriving in the colony of New York nearly thirty years after the English had taken it from the Dutch, Heathcote found only one Anglican service being held on a regular basis, and out of a total of thirty churches, none was Anglican. By 1700 there was just one Anglican church—Trinity, in the City of New York, which Heathcote had helped to found—out of a total of thirty-five churches.[34] The New York region had been settled by the Dutch, who established a climate of religious tolerance, as well as by New England Puritans, French Huguenots, and others not of the Anglican faith. The English, though much in the minority in New York, referred to anyone not affiliated with the Church of England as a "dissenter" or a heathen. Authorities in Great Britain expected both governors and lords of manors to promote the Anglican faith in the colonies.

Having overseen the spiritual and moral well-being of the three hundred families living in Westchester County when he first arrived there as a militia colonel and judge, Heathcote took his continuing ecclesiastical role seriously. By 1693 he had taken steps to improve what he perceived to be a morally bankrupt environment by initiating a call for clergymen to four towns in Westchester.[35] In 1704 the Society for the Propagation of the Gospel in Foreign Parts (the S.P.G.) invited Heathcote to become a member. The S.P.G., also known as the Venerable Society, was organized in England in 1701 to spread the gospel among Native Americans and others not of the Anglican faith—whose conversion would help secure their loyalty to the British government.

With the Native American population in Westchester County waning, however, Heathcote's main interest was the European settlers in the area. Demonstrating his concern for them in a 1704 letter to the secretary of the S.P.G., he wrote,

> From the time I first came amongst them, . . . I found it the most rude and heathenish count[r]y I ever saw in my whole life, which call themselves christians, there being not so much as the least marks or footsteps of religion of any sort. Sundays being the only time sett apart by them for all matter of vain sports and lewd diversions, and they were grown to such a degree of rudeness, that it was intolerable; and having then the command of the militia, I sent an order to all the captains, requiring them to . . . pass the Sabbath in the best manner they could, till such times as they could be better provided.[36]

He had passed a 1693 ordinance in response to the "great Debaucheries & Profainness . . . committed on the Lords day" ordering "that noe person shall sitt Tippleing in a publick ordinary on the Lords day, . . . that any Persons Inhabiting within this County shall not travill on the Lords day without permition. . . . Likewise noe person or persons shall presume to goe A ffishing shooteing or hunting of horses or Any other Sports which makes breach of the

Sabbath Upon ye penalty as aforesaid. . . ."[37] The penalty included being confined to the stocks for one hour or paying a fine of ten shillings.

As an S.P.G. "watch," a position that entailed gathering information for the society's leadership in England, Heathcote found in 1714 that in the colony of New York, of a population of forty-five thousand, only twelve hundred were Anglicans, and of them, just 450 were communicants. With such statistics, he must have felt compelled to do some proselytizing both within and beyond the borders of New York. Utilizing the church he had helped to establish in Rye as his base, he and the church's minister ventured into Connecticut on several occasions with the express purpose of converting "dissenters," of which there were many in this area settled by New Englanders of Puritan stock. On these missions the two rode on horseback, their saddlebags stuffed with prayer books and Heathcote "always . . . *fully armed*, as . . . it was as much as a man's life was worth even to talk of the Church in Connecticut, without the means of self defense."[38] His efforts bore fruit as he converted some to the Anglican faith and succeeded in introducing the Church of England into Connecticut.[39]

HEATHCOTE'S LEGACY

With all of his success in business, civic, judicial, and ecclesiastical endeavors, it was in his land acquisitions and in his role as manor lord that Caleb Heathcote made his greatest mark. In 1788 the land comprising his Manor of Scarsdale produced both the town that still bears its name, Scarsdale, and Mamaroneck. A number of entities, in addition to the road and the school so familiar to me, bear his name—Heathcote Hill, Heathcote Corners, assorted local businesses, a foundation, and a neighborhood in Scarsdale. A large New Deal-era mural in the Scarsdale Post Office depicts Heathcote negotiating the purchase of the property with Anne Richbell, as associates study a map and servants attend to his saddle and draw water from a well.[40]

Heathcote died suddenly in early 1720/21 at the age of fifty-four. His brief obituary in a Philadelphia newspaper read:

> New-York, March 6. On the 28th Day of February last died here the Honorable Caleb Heathcote, Esq., Surveyor General of His Majesty's Customs for the Eastern District of North America, Judge of the Court of Admiralty for the Provinces of New-York and New-Jersey, and the Colony of Connecticut, one of His Majesty's Council for the Province of New-York, and Brother of Sir Gilbert Heathcote of London. He was a Gentleman of rare Qualities, excellent Temper and Virtuous Life and Conversation, and his Loss lamented by all who knew him, who on the Day of his Death went about doing Good, in procuring a Charitable Subscription, in which he made a very great progress.[41]

His will named his eldest son as heir to his dwelling and farm on the East Neck in Mamaroneck and a large portion of his manor lands,[42] but as he died young, Heathcote's wife took possession of the properties. Upon her death, they passed to the only surviving two of their six children, who during the next fifty years sold much of the property to tenants and others. The rest of the manor stayed in the family until heirs asked that the unsold parts be surveyed and partitioned by an unbiased panel of commissioners pursuant to a 1762 act of the provincial legislature. The commissioners completed the sale of the remaining property in 1774, just before all attention in the county turned toward the American Revolution.

Heathcote, however, did sell some of his manor lands during his lifetime. As the lord of a manor, he maintained the right to sell or give away land as he saw fit. Although most of the Manor of Scarsdale residents held their land in the form of long-term leases, some purchased their property. Heathcote sold off thirteen parcels ranging from fifty to 250 acres over the course of his two decades as manor lord. Most of Heathcote's grantees acquired their land for the price of a New York pound per acre,[43] although Eliezer Gedney, the next in line of the owners of my property, got a somewhat better deal four years before Heathcote's death. By this time a Richbell/Heathcote/Gedney familial relationship had developed. In her 1700 will Anne Richbell, having already sold most of her property to Heathcote, named him one of her executors, requested a "decent and comly buriall at the discretion of Coll. Caleb Heathcote," and left forty pounds to a granddaughter, Anna,[44] who had recently married Eliezer Gedney. In 1716, Eliezer and Anna Gedney bought their eighty acres from Heathcote, a bargain at just sixty-two pounds,[45] perhaps because of the nature of their connection to the lord of the manor.

With his imperialist outlook, or, as his biographer put it, his "temper of a loyalist,"[46] Caleb Heathcote probably would have been pleased to know that his grandson and the heir to his Mamaroneck property, John Peter De Lancey, was a Loyalist during the American Revolution. Educated in England, De Lancey stayed abroad to enter the British army and later returned to America and became a major in the Pennsylvania Loyalists.[47] Likewise, it might have pleased Caleb Heathcote that Isaac Gedney, the grandson and heir of his grantee, Eliezer Gedney, acted upon his own Loyalist disposition, presented as he was with a choice—to support the British Crown or the colonists' move toward independence—some sixty years and two generations after a portion of the Heathcote property came into the hands of the Gedney family.

Wills and Probate:
A Cautionary Tale

Wills are great sources of information about people's lives. They can include places of residence, occupations, and, especially important for genealogical purposes, names of relatives. Sometimes they contain inventories of possessions and property. For example, in John Richbell's will of 1684, his estate was valued at sixty-two pounds, seven shillings. The inventory, with the value of each item listed, includes: "one pair of oxen, . . . ; four cows, . . . ; two yearlings, . . . ; four calves, . . . ; a horse bridle and saddle, . . . ; a cart and wheels, . . . ; a yoke and chain, . . . ; a sick Negro woman, . . . ; his wearing apparel, . . . ; pewter, . . . ; half a dozen chairs, . . . ; a bed and furniture, . . . ; a couch and what belongs to it, . . . ; a cold still, . . . ; two iron pots, . . . ; two pair of andirons and two brass candlesticks, . . . ; a cupboard."[1] The "sick Negro woman" at twelve pounds had the highest value of all the items listed. Other places to look for estate inventories are in manuscript collections, the result of families keeping them.

Wills go through a legal process known as probate, which simply means legally establishing the validity of a will; to prove a will is to establish its authenticity before a judicial authority. In cases where a person dies intestate (without a will), the government issues letters of administration when an estate requires legal action. These documents can be helpful too.

The records and procedures in each state are different. For New York State, the New York Genealogical & Biographical Society offers guidance on sorting through the complexities of probate records, which are particularly confusing for those issued earlier than the end of the colonial period. For example, before 1664 the Dutch ruled what is now New York; then up until the Revolution, the British ruled. There was even a period from 1688 to 1691 when New York was part of the "Dominion of New England," resulting in wills being proved in Boston for those years. At times the records were held locally by counties and even towns; at other times they were centralized for the whole colony. Some of them were moved depending on various factors including the location of the state capital.[2] Focusing in on the state in question and looking for "how-to" books and guides, which address finding aids such as indexes and abstracts for probate records in that state, is the best way to find wills. It may be no longer important to see the original or paper record because much material is now in microform, but it is important to get beyond an abstracted version of a will.

One example serves to demonstrate the importance of learning about where probate records are kept in a given state before making assumptions about the accuracy of a will, which one might do just because it has been published. For the will of Anne Richbell, who died in 1700, the widow of John Richbell, I found two different published abstracts, a published extract, and a published "copy," before finding the official original will on microfilm at the New York Public Library.[3] The abstracts and the extract were especially frustrating. The former were in a book of will abstracts entitled *Early Wills of Westchester County, New York from 1664 to 1784* and in an online source, *Ancestry Library Edition (ALE)*, the library version of *Ancestry.com*. The extract was in a history of Westchester County published in 1848. With these sources, I was confused by small differences I found such as a gold chain left to a daughter, Ann, in two of the sources as opposed to a gold ring left to her in the third, or forty pounds left to three granddaughters in two of the sources and just ten pounds left in the other one. Also confusing were the witnesses, which included a John Wickham in one source and a John Wortham in another, apparently the same person.

Needless to say, I was pleased to find what claimed to be a copy of the complete will in a family history published in 1890, digitized by Google and available online. The author even stated that he had copied the official will from the same volume and page number where I eventually found it in the library. In this copy I discovered that neither Wickham nor Wortham was correct. It was John Washburn—a small error perhaps, but an important one depending on the goals of one's research.

More significant was the following statement, omitted from the abstracts and the extract: "I give and bequeath to my negro woman her freedom and one suit of apparell from head to foot besides what she hath allready and a cow and twenty shillings in currant money." Later, when I read the actual official deed in the library, I found that in the family history "copy" the words of Anne's request that she be given "a country burial" were actually "a comly buriall," and her name was spelled *Ann*, not *Anne*, as it appears in most of the other sources. The spelling notwithstanding, a country burial is very different from a comely burial. And one of her granddaughters, listed in all the sources except the official one as Mary Mott, was actually Grace Mott. The lessons to be learned are to be leery of wills "copied in full" and not to trust will abstracts and extracts at all.

six

Isaac Gedney Jr.: The Neutral Ground

> The history of nations is the history of the men who make up nations; it is in the homes of the common people, their daily lives and their ambitions that we find the motives, which actuate the most important national events, revolutionize governments and change the political geography of continents.[1]
>
> —Hippolyte Taine, nineteenth-century French historian

On the Fourth of July in 2006, my nineteen-year-old daughter and I set out to share a mother/child venture through which I hoped to transmit some family lore. We boarded a train at New York City's Penn Station for the two-hour trip to Philadelphia, where we would participate in an annual event, a reading of the Declaration of Independence by descendants of the document's signers in Independence Hall, the very spot where the historic event took place. As a descendant of two signers, Arthur Middleton and Edward Rutledge of South Carolina, I was proud to be introducing my daughter to this lineage. Plus, the sponsoring organization had generously awarded her a college scholarship.

My family's history is well documented on both sides. I grew up surrounded by relatives who regularly lauded and applauded the family's two signers, along with other Patriot ancestors. And as a young teacher starting a new job, I moved to the Boston area, where I learned that the third Monday in April, Patriots' Day—an annual holiday I had never heard of—would be not only a day off from work but also a commemoration celebrated across the commonwealth. Observances and re-enactments of the events leading to the American Revolution seemed to be everywhere in and around Boston, with the mounted Paul Revere re-enactor and his state police escort riding right past both my school in Arlington and my apartment in Cambridge. So for me, with a definite gap in my knowledge of American history, it was surprising and compelling to learn years later how many citizens had sided with the British, especially in New York.

The American Revolution (1776–1783) presented the citizens of Westchester County, like the rest of colonial America, with a difficult choice—to side with the movement for independence or to support the preservation of the status quo as a colony of Great Britain. The inhabitants of Westchester County, living in what was called the Neutral Ground, were divided in their allegiances, perhaps more so than people in other parts of the colonies. Neutral, however, was truly a misnomer. With neighbor clashing against neighbor, families sometimes at odds, and the enemy often not clearly defined, the war in Westchester was very much a civil war. Living in Westchester during the more than seven long years of the war was to be in a partisan, chaotic, confusing, violent, threatening, and fundamentally lawless place.

In hindsight, the Revolution surely seems to have been a good idea, but at the time, it was not so clear. Patriots or Whigs, who fought for American independence, are the ones we most often hear about, the ones we remember and revere, the forefathers of our country. We hear less often the stories of those in the Loyalist or Tory camp, particularly those not in positions of power or prominence.

Geographically, the northern boundary of the Neutral Ground was an east-west line that ran just north of the Croton and Cross Rivers from the Hudson River to Connecticut. To the south, the line ran just above what is today the border between New York City and Westchester County. From November 1776 until the war ended in 1783, the American Continental army almost continually occupied the region to the north of the Neutral Ground, and the British troops and their American Loyalist supporters generally were south of it in New York City. Neither side had the military capacity to control the area between the lines. This no-man's land came to be known as the Neutral Ground, and Isaac Gedney Jr., a Loyalist, lived in the heart of it.

Isaac Gedney Jr. (ca. 1740–1802), a farmer in eighteenth-century Mamaroneck, happened to possess a surname well known in the county then, and now. Isaac Jr. was descended from one of Westchester County's early settlers. His great-great-grandfather, weaver John Gedney, emigrated from England in 1637 and settled in Salem, Massachusetts, where the family prospered in the shipbuilding business. Eliezer Gedney,[2] Isaac Jr.'s shipwright grandfather, left Salem and was the first Gedney to settle in Westchester around 1697. Eliezer (also spelled Eleazor) soon married the daughter of John Richbell. In 1716 he bought eighty acres in Mamaroneck, in the area now known as Harbor Heights, from Caleb Heathcote and then sold the property, along with the house and other buildings, to his son Isaac Sr. in 1722. Of Eliezer's five sons, only Isaac Sr. stayed in Mamaroneck, but lines of the family stemming from at least three of Eliezer's sons resided in Mamaroneck through much of the 1700s and into the 1800s; some descendants are still in the area today. The other sons settled elsewhere in Westchester County—including Rye, Scarsdale, and Philipsburgh—establishing branches of the family in those areas and, later, in White Plains. The Harbor Heights property passed to Isaac Jr. upon his father's death in 1771, a few years before the Revolution, remaining in his possession until just after the war.

Consulting scores of histories and documents for the preparation of this chapter turned up the name Isaac Gedney Jr. only a few times. He did hold elective office, but his positions were limited to "overseer of highways" and "fence and damage viewer."[3] A very ordinary man, Isaac Gedney Jr., happened to live at an extraordinary time—a time when a war was fought for all intents and purposes in his front yard.

WESTCHESTER COUNTY BEFORE THE NEUTRAL GROUND

Before the Revolution, Westchester County was an agrarian community with tiny towns, scattered farms, and no local newspapers. Farmers constituted by far the largest occupation group, many of them tenants of the county's six manors, which together comprised the largest part of its area. The tenants held long-term leases, making for relatively stable communities.[4] Freeholders, like Isaac Gedney Jr., in the social hierarchy just below the truly wealthy aristocracy, were citizens who owned property worth sixty pounds or more, free of debt, and had the rights to vote and serve on juries. They made up about 22 percent of the white male population between the ages of twenty-one and seventy.[5] With day laborers, enslaved people,[6] many tenant farmers, and those with very small properties excluded from voting, attendance at political gatherings was often thin. On the whole, both freeholders and tenants primarily concentrated on tending their farms, producing what they needed for home consumption, and trading or selling their surplus locally or in New York City.

Market-sloops regularly traveled along the major waterways bordering the county—Long Island Sound, where Mamaroneck and Rye are located, and the Hudson River—transporting both people and produce. The most prosperous farmers living near the water owned a sloop,[7] as did Isaac Gedney Jr until 1775.[8] Yeomen farmers, whose produce included wheat, rye, corn, oats, hay, flaxseed, beef, pork, butter, and cheese,[9] constituted 85 percent of the freeholders, the rest made up of various artisans. Mamaroneck, for example, in 1763 had a total of twenty-three freeholders, nineteen of whom were yeomen, with a miller, a shoemaker, and two merchants. Rye, adjacent to Mamaroneck and quite a bit larger at the time, had 124 freeholding yeomen and twenty-seven artisans—seven carpenters, five blacksmiths, three shoemakers, three weavers, and one each of a boatman, cooper, currier, mason, merchant, miller, rope maker, tailor, and tanner.[10] A large town, such as Rye, in eighteenth-century Westchester County typically would have had a church, a tavern, and a store, in addition to the various artisans' shops. Artisans were, however, more often than not, small-scale farmers as well.[11]

Westchester County's population increased from 1,063 in 1698, around the time of the first Gedney's arrival, to 23,941 in 1790.[12] The town of Mamaroneck grew at a slower rate, from just sixteen households and approximately seventy-three people in 1698[13] to 436 residents in 1790.[14] Elected town officials always included a tax assessor, clerk, recorder, and overseer of highways, the latter a position held by Isaac Gedney Jr. in 1789 and 1790.[15] The town's first school took the form of a visiting schoolmaster who taught in successive four-month periods at Mamaroneck, Rye, and Bedford beginning in 1704.[16] Mamaroneck, being relatively small, would have had few of the conveniences of a town such as Rye and was not large enough to support its own Anglican church until 1814. Before that, its Anglican citizens, such as Isaac Jr., would have had to travel to Christ's Church in the parish of Rye to attend church.[17] The serene and quiet life of the tiny Mamaroneck farming community, along with that of many others in the area, changed dramatically with the onset of the war.

The first bloodshed of the Revolution in Westchester County actually took place in Mamaroneck on August 29, 1776, when American soldiers attacked a gathering of fourteen Loyalists.[18] As early as mid-1774, however, the controversy was well under way with residents taking sides for and against independence, a circumstance that helped to create the Neutral Ground.

In our own postcolonial era, it is obvious to us why Americans would have wanted to be free of British rule. As one historian has pointed out, "The independence of the United States is so firmly established and universally accepted that it is virtually impossible to imagine that things could have been otherwise."[19] Why would Isaac Gedney Jr. and many of his fellow Westchester farmers have been Loyalists? Blessed with soil still fertile, a temperate climate, minimal taxes, proximity to a huge market for their produce, and distance from the frontier and hostile contact with Native Americans, the land-owning, farming residents of Westchester were, for the most part, reasonably comfortable and, by the mid-1770s, happy to maintain the political status quo.[20] Harold Drimmer, in an examination of Revolutionary War militia service in Westchester, speculates that rampant inflation in the price of agricultural goods during the war contributed to the Westchester farmer's reluctance to serve in the militia and to support the independence movement in general.[21] Even as the American-British controversies over taxation and control intensified, many of the farmers of Westchester County continued to maintain their loyalty to the British Crown.

THE CONTROVERSY—1764–1774

In 1764 the British Parliament changed the rules of empire by passing a series of new laws in the colonies to raise funds to reduce the British national debt. The Sugar Act of 1764, the Stamp Act of 1765, and the Townshend Acts of 1767 imposed taxes on the purchase and use of various products in the colonies. The Townshend Acts also legalized general search warrants, the 1765 Quartering Act required colonists to feed and house British soldiers, and the Declaratory Act of 1766 obliged colonists to obey laws enacted by Parliament. Many colonists grew increasingly resentful, and the Sons of Liberty, led by Samuel Adams in Boston, instituted official resistance calling for the boycott of British goods. Allowing the British East India Company to sell tea at lower prices than the colonial importers, the 1773 Tea Act provoked members of the Sons of Liberty to climb on board British ships anchored in Boston Harbor and dump their cargoes of tea into the water. Retaliating to this famed 1773 event, the Boston Tea Party, the British Parliament closed Boston Harbor in March 1774 and passed the Coercive Acts, known to Americans as the Intolerable Acts. These measures shocked the colonists; resistance to Parliament's actions intensified throughout the colonies.

Westchester County residents held a meeting at the courthouse in White Plains on August 22, 1774, and, like other counties in New York, authorized the delegates elected by the City of New York to represent them as well at the upcoming Continental Congress.[22] At this point, many citizens believed that America could resolve her differences with Great Britain. The lieutenant governor of New York, Cadwallader Colden, an appointee of the British Crown, observed in a letter dated July 6, 1774, to the Earl of Dartmouth, "The present political zeal and Frenzy is almost entirely confined to the City of New York. The People in the Counties are noways disposed to become active or bear any part in what is proposed by the citizens. . . . This Province is everywhere, except in the City of New York, perfectly quiet and in good order. . . ."[23] The state of affairs he described was about to change dramatically, with Westchester County residents not only taking sides in the controversy, but also becoming political activists.

In Rye a group of freeholders and tenants met September 24, 1774, and subsequently published in a New York City newspaper, *Rivington's New-York Gazetteer*, the most aggressively pro-British newspaper in America, a statement supporting the British Crown:[24]

> We the Subscribers, Freeholders and Inhabitants of the town of Rye, in the county of Westchester, being much concerned with the unhappy situation of public affairs, think it our duty to our King and country, to declare that we have not been concerned in any resolutions entered into, or measures taken, with regard to the disputes at present subsisting with the mother country; we also testify our dislike to many hot and furious proceedings, in consequence of said disputes, which we think are more likely to ruin this once happy country, than remove grievances, if any there are.

We also declare our great desire and full resolution to live and die peaceable subjects to our gracious sovereign, King George the third, and his laws.[25]

The signatures of eighty-three men, including two Gidneys and three Gedneys, all cousins of Isaac Jr. of Mamaroneck, followed the statement.[26]

Even Paul Revere's May 1774 ride to spread the news of the Intolerable Acts, a ride that took him right through Rye and Mamaroneck along the Boston Post Road, barely a mile from Isaac Gedney Jr.'s farm, had failed to rally widespread support for the Patriot cause among the inhabitants of Westchester County.[27] The number of Loyalists in the colony of New York as a whole is unknown but often estimated at roughly 50 percent of the population. Historians generally agree that there was a significantly higher proportion of them in New York and that the lines between the Loyalist and Patriot camps were less distinct and more changing in New York than elsewhere in the colonies.[28]

In the absence of written records, it is impossible to know precisely what motivated Isaac Jr. and others like him to be Loyalists and, more specifically, to take action in support of the British. Yet it is possible they heard about, or perhaps read, the four contemporaneously notorious Westchester Farmer pamphlets, the first one published on November 16, 1774, just a month after the Continental Congress adjourned. Written by Westchester Anglican clergyman Reverend Samuel Seabury Jr. under the pseudonym, "A. W. Farmer," the pamphlets, calling upon the sympathies of New York farmers and responding to the actions of the Continental Congress, were the most complete of the Tory efforts to reject the pre-Revolutionary movement.[29]

The Continental Congress delegates had agreed that if the British Parliament refused to repeal the Intolerable Acts, they would boycott colonial trade with Great Britain and the West Indies. Seabury wrote in the first of his pamphlets,

> I choose to address myself principally to You the *Farmers* of . . . New-York, because I am most nearly connected with you, being one of your number . . . and also, because the interest of the farmers in general will be more sensibly affected, and more deeply injured by these agreements, than the interest of any body of people on the continent. Another reason why I choose to address myself to you is, because the Farmers are of the greatest benefit to the state, of any people in it: . . . be then convinced of your own importance and think and act accordingly. . . .

He made the point that both farms and farm products would be greatly reduced in value.

> We shall have no trade at all, and consequently no vent for the produce of our farms. Such part of our wheat, flax-seed, corn, beef, pork, butter, cheese, as was not consumed in the province, must be left to rot and stink on our hands. . . . Look well to yourselves, I beseech you. From the day that the exports from this province are stopped, the farmers may date the commencement of their ruin. . . .
>
> Nor, under the circumstances, will your farms fetch half what they cost you. What is a farm good for, the produce of which cannot be sold? . . . You are ruined, stripped of your farm, and very probably of the means of subsistence for yourself and family. Glorious effect of Non-exportation! Think a little, and then tell me—when the Congress adopted this accursed scheme, did they in the least consider your interest? No, impossible! they ignorantly misunderstood, carelessly neglected, or basely betrayed you.[30]

Understandably angered, Patriots attempted to prevent the pamphlet's distribution, burned copies in bonfires, and,

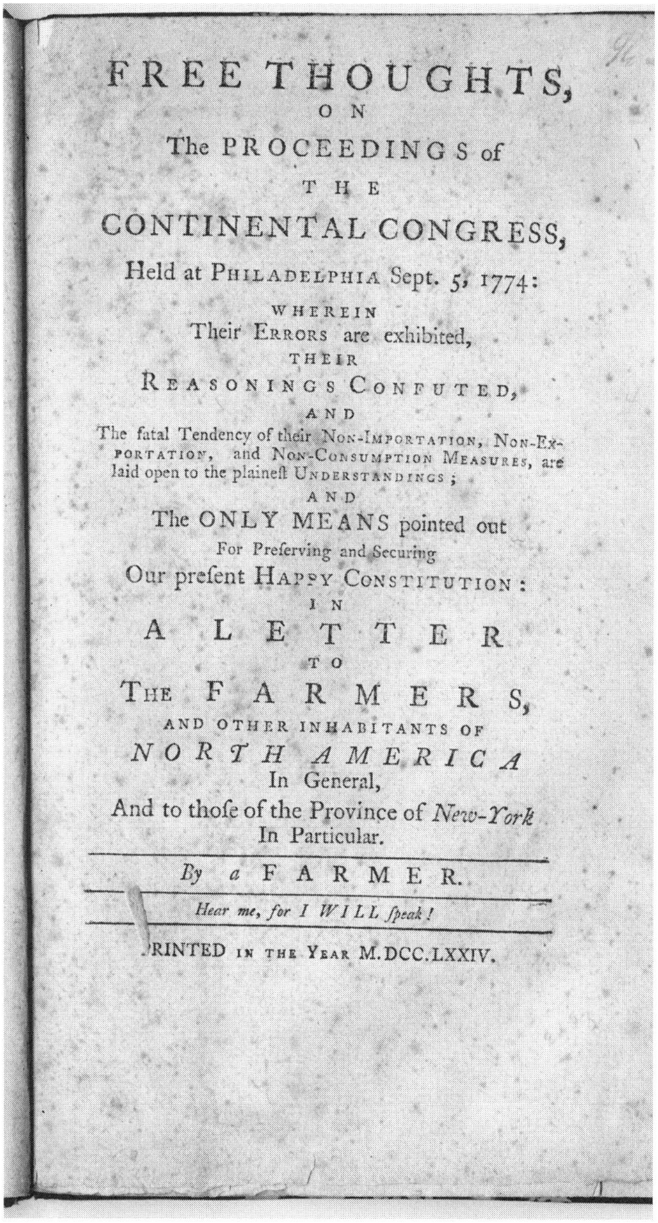

FREE THOUGHTS,
ON
The PROCEEDINGS of
THE
CONTINENTAL CONGRESS,
Held at PHILADELPHIA Sept. 5, 1774:
WHEREIN
Their ERRORS are exhibited,
THEIR
REASONINGS CONFUTED,
AND
The fatal Tendency of their NON-IMPORTATION, NON-EXPORTATION, and NON-CONSUMPTION MEASURES, are laid open to the plaineſt UNDERSTANDINGS;
AND
The ONLY MEANS pointed out
For Preſerving and Securing
Our preſent HAPPY CONSTITUTION:
IN
A LETTER
TO
THE FARMERS,
AND OTHER INHABITANTS OF
NORTH AMERICA
In General,
And to thoſe of the Province of *New-York*
In Particular.

By a FARMER.

Hear me, for I WILL ſpeak!

PRINTED IN THE YEAR M.DCC.LXXIV.

FIGURE 6.1 The cover of [Samuel Seabury]. *Free Thoughts on the Proceedings of the Continental Congress . . . in a Letter to the Farmers . . . ,* 1774. *(Photograph courtesy of the Westchester County Historical Society.)*

in one instance, coated them with tar and turkey buzzard feathers.[31] Over the next two months, Seabury made similar arguments, published in three more of his Westchester Farmer pamphlets.

THE LOYALIST IDEOLOGY

Understanding the Loyalist ideology helps place the Westchester Farmer pamphlets and their possible sway on Isaac Gedney Jr. into context. By 1774 the independence movement had become a concern everywhere in the colonies, thus engendering both a collection of ideas justifying it as well as an opposing Loyalist ideology. Patriots and Loyalists differed fundamentally in their views on liberty and government. To the Patriots, individual liberty had to be protected from the possible tyranny of government. Loyalists, on the other hand, feared that liberty could readily degenerate into licentiousness and anarchy, a greater peril than the power of the British government, which Loyalists believed could actually ensure individual rights to life, liberty, and property.[32]

As the colonial controversy grew from 1773 to 1776, Patriots perceived the greatest threat to freedom to be an external one, the British government, whereas Loyalists believed the threat was internal. Addressing the inhabitants of the City of New York in a newspaper in 1773, a Loyalist wrote, "while we are watchful against *external* attacks on our freedom, let us be on our guard, lest we become *enslaved* by dangerous tyrants within."[33] Particularly alarming to Loyalists were certain actions being taken by the extra-legal revolutionary committees, proliferating all over the colonies, depriving citizens of trial by jury, search without warrant, and freedom of expression—long-valued British institutions.[34]

Loyalists maintained what historian Janice Potter calls an "Anglo-American vision," a union between Great Britain and her American colonies, beneficial to both and rooted in language, religion, and a shared history"[35] Samuel Seabury, in one of the Westchester Farmer pamphlets, compared America to a limb: "To talk of a colony independent of the mother-country, is no better sense than to talk of a limb independent of the body to which it belongs."[36] Many considered breaking with Britain to be destabilizing, unnatural, and fratricidal.

The most compelling reason for maintaining unity with the British Empire, according to Loyalists, was the American benefit from the transatlantic trade. Americans, even those of modest means, valued the opportunity to obtain products manufactured in England. Elegant, stylish imports, especially cloth, eventually became an indication of moral decay in the eyes of Patriots, who favored the wearing of homespun fabric as a sign of patriotism.[37] For Loyalists, numerous cultural links as well as trade ties tightly bound America to Great Britain.

Using several media, standard for eighteenth-century political discussions—pamphlets, broadsides, and newspapers—Loyalists communicated their ideology. Consisting of pages stitched together, pamphlets could be produced quickly and sold inexpensively. Described by Moses Coit Tyler in *The Literary History of the American Revolution, 1763–1783* as "the chief weapon in the intellectual warfare of the American Revolution,"[38] the pamphlets typically had long titles and were signed with pseudonyms to hide their authors' identities. Broadsides were notices, lists, or essays posted in public places to be read by passersby.[39] Weekly newspapers, such as *Rivington's New-York Gazetteer*, published numerous articles, essays, declarations, and testimonials produced by ordinary Loyalist citizens. Each of these means of communication helped spread the Loyalist ideology, particularly to those who were literate.

Even illiterate citizens in Westchester County, however, could have heard directly from a Loyalist polemicist like Samuel Seabury, who, in addition to writing pamphlets, used the church sermon as an effective propaganda vehicle. His parish was St. Peter's in the town of Westchester, near the present-day Throggs Neck area of the Bronx, but he claimed to have ridden around the county almost daily, speaking for the Loyalist cause and trying to convince people to discredit the actions of the Continental Congress.[40] Another local resident, Timothy Wetmore, a signer of the September 1774 Rye declaration, the schoolmaster of Christ's Church in Rye from 1754 to 1769, the son of its former rector, and an influential man in the county, also organized members of his community to resist the movement toward independence.[41] Living near the Christ's Church parish, Isaac Gedney Jr. may have worshipped there and presumably would have heard from Mr. Wetmore. Thus, there were a number of avenues through which his Loyalist proclivities could have developed.

ISAAC SIGNS A DECLARATION—1775

Patriot leaders throughout the colonies called for delegates to a second Continental Congress scheduled for May 1775. On April 11, 1775, a group of freeholders and others met at the courthouse in White Plains to appoint deputies to represent Westchester County at the April 20 Provincial Convention in New York City, which would, in turn, elect representatives to the Continental Congress. A contemporary account of the courthouse gathering states that some of those present declared that they would have nothing to do with the business of the day and left en masse. The meeting proceeded without them, the remaining Patriot group appointing eight deputies to attend the convention.[42]

The protesters, meanwhile, reconvened the same day at Captain Hatfield's Tavern nearby, where they drew up a declaration signed by 312 men. This gathering was the largest spontaneous Loyalist gathering of the pre-Revolutionary period.[43] In a newspaper narrative describing the events, published along with the declaration, the group called themselves "friends of government" and "declared their determined resolution to continue stedfast in their allegiance of gracious and merciful sovereign King George the Third." The declaration itself stated, "We the subscribers, freeholders and inhabitants of the county of Westchester, having assembled at the White Plains, in consequence of certain advertisements, do now declare, that we met here to express our honest abhorrence of all unlawful congresses and committees, and that we are determined at the hazard of our lives and properties, to support the King and Constitution. . . ."[44] Samuel Seabury claimed to have gathered four hundred people in White Plains in 1775, and though no record of a speech remains,[45] it is likely that he was one of the organizers and speakers at the Hatfield's Tavern gathering. Among the declaration's signatures were those of Seabury, right at the top of the list, Isaac Gidney (undoubtedly Isaac Jr. of Mamaroneck), and eleven other Gidneys.[46] According to one historian, at the conclusion of this event, the farmers of Westchester returned to their farms, and the whole episode subsided into a thing of the past.[47] That was not the case for everyone, however, as Isaac Gedney Jr. and many of his peers, during the next fourteen months, challenged the developing Patriot cause.

Beginning in August 1775, in the wake of the Battles of Lexington and Concord and the second Continental Congress, the New York Provincial Congress adopted a series of drastic regulations to limit objectionable language and prevent and punish unacceptable actions by Loyalists. The measures prohibited supplying provisions or communicating information detrimental to the Patriot cause to the British military. In September the Committee of Safety for the Colony of New York ordered all citizens who had not signed the general association[48]—boycotting British goods and agreeing to defend the colonies against the British—to give up their arms to the Continental army, which had been deemed inadequately armed. All attempts to purchase a sufficient quantity of guns had failed, so the need was great.[49] Each confiscated musket, gun, or firelock was to be marked, recorded, and appraised so that the owner could be reimbursed at the end of the war. A county-level Committee of Safety examined anyone accused or even suspected of refusing to comply with the order. The consequences for those found guilty included disarmament, fines, or imprisonment, a second offense warranting banishment from the colony for seven years.

The extensive and strict enforcement of these laws in Westchester County resulted in a particularly high number of instances of neighbor informing against neighbor. The situation in Westchester differed from that in the nearby counties of Kings, Queens, Suffolk, and Richmond, which also contained large Loyalist populations. From 1776 on, these counties were under more definitive British occupation affording their citizenry greater protection. Westchester's British sympathizers, on the other hand, residing within the conflict-ridden Neutral Ground, were subject to what historians have likened to the Inquisition.[50]

ISAAC ACTS OUT—1775–1776

Among those who received this kind of inquisitorial treatment were Issac Gedney Jr. and Elijah Weeks. Arrested in the fall of 1775 on unnamed charges, Loyalist Elijah Weeks was brought before the Westchester committee. It was Isaac Jr.'s immediate neighbor to the north, Job Haddon, who had made the arrest and subsequently was a witness for the prosecution. An armed group of eight Loyalist sympathizers, including Isaac Jr., attempted to rescue Weeks, apparently unsuccessfully.[51] This was the first in a series of Isaac Jr.'s activities in support of the Loyalist cause that resulted in conflicts with neighbors.

More dramatic was the case of Godfrey Haines, a Rye rope maker.[52] Haines was among a group of thirty-one suspected of aiding the enemy; the Patriot authorities eventually convicted and imprisoned at least twenty of them.[53] Haines's arrest in September 1775 resulted from the testimony of a woman who stated that he had "damned the Congresses and Committees frequently, and . . . that he wished the men-of-war would come along the Sound, and that he would be one to shew them who to fire upon. . . ."[54] Based on only this sworn statement as evidence and the suspicion that he had plotted to seize distinguished Westchester citizens and take them as captives to the British military, the Westchester committee ordered Haines to disarm. His refusal to relinquish his gun, pistol, and sword landed him in a New York City jail; escaping a few days later, he headed for the East River, where he found refuge on board the *Asia*, a British man-of-war. The captain took Haines home to Rye and asked him if he could be of assistance in procuring some oars.[55] It was Isaac Gedney Jr. of Mamaroneck who subsequently made the oars for the British captain, and in so doing, aided the enemy, according to testimony of Colonel Gilbert Budd, the town clerk and Gedney's immediate neighbor to the south.[56]

Implicated in a conspiracy to "carry off" Patriots, Isaac Jr. persisted in his efforts to support the Loyalist cause. The Westchester committee met November 1, 1775, to investigate a plot and wrote in a letter to the Provincial Congress that Isaac Gedney Jr. and others "were minute men, . . . ready, at a moment's warning, to take off some persons who were the most obnoxious." Believing itself "too weak" to handle such an issue, the committee recommended that a hearing be held before the Provincial Congress and that Gedney's next-door neighbors, Colonel Gilbert Budd and Job Haddon, be called as witnesses.[57] As close neighbors in conflict, the three men found themselves in an all-too-common situation in the Neutral Ground.

On November 3, 1775, Colonel Budd testified against Isaac Jr., using information given to him by an informant. His testimony stated, "The tories are getting the upper hand of and threaten [us] daily, and have injured [our] private property, by throwing down stone fences and cropping . . . horses' tails and manes." Budd reported that he had been told that "there would be bad times in Mamaroneck, before long" and that some of the residents would be forcibly gathered onto barges and then taken to a tender in the harbor to be transported to the British army. Having been told he was among the men to be kidnapped and his neighbor Isaac Gedney Jr. "stood ready to assist the tender in order to take them," Budd went on to state that the informant had warned him it was not safe for him to sleep in his house and that "the tories are equipped, and constantly in arms walking about at night, 6, 8 and 10 at a time, . . . determined to defend themselves, and that if any body came to their houses to take away their arms, they would fire upon them."[58]

After Budd testified, for unknown reasons, the chairman of the meeting asked that the matter be kept a secret. The Congress then forwarded a letter to the Westchester committee recommending that it make an inquiry into the matter and, if necessary, institute measures to protect those Patriots who felt threatened.[59] What action the Westchester committee took, if any, is not known.

Isaac Gedney Jr., however, continued his Loyalist involvement with Godfrey Haines. Gedney sold his sloop, the *Polly and Ann*, to Haines in December 1775 and then, with Haines and two other men, loaded it with beef, port, Madeira, turnips, other provisions, and seven passengers and sailed for Boston, with plans to deliver the goods to the British general Sir William Howe. Foul weather drove the sloop far from its intended route; it went ashore at Squam Beach in New Jersey, sometimes called the "graveyard" of the merchant marine. The revolutionary Monmouth County committee seized Captain Godfrey Haines and sent him to New York City to be jailed.[60] It is not known precisely how Isaac Jr., the sloop's master, and the others fared in the immediate aftermath, though Isaac somehow did find his way back to Westchester.

Another major Loyalist escapade was the "spiking of the cannon." Patriots had gathered more than two hundred cannon in at least two locations at Kingsbridge in the Bronx, near the northern tip of Manhattan. Late on the night of January 17, 1776, a group of Loyalists inserted into many of the guns files that had been worked into spikes by blacksmith Isaac Gedney, rendering them useless. It turns out that this Isaac Gedney was not Isaac Jr. but instead a contemporary and first cousin living in Rye. This blacksmith was also one of the Gidneys or Gedneys who signed the September 1774 Rye declaration as well as the Lieut. Isaac Gidney who signed the Hatfield's Tavern declaration of April 1775 along with Isaac Jr. and the other ten Gidneys.[61] Apparently, the goal in disarming the cannon was to save the city by keeping it from burning. The Loyalist perpetrators escaped undiscovered. Over the course of a week, the Committee of Safety apprehended and examined various suspects. Some in the group claimed that they had visited British-appointed Governor William Tryon of New York, who had put them up to it. The committee released a few of the suspects, but imprisoned blacksmith Isaac and several others, manacled and shackled some, and denied all the use of pen, ink, and paper.[62] Two months later a Colonel Joseph Bull paid a two-thousand-pound bond to have Gedney moved to a prison in White Plains.[63] On April 20, 1776, the prisoner sent a letter to the Provincial Congress asking for mercy and his release:

> Gentlemen
>
> I am to acknowledge your kindness in removing me from New-York jail to this place, but am still unhappy in being detained from my family, who at this season, want my assistance very much. It is not only the aid I might give in keeping my interest together, (all of which has been earned by the sweat of my brow,) but adding happiness to my family, and saving a large family of [seven] children from running into many vices. . . . If you, gentlemen, think that giving you good bail for my appearance as well as for my peaceable behavior, will answer the intention of the law, I can, and shall with pleasure give it, in any sum which may be asked. . . .
>
> Your unhappy humble servt.
> Isaac Gedney[64]

He was released sometime soon thereafter. It seems that this incident put an end to blacksmith Isaac's Loyalist activity.

Isaac Jr.'s last Loyalist involvement was paying a visit, with a group of about eight other Westchester men, to Governor Tryon in early 1776.[65] The exact nature of Isaac Jr.'s visit is unknown, but one of the governor's letters provides a hint. In October 1775 Tryon had taken refuge from Patriot hostilities on board the *Duchess of Gordon*, anchored in New York Harbor under the protection of the man-of-war *Asia*. In a letter of November 11, 1775, to the Earl of Dartmouth, who was back in England, Tryon reported that "the Friends of Government freely come to me. . . . [The inhabitants of the County of] Westchester . . . call for protection as the enemies to Government [Patriots] are daily insulting and disarming them. . . ."[66] If this was Isaac Jr.'s final Loyalist action—begging the governor for help and protection and possibly bringing him provisions—it is not surprising that he chose to make it his last. Not only was his cousin in prison, but also, in the face of New York's high number of Loyalists, Patriots were developing a strong, centralized apparatus for containing enemy activity and ferreting out traitors to the revolutionary cause.

On June 5, 1776, the Provincial Congress took a momentous step by defining citizenship and treason. With the expectation that soon a British "hostile armament" would arrive, it became "expedient and necessary" that the inhabitants of New York "not be injured or annoyed by domestic enemies." Anyone who aided the British military, actively dissuaded colonists from "associating for the defense of the United Colonies," questioned the value of Continental currency, or "engaged in any schemes to defeat, retard or oppose" the "American cause" would be arrested and, if found guilty, be subject to imprisonment or exile to another colony.[67] As the number of suspects grew, the Convention (previously known as the Congress[68]) on September 21, 1776, resolved to appoint a formal body, a committee for "detecting and defeating all conspiracies."[69] By mid-1776 the records no longer reflect any Loyalist activity on Isaac Gedney Jr.'s part. With the stakes this high, it is easy to understand why he modified his behavior and began to show restraint at the moment the American War of Independence was beginning to accelerate in New York.

WAR IN WESTCHESTER AND PITCHERS OF CIDER—1776–1783

In the summer of 1776 things began to move quickly toward all-out war in Westchester County. General George Washington and his army had arrived in New York on April 13; the British, with troops better trained, equipped, and more cohesive, brought 120 warships into New York Harbor in early July. Patriot citizens read the Declaration of Independence from the courthouse steps in White Plains on July 11. By August 15 the British had armed and equipped their soldiers for battle in New York.

After the Battle of Long Island, British troops landed at Throggs Neck, at the southeastern edge of the Bronx, on October 12. In the week or two leading up to Westchester's most significant battle, the Battle of White Plains, British troops marched north and set up camp in and around Mamaroneck. Upon learning that a regiment of Loyalists was at Heathcote Hill in Mamaroneck, Washington sent troops who took more than thirty Loyalists prisoner in the ensuing skirmish of Heathcote Hill. The two full

FIGURE 6.2 Charles Willson Peale (1741–1827). *George Washington*. ca. 1779–1781. Oil on canvas. 95 x 61¾ in. The Metropolitan Museum of Art, New York, NY, U.S.A. Gift of Collis P. Huntington, 1897 (97.33). *(Image copyright © The Metropolitan Museum of Art / Art Resource, NY.)*

FIGURE 6.3 John Trumbull (1756–1843). *The Declaration of Independence, July 4, 1776*. 1786–1820. Oil on canvas. 20⅞ x 31 in. Yale University Art Gallery. Trumbull Collection, 1832.3. *(Photograph courtesy of Yale University Art Gallery.)*

armies fought the Battle of White Plains on October 28. Although the British, who far outnumbered the ill-equipped Americans, technically won the battle, some consider it to have been a stand-off. It was, according to early twentieth-century historian Otto Hufeland, "... a barren victory for the royal army, and their elaborate campaign of a month had left the Americans in a position less exposed, with all their lines of communication open.... Howe's splendidly appointed army, assisted by the ships of the Navy with all the conditions in his favor, had permitted an equal number of untrained and ill-equipped troops to escape from an untenable position ... Howe and his staff had been completely outgeneraled by Washington...."[70] On November 4, following the battle, General William Howe issued an order from his headquarters in Scarsdale that the army was "to strike their Tents, load their Wagons, and be in readiness to march to-morrow morning at day-break."[71] By the next day the British had moved south to Dobbs Ferry, leaving White Plains and its environs free of the enemy.

Only the area was not, at this point, completely free of the "enemy." Although no more major battles occurred in Westchester, there were numerous skirmishes throughout the county and several in Mamaroneck during the remaining years of the war. The American Continental army placed its regular units so as to protect the Hudson River, and, as the lines extended eastward across the county toward Long Island Sound, they increasingly consisted of weaker militia units, allowing the British to penetrate the lines on nearly a weekly basis. These maneuvers were of little military value but served to keep the populace in a constant state of terror.[72]

Stone Walls: What They Tell Us

The stone walls of Westchester County, many of them still very much in evidence today, are a story unto themselves. One remnant of a stone wall still stands on my property; another stone wall in my neighborhood was a property line marker in deeds for the property from 1784 to 1826.[1] Created from the rock-strewn terrain as farmers cleared the land for farming, stone walls served to keep animals out of cultivated fields. The old stone walls still in existence today are, in many cases, only the bottom part of what would have been a four-foot-high fence, the top part made of rail, brush, or stumps. By 1871, New York had 529,802 miles of fencing, of which 18 percent was "stone-wall and other kinds, including a small amount of wire, picket, hedge, &c." Stone walls were time-consuming to build; thus, farmers tended to build them over time and after first building other types. Even in 1871, 45 percent of fences in New York were still "worm fences," built of crossed rails in a zigzag pattern, the remainder post and rail or board.[2]

In Mamaroneck's town records of the 1700s, a "fence viewer" or "fence and damage viewer" was always among the elected officials. As fence viewer, Isaac Gedney Jr.'s job was to regularly survey the condition of the stone walls and timber rail fences, see that they were maintained to the proper height, and arbitrate disputes involving them. Stone walls could become the locus for expression of conflict as when Isaac Jr.'s neighbor testified that Tories had damaged private property by "throwing down stone fences."[3]

Stone walls also played a tactical military role during the Revolution. As British troops advanced northward through Westchester County in the autumn of 1776, a myriad of them, crisscrossing the landscape, offered American troops much-needed protection.[4] Riflemen hid behind them as invading British lines approached, not only in Westchester County but also throughout New York and New England. So strategically important were they to the Americans that Otto Hufeland in his *Westchester County During the American Revolution* mentions them at least fourteen times in his discussions of various battles, skirmishes, and military maneuvers.[5]

Picturesque and romantic reminders of the past, stone walls were perhaps expedient ways to address the problem of rocky soil, but they also served as boundary markers for property and, because of their longevity, continue to help us understand our past.

FIGURE 6.4 Stone walls are common in wooded areas of Westchester County and other parts of the Northeast where rocky soil led early settlers to build "sheep fence" as they cleared the land for planting. The fences served to contain animals and to define property boundaries. *(Photo by Michael Torlen.)*

Even more distressing to the residents of Westchester County than the armed conflict was the continual marauding and pillaging that began immediately after the Battle of White Plains. A great number of the troops fighting for the British were mercenaries, and together with "camp followers," many of them women, they were at times unruly and difficult for the British commanders to control. On October 31, 1776, General Howe issued an order stating, "the Commander in Chief is under the necessity of issuing his warrant to the Provost Martial for Executing upon the Spot, any Soldier, Seaman, or follower of the Army, found Guilty of Plundering or Marauding."[73] The behavior apparently continued in spite of the order. Lieutenant Colonel Stephen Kemble, Howe's adjutant general, wrote in his journal on November 2, "The Country all this time unmercifully Pillaged by our Troops, Hessians [German mercenary soldiers fighting for the British] in particular, no wonder if the Country People refuse to join us."[74] The British dismantled whole houses in Westchester to provide lumber to build barracks for the soldiers' winter quarters, scavenging fifty wagonloads of doors, windows, and lumber in the process as part of the effort at one house.[75]

By pure coincidence, on the day of Howe's order to cease the plundering, General Washington issued a similar, if somewhat milder, one to his troops: "It is with astonishment the General hears, that some officers have taken Horses, between Enemy's Camp and ours, and sent them into the Country for their private use: Can it be possible, that persons bearing Commissions, and fighting in such a Cause, can degrade themselves into Plunderers of horses? . . ."[76] Stealing horses was not the only crime. On November 2, Washington issued more orders in an attempt to control the situation. "The General expressly forbids any person, or soldier, belonging to the Army, to set fire to any House, or Barn, on any pretence, without a special order from some General Officer."[77]

In spite of Washington's efforts, his troops continued to disobey orders. One Patriot tavern owner, Miles Oakley, writing in the third person, as was the custom in such documents, complained in a petition to General Washington in November 1776 that his house and business had been ". . . robbed and pillaged, his desk split to pieces, his money, books, and papers taken and carried away by our own troops, by which means he is left without a second bed and scarce a change of clothes for himself, his wife or his children. . . ." Later his house and barn were ". . . by some of the *American* troops burnt to the ground. . . ."[78] Knowledge of the problem was widespread at the time. On November 28, 1776, Governor Tryon wrote to Lord George Germain in England, ". . . what with the Conflagrations of the Rebels, and the marauding of both armies, the inhabitants of that [Westchester] County are reduced to great distress."[79]

People who had farm produce had difficulty keeping soldiers and ordinary thieves from taking it, and those who needed food had problems finding anything to buy. In October 1776 the New York Committee of Safety had begun requisitioning for use by the army all cattle and produce from the farmers of Westchester County over and above what was barely adequate for survival. The committee also authorized the Continental army to purchase farm animals and hay for the soldiers' use and to remove or destroy any that were in danger of falling into enemy hands.[80] Even thus empowered, the army had difficulty obtaining adequate provisions for the troops. In 1779 a purchasing agent wrote to George Clinton, the first governor of the state of New York:

> The Confused State in which the County of West Chester hath been for Some time, by the Ravages of the Enemy, hath Disabled me from procuring a Supply of flour for the Guards of this County & Fairfield County,—while a Considerable Quantity

of wheat is yet in this County, which the proprietors Refuse to Sell, and now Since this present alarm, I am informed that Many Disaffected persons are Threshing out their Wheat, (which we Suppose is for the Enemy) and unless authority is Vested in Some person for Seizing and Securing the wheat & flour in the County . . . for the army Very Soon, our Guards on their Frontiers will Soon be Discharged for want of Bread.[81]

The lawlessness continued in Westchester throughout the war. Officers on both sides routinely looked the other way when troops ignored orders against pillaging. A Hessian soldier, Lieutenant John Charles Philip von Krafft, occupied several locations in southern Westchester and left a journal. Entries from September and October of 1778 reveal aspects of what life was like for Westchester residents during this time:

> We opened the pretty church there [in Yonkers] and quartered ourselves in it—. . . in all about 30 men. Finally a search was begun and a large potato-field was cleaned out and many other luxuries brought in. Fowls, pigs and beef slaughtered, although everything had to be done secretly. As usual when on the march we received nothing but salt pork, crackers and rum for rations. . . . We gathered hay and straw and made ourselves good beds. . . . We . . . marched . . . and . . . were obliged to build huts to camp in until further orders. The foraging commenced again immediately, during which some of the soldiers began to plunder. Many of the houses, which I saw afterwards, had been left in a deplorable condition and the soldiers had made a good haul. We were not forbidden to get provisions, but were very strictly admonished not to take anything from the people in their houses. However, even

Eyewitness Accounts

By eyewitness accounts I mean any firsthand reporting by someone present at an event. Such a narrative enhances any historical study. An eyewitness account can be found in many forms—letters, journals, memoirs, government reports, court records, oral histories, published quotations from reliable contemporary sources, and interviews by you or someone else.

In the First Person is a database index to diaries, letters, oral histories, and personal narratives from the past four hundred years. The *Eyewitness to History* website, http://www.eyewitnesstohistory.com, contains an interesting selection of eyewitness accounts organized chronologically, but none of the ones I used are to be found there. Citations for mine were most often found buried in footnotes of published sources.

What follows are a few ways to consider various kinds of firsthand accounts found in this book and thoughts on authors' possible motives and considerations for interpreting the material. A journal is normally regarded as the private thoughts and observations of a writer. John Charles Philip von Krafft, a mercenary fighting for the British during the American Revolution, wrote in his journal about the foraging excursions he and his comrades undertook in order to feed themselves. His descriptions certainly square with the historical record, but his words—"when on the march we received nothing but salt pork, crackers and rum for rations"; "a large potato-field was cleaned out"; "all the field fruit we could carry"[1]—add richness and specificity.

In another example of a journal entry, Sarah Kemble Knight, the woman who accompanied the postriders from Boston to New York City in 1704–05, describes their route, "the way being very narrow, and on each side the Trees and bushes gave us very unpleasent welcomes wth their Branches and bow's, wch wee could not avoid,"[2] offering a vivid picture of just how small was the path used by the long-distance mail carriers. It is difficult to know if the author considered whether his or her work would be published some day—in each of these two cases, the journal was not published until the nineteenth century. Because both authors were involved in something out of the ordinary, it seems they may have written with thoughts of sharing their adventures with others and with an eye to posterity.

Interviews offer the possibility to hear the account of someone who either cannot write or who is not inclined to write but is willing to talk about an experience. The words of formerly enslaved Prince Gedney in his 1850 interview about life in the Neutral Ground lend humanness to an otherwise difficult circumstance. He mentions the specifics of his mission, "to sell chickens, butter and provisions for my master," relates a story of how he lost his pass and had to go back for another, provoking the general, who, after scolding him, asked, " 'Vat vill you trink? Here's brandy, rum and gin,' "[3] an offer Prince could not refuse. The bit of humor is a welcome addition too.

An emissary sent by a governmental or corporate entity who reports back to the authorities on his findings may have a political or profit-driven bias. For example, Adriaen van der Donck came to the New World as a legal officer working for the Dutch West India Company. His primary goals were to invest in property and encourage his fellow Dutchmen to settle in New Netherland. His positive, descriptive reports of the Native Americans he met, including comments such as, "Congenital defects and deformities are very seldom seen. . . . One finds no fools, madmen, maniacs, or lunatics among them,"[4] may well have been influenced by the incentive to encourage settlers.

With a court record such as the one in which Isaac Gedney Jr.'s neighbor Gilbert Budd testified against Gedney during the American Revolution, stating that Gedney and others "were minute men, . . . ready, at a moment's warning, to take off some persons who were the most obnoxious" and had destroyed stone fences and cropped "horses' tails and manes,"[5] the real motive cannot be known. It may have been motivated by ideology and pure politics, but on the other hand, it could have been partly a back-fence feud. In either case, the words lend a feeling of an experience lived.

Another court document from the same period tells us not only about the events of the war but also about ordinary possessions of the day. The list of items stored in one family's trunk included: "Linen & cloaths . . . five feather beads & bedding, one looking glass, one Copper Coffey-Kettle, with lamp and stand, two muffs in cases, a long blue cloth cloak, one pair of brass knobbed hand irons, one painted and one woolen floor-cloth, one copper Tea Kettle, two Pewter dishes & one dozen of plates, a whole set of Tea China, and a small red trunk . . . a pair of boots almost new, a pair of brass Candle-sticks and some books."[6] The owner's claim was that all this had been looted by American troops after the Battle of White Plains.

An eyewitness account standing alone lacks interpretation, something that has to be supplied by others. With hindsight and greater objectivity, placing information into a larger context, supported by other sources, creates a convincing picture. The motives behind the reporting in an eyewitness account vary depending on many factors and must be taken into consideration when interpreting what was said. However, seeing events through the eyes of someone who was there, even when the first-person reporting is done with hindsight, as in a memoir or an interview, adds a freshness and an intensity that are difficult to capture when the story is told by someone who was not there.

when they were caught in the act, the punishment was not equal to the prohibition. For a few days we had an abundance of good food. . . . Then we left and marched further on . . . to what was called *Weit Blene* [probably his phonetic spelling of White Plains]. Here we halted at a pretty house. Many of the men of our Corps went about and snatched up all the fowls and pigs, which was not forbidden them. I was thirsty, so I went into the house to get a drink. It was quite full of soldiers and everything was in confusion. . . . The people lamented greatly. . . . We also took all the field fruit we could carry. Most of the soldiers and Yagers, going in couples, had a stick between them for carrying meat and chickens. So we marched on and from out the bushes and hills on the way the farmers frequently fired upon us, when our men showed themselves with their pigs and chickens.[82]

The colonial militias were no less guilty of plundering. A citizen wrote to the Provincial Convention on behalf of the inhabitants of Westchester County in December 1776: "Many of the eastern troops [militiamen], while in our county, instead of protecting its inhabitants from the enemy, did plunder and distress them more than the enemy themselves, taking off with them our stock, household furniture, and even our farming utensils."[83] In 1780 an American colonel informed General Robert Howe of the activities of the colonial militia and an incident in Mamaroneck:

> The militia are very laborious in plundering and distressing the Inhabitants, about us, especially between us and the Enemies Lines, there is scarcely anyone who escaped their notice.
>
> A scout of mine has just arrived, by whom I am informed that they fell in with a party of Militia last night, at Marrineck, who rob'd & plundered the Inhabitants indiscriminately, which conduct is so infamous, I think an immediate stop ought to be put to it, for the safety of those Inhabitants, who are Friends to their country. . . .[84]

Referring to American militiamen, who were poorly trained and unreliable, an American general in a 1780 letter to Governor Clinton wrote, "I am informed that there is great reason to suspect that some of these people have driven off the Cattle of the Inhabitants, . . . pretending that they had defeated a party of cow boys [Loyalist irregular soldiers] and retook the cattle, which they claim as a lawful prize and sell at vendue. Thus plunder being the object, every one who is exposed, when it can be done with impunity, will be plundered."[85] Continually bearing the burden of providing provisions both legally and illegally for a starving American army and militia and, because of their geographic location, easily accessible to the foraging of the British troops occupying New York City, Westchester County's farms were nearly obliterated.

The lawlessness grew out of the necessity of the soldiers to survive. It was wartime, and both sides fed and paid their soldiers poorly. In addition to the plundering of the regular army and the militia was that of the Cowboys and the Skinners, variously characterized by witnesses and historians as either rogue criminals who took advantage of a lawless and chaotic situation or guerrilla fighters acting under military authority[86]—the Cowboys for the British, the Skinners on the American side. A lieutenant colonel appeared before the New York Council of Safety in early January 1778 and reported that Westchester County ". . . is almost entirely undefended, exposed to the incursions of the enemy and infested with villains who daily commit murders, robberies and other outrages. . . ."[87] Whether the perpetrators adhered to the established rules of conventional warfare, fought a modern guerrilla-style war, or engaged in law-breaking pure and simple, Westchester residents suffered the constant threat as well as the reality of property loss and violence.

The absence of effective administrative, legislative, and judicial systems exacerbated the crisis. Travel between towns was difficult because roads became increasingly rutted and poorly maintained. Money grew almost worthless. During 1779 the paper dollar went from being worth just sixteen cents to only two cents; by the following year it took ten dollars to equal one cent.[88] Doubt and suspicion were rampant. No one knew whom he or she could trust.

The Provincial Convention made efforts to aid the county, approving at least three resolutions in late 1776 and the spring of 1777 to send troops to provide for the security and protection of Westchester County[89] and to appoint a committee to develop a plan for a permanent defense of the county.[90] By 1781 things did begin to improve slightly. The American troops had moved south to within nine miles of the British line, greatly shrinking the size of the Neutral Ground, though Mamaroneck was still well within it. The constant military and foraging raids that had reduced Westchester to an almost primitive condition could no longer take place, but sporadic lawlessness continued. A letter written at the end of 1780 by a New York assemblyman summed up the situation concisely: "I was in Westchester County last Saturday and found that . . . the People of Westchester County think themselves given up to ruin, are discouraged and worn out, and believe they shall receive no further help. . . . I believe that unless something is done, Westchester County, in less than a month, will be totally in the Enemy's power; their exposed situation occasions those who were once good men to become corrupt by trading with the Enemy. . . ."[91]

A more eloquent account by Reverend Dr. Timothy Dwight, who lived in Westchester County for a time during the years of the Neutral Ground, is an oft-quoted passage from his *Travels in New-England and New-York*, where he described in vivid detail what life was like in and around Mamaroneck from his perspective as a visitor:

> In the autumn of 1777, I resided for some time in this County. The lines of the British were then in the neighbourhood of King's bridge; and those of the Americans at Byram river. These unhappy people were, therefore, exposed to the depredations of both. Often they were actually plundered; and always were liable to this calamity. They feared every body whom they saw; and loved nobody. . . . The power of volition seemed to have deserted them. They were not civil, but obsequious; not obliging, but subservient. . . . Both their countenances, and their motions had lost every trace of animation and of feeling. Their features were smoothed, not into serenity, but apathy. . . .
>
> Their houses, in the mean time, were in a great measure scenes of desolation. Their furniture was extensively plundered, or broken to pieces. The walls, floors, and windows were injured both by violence, and decay; and were not repaired, because they had not the means of repairing them, and because they were exposed to the repetition of the same injuries. Their cattle were gone. Their enclosures were burnt, where they were capable of becoming fuel; and in many cases thrown down, where they were not. Their fields were covered with a rank of growth of weeds, and wild grass. Amid all this appearance of desolation, nothing struck my eye more forcibly than the sight of this great road; the passage from New-York to Boston [the Boston Post Road, which passes through Mamaroneck and Rye]. Where I had heretofore seen a continual suc-

cession of horses and carriages; and life and bustle lent a sprightliness to all the environing objects; not a single, solitary traveller was visible, from week to week, or from month to month. . . . The very tracks of the carriages were grown over, and obliterated: and, where they were discernable, resembled the faint impressions of chariot wheels, said to be left on the pavements of Herculaneum. The grass was of full height for the scythe, and strongly realized to my own mind, for the first time, the proper import of that picturesque declaration in the Song of Deborah:—"In the days of Shamgar, the son of Anath, in the days of Jael, the highways were unoccupied; and the travelers walked through by-paths. The inhabitants of the villages ceased: they ceased in Israel."[92]

Apparently, life during the war was too chaotic even for annual town meetings and elections to be held. The minutes of the Mamaroneck town meetings for the year 1776 end and the minutes for the year 1783 begin on the same page, without so much as a notation or the drawing of a line across the paper, implying that governmental activity, in effect, had nearly ceased, and everyone simply assumed it would be so.[93]

On occasion, some fortunate Westchester residents fared better in the Neutral Ground. When twenty-two-year-old Lieutenant Colonel Aaron Burr (Thomas Jefferson's vice president who subsequently killed Alexander Hamilton in a famous duel over a political disagreement) took command of American troops at White Plains in early 1779, he found all his horsemen anxious to act as scouts, soon discovering their real objective. He wrote in a letter dated January 13, 1779 to General Alexander McDougall, "Notwithstanding the cautions I gave, . . . I blush to tell you that the party returned loaded with plunder. . . . The party had not been returned an hour, before I had six or seven persons from New-Rochelle and Frog's Neck [Throgg's Neck], with piteous applications for stolen goods and horses. Some of these persons are of the most friendly families. . . . I have at least a fortnight's work before me to undo the doings of last night."[94] Burr meted out strict disciplinary measures and forced his soldiers to return everything immediately. When some of his men subsequently went to Mamaroneck and plundered Isaac Gedney Jr.'s house, taking beds and bedding to make their tents more comfortable, Burr again commanded his troops to return the stolen goods.[95]

Some aspects of life in the Neutral Ground were merely inconvenient or perhaps even exhilarating. Between 1844 and 1851, John MacLean McDonald interviewed over one hundred elderly Westchester County residents who had memories of the Revolution. Among them was Prince Gedney, who around 1758 had been born enslaved into the Scarsdale family of John Gedney, an uncle of both Isaac Jr. and blacksmith Isaac. When he was ten, Prince's master died, leaving a widow who subsequently married Captain Absalom Gedney, a cousin of the two Isaacs. At age eighteen Prince witnessed the advance of the British army to White Plains from the top of his new master's house. In his interview, he told of having witnessed Loyalists steal cattle to send to the British in New York City and of having experienced certain restrictions in his everyday life in the Neutral Ground:

> I used often to go below [the Neutral Ground] to sell chickens, butter and provisions for my master. . . . Sometimes, I went into New York to buy. On such occasions I got a pass from General Horriman or some other Hessian officer. . . . The pass allowed me to go in the city and purchase the articles which were specified. Once I lost my pass and went back for another. This provoked General Horriman who said, "What for you lose your pass? Be careful. Suppose you lose this, I give you no

more." After scolding awhile he gave me a new permit and then asked, "Vat vill you trink? Here's brandy, rum and gin." I answered that I would take a glass of spirits which he gave me accordingly.[96]

Major William Hull succeeded Aaron Burr in his Continental army position in 1779. He, like Burr, found service in Westchester County difficult. The many Tories in the area reported his troops' every move to the enemy. To combat this disadvantage, Hull devised an ingenious way of gaining information. He directed the Patriots who lived nearest Kingsbridge, where British troops were headquartered, as soon as they noticed any movement of the troops, to nonchalantly take a pitcher of cider, milk, or beer to a neighbor, who in turn would do the same. Each Patriot in the chain would pass on the crucial information, along with the cider, until it reached its destination.[97] Ordinary people on both sides contributed quietly, and at times, not so quietly, to the war effort.

THE END OF THE WAR

The final show of British military might occurred on September 16, 1782, a massive search for provisions that moved north from New York City to Yonkers. The American army departed on October 27, 1782, and the last of the British army finally exited Westchester on May 13, 1783.[98] Hufeland summed up the war experience of county residents thus: "In these seven years and four months, Westchester County was never free from the enemy—for every week and perhaps every day, it could furnish a record of bloodshed, either in open fight or in atrocious misdeed of sneaking robber, and the strain of consuming anxiety was never absent from its people. They fought longer and suffered more than any other community in all the thirteen colonies, and its fields, its hills and valleys, are consecrated by their valor, their patriotism and their suffering."[99]

After the war Isaac Gedney Jr.—by now probably in his mid-forties or somewhat older—his wife, Marcia (also spelled Maria, Mercie, Mercey, and Marcey), and his mother, Sebe, sold their Harbor Heights property to cousin Captain Absalom Gedney in June 1784.[100] The property had been in their immediate family for nearly seventy years. Had the long years of hardship, living in the Neutral Ground, left the Isaac Gedney Jr. family too exhausted, risk-averse, or financially depleted to maintain their large farm? Were Isaac Jr.'s sympathies still with the British, or had he come around to support the Patriot point of view? He was not among the 109 Westchester freeholders who belatedly signed an oath of allegiance to the state of New York in December of 1777.[101] Unlike cousins John Gidney[102] and Joseph Gedney, a truly infamous Loyalist,[103] and roughly one hundred thousand others, Isaac Jr. never had to leave the country as a result of his Loyalist activity. His status as a common man undoubtedly helped to protect him from that fate. In fact, in selling his big farm, perhaps he was simply scaling back and shifting the direction of his vocation. On the day of the sale of the family farm, he bought a smaller, thirty-four-acre farm in Mamaroneck near the Boston Post Road[104] and the following year in a mortgage document listed himself as a carpenter.[105] He died seventeen years later in 1802. The rector of Christ's Church in Rye conducted his burial service,[106] indicating that though he had left the house and property of his birth, Isaac Gedney Jr. probably continued his relatively ordinary life residing and working in Westchester County after the Revolution. Even though the agrarian life in Westchester County continued on for several decades after the massive disruption of the Revolution, even greater changes lay ahead in the century to come.

FIGURE 6.5 The Eleazor Gedney Cemetery, Mamaroneck, New York, is entirely surrounded by an Interstate 95 cloverleaf entrance/exit ramp, just visible in the background. *(Photo by author.)*

seven

Louis Block and Harry Rich Mooney: From Farm to Subdivision

Vast Areas Being Brought Close to the Heart of the City[1]

—*New York Times* headline, 1896

When my husband and I embarked on a search for a house in the same suburban area where I had been living, I had no way of knowing that the house we would find and subsequently buy would lead me not only to learn much about the property's history, but also to discover some surprising connections between the house and the apartment building where I then resided. From a childhood spent in a Pittsburgh suburb to adulthood in several cities on both the East and West Coasts and in a small Midwestern town, I was well attuned to what suburbs are and are not. It was only after spending months researching the historical agrarian aspects of Westchester County that I became curious about how my surroundings had been transformed from a rural, agricultural place into a well-known suburb.

Caleb Heathcote might be regarded as New York City's first suburban commuter, for to get from his house to the city where he worked, he could have boarded a sloop in the Mamaroneck Harbor right in front of his house, ridden a horse, presumably down the Shore Path all the way to Manhattan, or had a driver take him there by horse-drawn carriage. The Mamaroneck of Heathcote's day was, however, a far cry from the suburbs as we know them today. And Heathcote undoubtedly did not commute on a daily basis as he also had a home in the city. Two of the property's subsequent owners, however—one who commuted to the city by trolley and train, the other who depended for his livelihood on automobile commutation—exemplify true suburban development, a phenomenon that occurred two hundred years after Heathcote's lifespan. How do we account for the transformation of this land from the site of a family farm to that of a suburban Cape Cod in a bedroom community?

FROM WORKING FARM TO "COUNTRY SEAT"

The land that the Gedneys had consolidated into a 135-acre, working family farm by the time Isaac Jr. inherited it in 1771 remained a family farm for several more decades. It passed into the hands of one more Gedney, Absalom, in 1784. Having made the transition from tenant farmer to land owner,[2] Absalom Gedney was elected by his fellow Mamaroneck yeomen to several positions of town leadership, including overseer of highways and overseer of the poor.[3]

A decade later, Captain William Gray, a man of some note in the area, acquired the property. A 1797 Mamaroneck map of unknown authorship indicates a number of geographic features such as roads, bridges, rivers, and harbor, but includes and labels tiny drawings of just three houses—"Heathcoot's [*sic*] Hill," "Widow Griffens," and "Capt. Gray's"—at a time when there must have been at least fifty households in the town.[4] Captain Gray, as a young lieutenant, fought for the British in the Seven Years' War (French and Indian War), signed the 1775 oath of loyalty to the king in White Plains, but then switched allegiances and became the captain of a regiment of Westchester County minutemen during the Revolution.[5] Ordered to protect Westchester County farmers "exposed to the depredations of the enemy" in 1777,[6] he must have succeeded in his task and, in doing so, endeared himself to his neighbors, which may explain the prominence given his house on the map twenty years later.

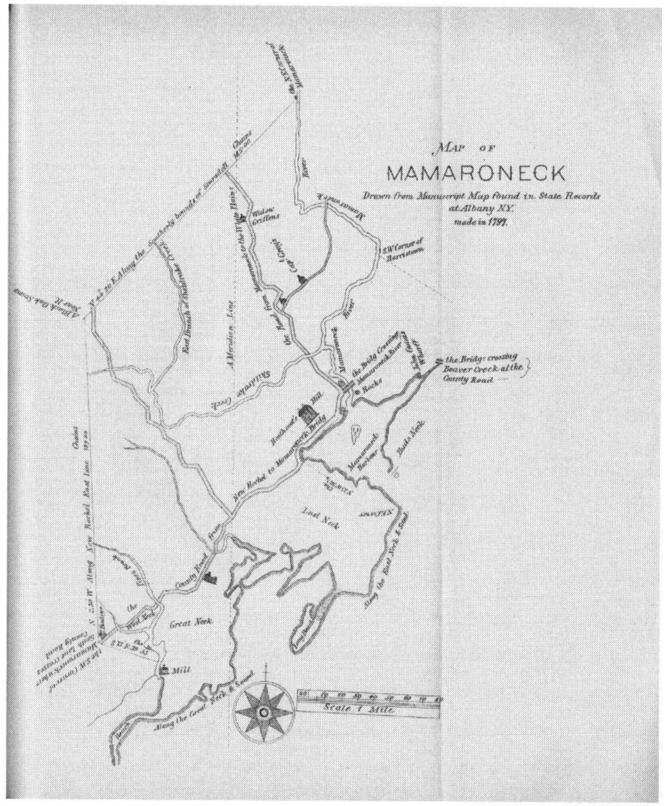

FIGURE 7.1 Map of Mamaroneck, 1797, showing Captain Gray's house. Drawn by nineteenth-century historian Edward Delancey from a manuscript map found in New York State records in Albany. *(Reprinted from Scharf,* History of Westchester County*, 1886, vol. 1, opp. p. 846. Photo by author.)*

In 1818 the captain turned over the property for one dollar to his son James, a New York City distiller, who maintained both home and business addresses in the city until 1821.[7] The only other fact I could find about him was that he manumitted two enslaved workers, Telemaque and Rose, in Mamaroneck in 1810.[8] From him the farm passed two years later to one New York City grocer and then another in the 1820s. The first, David Lewis, soon ceased to be listed in the New York City directories. Three years after Lewis acquired the property, his fellow citizens elected him overseer of highways for the northern district of Mamaroneck.[9] The second grocer, Jacob Richee, also appears to have given up his New York City business soon after he purchased the property, and perhaps he, too, moved and took up farming in Mamaroneck.[10]

Around this time, Westchester County's four thousand farms produced wheat, rye, oats, corn, potatoes, hay, buckwheat, wool, and fruit, shipping surpluses to New York City markets via sloop.[11] By mid-century, however, farming in the region was becoming a thing of the past. The Erie Canal had opened in 1825, and the railroad followed soon after, allowing distant markets to expand. Also significant was the 1840s introduction of the refrigerated railroad boxcar, which permitted meat and other perishables to be transported longer distances, from Ohio, Indiana, and Illinois, where they could be produced more cheaply and more abundantly. Suddenly, the transportation advantage that Westchester County had enjoyed because of its proximity to a large metropolitan center disappeared. Soil depletion further diminished Westchester's productivity and market domination, forcing farmers to move toward dairy farming. One observer noted in 1850 that the country residences of Westchester County were "mainly supplied with marketing from the city, instead of their own vicinity" (much like today's suburbs) and that milk was a farmer's most profitable product.[12]

In this transitional period, when Westchester County changed from a diversified farming community into something new, some observers mourned the impending loss of an idyllic, pastoral retreat. Four years after he purchased his beloved Westchester County home, Sunnyside, renowned author Washington Irving wrote in *Knickerbocker Magazine* in 1839 of his return to his childhood home where, contrary to his fears, he had found little changed from his youth. With a bank about to be built in the area, however, he lamented, "The fate of the neighborhood is therefore sealed. I see no hope of averting it. . . . The country is suddenly to be deluged with wealth."[13] Others, however, focused on the positive aspects of creating a new spatial order, characterized by gentleman farmers moving in to build "country seats," the loci for gracious living.[14]

During this mid-century period of transition, still other observers noted an aura of slovenliness, decay, and imminent abandonment, blaming the farms' untidy appearance and failure to prosper on the farmers' moral weakness,[15] whereas in reality, basic economics was the more likely cause. Across the Northeast a tension arose between farmers who wanted to use the land to earn a living and others who wanted to live in the country but make their money in cities. The ongoing economic pressure eventually led to real estate development and the subdivision of what once had been farms.[16] In Westchester County the uses of land quickly shifted in that direction; from 1850 to 1880, at least one thousand farms vanished.[17]

A look at population statistics tells us much about the story too. Mamaroneck's population increased slowly and steadily from 1790 to 1840; it then grew little in the three decades from 1840 to 1870, probably a consequence of the failing farms. Growth picked up in the last quarter of the nineteenth century with Westchester County's population as a whole doubling in each of the two twenty-year periods between 1870 and 1910, making it the world's first large suburb.[18] The largest population increase took place in the decades from 1890 to 1900 and from 1920 to 1930, the two phases of suburban development under consideration here.[19]

Fitting the overall countywide pattern, the Gedney-Gray property was carved up sometime after 1826 and before 1847, when there is evidence of a State Supreme Court action and a public auction, probably the outcome of a bankruptcy declaration. A second Supreme Court action resulted in the Mutual Life Insurance Company of New York acquiring and consolidating two parcels into a property of about twelve acres in 1884. Owned by a series of absentee New York City and New Jersey investors, undoubtedly speculators banking on the coming trolley line to inflate land value, it changed hands five times in the six years from 1890 to 1895, when Louis Block, probably the property's first true commuting suburbanite, purchased it.[20] His use of the land as both gentleman farmer and commuting businessman is emblematic of the transition from farm to subdivision.

LEADING PRINCIPLES FOR RURAL RESIDENCES

By the mid-1830s New York City was a booming metropolis with a population of more than 250,000.[21] At first, those who could afford it escaped the summer heat and seasonal epidemics by migrating to second homes in the country. From summer places developed the fashion for year-round country living. "Country seats" began to spring up around this time along the Hudson and in other places of natural beauty.[22] Andrew Jackson Downing's 1841 *A Treatise on the Theory and Practice of Landscape Gardening*, followed the next year by his *Cottage Residences*, in many ways established the template for suburban country living.

In these influential and enormously popular books, Downing set forth his "leading principles" for amateurs to follow to embellish their "Rural Residences." Readily acknowledging his debt to English landscape gardening writers such as John Claudius Loudon, he adapted the British author's suggestions to an American audience, speaking in accessible language directly to the owner rather than to the builder. Assuring his readers that successful landscape gardening could be practiced on as little as ten well-situated acres, Downing demonstrated to the owner of a country property how to create a residence of "*tasteful simplicity*." Included in *A Treatise* were plans for a suburban cottage, just as worthy, he emphasized, as a mansion.[23] *Cottage Residences* expanded his ideas more broadly for a collection of modest homes.[24]

His were surely publications in the right place at the right time. *A Treatise* went through more than fifteen editions and printings before 1880, and there were five editions of *Cottage Residences*, the fourth alone reissued seven times.[25] Downing, without doubt, helped promote and popularize a suburban way of life in the mid- and late-nineteenth century by showing people how to transform farmland, the wealthy and their estates setting an example for suburban living across the economic spectrum. Westchester County, a place of natural beauty close to New York City, was ideally suited for the application of Downing's principles.

A TRANSPORTATION REVOLUTION

Before the introduction of public transportation systems, an early nineteenth-century commuter in Mamaroneck would more than likely have traveled to New York City as described by Susan Fenimore Cooper, daughter of noted author James Fenimore Cooper and great-great granddaughter of Caleb Heathcote. She reported in a private family memoir that in the 1820s—while her family lived at Heathcote Hill, Heathcote's Mamaroneck homestead—her father made the trip to the city frequently and would travel "sometimes by the Mamaroneck stage, sometimes in his gig, occasionally on horse back, and I can remember his walking the 25 miles occasionally, and coming home very tired."[26] The subsequent development of public transportation systems would make the trip far easier and more accessible to many people.

Mass transit might be said to have begun on July 7, 1829, when London's *Morning Post* noted that omnibus service had begun in that city:

Saturday the new vehicle, called the Omnibus, commenced running from Paddington to the City, and excited considerable notice, both from the novel form of the carriage, and the elegance with which it is fitted out. It is capable of accommodating 16 or 18 persons, all inside, and we apprehend it would be almost impossible to make it overturn, owing to the great width of the carriage. It was drawn by three beautiful bays abreast, after the French fashion. The Omnibus is a handsome machine, in the shape of a van. The width the horses occupy will render the vehicle rather inconvenient to be turned or driven through some of the streets of London.[27]

The omnibus, a kind of stagecoach with set routes and fares, soon made its way to New York in the form of a single-route line along Broadway. In less than a decade one New Yorker noted that twenty-five thousand people rode omnibuses each day and observed, "We daily see persons waiting at the crossing places, for some minutes, before they can find an opening, and a chance to get over, between the omnibuses, coaches, and other vehicles, that are constantly dashing up and down the street. . . ."[28] In 1853 there were 683 coaches in twenty-two firms competing for business in New York City.[29]

For suburbanites at mid-century, the railroad offered transportation to and from the city. Westchester County, the only land link between New York City and New England, enjoyed access to four railroad lines by the mid-1800s. The New York and New Haven Railroad had been completed by 1849, with commuters from Mamaroneck using it soon afterward. As early as the end of the Civil War, it carried forty-four Mamaroneck daily commuters to and from the city.[30] Well established by 1896, the line offered a Mamaroneck commuter frequent daily trains and a choice of seven ticket classes for the twenty-one-mile trip to Grand Central Station.[31]

By the 1890s, the formation of the transportation infrastructure for the New York City metropolitan region was underway. A new technology, the electric trolleybus, also known as the trackless trolley, or simply the trolley, powered by electricity through a system of poles attached to paired overhead wires, had come to New York City in the 1880s and to its suburbs a decade later. An 1896 *New York Times* article with the subhead, "Vast Areas Being Brought Close to the Heart of the City," stated that twenty years earlier the trolley had not even been dreamed of. The article reviewed the current state of public transportation in Westchester County: forty miles of trolley tracks in place and more to open within a few months, including a line connecting Mamaroneck to White Plains and Tarrytown. Although at least one scholar maintains that none of the several new transportation technologies that advanced in the nineteenth century single-handedly caused suburban development, public transportation unquestionably supported it, especially when railroad companies invested in real estate for development and real estate developers joined the railroad lines in promoting suburban living as a kind of ongoing vacation.[32]

REFRIGERATION AND THE DEMISE OF FARMING IN WESTCHESTER

With farming but a remnant of a bygone era in Westchester County and the advances in long-distance-transportation refrigeration among the several causes of that change in land use, it is perhaps ironic that my property's first real daily commuter was the chief engineer of the pioneering De La Vergne Refrigerating Machine Company in the Bronx. After his time with De La Vergne, Louis Block (ca. 1850–1926) became a consulting mechanical refrigeration engineer with an office on Forty-second Street in midtown Manhattan, just a couple of blocks from Grand Central Station.[33] Although the refrigerated railroad car, developed beginning in the 1840s, used natural ice in bunkers and circulating air to chill insulated boxcars, the development of mechanical refrigeration technology, utilizing compressed ammonia, brought about a major increase in the distances food could be transported. Block's role as an inventor and consultant in that industry brought him the material success that allowed him to be the owner of a small estate in suburban Westchester County.[34] Block was not alone. A 1903 article in the *New York Times* commented that of Mamaroneck's population of about four thousand, five hundred were "New York business men, who in settling [t]here shrewdly gauged the possibilities and merit of the place as a home centre."[35] Born in Germany in 1850 or 1851, Block emigrated in his early twenties. By 1900, established in Mamaroneck and married to American-born Celia, he had three children ages fifteen, eleven, and nine, and three Irish live-in servants to help run his nearly twelve-acre property.[36]

The Census

For the researcher of history, the census is much more than a mere headcount. The United States Census, the one we hear about every ten years, is mandated by the Constitution and is used to apportion seats in the U.S. House of Representatives, to allocate federal government funding, and to analyze demographic trends. The first federal census took place in 1790, and there have been twenty-two of them since.

The place to begin a search of United States Census data is the National Archives and Records Administration (NARA), http://www.archives.gov. The actual census records are not online here, but this website contains a wealth of information. Also at this website are catalogues which can be used to help prepare for a visit to the archives, one of their regional satellite sites, or a state archive or library that licenses their digitized data through *Ancestry.com* or *Heritagequest.com*. Partial census records from some states have been transcribed and are available free of charge through the USGenWeb project at http://www.uscensus.org, and http://www.rootsweb.com. Certain limitations on census data include the facts that most of the 1890 census was destroyed in a fire and the most recent population census data available is for 1940 because of a law preventing the release of the data for seventy-two years. In addition to census records, NARA's holdings include military, immigration, naturalization, and land records, among other things.

Early censuses listed by name only the head of household but did include the age range and gender of each member of the household, and whether they were free or enslaved. The 1820 census designated persons who worked in agriculture, manufacturing, and commerce. For people engaged in manufacturing, more information is available in the 1820 Census of Manufactures, a kind of addendum to the census that year. It gives information such as the type and size of the business, the kinds of materials used, and the goods produced annually. You may have to ask for this material because it is held separately from the rest of the 1820 census data and seems not to be in Ancestry.com. Because the questions used by census-takers were often open-ended, this information can provide firsthand accounts of business operations.

The level of detail increases in the censuses from 1850 onward. Though they vary from year to year, data available can include: the person's date and place of birth, date of marriage, years of immigration and naturalization, place of parents' births, military service, property ownership, and occupation. Information on occupations can lead a researcher to check other pertinent resources such as deeds and tax records.

To take just one example of ways census data can be used, through a close look at the census of 1870, I was able to learn much about the sociological makeup of my town, particularly through the column marked "occupations." Such information can help place the person you are researching into the social structure of the place where he or she lived. In 1870, during the period of declining agriculture in Westchester County, my town was clearly still hanging on as a partly agricultural town. The second-largest single category was farmer, and most of those in it were property owners. The categories that included just one or a very few individuals were: blacksmith, bricklayer, butcher, cattle dealer, gardener, ice dealer, inn keeper, mason, painter, peddler, plasterer, policeman, seamstress, shoemaker, teamster, and wood chopper. There were several people listed in each of the categories of carpenter, coachman, domestic, and merchant. A few fell into the categories of lawyer, insurance agent, real estate agent, and stockbroker, a harbinger of the urban bedroom community that would develop in the next few decades. The largest single group was "laborer," all of them born in Ireland or Italy. Some lived with families, others in boarding houses. In a single boarding house were listed ninety-five Italian men, most of them illiterate. The proportionately high number of laborers suggests that many of them worked in nearby towns. Out of a total of more than two hundred households, ninety were headed by someone who owned land.

Sometimes census information has to be used with caution and put together with data from other sources. For example, the 1900 census listed Louis Block—the refrigeration engineer and inventor with several U.S. patents to his name who commuted to a midtown Manhattan office—as a carpenter, most likely an error.

Census research should not be limited to just the "United States Census" because there have been other censuses, state and local, equally useful to research on historical topics, and they are worth looking for. For population information before 1790, a good source is Evarts B. Greene and Virginia D. Harrington, *American Population Before the Federal Census of 1790* (New York: Columbia University Press, 1932).

With railroad commutation to New York City well established in Mamaroneck by the time Block purchased the property in 1895, it was undoubtedly the imminent arrival of the trolley that influenced him to settle just where and when he did. At the time, only the very wealthiest Americans could afford a horse and driver.[37] Within a year of his purchase of the land, Block could have taken the trolley from his house to the station less than a mile away and from there boarded a train to New York City, a thirty- to forty-minute commute. By 1926 there was even a second commuter train line, the New York, Westchester & Boston, running through Mamaroneck as well.[38]

Block's tenure in Mamaroneck from 1895 to 1926 precisely positioned him to experience trolley/train commuter transportation and to witness the start of automobile commutation. Although I have not been able to determine what buildings were on the property when Block purchased it, a 1919 Sanborn fire insurance map shows the outline of his house and, nearby, a large barn structure labeled "auto," located directly in front of where my house is today.[39] In 1898 there was just one car for every eighteen thousand people in the United States. From 1905 to 1925, the number of automobiles jumped from 8,000 to 17.5 million. By 1927, the year the Model T ceased production (after twenty years on the market) and the recently widowed Celia Block sold the property, a car had become an essential part of middle-class life.[40] The stage was set for the next phase of suburban development in Westchester County.

THE AUTOMOBILE SUBURB

By the early 1920s, a building boom was underway in Westchester County, the region fast becoming an automobile suburb. The property's newest owner was Harry Rich Mooney (1884–1957), a 1905 Columbia University graduate[41] and established local real estate developer. As president

FIGURE 7.2 Sanborn Map of Mamaroneck, New York, 1919, showing the Louis Block property. *(Use of 1919 Map of Mamaroneck, NY reprinted / used with permission from The Sanborn Library, LLC.)*

Maps

Maps, for the purpose of tracing property ownership, are invaluable, particularly for transactions that use the metes-and-bounds system of property descriptions. Perhaps more importantly, though, maps tell stories. Maps not only represent the physical features of the land, they also document human activity through the depiction of political borders, personal property boundaries, roads, locations of towns, and even individual houses. Far from being the neutral documents they may appear to be, maps often reveal biases and political motives and therefore require interpretation. And assuming the map can be dated, the stories become historical.

Even in times in North America before published maps, the Native Americans used place names that were descriptive of what could be done in a given place. In other words, they described places rather than naming them as we do today. In Westchester County alone there are dozens of such names still in use; for example: *Nepperhan*, a river—"running cold water"; *Senasqua*, a park—"the grassy place"; *Ossining*, a town—"a place of stones"; and *Chappaqua*, also a town—"place where the brush makes a rustling sound when you walk through." Others, unfamiliar today to most local residents, include *Alipkonk*, an Indian settlement—"where the elm trees grow"; *Asoquatah*, a mountain—"pine tree sap place"; and *Appamaghpogh*, an area—"where the cattails used for covering lodges grow."[1] By doing this, the Native Americans made the land itself into a kind of map and more, not only helping people find their way, but also giving them information they needed to sustain themselves.[2]

Maps by sixteenth- and seventeenth-century European cartographers are, of course, far from topographically accurate by today's standards, but they can give us plenty of information about people's observations, beliefs, and attitudes. They often include information and instructive images distributed across the surface of the map itself as well as in accompanying insets. For example, the well-known Visscher map (see fig. 4.3) of the mid-1600s includes the names of Indian peoples, including the Siwanoys, drawings of Native American villages as described by explorers, and images of the animals they found—bears, beavers, turkeys, and others. The inset view of the Dutch settlement of New Amsterdam shows houses, government buildings, a crane for lifting ships' cargoes, a windmill, and a flag flying atop a pole, a signal that ships were nearing the harbor. Herman Moll's 1715 "Beaver Map" (see fig. 4.5) includes fanciful but hard-working beavers, a sign of the importance placed on the beaver pelt trade at the time.

Maps greatly aided my work finding the owners of my property. Sometimes the property descriptions in the deeds were too vague for me to fully understand the transactions. With the aid of maps and certain mostly unchanging topographical features—river, cemetery, pond—the property boundaries became clear. With the property progressively sliced down into smaller and smaller parcels, consulting maps reaffirmed what properties belonged to whom. Maps, even those done by amateurs, also sometimes contain useful bits of information. For example, the placement of the tiny drawing of Captain Gray's house on a 1797 map of Mamaroneck (see fig. 7.1) indicates either his importance in the community or his connection to the mapmaker; either way he was probably a citizen of some local note.

Old maps may be found in a number of places including libraries (usually in bound volumes), archives, places where land records are kept, real estate attorneys' offices, municipal tax records offices, and the Web. *Google Earth* offers a myriad of features and tools worth exploring. One of my favorites is the very basic measuring tool, which I use to determine the distances between things in my own neighborhood. *Google Earth User Guide*, http://earth.google.com/userguide/v4/, explains how to use the many features it offers once you have downloaded the free program onto your computer.

The purpose for which a map was made determines what one might find on it. Specific purposes beyond laying out topographical and geographical features and delineating travel routes include, among others: designing municipal parklands, building highways, assessing property taxes, defining election districts, surveying a private property, developing a subdivision, and determining insurance valuations.

Sanborn fire insurance maps are an especially valuable historical tool, particularly for urban and suburban areas and town centers, because they include details such as property boundaries, the location, outline, purpose, height, number of stories, and construction material of buildings, as well as water lines and hydrants, which in many communities have not changed since they were first installed. The Sanborn Map Company produced them beginning in 1867 and has updated them periodically to account for new construction. A complete collection of them is in the Library of Congress, with local libraries often in possession of the older versions of local maps bound into books. And now many libraries have access to *Digital Sanborn Maps* with 660,000 maps of more than 12,000 American towns and cities. A researcher can buy selected digital or 18-by-17-inch paper maps from Environmental Data Resources, Inc., http://www.edrnet.com, which now owns the copyright to them.

Finally, a sophisticated way to understand a piece of property through maps is to georeference a place using Geographic Information System (GIS) software. GIS is a computer program for creating, managing, and analyzing geographic data. Maps in GIS can be represented as layers where each layer holds data about a geographic characteristic linked to a coordinate position, in terms of longitude and latitude, on the earth's surface. In order to use data in GIS you have to align a selected location with existing geographically known points on the earth. For example, if you have an old map of a property and you want to compare it to a contemporary map that you know is accurate, you select control points on each map—ones that can be confirmed as representing the same geographic location (landmark, political boundary, or street intersection). GIS matches up the pairs of points and integrates the data so that the old map is put into a consistent coordinate system, allowing you to see where things once were.

of Mamaroneck Knolls, Inc., his vision in 1926 was to subdivide most of the twelve-acre site into roughly quarter-acre lots and build single-family homes, reserving a section of the property for the construction of two large apartment houses. This model had already been successfully carried out in the adjoining village of Larchmont, where the year before, Mooney had completed his only other major real estate development undertaking, Larchmont Knolls. In an odd coincidence, the cooperative apartment I lived in for ten years and sold just before moving to my house in Mamaroneck was in the building known as Larchmont Gables, part of Mooney's Larchmont Knolls development.

This type of planned suburban complex, combining houses and apartment buildings, was not unique. For example, in the New York City borough of Queens a similar kind of development, Sunnyside Gardens, went up beginning in 1924. Drawing inspiration from the Garden City movement in England, such developments included moderate-sized private homes and apartment buildings, with shared playgrounds and other recreational spaces.[42] The National Recreation Society recognized Mooney in 1931 as one of a number of developers involved in New York real estate who had donated land for "recreation features for the new community, as parks, children's playgrounds, [and] facilities for sports and healthful exercise add materially to the attractiveness of a certain locality as a home centre."[43]

Harry Rich Mooney embraced his real estate projects with gusto, producing promotional newsletters and placing newspaper advertisements frequently. *Larchmont Fables*, his Larchmont Knolls newsletter, presented the scope of his Larchmont development—ninety-two houses and an apartment building (where I had lived) with forty rental units, a tennis court and playground with canopied sandbox, seesaw, swings, shoot-the-chutes, tether ball, and quoits, providing recreational opportunities for all ages.

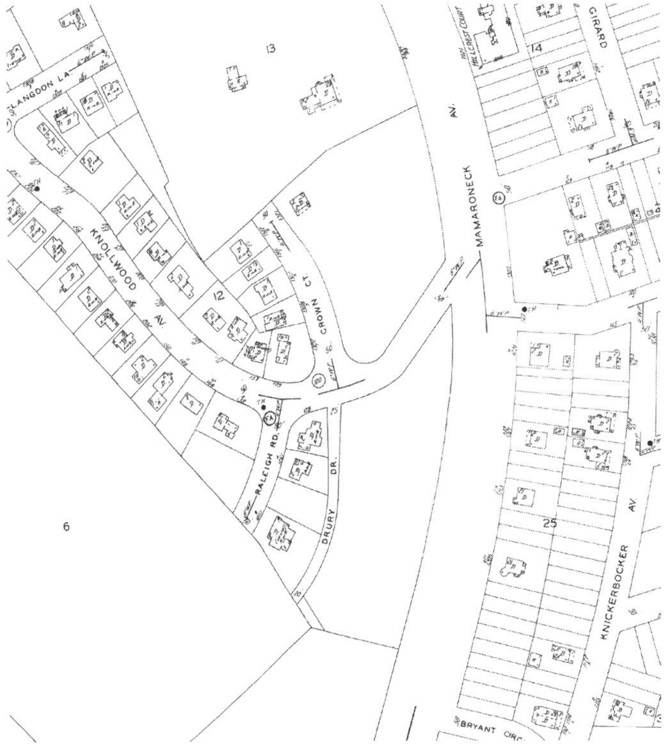

FIGURE 7.3 Sanborn Map of Mamaroneck, New York, 1934, showing the property after Harry Rich Mooney had developed the neighborhood and sold his remaining empty lots at the onset of the Great Depression. *(Use of 1934 Map of Mamaroneck, NY reprinted / used with permission from The Sanborn Library, LLC.)*

FIGURE 7.4 Larchmont Gables as shown in *Mooney's Megaphone* in 1928. *(Photo by author.)*

Residents of the apartment building, or as he referred to it, the "apartment hotel," had access to maid service by the hour, individual garage spaces, and a restaurant, the Gables Grill, catering directly to residents' apartments and featuring a "conservatively conducted" dance orchestra after 8:00 in the evening.[44] (None of these "hotel" amenities existed when I lived there, nor did the tennis court and playground.) Mooney even lived there himself for a time, exploiting that fact for promotional purposes.[45]

Mooney announced his plans for his second development, Mamaroneck Knolls, in December 1926, describing it in his newsletter as a "marvelous situation on a high hill with stately elms and verdant pines," and adding, "our home designers have made of this old country estate one of the most interesting places in Westchester."[46] Within a few months of taking possession of the property, Mooney had begun publishing *Mooney's Megaphone*, a more elaborate version of *Larchmont Fables*. A jaunty, twenty-four-page promotional piece, published twice, in 1927 and 1928, it overflowed with information on parks, transportation, and other amenities in the area. Transportation, in particular, was a superior selling point for Mooney's project. As his *Megaphone* put it, "Mamaroneck Knolls is located in the hub of the new Westchester County Parkway System. . . . Here Saxon Woods Parkway is joined by the Pelham-Port Chester."[47] The Pelham-Port Chester Parkway at the time, of course, was still just a long strip of parkland with no highway and remained so until the interstate came along in the 1950s and swallowed up all the land. The Saxon Woods Parkway was also just a strip of land, eventually becoming a large, wooded county park. Yet another in the network of county parkways, the Hutchinson River Parkway, had just opened its new highway to automobile traffic, the nearest entrance just one mile away. Even though most residents of the development probably had cars by this time (Mooney's houses all had steam-heated, attached garages), there was the readily accessible trolley line, in place until the county tore out the tracks just before World War II,[48] and the nearby commuter train station serving two train lines. *Mooney's Megaphone* notes that there were 169 daily trains between Mamaroneck and New York City,[49] compared to fewer than one hundred today. In a lovely setting, ideally situated for transportation access, its houses designed to include all the latest modern conveniences, the development promised to be a great success.

The *Megaphone* also included letters to the editor praising the development, staff professional profiles, photographs, advertisements, cartoons, jokes, contests, artist renderings with elaborate descriptions of the houses, as well as information on the progress of the project as a whole. The two issues reveal that by November 1927, when six of the homeowners had already moved in to their new dwellings, Mooney had constructed a playground, demolished the old barn (Louis Block's "auto" barn), and drawn up plans for two large apartment houses, one of them to be built right where my house stands today. It was to be a four-story building, in a "French Chateau district" style, much like Larchmont Gables. The drawing of it even shows how the architect jogged the building's perimeter around the large rock outcrop. Fireplaces, incinerators, Frigidaires, and dishwashers would have enhanced these rental apartments. The other building was to include a number of additional

FIGURE 7.5 The cover of *Mooney's Megaphone* newsletter promoted the residential real estate development of Harry Rich Mooney in 1928. *(Photo by author.)*

impressive amenities, such as underground parking for fifty cars, hidden beneath a terrace, a roof garden restaurant and solarium, and in the basement a swimming pool and Turkish bath.[50]

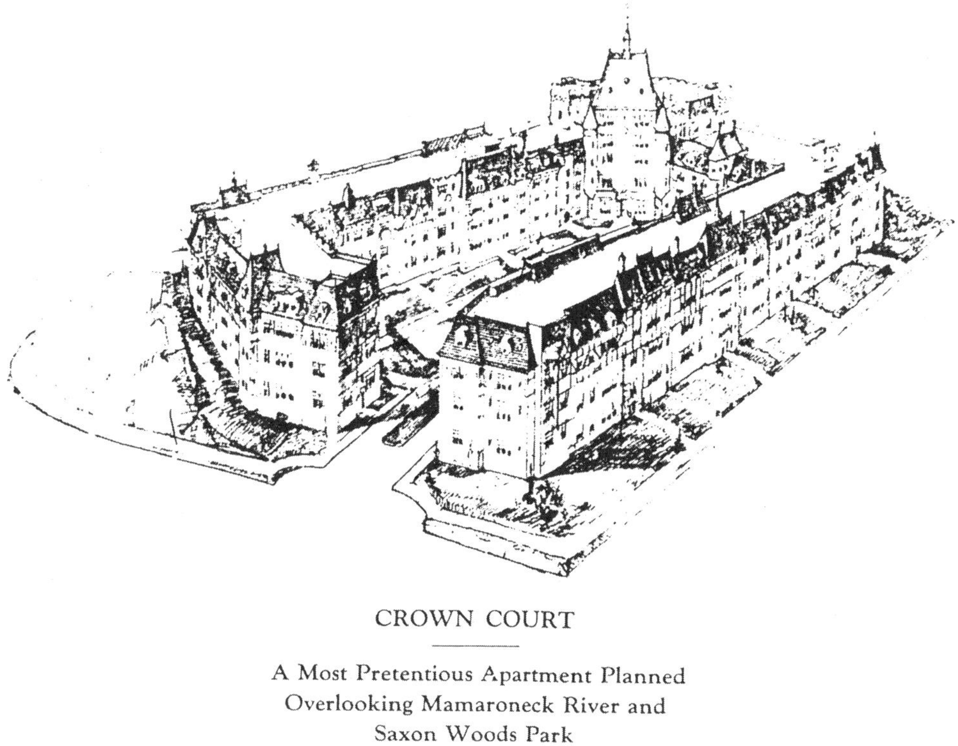

FIGURE 7.6 Artist's rendering in *Mooney's Megaphone* of the proposed apartment building where my house is today. The drawing shows the sliced-off corner of the building, designed to accommodate the rock outcropping, in the left foreground. *(Photo by author.)*

The variety of styles offered for the relatively modest houses was notable. Promotional materials designated and described them as: the Quaker, a "true colonial, typical of sleepy Philadelphia"; the Provincetown, "a true importation from Cape Cod"; the Rensselaer, a "dainty Colonial cottage"; and the Wayside Cottage, "from the countryside of Devonshire." Warwick House was "reminiscent of Merrie England in the eighteenth century"; the Gainsborough was "an English type of Norman extraction"; Old English had been "brought from old England"; and Le Bourget was "imbued with the quaint charm of old Versailles."[51]

One of Mooney's more spectacular advertising campaigns centered on the Mamaroneck Knolls home number thirteen, "copied after a country dwelling in Normandy," the Burgundy Villa, which had been selected as a model home by the *New York Herald-Tribune* in conjunction with the Home Owners Institute, Inc. Opened to the public for several weekends in late 1927, Mooney's house was featured in an elaborate, full-page spread on the front page of the Sunday Gravure Section, which showed the house in two photographs and a drawing, surrounded by an "abandoned moat" with a mock drawbridge leading to the front door.

Mooney's Megaphone

WARWICK HOUSE

An impressive entrance through a massive stone chimney with broad expanses of stucco on each side, and weathered green copper bay window lending charm to the exterior. A beamed studio living room with "pecky" cypress walls, sun porch, dining room, breakfast nook, kitchen and large bedroom, and tiled bath on the ground [illegible]r. On the second floor, two large bedrooms and beauti[illegible]y tiled bath, large closets, one of them cedar, topped by a spacious attic.

GAINSBOROUGH

An English type, best suited for the artist, or one artistically inclined. Large studio living room with beamed ceiling, emphasis being placed on wide and high windows, affording north light, and a charming balcony overlooking living room. Dining room, kitchen, private suite of room and bath, complete the first floor. Upstairs, two bedrooms and tiled bath, with large spacious attic above.

LE BOURGET

A true replica from famous French antecedent. The te[illegible]re of the stucco with its massive quoins, the high sloping roof and massive stone chimney materially add to its charm. Large living room, dining room, kitchen, two bedrooms and tiled bath. A large stone terrace in the rear, surrounded by an imported French fence, assures the privacy of the occupant.

OLD ENGLISH

We have brought from old England the lines of this adorable and lovable little home. The mellow reds of the rugged, over-burnt brick walls, the high ridges of the roof lines, the artistic entrance way with its slate walk and iron rail, make the picture one of appealing beauty. The living room is unique. High vaulted ceiling, cast stone fire-place, a hanging balcony across the full width at one end serving as an entrance to the second floor. Under the balcony are three steps down to a lovely dining room. Then there is a bedroom and bath and kitchen with pantry. Upstairs are two corner bedrooms with colored tiled bath between. Ample closets. Garage in cellar.

FIGURE 7.7 A page from *Mooney's Megaphone* depicting four of the houses Harry Rich Mooney offered for sale in November 1927. *(Photo by author.)*

FIGURE 7.8 The Gainsborough, one of Mooney's houses, in 2011. *(Courtesy of Kira and Brian Nickerson. Photo by author.)*

Also included were floor plans of the house's first and second stories, a photograph of Mooney's nearby Cape Cod-type house, and a view of an enormous crowd milling outside another Home Owners Institute model home. A large crowd also visited Mooney's house on one day (six thousand, if one of Mooney's ads is to be believed), seeking a look at it and the other two dozen completed homes. Mooney summed up the project in a *New York Times* ad during the run of the open house: "Mamaroneck Knolls, the gem of Westchester County, . . . [has twenty-five homes] designed for quaintness in structure, housekeeping simplicity and hominess. Some are little story and a half Cape Cod Cottages of five rooms, bath and garage; others are large Colonial[s] with seven or [in a single case] eight exceptionally large rooms. . . ."[52] The publicity had the desired effect because within a year Mooney had sold nearly all the houses.

Mooney proudly promoted his entire organization, built around the premise that all work was to be done directly, without the use of subcontractors, much of it on site. He owned a mill shop, steam shovels, compressor, pumps, truck, and concrete mixers, retaining on his staff a civil engineer, an architect, a draftsman, an accountant, and a salesman, along with foremen for the various trades.[53] Mooney "autographed" each house with a bronze tablet sporting a logo suggestive of his name—a sliver of a moon embracing a large "E," dating and emblazoning each tablet with the words "Seal of Integrity" and "This home built with the pride of the true craftsman by the organization of Harry Rich Mooney."[54]

Mooney's lifespan put him smack in the middle of the train/trolley-to-automobile transition, and it happens that he survived two dramatic transportation accidents. As a young man accompanying a train car full of boys returning to New York from summer camp in Maine, he lived through one of the deadliest train wrecks in the history of a train line that ran through Mamaroneck—the New York, New Haven & Hartford Railroad. Interviewed at the time and quoted extensively by the *New York Times*, Mooney gave a dramatic, first-hand report of the harrowing 1913 accident near New Haven that left twenty-one dead and fifty injured.[55] Years later, in 1928, Mooney survived a Florida automobile crash in which his wife suffered injuries and his mother-in-law perished.[56]

Business challenges beset him too. A 1925 article in a local newspaper reported on forty Larchmont Knolls property owners indignant over Mooney's failure to complete the installation of sewers and street lights and to pave roads in their development. He further frustrated the residents by being unreachable via telegram at his Florida winter home.[57] Contrary to all the glowing words that characterize his newsletters and advertising, his real estate development business, like his life, was not all smooth sailing.

FIGURE 7.9 Harry Rich Mooney's bronze "Seal of Integrity" appeared somewhere on each of his houses. *(Courtesy of Wendy Satin. Photo by author.)*

THE APARTMENT HOUSE THAT NEVER WAS

Despite the controversy and the challenges, Mooney continued on his real estate roll through the 1920s. By the time of the 1929 stock market crash, in less than three years from the time he purchased the Block estate, Mooney had built and sold thirty-five houses. He managed to sell another four to individual homeowners by the end of 1931, when he sold to a realty company the remaining five empty lots and the two large parcels that he had earmarked for the apartment buildings. With those apartment houses still on the drawing board, Harry Rich Mooney abandoned Mamaroneck Knolls, Inc., selling its assets for just one hundred dollars and the substantial mortgage liens on the property, yet newspaper articles through the 1930s indicate that he stayed in the real estate development business, at least marginally. In late 1938 and early 1939 he lost two sizeable lawsuits against one of his realty companies.[58]

Shortly thereafter, Mooney became president of Trailer Town, a site in the Bronx designated by the city to house five thousand trailers for visitors to the 1939 World's Fair, which would open in April. That project became embroiled in controversy when Robert Moses, New York City's powerful master builder, criticized and then closed the trailer camp on grounds that it might attract Gypsies to the area and would spoil the beauty of the Bronx-Whitestone Bridge, one of his recently completed public works. Citing a need to boost attendance at the fair, the project organizers moved ahead. A proposal from the Bronx borough president for an alternative location found that the Trailer Town operator had never completed the camp to conform to the Building Department's health and sanitary standards,[59] seemingly implicating Mooney as the responsible party. Though his 1957 obituary calls him a retired realty developer, a newspaper article in the mid-1940s describes Mooney as a hearing aids dealer,[60] suggesting that he had suffered a reversal of fortune. Evidently for him, as for most others, real estate development was not a lucrative way to make a living during the 1930s and early 1940s.

The Great Depression definitively ended the housing boom that Mooney had profited from, with residential property construction declining 95 percent between 1928 and 1933.[61] The weak economy and the ensuing war meant the remnants of Mamaroneck Knolls stayed in limbo for over fifteen years. Eventually, the Village of Mamaroneck took over the property following a 1945 tax

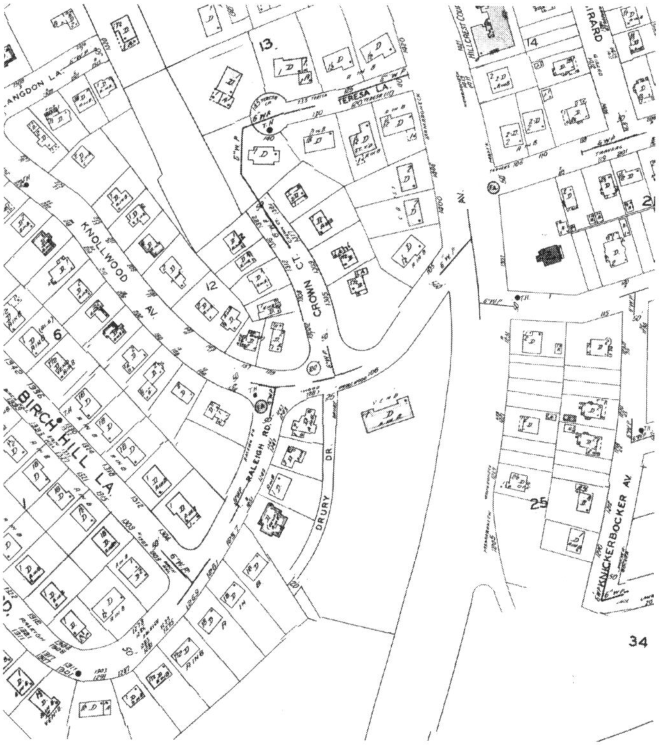

FIGURE 7.10 Sanborn Map of Mamaroneck, New York, 1963. After the real estate development of the 1920s, the greatest changes in the neighborhood took place in the fifteen years following the Second World War. *(Use of 1963 Map of Mamaroneck, NY reprinted / used with permission from The Sanborn Library, LLC.)*

FIGURE 7.11 Sanborn Map of Mamaroneck, New York, 2003. The neighborhood has changed little since the early 1960s. *(Use of 2003 Map of Mamaroneck, NY reprinted / used with permission from The Sanborn Library, LLC.)*

lien foreclosure proceeding for taxes unpaid from 1934 to 1945. Along with a large number of other properties that had suffered the same fate, the village auctioned the land in 1946 to yet another real estate developer, who created seven lots from the parcel that was to have been the site of one of Mooney's apartment buildings. One of the lots went to Mr. and Mrs. T——— who in 1956 moved the *McCall's* "Home of the Month" to where it is today in the neighborhood now known as Harbor Heights rather than as Mooney's Mamaroneck Knolls.[62]

PART III

MYSTERIES OF THE LAND

eight
In New York or In Connecticut?

[It was] one of the most remarkable boundary disputes on record.[1]
—Commissioners Appointed to Ascertain the
Boundary Line Between the States of New-York and
Connecticut, New York State Senate, 1857

One of the most surprising findings in my research was the discovery that my little portion of New York had once been a part of Connecticut, the border of which today is about four miles from my house. Still more surprising was that Caleb Heathcote had a role, albeit a peripheral one, in this odd footnote regarding the property's history. Unlike my house, the land never moved; however, the boundary between New York and Connecticut did—several times. Not only did its location change, placing my property in Connecticut for nineteen years, but both the colonies and the states of Connecticut and New York disputed the boundary's location for two and one-half centuries, from 1632 to 1881, with discussions about the issue reemerging half a dozen times at periodic intervals. The controversy, deemed by commissioners of the New York State Senate "one of the most remarkable boundary disputes on record,"[2] proceeded in fits and starts, partly because the two sides failed to reach agreements, partly because there were more pressing issues to attend to, and partly because, at the time, communication took place at a snail's pace.[3]

THE BOUNDARY

The Hudson River determines the western edge of Westchester County; Long Island Sound and New York City mark its southern boundary. New York colonial leaders divided the colony into counties in 1683 and thereby established the northern boundary

Libraries

Libraries are the backbone of most any broad-based research project. First and foremost is often the one nearest you—your local library. Researching a specific piece of property makes your realm of needed information automatically of concern to nearby libraries. They therefore often have focused, specialized information not found anywhere else. And if the focus is history, certain older materials will be on paper only in a library and not on the Web.

To use a library effectively, start by gathering your facts. Then formulate the question you seek to answer. Then set limits for yourself. Do you need a simple definition, more than a one-sentence answer, a few paragraphs, or everything ever written on the subject? Knowing this information will help you and any librarian helping you to plan your research strategy. From any given source, there are ways to cast your research net more widely. When you find a helpful book, check its bibliography for more sources. Read footnotes carefully; they can lead you to much useful information. Once you locate a pertinent book, browse the library shelves around it to see what else on the topic is there.

Putting your questions into a context is important. General background reading of materials I found in libraries helped me create a framework for understanding many topics: the history of magazines, Eastern Woodland Indian customs and attitudes, slavery, the American Revolution, domestic architecture, suburban growth, the development of the highway systems in metropolitan New York, and more. Regional histories are good sources but sometimes have not been written by professional historians. They therefore need to have their facts checked.

Libraries are all different, but they share some features. One is the reference librarian who can be a goldmine—helping people find information is why he or she is there. Do not hesitate to ask. And ask more than one librarian the same question because you will often get different answers about where to look for information. I once asked the same question of four different reference librarians in the same library over the course of an afternoon (in big libraries, they rotate, taking turns at the reference desk). I got four different responses, pointers on places to look, all useful. You will find, too, that repeated asking enables you to hone your question to better communicate what you are looking for. Reference librarians will not necessarily give you answers to your questions, but they will offer ideas on where to find answers.

Another common feature is the library catalogue, most of them generally now computerized. Using online catalogues from home saves an enormous amount of time. Once you have the call number, you can make the most efficient use of your time during a visit to a library. Be sure to ask whether you can renew borrowed material via the Internet. That will save travel time and fuel. Rarely is one library going to have everything you will want to see. Many libraries offer interlibrary loan services to get material from other libraries. Some are networked into a consortium with like institutions, which share their catalogues and collections on a regular basis and deliver what you need to your library of choice.

Libraries, large and small, often maintain old-fashioned clipping or ephemera files, which are full of materials that are considered not worthy of cataloguing and are not currently in digital form but are nonetheless of value to someone. Those files might have just what you are looking for. I have found this to be the case both in huge operations like the New York Public Library and in a local historical society's library. Such resources are usually not on display, nor are they publicized, so you have to ask about them.

The digital age has naturally brought huge changes to libraries. A library often licenses a selection of databases. Ask what they have that you can use free of charge, either from your home computer or from computers at their facility. And ask the reference librarian which databases are your best bet for finding what you want. Remember though, not everything is digital. Even periodicals now found in electronic form in databases or on the Web sometimes have digitized issues going back only a decade or so. To see older issues, you may have to use the library's bound volumes or microforms. This is continually changing, of course. I recently learned that my local library's collection of back issues of a certain local newspaper was no longer on the shelves where I had always found it for browsing. It had just been sent out for digital scanning. When it comes back in electronic form, accessible on a computer in the library, it will be full-text searchable with keywords, thankfully putting an end to my tedious page-flipping.

As the president of the New York Public Library has said, even in the digital age, the library's "fundamental responsibility" remains the same—"to acquire materials, keep them and let people look at them."[1] Libraries are the place for books and more, and it is in libraries that you can find the history, the stories that will give flesh to the bones of the facts you find. And best of all, generally speaking, using a library to access reference material and to borrow books is free.

with no ensuing controversy. Only the eastern border has a convoluted history. The origin of its dispute stemmed from the colonial charters granted respectively by the Dutch and the English governments in the 1600s.

In 1614 the Dutch States-General granted a monopoly to a trading company for the territory between the fortieth and forty-fifth parallels of latitude, or roughly from Philadelphia to the New Hampshire/Canada border. Within a few years Dutch settlers had established a trading post on the Connecticut River in addition to one at New Amsterdam, today's Manhattan. Then in 1620 King James I of England chartered to the Plymouth Company a territory between the thirty-fourth and forty-eighth parallels, from South Carolina to the northern tip of Maine, completely encompassing the Dutch claim. English immigrants soon settled Connecticut, pushing westward into Dutch territory, particularly after 1630, setting the stage for a fight.

Complaints aired on both sides of the Atlantic, with territorial claims and counter-claims bouncing back and forth, a confrontation finally erupting in 1632 when the English seized a beaver pelt-laden Dutch ship that had been forced by weather conditions into their port at Plymouth, England, the first in a series of flare-ups over the issue. As their rationale for the seizure, the English maintained that the Dutch had conducted trade activities in North American territory belonging to Great Britain.[4] The Dutch government denied any wrongdoing and, in response to this affront, articulated the details of the conflicting territorial claims, insisting on its right to the land between the thirty-ninth and forty-first parallels, from the Chesapeake Bay to Long Island Sound. King Charles I, on the other hand, asserted that "the right his Majesty's subjects have in that country, is justified by first discovery, occupation and the possession which they have taken thereof, and by the concessions and letters patents they have had from our Sovereigns, who were, for the above reasons, the true and legitimate proprietors thereof in those parts. . . ."[5]

The situation remained a standoff even after the English released the Dutch ship.

THE CONFLICT CONTINUES

The next round of negotiations resulted in an agreed-upon, though short-lived, boundary. The New Netherland governors had continued their claims to the territory of the four English colonies of New England—Massachusetts, Plymouth, Connecticut, and New Haven—in the face of the tide of English settlement, which was growing much more rapidly than that of the Dutch. In 1647 Governor Stuyvesant of New Netherland seized on an opportunity to force the issue of the boundary back into the forefront. After deciding that the *St. Beninio*, a Dutch trading vessel anchored at New Haven, had been involved in smuggling, a violation of the Dutch West India Company charter, he sent another ship—one that he had just sold to the English—into the New Haven harbor under the guise of delivering it to them. Unbeknownst to the English, he had crammed his ship with Dutch soldiers who, upon entering the harbor, leapt aboard the *St. Beninio*, seized it, and took it back to New Amsterdam. The English governor of New Haven, incensed that his territory had been invaded, voiced his objection. Stuyvesant's nominal justification for the action was to make an example of the ship, which was in violation of Dutch laws in territory claimed by the Dutch. His real motivation, however, was to resurrect the Dutch claim to the territory and force the governors of the English colonies to negotiate with him on its boundary.[6] Meeting with representatives of the four colonies of the New England Confederation in Hartford in September 1650, Stuyvesant managed to gain an agreement on a boundary that went due north from Greenwich, Connecticut, a division that put the territory east of Greenwich in English hands, the rest under Dutch control. The line held only as long as the Dutch colony of New Netherland lasted, another fourteen years.[7]

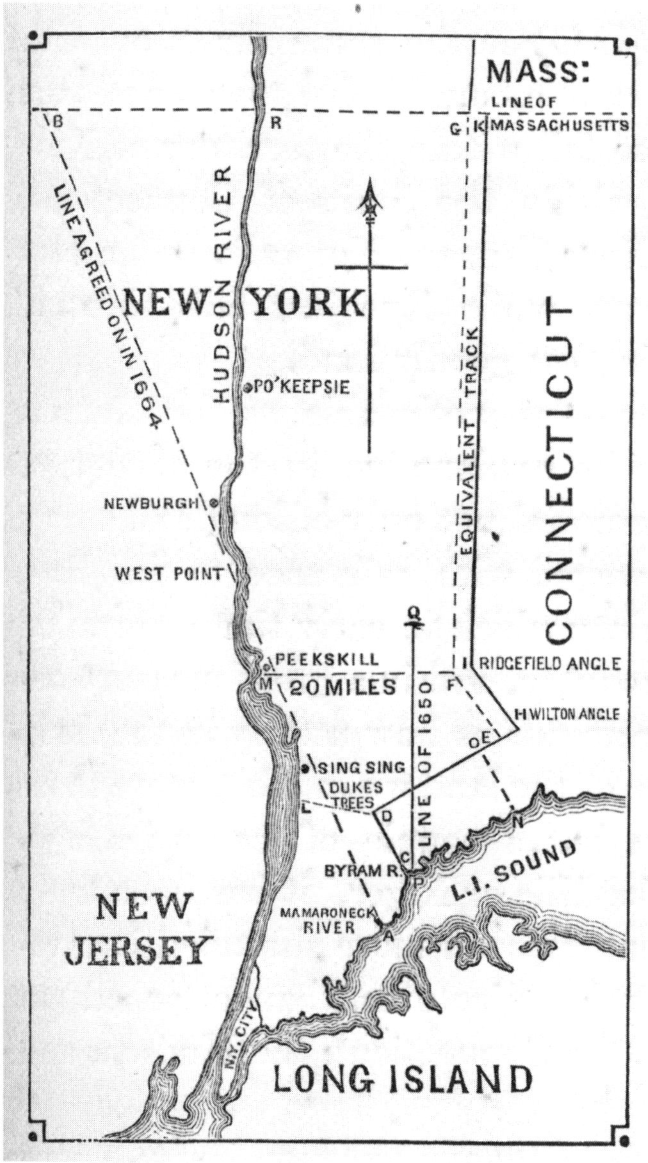

FIGURE 8.1 Map graphically summarizes the 250-year boundary dispute between Connecticut and New York. *(Reprinted from Baird,* Chronicle of a Border Town, *1871, p. 105. Photo by author.)*

Round three developed out of two conflicting decisions made by King Charles II. Responding to Connecticut Governor Winthrop's 1662 petition for a colonial charter, the king granted him not only Connecticut, but also a territory that extended west as far as the Pacific and south to Virginia. The enormous tract also encompassed New Netherland. But then in a contradictory maneuver less than two years later, the king granted a vast tract of the North American continent—from the Delaware Bay to Cape Cod—to his brother, James, the Duke of York. So, in effect, in less than two years the king granted the Dutch colony of New Netherland to his own colony, Connecticut, and made most of Connecticut part of a new claim, which was soon to become New York. The king's apparent confusion was no accident. He and his advisors had identified Manhattan as the strategic geographic key to the American colonies and, in planning for their future expansion, decided they did not trust the New England colonial leadership to manage the task. Hence, they sought to correct their mistake by putting New Netherland into the hands of the king's closest associates. Six months later, England took possession of New Netherland without bloodshed and renamed it New York.[8]

At this point, driven by fears that their border had been disregarded by the king's actions, the residents of Connecticut sent delegates to the newly installed Governor Nicolls of New York to press for a resolution to the boundary dispute. The 1664 discussions resulted in a new understanding that the line between the two English colonies should run parallel to the Hudson River twenty miles to the east.[9] The New York governor, however, followed up with a statement, signed and endorsed by representatives from Connecticut, ordering and declaring "that the Creeke or River called Momoronock, . . . and a Line drawne from the East point or side, where the ffresh water falls into the Salt, at high water Marke, North North West to the Line of the Massachusetts, be the westerne bounds, of the said Colony of Conecticutt . . ."[10] Where the "North North West line" came from is unknown, but the New York governor apparently thought this new boundary line was parallel to the Hudson River. Adding to the confusion was the fact that Mamaroneck is only about nine miles east of the Hudson, not twenty. It seems the King's commissioners believed they were agreeing to a line twenty miles from and parallel to the Hudson, whereas in the document they signed, the border, drawn in a north northwest direction, actually crossed the Hudson below West Point, giving Connecticut a large chunk of new territory.[11] So with this strange move, seemingly the consequence of either the geographic ignorance of the time or strategic manipulation on the part of the Connecticut authorities (who were negotiating with relative newcomers, the King's commissioners representing New York), my property was suddenly a part of Connecticut.

The Mamaroneck locals, however, disregarded the north northwest direction of the official line and used the more logical and expected geographic marker of the Mamaroneck River's northward path. For example, John Richbell's 1668 patent from the king reads, "a Certain parcell or tract of Land within this Government upon the Main Contained in three Necks of which the Eastermost is bounded with a Small river commonly Called Mamaroneck river being also the East bounds or limits of this Government upon the Maine. . . ."[12] The key words here are "within this Government" and "being also the East bounds or limits of this Government," a choice indicating that the British government still considered the Richbell property to be in New York and the Mamaroneck River to be the colony's boundary, the north northwest line to Massachusetts notwithstanding.

STILL IN LIMBO

By 1683 it had become apparent that there was a problem with the newest boundary, so the colonies once again began negotiations to clarify the confusion. This time the negotiators drew a new line beginning slightly closer to the agreed-upon twenty miles from the Hudson at the mouth of the Byram River, but then, because Connecticut objected to the loss of certain strategically located towns, the negotiators made an accommodation, resulting in today's zigzag line of the southern part of the state's western border. To compensate, Connecticut gave New York a long, narrow strip of land along its western border from Greenwich to Massachusetts.[13] The new boundary line, running northward from the mouth of the Byram River, placed my property back into New York.

Neither side ever legally set the 1683 boundary, however, so it remained indeterminate until 1718, when both governments appointed a group of commissioners, among them Caleb Heathcote, to negotiate yet another line. Their meeting in Rye failed to reach an agreement, the whole issue dragging on way past Heathcote's death four years later. In 1731, with a survey complete, both sides finally ratified the newest boundary.[14]

FINALLY A RESOLUTION

But that, believe it or not, was not the end of the story. In 1855 Connecticut concluded that the 1731 survey was no longer valid. Why? Because the markers used in the survey description, typical of the time, included items like a "heap of stone" and "marked trees."[15] Such transient markers had long since disappeared in the intervening 124 years, and thus there was great uncertainty as to the actual boundary line. As a result, people had been taking advantage of the situation by not voting in, and not paying taxes to, either state. To remedy the situation, the two state governments hired an engineer to conduct a new survey along the old 1731 boundary. Concluded in 1860, the survey produced a somewhat irregular, point-to-point line, which still failed to settle the issue. The controversy persisted with Connecticut arguing for a geometrically straight line and New York pressing for the irregular 1860 survey line. Finally, in the late 1870s the two states reached an agreement. In exchange for the twenty-six hundred acres Connecticut had to relinquish due to the acceptance of the 1860 survey line, the representatives of each side authorized Connecticut to extend her southern boundary further into Long Island Sound. Both state legislatures ratified the agreement, and the U.S. Congress confirmed it during its 1880–81 session, at long last putting to an end the 250-year controversy.[16]

The significance of this bizarre, episodic, and protracted affair lies in what it tells us about how persistent people can be when it comes to land claims. The tenacity brought, for as many as ten generations, to defending this territory and delineating its boundaries is astounding given the absence of any significant cultural differences, serious conflict, or real animosity between the two sides. It is an indication of the role the concept of land ownership plays in our society. Yet how people use the land also tells us much about our attitudes toward it. For example, unlike the other people discussed here, noted photographer Edward Steichen made aesthetic use of the land in his work. A brief examination of one famous photograph he took while in Mamaroneck provides a respite from talk of boundaries, deeds, and property as a source of revenue, as an asset, as an investment, or as a status symbol, taking us, perhaps, from the ridiculous to the sublime.

nine

Moon Over Mamaroneck: When and Where

> Because I found nature most beautiful in twilight and moonlight, all my efforts were directed toward finding a way of interpreting such moments.[1]
>
> —Edward Steichen, 1963

Sometime after my move to Mamaroneck, someone mentioned to me that Edward Steichen (1879–1973) had taken his well-known 1904 photograph (variously titled in its three existing prints as *Moonrise—Mamaroneck, New York*; *The Pond—Moonrise*; and *The Pond—Moonlight*),[2] not far from my property, at Gedney Pond, a part of the original Gedney family farm. The comment stayed with me. The photograph, in Steichen's own words, captures the "haunting, elusive quality of twilight,"[3] that liminal instant when the full moon first peeks above the horizon line, the moment of transition from day to night, a moment that can be regularly experienced by people in any time and in any place. The water's reflection of the centralized moon shining through the trees creates symmetry both horizontally and vertically and forms two triangles, one atop the other. Although on a literal level, the photograph depicts trees in the distance reflected in a foreground body of water at the time of the full moon rising, it is in many ways also an abstract composition with broad and enduring appeal. The image is arresting and might be described by many as mysterious and sublime. When in 2006 one of the three prints of the photograph sold at auction for a record-breaking price, it caught my attention as well as that of the press and many people in the art world.

The day of the sale, the Associated Press issued a wire story that Steichen's "photograph of a pond" had sold for more than $2.9 million, "easily setting a world record for the highest amount a photograph has sold for at auction." The story went on to say that "the photograph, titled 'The Pond—Moonlight' and taken on Long Island in 1904," broke the previous record set the year before by over $1.6 million.[4] The location mentioned, of course, did not square with what I had been told, but more about that later. Two days after the news broke, the *New York Times* ran an article titled "A Big Sale Spurs Talk of a Photography Gold Rush" and quoted an art dealer: "'It's all anybody in photography

FIGURE 9.1 Edward Steichen (1879–1973). *The Pond—Moonrise*, 1904. Platinum print with applied color, 15⅝ x 19 in., The Metropolitan Museum of Art, New York, NY, U.S.A. Alfred Stieglitz Collection, 1933 (33.43.40). *(Permission of the Estate of Edward Steichen. Image copyright © The Metropolitan Museum of Art / Art Resource, NY.)*

is talking about.'" In light of its original sale price of $75 in 1906, the equivalent of roughly $1,700 today, the reporter cited two factors, in addition to the quality of the image, contributing to its remarkably high selling price in 2006: one, its rarity—the only other two prints of it are in the collections of the Museum of Modern Art and the Metropolitan Museum of Art; two, the growing appreciation for handwork in today's digital photography world—Steichen's methods in this work were complex, labor intensive, and involved a painter's touch.[5]

What is striking, however, in addition to the exceptionally high price the photograph commanded, is the concern displayed in the press for just where Steichen took it. The AP issued a correction the day of its original story, stating that, instead of on Long Island, the photograph actually had been taken in Mamaroneck. Reporters for the *Journal News*, a Westchester County newspaper, picked up the mistake, and one of them took it a step further by contacting the Mamaroneck Village historian, who remarked she was convinced the pond in the photograph was Gedney Pond. Then, the next day, perhaps influenced by the words in the auction house's sale catalogue, "made in the wetlands around Mamaroneck," which the reporter probably brought to her attention, the village historian recanted, saying she now believed the photograph had been taken in a different part of the village near Long Island Sound.[6] I wanted to know exactly where in Mamaroneck it had been taken and what was at the root of the location equivocation.

FROM MILWAUKEE TO MAMARONECK—STEICHEN'S CAREER

Edward Steichen wrote in his 1963 autobiography that he acquired his first camera at the age of sixteen in 1895. A short time later, while enrolled in a four-year apprenticeship at a Milwaukee lithographic firm, he suggested to his boss that, instead of copying woodcut images from old German books to illustrate the firm's advertising posters for breweries, flour mills, and pork-packing plants, they use photographs, which he would take. The firm agreed to give him the time off to take the pictures if he bought the appropriate camera, which he did, with help from his mother. His excursions into the country during the summer resulted in photographs of hop vines, wheat fields, and pigs, which he taught himself to print in a darkroom he had constructed at home in the cellar. From these commercial photographs developed his interest in subjects of more a personal and aesthetic nature.

Steichen was also painting in his spare time and, looking back on his youth, he noted years later, "The romantic and mysterious quality of moonlight, the lyric aspect of nature made the strongest appeal to me. Most of the paintings—watercolors—that I did at that time were of moonlight subjects."[7] Although at this point in his career he occasionally made portraits, it was mainly landscapes—especially the woods at dusk—that interested him as subjects for both his painting and his photography. He wrote in regard to his early photographs:

> Because I found nature most beautiful in twilight and moonlight, all my efforts were directed toward finding a way of interpreting such moments. By taking a streetcar out to the end of the line and walking a short distance, I could find a few wood lots. These became my stamping grounds, especially during the autumn, winter, and early spring. They were particularly appealing . . . at twilight. Under those conditions the woods had moods, and the moods aroused emotional reactions that I tried to render in photographs. . . . The haunting, elusive quality of twilight excited in me an emotion that I felt compelled to evoke in the images I was making.[8]

In the late 1890s, Steichen formed a young artists' group, later the Art Students League of Milwaukee. When a review of the Pennsylvania Academy of Fine Arts' Philadelphia Photographic Salon, the first such museum exhibition to be held in America, appeared in the November 5, 1898 *Harper's Weekly*,[9] it so impressed Steichen that he read it before his fellow artists, whereupon someone suggested he send his photographs to the next exhibition. He made up his mind then and there that he would. The following year, when the academy announced its second salon, Steichen submitted two of his photographs. The jury accepted them both.[10]

After having work accepted into yet another photographic salon, this time in Chicago, Steichen made plans to travel to Europe. In the spring of 1900, barely twenty-two, he left Milwaukee for New York en route to Paris. While in New York City, he stopped at the Camera Club to see Alfred Stieglitz, the noted photographer and modern art promoter, who received him warmly with encouraging words. Before their brief meeting ended, Stieglitz had bought three of the photographs in Steichen's portfolio, two of them landscapes taken in the woodlands on the outskirts of Milwaukee.[11] In a review published that summer, a critic commented on the young photographer's work in the Chicago Salon: "There is special attraction in the remarkable advance made by . . . [Edward Steichen]. Here is a worker with a soul full of feeling, a thoughtful mind, and skilled hand. His future is sure to be most interesting."[12]

Steichen's time abroad was fruitful. By 1902, he had exhibited widely throughout Europe, as well as in New York. While living abroad, he had his photographs reproduced and his review of two London exhibitions published in *Camera Notes*, Stieglitz's quarterly photography journal.[13] In the July 1902 issue, a critic commented that over a year before, the journal had decided to devote an entire issue to Steichen's work, though circumstances with the publication had prevented it from happening.[14] The young artist was off to a very good start at a time when photography was just beginning to become a self-consciously artistic endeavor.

The year following his return to the United States, Steichen married Clara E. Smith, a young American singer he had met in Paris. After a difficult childbirth with their firstborn in July 1904, the couple sought a respite from their stifling New York City apartment and accepted the invitation of Charles H. Caffin and his wife to spend time in their Mamaroneck home.[15] Caffin, the author of the *Harper's Weekly* article that had so influenced Steichen six years earlier, had by this time published *Photography as a Fine Art,* in which he argued that photography should be lifted to the level of one of the fine arts. Devoting a chapter to landscape as a subject for photography, to illustrate his views he used six works by the then twenty-one-year-old Steichen, whom he described as "to the marrow an artist."[16] Steichen's relationship with Caffin continued, and the young artist took advantage of the woodlands near Caffin's Mamaroneck house to do more of the work he had started in Milwaukee. It was during a visit to Mamaroneck that Steichen took his now famous photograph, *The Pond—Moonlight.*

By 1902 Steichen had joined Stieglitz's Camera Club, where he had access to a state-of-the-art darkroom. Remarking on the technical difficulty and the painstaking nature of his work in a letter to Stieglitz, he offered a cursory description of a labor-intensive process,[17] similar to the one he used for the Mamaroneck image. Working in the studio, his initial preparatory step was to create an enlarged (16- x 19-inch) negative, the approximate size of his final prints. From this "internegative" he made platinum prints (black and white) on which he worked in gum bichromate, a process that offers great fluidity and flexibility and results in a painterly and sometimes gestural expression. After coating the platinum print surface with an ultraviolet light-sensitive emulsion and a pigment, he re-exposed it to

Archives

An archive or archives (the latter is used for both the singular and the plural) is a collection of historical records, usually primary sources; it is also a place where such a collection is housed. Archival materials can also be housed in a library and, in that case, are often referred to as special collections. Normally archival records are unique, have not been published, and may include a wide variety of items—letters, journals, scrapbooks, manuscripts, photographs, maps, objects, audio/video and digital tapes, and more. The purpose of an archives is preservation. I once heard someone say in reference to the preservation of wildlife species that such an endeavor can hold answers to questions we have not yet learned how to ask, a comment also applicable to the preservation of historical records and documents.

Archives vary from the most highly professionalized to ones run by volunteers. The former is likely to have fully developed and detailed finding aids, whereas the latter can be merely boxes full of old papers, perhaps organized somehow and perhaps not. I have encountered a volunteer-run local archives where access is restricted to the point that no one but the volunteer archivist is allowed in and that person will look for things for you. In using that resource, I just had to ask repeated questions and hope for the best.

In order to find what you are looking for in an archives, you use a finding aid or an inventory, assuming that one has been created. A tool to help you determine whether the archival holdings are relevant to your research, a finding aid might be simply a kind of rudimentary list of what is in each box, or it might be a highly detailed, digitized, and thus searchable, database. Do your homework ahead of time. Find out if the finding aid for your archives is available online. If so, you can know a lot about what you are looking for before you get there. It saves time, and the archivist will probably be more inclined to help you if you have honed your goals and questions ahead of time. Call or write to make sure the specific material you want to see is available. Occasionally, materials are in some state of transition and are temporarily unavailable.

Because the purpose of archives is to preserve documents and records, they will have stringent regulations governing the use of materials. Do not be put off by them, but rather appreciate them, for without those rules, the material might no longer exist and you would not be able to do the research you want to do. Many archives have limited hours. Some you can simply walk into, others require preregistration or confirmed appointments. To give you an idea of what might await you at an archives or in the special collections division of a library, here is the story of my visit to one of the nine I used in my research for this book.

I made my appointment and had it confirmed by e-mail. After arriving at the address I had been given, a receptionist had me sign in and then made a call to my final destination to be sure the staff there was expecting me. She then asked a security guard to escort me to an elevator requiring a swipe of an electronic card. As I exited the elevator, another receptionist instructed me to leave all my belongings—jacket, purse, bag, books, water bottle—in a closet where she would watch them for me and to take with me only papers, pencil, and a laptop. Another person then led me into the reading room and asked me to wash and thoroughly dry my hands and to remove my rings. Next she asked me to fill out a form with information such as name, address, and phone numbers.

Since the staff knew I was coming, they had pulled out the material I had asked for. Never for even an instant was I left alone. When I had questions the assistant could not answer, she asked someone with more knowledge to come out from the inner offices for me to speak to. At one point, as I chatted with the archivist, she suddenly reached for a piece of acid-free tissue paper and used it to cover the item, explaining that she was worried about spit. "Oh dear, was I spitting?" I asked. No, I was not spitting, it was just a precaution they routinely take to protect the delicate surface of the historic material. It was also made clear that I was not to touch any of the materials but rather to ask one of the staff to lift, turn, or otherwise make them accessible.

Other things you might encounter in using an archives or a rare-book collection: The staff might ask you for one or two photo IDs, which they will hold until you sign out at the end of your visit. You might be asked to stow your belongings in a locker. Sometimes cameras and tripods are allowed, though flashes are not, as intense light can damage paper. Some archives allow traditional wooden pencils only—no mechanical pencils because pieces of lead can slip out and go unnoticed on the table, where they then might mar a document. Sometimes only the paper they supply is allowed—in one case, the paper was yellow to distinguish it from the archival papers. You undoubtedly will be instructed not to use Post-its as bookmarks because they leave a residue on paper surfaces. Bound books may need to be supported on a table with special wedge-shaped devices. And, depending on the materials being examined, only those wearing white cotton gloves are allowed to touch them.

At the other end of the spectrum, in a less professional town archives where the material was stored in a locked room in a local library and no one was to be granted access, I befriended the librarian, who one day sneaked into the archives storage room to retrieve something I wanted to look at. While this tactic is not recommended, sometimes a researcher can get desperate.

Finally, an excellent guide to using archives, "Using Manuscripts & Archives: A Tutorial," may be found at the Yale University website http://www.library.yale.edu.

sunlight through the negative to harden parts of the emulsion. When the paper was dry, he submerged it in a water bath to soak and rinse away the less hard, less exposed areas for varying amounts of time to alter the contrast and to achieve a range of effects. He might have brushed, sponged, or scraped the print to otherwise enhance it. The results were subtly pigmented images, enlarged and transformed from the original negatives, produced some three years before the advent of color photography.

Steichen had joined forces with Stieglitz and others soon after his 1902 return from Europe to found the New York-based Photo-Secession, a group of photographers who broke from established photographic customs and traditions and worked to establish photography as a fine art. Three years later Stieglitz founded his gallery (known as 291 for its address at 291 Fifth Avenue in New York City), where the Photo-Secessionists showed their work. Steichen's photographs from the turn of the century and the early 291 years, including *The Pond—Moonlight*, were part of art photography's pictorialist movement, characterized by softly focused images, painterly qualities, and the mark of the artist's hand.

Steichen's later photographic career moved in other directions. He became a noted military photographer, designing strategy for aerial reconnaissance in the photographic division of the American Expeditionary Force in World War I and documenting World War II as the director of the U.S. Navy Photographic Institute.[18] His work as a highly paid commercial fashion photographer for *Vogue* and *Vanity Fair* in the 1920s and 1930s earned him recognition, as did his position as director of the Museum of Modern Art photography department from 1946 to 1962. There in 1955 he assembled the celebrated exhibition and publication *The Family of Man*, featuring the work of twentieth-century photographers from around the globe.

CORRECTIONS FOR THE RECORD

After initial reports of the newsworthy 2006 sale, the press coverage continued. The *New York Times* printed in its "Corrections: For the Record" section its own adjustment to the story: "An article by The Associated Press on Wednesday about the record-setting $2.9 million sale of a 1904 photograph by Edward Steichen, 'The Pond—Moonlight,' at a Sotheby's auction misstated the location of the pond. It was in Mamaroneck, in Westchester County, not on Long Island."[19] Even with the error duly noted, the *New York Times*, like the *Journal News*, seemed not satisfied with the precision of the reported location. The *Times* ran a story the following week with a teaser on the section's front page: "Steichen's pricey pond. Exactly where was this photo taken?" The *Times* reporter covering the story also had contacted the Mamaroneck village historian. What she told him became the basis for his article, which was full of troubling inconsistencies and faulty assumptions.

First, the village historian told the reporter that although it had often been said that Steichen took the photograph at Gedney Pond, she believed he would not have gone to such trouble as to trudge into the woods one mile away from where she believed he stayed during his visits, but rather would have merely "'wandered down toward the sand'" of the Long Island Sound shore near what is today a golf course, a "'short distance'" away.[20] The comment suggests the notion of working spontaneously with a point-and-shoot camera, rather than with the boxy camera and bulky tripod that Steichen undoubtedly used. What is most peculiar about the historian's assertion is that Gedney Pond is actually slightly closer to where she thought Steichen was staying with Caffin in a rented house than is the golf course, her purported site of the photograph's image. Knowing what I did about Steichen's inclination to photograph in the woods and to travel some distance (to the end of the streetcar line) to do so, it seemed to me not so unlikely he would have traveled the one mile to get to Gedney Pond. I remembered the words from his autobiography, "wood lots . . . became my stamping grounds, especially during the autumn, winter, and early spring. They were particularly appealing . . . at twilight."[21] Steichen is also known to have set up his camera to photograph a single outdoor motif all night long.[22] All in all, he was hardly a man to limit his photographic ventures to places he could simply wander to a short distance away.

There were other problems with the village historian's assertions. She seemed unaware that Caffin, Steichen's host the summer of 1904, had purchased a twelve-room house in Mamaroneck in 1901 and that Steichen had likely stayed there,[23] rather than at the rented house close to today's golf course where Caffin had previously stayed. And although the title of the photograph in question is *Moonlight*, the titles of the two other existing prints of it contain the word *Moonrise*, including the one given to the Museum of Modern Art by the artist. The historian, on the other hand, found "trees facing the direction in which the moon sets in the west"[24] to be the likely motif in the photograph. But, of course, if the image is of a moonrise, Steichen would have had to be facing east, where the full moon rises, when he took the photograph.

The author of the *Times* article does admit that all the evidence he presented is less than overwhelming. Given Steichen's inconsistent record-keeping and the possibility that in the one hundred intervening years the landscape had been altered, he concluded we may never know where the photograph was taken, but I believed the information put forth was more than inconclusive. It was misleading and deserved yet another correction. So I composed a letter to the editor, which the *New York Times* published, much to my delight. My hope that the letter might provoke further discussion among Steichen scholars or other people in the community, however, did not materialize. I decided, nonetheless, not only to continue researching Steichen's work to find facts about the photograph, but also to make observations of the topography, the vegetation, and the moon risings at Gedney Pond in an effort to develop my case that Steichen took the photograph there. Why? Just for the fun of it.

FOREST FORAYS

My first trip into the woods, accompanied by my husband, focused on simply finding a way to get to Gedney Pond, a narrow body of water about the width of a football field and half again as long. It was on maps and easily visible on Google Earth in a low-lying area on the edge of a wooded county park near our house. And we could catch a fleeting glimpse of it down below us as we drove along an interstate entrance ramp. But access to it from that direction was unsafe. The only other short-distance way to it involved going down someone's driveway and across their front yard, which abutted the pond. The property had a

LETTERS TO THE EDITOR

A Familiar Photo, Reconsidered

To the Editor:

"Hey Mamaroneck, Recognize This Pond?" (Feb. 26), proposes, with input from a local historian, that Edward Steichen may have taken his now-famous photograph, "The Pond — Moonlight," at what is today the Hampshire Country Club golf course, conveniently close to where the photographer was supposedly staying during the summer of 1904. Steichen's host, the art critic Charles H. Caffin, according to The New York Times (April 14, 1901), had purchased a 12-room house at Orienta Point in 1901. It is more likely Steichen stayed there and not at the rented house on Prospect Avenue.

Regardless of where Steichen resided that summer, proximity is not a convincing argument for a photographer's choice of motif. Photographers of the era toted their large-format cameras considerable distances, and Steichen's host easily could have provided him with transportation.

The photo may be of a full moon rising, rather than setting. If so, Steichen's camera would have to have been facing east. Based on visual evidence, including the rock formations in the image, a feature that would change little in a hundred years, an eastward view across Gedney Pond is a plausible site for "The Pond — Moonlight."

ELEANOR PHILLIPS BRACKBILL
Mamaroneck

The writer is an art historian.

FIGURE 9.2 Author's letter to the editor of the *New York Times*. *(Photo by author.)*

"no trespassing" sign at the entrance to the driveway, along with stone pillars and a chain, although the latter lay on the ground. Aside from the sign, the chain, and a string of large Tibetan prayer flags flying in the front yard, it was a typical suburban contemporary with walls of glass. We tried a direct approach on several occasions during the day, seeking permission to gain access to the pond, by knocking on the door, an approach that yielded no response, so we decided to try reaching the pond from a public parking area on the far side of the park about one-half mile away.

The pond was more difficult to find by hiking through the woods than we had anticipated. On a frigid, sunny day in January, armed with compass, map, camera, and boots, my husband, daughter, and I hiked until we found it. We were able to scope it out, noting that the terrain is rocky and uneven, trees surround the pond, and to the east, just beyond the pond, the earth rises gently. But it was daytime. We needed to return at moonrise on the evening of a full moon. Getting there at dusk would be bad enough; finding our way out of the woods in the dark of night, even under a full moon, would be another matter, so we decided to seek permission to use the driveway/yard approach again, our only reasonable option. Not wanting to risk coming unannounced the night of the full moon and find no one at home, only to have a neighbor call the police, we made a daytime visit, knocking on the door once again.

A carefully assembled notebook containing moon chart, photographs, copies of the newspaper articles, and my letter to the editor in hand to lend legitimacy to our request, we once again sought the okay to walk across the yard to avoid the very long and dark trek through the woods. The woman who came to the door this time had no interest whatsoever in my handsome notebook, and her frustration with recurrent trespassers was evident. I tried to explain our mission and took pains to make clear that we would stay at a distance from her house, be very quiet, and not disturb any of her landscaping. Annoyed and befuddled by our unusual request, she impatiently waved us on, indicating we had her permission to walk across her property as long as we parked in a designated spot—even if we returned each month. We made plans to return at the next full moon.

With our own near-trespassing experience in mind, I wondered, if Steichen did go to Gedney Pond to shoot his photograph, whose property was he entering and was he trespassing? At the time, it was not parkland, as some scholars have suggested, but rather privately owned property, a former estate and horse farm slated for development, which never took place. It remained in limbo until 1927, when it became a part of Saxon Woods Park, owned and managed by Westchester County.[25] Gedney Pond, then, at the time of Steichen's photograph, was situated on the edge of an unoccupied estate. Steichen, in turn, may or may not have gained permission to photograph there.

As an aside, it is worth noting that Louis Block, along with a dozen other owners whose property abutted Saxon Woods, had been asked to sell a small section of his land to help complete the park. In the end, because Block had died and the property had been sold, it was developer Harry Rich Mooney who turned the transaction into a marketing opportunity—never mind that it was probably an eminent domain situation in which he had no choice. His newsletter proudly informed readers that one of his first acts as the new owner of the property "was to deed part of it [a triangular sliver of less than one-third acre, ill-suited to building on] to the Park Commission, at a nominal price, thereby showing his fine spirit toward the County as well as securing for his development, or MAMARONECK KNOLLS, as it is called, an immediate link of the parkway system."[26]

We made our initial evening visit the next time the full moon promised to rise into a clear eastern sky, only to be accosted by an angry husband. After a full explanation and reference to his wife's earlier permission, he, too, kindly gave us his blessing to continue our quest. That evening was just the first of many excursions to the pond over the course of a couple of years. Since the moon rises at a different place along the eastern horizon each month of the year, from northeast at the winter solstice to southeast at the summer solstice and back again, it meant making multiple trips to try to see the moon in just the right spot. Going into the woods month after month—L.L. Bean headlamps in place, flashlights and camera in hand, and pants tucked into tick-repellant-sprayed socks—became an anticipated outing, scotched only when the eastern sky was overcast.

I knew the approximate dates of Steichen's stay in Mamaroneck during the summer of 1904, bracketed as it was by the July 1 birth of his daughter, his wife's three-week postpartum bed rest in New York City, and the family's visit to Lake George in October.[27] Some scholars imply that Steichen took the photograph during that stay; however, my visits to the pond caused me to think otherwise. I was reminded that in southern New York, late summer and early fall guarantee a thick blanket of weeds and undergrowth around any pond in a wooded area and probably water lilies floating on the water's surface. In addition, I observed that when the trees around Gedney Pond are in full leaf, they create a dense screen behind the pond, making the moon impossible to see as it clears the eastern horizon. So the photograph had to have been taken when the vegetation was gone—winter or early spring. Careful examination of the photograph reinforces this supposition. In the foreground, where the reflectivity of the water's surface is absent, it appears that a swath of ice is receding, and near the far edge of the pond are white patches that look like remnants of snow. The dark, reedlike forms barely visible in the foreground may be the result of some kind of handwork on the negative or on the final prints, but they are more likely the spiky remains of water lilies in their dormant state, visible on the pond's surface in winter. No other vegetation is evident around the edges of the pond.

Assume Nothing

Sometimes bits of information can be misleading and threaten to send a researcher down the wrong path. Here is one example of what I mean. I was attempting to find who in the early 1900s owned the piece of land where Gedney Pond is located so that I could draw conclusions about whose property Edward Steichen might have been on when he took his famous photograph of what I believe to be Gedney Pond. At the same time, I questioned an art historian's published statement that Steichen had often photographed in "parklands" around Mamaroneck. While today the pond is in Saxon Woods, a county park of some seven hundred acres, I knew that most of the county parks had not been established until the 1920s. Steichen took his photograph in 1904, a time when the property was undoubtedly still in private hands.

My initial source for determining whether Steichen had photographed on public or private property consisted of photocopies of segments of maps of the area from 1893, 1907, and 1919 that a local historian had kindly given me. The earliest map contained the designation "E. Hyatt, 55 acres" right next to the pond. The 1907 map had a label for the area in question that read "S. W. Park, 55 acres." The 1919 map labeled the area surrounding the pond "Altonwood." My first thought was that the 1907 "S. W. Park" label stood for Saxon Woods Park, but it seemed much too early for such a designation. Possibly the parcel had been a fifty-five-acre estate throughout the period of the three maps, perhaps known as "Altonwood" by 1919. Either assumption would have been faulty. Since both ideas were unconvincing, I looked further.

I sought maps closer in time to the period of my interest. On the Web I found a map from 1901 that revealed that S.W. Park was in fact S. W. Parker (the "er" had been cut off in the photocopy I had been given—a compelling reason to look for originals and complete documents), "owner" of the fifty-five-acre tract and an adjoining 130 acres. A little Web research turned up a couple of newspaper articles revealing that he was S. Webber Parker and not, strictly speaking, the owner of the property in 1901. He was a member of a major New York real estate family who had once owned the property, used as a large horse-breeding farm of more than one hundred horses and known as Altonwood Stock Farm in 1881.[1]

By 1900 Parker had joined financial forces with other investors to create the Altonwood Park Realty and Investment Company, become its vice president, and made plans to develop the tract, now expanded to one thousand acres, into residential "villa plots" with an already-constructed amenity—undoubtedly a remnant of the horse-breeding farm—a stables to "furnish accommodations for a large number of horses, making the maintenance of separate stables unnecessary for residents of the section."[2] One of the largest suburban-development enterprises ever undertaken in the New York City area, it was apparently a bust. The stables would have soon been an amenity of little value, as the train, trolley, and automobile would replace horse-drawn carriages and the need for horses. Having already been purchased by another investor, the property was put up for auction in the summer of 1904.[3] Parts of it may well have remained tied up in the courts and retained the loose designation "Altonwood" until Westchester County purchased the property for the park in the mid-1920s.

Thus, I conclude that in 1904, when Steichen took his photograph, the property, while technically privately held, was in a sort of limbo—it had spent four years waiting to be developed and was on the verge of being auctioned off. Undoubtedly, no one would have been worried about the trespassing of a solitary photographer setting up his tripod near the perimeter of the tract. My quest to figure out the nature of the Gedney Pond property during these years succeeded because I did not stop with map labels but rather pushed further until I had more solid information. Maps are often a little out of date when it comes to property-owner labels and are best used in concert with deeds or other sources. A deed search would have yielded the information about the owner, but the additional information offered in the newspaper accounts enriched the story. It's often worth the effort to push beyond what seems to be an easy answer.

The result of my ventures into the woods was my conclusion that Steichen did, indeed, take his famous *The Pond—Moonlight* at Gedney Pond, not in the summer, but in the late winter or early spring, probably March. At that time of year, the moon comes up at just the right place (due east) and the underbrush and leaves are gone, allowing the rocks around the pond to be visible. In late spring, summer, and autumn, they are obliterated by underbrush. The only real change in the site today is the angle of the rise of the earth just beyond the pond. The terrain now slants slightly up to the north, on the left in the photograph, a result of the construction of the interstate entrance ramp. Given Steichen's relationship with Caffin, the proximity of Mamaroneck to New York City with easy access by train, and Steichen's inclination to photograph in the woods at twilight during the autumn, winter, and early spring (as he discussed in his autobiography), it is likely that he made a number of trips out of the city—in addition to the extended stay in the summer of 1904—to make photographs in the woodlands near Caffin's house.

THE UNIVERSAL VERSUS THE SPECIFIC

One might ask—and surely many art historians, critics, and collectors would, as well as anyone who responds to the image's aesthetic and poetic aspects—what difference does it make when and where Steichen took the photograph? The artist's intent, they would argue, was to create a universal or archetypical image without reference to a specific time or place. Poet Carl Sandburg, Steichen's brother-in-law, wrote an appreciation of the photographer's work in 1929, remarking, "He defines art as . . . 'the taking of the essence of an object or experience and giving it a new form so that it has an existence of its own and an essence of its own,'"[28] thus removing it from the specific. As curator Joel Smith put it in describing the Metropolitan Museum of Art's *The Pond—Moonrise*, "the landscape becomes a frame, or framing, of mind. . . . The image was sometimes exhibited under the title *Solitude*; the pictured moment of lunar dawning both prompts and mirrors a moment of contemplation, with the pool suggesting a primal site of self-reflection. . . ."[29] Charles Caffin described Steichen's landscape photographs of this period in *Camera Work* in 1910: "It is in the penumbra, between the clear visibility of things and their total extinction in darkness, when the concreteness of appearances becomes merged in half-realized, half-baffled vision, that spirit seems to disengage itself from matter and to envelop it with a mystery of soul-suggestion."[30] And more recently, in 2006, an art gallery owner responded when asked by a reporter where Steichen took *The Pond—Moonlight*, "It's kind of like asking what kind of camera he used—it really doesn't matter. It wouldn't have been important to him."[31]

Perhaps all true, yet the interest in where the photograph was taken lingers as evidenced by the extensive newspaper coverage surrounding the 2006 sale and my own curiosity. And though Steichen's primary concern may have been in the universality of the image, it is informative to note the specificity of the title of the print owned by the Museum of Modern Art, *Moonrise—Mamaroneck, New York*, in contrast to the generic titles held by the other two prints. Steichen not only spent fifteen years as the director of the museum's department of photography, but also, after his retirement, gave the print to the museum in 1964, indicating that he most likely had some say in its title. According to curatorial records in the Museum of Modern Art, the photograph had "Mamaroneck" in the title from the time Steichen donated it, an indication that the artist did, in fact, have some interest in specificity of location.[32] The question of where the photograph was taken is perhaps not important in a conversation about the photograph as a work of art. It is, however, important from the point of view of history. And Edward Steichen's acute sensitivity to the landscape reminds us of another dimension of the land aside from its use as property.

ten

Monkey Business and More: The Possibilities

This smugglers' paradise is crowned by a vast rock outcrop, providing a fine lookout post.[1]

—S.D. Smith, 2004

The great granite outcrop occupying the southwestern corner of my property has held a sense of mystery for me from the time my family moved in to our house. It is large, taller than any person, mountable by a large boulder staircase on one side, flat on top with remnants of rough cement apparently intended to further level the surface, and covered in vegetation—masses of tiger lilies, weeds of every description, assorted trees with trunks of dimensions from pencil-sized to three-feet across, and an impressive wisteria vine with a stem as thick as my wrist. In summer, a majestic, high canopy of leaves envelops the whole area, thanks to two ancient maples and their progeny. We have made a woodland retreat there, private, magical, a world away from the surrounding suburbia. A backdrop to the front yard, the rocky outcrop is a handsome landscape feature, so much so that the former owner placed spotlights on the side of the house to shine upon it.

Aside from the rock's natural beauty and charm as a secluded hideaway, it seems to hold secrets, remnants of human activity. But what activity? The quarter-ton granite steps alone are evidence that someone wanted to make access to it easier and was willing to go to considerable effort to place them there. Even more curious are the ten iron stakes, three-quarter-inch in diameter, protruding from the side of the rock near the top surface. Embedded into the granite, they seem rusted securely into place, and some have remnants of rusted chain hanging from the eyelets at the ends. So when Mrs. T———, the former owner, told me, "Someone a long time ago kept monkeys chained there," I repeated the story over and over to anyone who would listen. The reaction was always the same: Wow! No kidding, no way, how weird! Based on that reaction, I made the assumption that such an endeavor would have been a hobby so exotic, it would have warranted some attention in the local press. Alas, a diligent search of old local newspapers failed to turn up any evidence that someone in town kept monkeys. I also consulted a few old-timers in the

FIGURE 10.1 The rock in four seasons. *(Photos by author.)*

area, but none of them had any awareness of the stakes or of any monkeys having been housed on the outcropping. So in my effort to find an explanation for the existence of the stakes, I soon abandoned the monkey story in search of another, more plausible one, a search I entered into with help. The stakes and their particular arrangement happen to intrigue people and motivate them to gamely enter into speculative exercises in an effort to explain their origins. So along with the typical reaction to the monkey story came a myriad of hypotheses developed through both research and conversations with assorted observers.

MONKEYS—A SUBURBAN LEGEND?

A first thought—if not exotic pets, then what about farm animals? I knew the property had been used by many farmers. The stakes, however, are not substantial enough to restrain horses or mules, and farmers in colonial New York allowed their smaller animals like pigs, sheep, and goats to roam freely, in later years keeping them within fenced areas.

The next hypothesis emerged as I researched Isaac Gedney Jr. (ca. 1740–1802) and learned that he, like many fellow landowners in eighteenth-century New York, had been a slave owner. One day, in a discussion about the mystery of the monkeys, my husband and teenaged daughter, with this newfound information about Gedney on their minds, simultaneously looked at me and said in unison, "Slaves?" Could the troubling truth of an explanation involving the sale of human beings have somehow morphed into the pet monkey story, an explanation more palatable to the twentieth-century mind? This disturbing and seemingly whacky idea demanded investigation.

Research on the eighteenth-century North American slave trade and the Gedney family genealogy revealed that Isaac Gedney was a cousin of Gedney Clarke, a major transatlantic merchant who traded in various commodities and captives to be sold as enslaved workers. Not only were Isaac Gedney Sr. (1700–1771) and Gedney Clarke Sr. (1711–1764) second cousins through a shared forebear, John Gedney, but a network of matrimonial alliances, going back several generations to the earliest English immigrants in the 1630s, further connected the Gedney and Clarke families, both of whom prospered in seventeenth- and eighteenth-century Salem, Massachusetts.[2] In the late 1690s Isaac Gedney Sr.'s father had migrated from Salem to Mamaroneck, where Isaac Jr. was born. In 1733 Gedney Clarke Sr. left Salem for Barbados where, soon after his arrival, he began supplying enslaved Barbadians of African descent to New England.[3]

By 1742 Clarke was one of Barbados's leading merchants, the island's customs collector, and a significant landholder. His son, Gedney Clarke Jr. (1735–1777), later joined him in the family businesses. As middlemen for other colonial slave importers in Barbados, South Carolina, London, and New York, they were significant players in the transatlantic slave trade triangle,[4] a lucrative arrangement for merchants who sold European manufactured goods, such as guns and cloth, in Africa, carried Africans to the Americas, where they were sold and enslaved, and transported produce from the slave-labor plantations in the continental Americas and the West Indies—cotton, sugar, molasses, rum, and tobacco—back to Europe.

In New York, the Clarkes' main business associate was John Watts, a major North American merchant, who in 1762 invested with Clarke Sr. in a slave vessel bound for the Guinea coast in Africa.[5] *The Letter Book of John Watts*, transcribed from a 276-page manuscript volume of his correspondence from 1762 to 1765 and published in 1928, reveals much about Watts's own business involving the buying, transporting, and selling of all manner of goods with rum a primary focus, as well as the transatlantic trade of the mid-seventeenth century as a whole.[6] Most ships coming into New York from Africa brought back mixed cargoes, with much of the non-slave goods then exported to

Genealogy

Most people use genealogical resources to learn about their own families, but why not use the myriad of genealogy websites and library and archival resources used by genealogists to find information on former owners of your property? It was through genealogical research that I was able to establish that the slave-trader Gedney Clarke was a cousin of Isaac Gedney Jr., that the Gedneys of New York had first settled in Salem, Massachusetts, and that the New York Gedneys' ancestor had migrated to Mamaroneck shortly after the Salem witch trials took place.

If no genealogy exists for the person you are investigating and you have to do your own primary research, many libraries or genealogical societies can get you started. There you can often find the library edition of *Ancestry.com, Ancestry Library Edition (ALE),* usually available without charge. There are a number of Web sources that you can subscribe to—*Ancestry.com, RootsWeb.com,* and *FamilySearch.org. Cyndi's List,* http://www.cyndislist.com, offers a list of free genealogy databases as well as free online learning centers where anyone can delve into a number of topics related to genealogical research.

A published obituary, if one exists, is always a good place to begin. It will give you essential facts and ideas for places to go next in your research. Other good places for leads are cemetery tombstones and indexes of them either on the Web, in books, or in historical societies' files. Among the other resources you may find helpful are: almshouse records, cemetery indexes, census data, church and synagogue records, city directories, court proceeding records and transcripts, deeds, estate documents, immigration records, incorporation papers, maps, military service records, mortgage records, naturalization records, newspapers for birth, marriage, and death announcements, orphanage records, school reports, ship passenger manifests, telephone books, vital records (births, deaths, and marriages), voter registries, and wills.

In order to access governmental records, you need to know at what level they are kept. For example, in New York State, vital records for birth, death, and marriage are filed with the clerk of the city, town, or village where the event took place (births and deaths) or where the license was issued (marriages). Land records are usually kept at the county level. Most census records are kept at the federal level, but also at times in the past at state and local levels.

Most important when using existing genealogies or published family histories as opposed to primary documents is to consider the source as well as the motivation and credentials of the author. Particularly in the online genealogies you will find much conflicting information to be wary of. It is best, when possible, to confirm all information with two or more primary sources.

England and other places. Though enslaved workers made up less than 2 percent of the overseas trade in and out of New York and vessels returning from Africa also carried ebony, dyewood, beeswax, and elephant tusks or ivory,[7] the buying and selling of Africans was an ongoing part of the mercantile community.

Several facts make plausible my so-called slave hypothesis on what purpose the stakes served. First, bringing enslaved people into New York was routine from the late 1740s until the American Revolution; for example, during 1748–74, there were at least 103 vessels that made 130 separate slave-trading voyages in and out of the port of New York.[8] Second, smugglers regularly made use of the many coves and other sheltered spots along Long Island Sound where they could unload some of their cargo, human or otherwise, and thereby avoid paying duties in the New York City port, where they would have to clear customs. Though the practice was illegal, the slave traders barely hid the facts of their involvement; colonial government officials knew well what was going on. In fact, so lax was government control that during the entire colonial era, New York authorities prosecuted only one ship for slave smuggling.[9]

Third, according to census records, members of the Gedney family in Westchester County owned enslaved workers. Isaac Gedney Sr.'s brother John, living in an adjoining town, owned two in 1755,[10] and Isaac Jr. owned one by 1790.[11] Fourth, in 1762–63, Gedney Clarke Jr., by now an active partner in his family's business, was living in New York City and involved both personally and professionally with John Watts.[12] And fifth, a scholar by the name of Simon D. Smith observed in a 2003 article that the Clarkes were in the habit of going to extraordinary lengths to maintain contact with, rely on, and give preference to kin on both sides of the Atlantic.[13]

So could the Clarkes have turned to their cousins, Isaac Gedney Sr. and Isaac Jr., and their property, just a mile up the Mamaroneck River from the coast of Long Island Sound, and used that property as a way station for transporting Africans bound for slavery? The river, though small, is navigable today by kayak or canoe. Described by Sarah Kemble Knight, who passed through the town in 1704, as "navigable,"[14] it was likely a waterway big enough for a raft used to transport people and produce between the harbor and the Gedney property. Could those stakes in the rock with the chains hanging from the ends possibly have been used as human restraints?

I thought this idea to be preposterous, but after stumbling upon Simon D. Smith's website through a Google search of the name Gedney Clarke and then reading his 2003 article, "Gedney Clarke of Salem and Barbados: Transatlantic Super-Merchant," in the highly respected journal *The William and Mary Quarterly*, I decided to write to Dr. Smith—a professor of modern history and diaspora studies and scholar of the Caribbean and the British Atlantic world during the period of enslavement—in England about my idea to see what he thought. To my surprise, he responded, "I didn't know of this New York property. Its existence certainly makes sense of Gedney Clarke's decision to settle temporarily in New York before returning to London. . . . My opinion (for what it's worth) is that the Clarkes made up their own commercial rules and that, if there was money to be made, it is highly likely that they drew on kinship links in the way you suggest."[15] Though I believed Dr. Smith's suggestion that merchants like the Clarkes would have done whatever was expedient and lucrative and may well have worked with their Gedney cousins in smuggling enslaved Africans to avoid paying New York port duties, his comments and my own observations had not completely convinced me of the plausibility of this explanation for how the stakes ended up in my rocky outcrop.[16]

Imagine my surprise, then, when Dr. Smith's book, *Slavery, Family, and Gentry Capitalism in the British Atlantic: The World of the Lascelles, 1646–1834*, published by

FIGURE 10.2 A view looking down on the top surface of the rock. The 48-inch measuring stick is centered in a rectangle marked by four broken vertical stakes. From the center point, marked by the rectangular block of rock, strings extend out to nine of the ten stakes on the periphery of the rock. The tenth stake, off toward the left, was found later. The strings mark the angles and the roughly symmetrical placement of the stakes. *(Photo by author.)*

FIGURE 10.3 A stake, about twelve inches long with the eyehole visible. *(Photo by author.)*

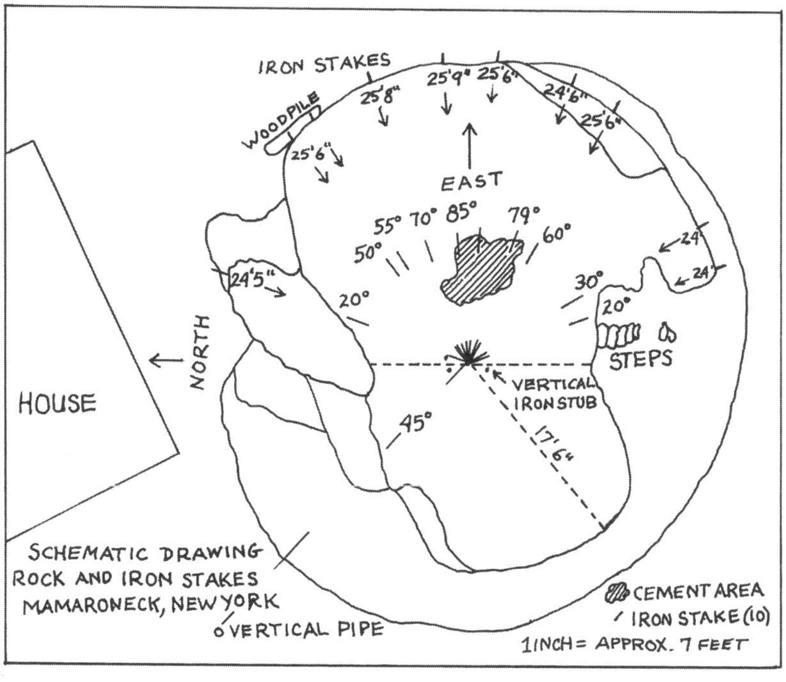

FIGURE 10.4 A bird's-eye-view schematic drawing of the rock indicating its orientation, its relationship to the house, and the location of the ten stakes. *(Map by author and Liz Blake.)*

Cambridge University Press, came out in 2006 and included the following statement in a footnote referencing his correspondence with me: "Watts and Clarke . . . smuggled slaves into New York itself, making use of the coves and inlets of Long Island. The illicit trade was probably assisted by the Gedney family's ownership of a 200-acre plot close to Long Island Sound, bordered by the Mamaroneck River, which empties into a fine natural harbour. This smugglers' paradise is crowned by a vast rock outcrop, providing a fine lookout post."[17] My property a smugglers' paradise! Wow! Yet as exciting as these confirming ideas were, I still was not persuaded, especially after I discovered that the placement of the stakes seemed far too symmetrical and calculated to have been put there as a temporary place for enslaved workers or as a playground for pet monkeys.

Ask the Experts

When you make observations or encounter a question that lies outside your realm of expertise and does not lend itself easily to library or archival research, ask an expert. It may take time and effort to find that person, so be persistent.

For example, if you find something buried in the yard or tucked in a corner of the attic, show it to a specialist. One idea is to take what you have to antique shops. You will get lots of suggestions and perhaps eventually find a consensus. Emulating the popular public television series *Antiques Roadshow*, local places such as adult education schools and historical societies sometimes hold their own bring-your-treasure-to-our-expert sessions. If you have an object associated with your house or property, they might be able to help you determine what it is and when it was made. Better still, go to the real *Roadshow* when it comes to a city near you. I did try that, but was not among the lottery-lucky-ones to get a ticket.

It was at a local version of the *Roadshow* where I learned that the small object I had dug up in my garden is probably a match safe (see introduction) dating from the late nineteenth or early twentieth century. But since the information I gained from this exchange seemed a bit uncertain, I keep it with me on my occasional trips to antique shops and collections of historical material and show it to every dealer and curator I can. After several years, I am still getting differing opinions. Eventually I will come across someone who is truly an authority and knows for sure what it is.

The odd symmetrical arrangement of the iron stakes in my rock outcropping prompted me to contact my county historic preservation office. Someone there suggested I contact a certain architect with expertise in historical uses of metal. It was he who offered various hypotheses in regard to derricks. I found another expert, the scholar who had published an article on the transatlantic slave trade in the colonial era, through a Google search. He has his own website, which, in turn, led me to one of his published articles on the subject and to his e-mail address. And the fortunate fact of my friendship with an expert in old metal dating may lead to conclusions on the age of the stakes.

My work on Edward Steichen's photograph (see chapter 9) left me with questions about his methods, both with the camera and in the darkroom. I found a professor who teaches processes used by artist/photographers from 1840 to 1910, and he was able to answer my questions about Steichen's platinum prints and photogravures. Finding the answers helped me to better understand the resulting work of art and what Steichen must have done to create it.

The bottom line is, no one can become an authority in every field of endeavor, and research without specialized knowledge can take you only so far. That is when you need to turn to the pursuit of the expert.

THE SYMMETRY OF THE STAKES

The stakes that ring the side of the rock just above eye-level were a curiosity from our first winter in the house when the winter foliage die-back revealed them. But not until a couple of years later did I realize that someone had quite deliberately positioned them. Near the center of the top surface of the outcrop, rusted, jagged stubs of four additional stakes stick vertically out of the rock. They mark the corners of a narrow rectangle about fifty-two by eight inches, oriented with the longer sides running north-south. Through its center runs a deep six-inch-wide crevice, now filled with dirt and roots. A due-east line extended from the rectangle's center point forms the central axis of a 140-degree arc containing the ten stakes. By stretching strings from this center point to each stake and then measuring their angles, I found the stakes to be positioned almost symmetrically around the axis, the lines to the various stakes from that center point similar in arrangement to the ribs of an open paper fan. The distance from the rectangle's center to each stake along the periphery of the rock where it drops down to the yard below is roughly twenty-five feet. Of the ten stakes, the two that mark the ends of the arc are short, about two inches long, the others all about one foot. Thirty-five feet to the northwest of the center point, protruding about eleven inches from the earth surrounding the rock, is a two-inch-in-diameter steel pipe, which may have something or nothing to do with the stakes.

So why on earth would someone go to all the trouble of measuring and arranging the stakes in this way? The due-east orientation of their central axis, perfectly aligned with the rising sun on the March equinox, filled my imagination with thoughts of sun worship, primitive rituals, and an ancient celestial observatory. Those possibilities, however, seemed unlikely, so I moved on to consider more concrete possibilities, ones that would align with the measured way the stakes had been arranged. What about some sort of elaborate sundial? Sundials, it turns out, were fashionable around the turn of the twentieth century. A 1904 article in *House & Garden* cited the recent "sudden popularity" of sundials in American gardens;[18] however, the ones I could find pictured in magazines of the period were small discs mounted either on freestanding garden statuary or pedestals or on the sides of buildings.[19] And sundials are oriented due north, not east, with their gnomon (shadow-maker) angled to match the latitude of the sundial's location and positioned to create a moving shadow as the sun travels across the sky throughout the day. A sundial would have no need for the east-oriented arc of radiating lines. So a sundial, too, seemed an unlikely explanation for the stakes.

I considered my property in other time periods—before and after slavery in New York—and realized I had no idea when the stakes might have been inserted into the rock. I just knew they looked old. The technology for making holes in rock in order to split it is an ancient one, dating to circa 2500 BC when the Egyptians began building their pyramids at Giza.[20] My careful observations of the rock area yielded just one clue in regard to stone splitting—one of the boulder steps displays a nine-inch-long uniform groove along one of its surfaces, evidence of a compressed-air rock drill used for blasting in order to split stone. This kind of stone-drilling device came into use late in the nineteenth century. So at least that boulder would have been placed there sometime in the last 120 years.

The metal stakes, however, were another issue. Given their rusty surface, I assumed they were made of iron, which also has a long history, having been used since about 1200 BC. Wrought iron, an iron alloy wrought (shaped) by hand, is tough and, unlike cast iron, capable of being bent into shapes like my stakes. My initial efforts to glean information from historians and antiques specialists on dating wrought iron produced nothing definitive. I thought of carbon-dating and learned that recent work on dating iron-based materials has shown that carbon-containing wrought iron can be dated with certain limitations.[21] That knowledge gave me hope.

It then occurred to me to consult my friend Dr. Charles E. Lyman of Lehigh University's Department of Materials Science and Engineering, who told me that old iron sometimes can be roughly dated by determining which process was used for smelting the pig iron that the blacksmith used as his raw material. He made a proposal—if I sent him a sample of one of the stakes, he would take a look at it. And even better, he might make it the "mystery material" for the students in his materials lab course.

Given that various methods of making wrought iron result in differences in the iron's microstructure, the goal of the semesterlong assignment was to analyze the "mystery material" with various microscopes and analytical instruments. Through analysis of its microstructure, it was hoped that the process that made the pig iron the blacksmith used could be determined, and from the process an estimate could be made of the century in which the stake was fabricated. Off my husband went with his hacksaw to remove a couple of small chunks according to Dr. Lyman's instructions. I assembled a package containing the metal samples, photographs of the site and the stakes before and after the cuts, a schematic diagram of the rock, and a brief history of the property and sent them to the lab at Lehigh. There was just one problem: Professor Lyman was going on sabbatical, so I had to wait for a couple of semesters. At that moment, feeling impatient, I wished I had the vast research and investigative resources of the PBS television series *History Detectives* at my disposal. I do not, so I went on with my research.

ELEVATION

"A fine lookout post"—the words from Dr. Smith's book continued to resonate with me. And several visitors had remarked on the rock's elevation of 110 feet above sea level and the possibility it had served as a lookout spot because of the sweeping, unobstructed (except for trees) eastern view. The early European settlers would have cleared most of the land for farming, making it easy to see all the way to Long Island Sound from the top of the rock. Native Americans had likely cleared the land even earlier. What made those archaeologists who had come knocking at the door of my house, when the former owner lived in it, think that this rock was a likely site for finding Indian relics? The 1961 newspaper caption stating, "Indian-placed rocks in a semi-circle . . . where the Indian Council met"[22] (formerly in my backyard and the adjacent yard before the swimming pool went in), added credence to the idea that the area of the outcrop was a Native American gathering place. One enthusiastic friend ran up on the rock and proclaimed that surely George Washington had ridden his horse up there during the Revolution. Not that my friend really knew that to be true, but given that the general was in the area for some time in the fall of 1776, before and after the Battle of White Plains, it was a possibility. Once upon a time, a fine lookout post indeed. But there was one problem with this line of thinking—a lookout post would not necessarily have required carefully arranged stakes. Perhaps someone put them there to anchor some sort of structure that would have called for a high elevation and the kind of careful measuring a construction engineer would bring to the endeavor. That idea led to more hypotheses.

Less than five hundred yards from my house is a reservoir, formed by the damming of the Mamaroneck River in 1885 at the site of Caleb Heathcote's old saw mill.[23] Might there have been a water tower atop the rock? Advertisements for water towers for private home fire protection and crop watering appeared in *Country Life in America* in the early twentieth century, and though these small towers would have been the right fit for the rock, the pictures indicate that they were not tethered to the ground.[24] Perhaps the rock would have been the location of a public water tower. The spot is definitely a high point compared to the rest of the town below, the recipient of the reservoir's water. Yet research at the waterworks station near my house and in town documents turned up nothing to confirm that explanation.[25] Another idea was proposed by an acquaintance who knew of two windmills that had once been nearby. A series of photographs and drawings of eighteenth- and nineteenth-century windmills on Long Island, however, suggested that windmills of the period were much bigger than the rock would have accommodated.[26] What about a radio mast to support a transmission antenna in the early twentieth century? The guys required to pin such a tall mast might have been attached to the stakes. And the timing was right with radio invented in the 1890s and radio stations starting up in New York in 1922. Owners of the property during the Great Depression would have been eager to make whatever money they could from a piece of undeveloped, uninhabited land and perhaps would have rented out the rock for extra income. But I could find no information to support the radio mast idea either.

With the notion that I should learn more about the history of residential real estate development, I arranged to meet with a friend who had been in the business in the region in the 1950s. Our discussion of my property and my theories about towers prompted her to mention that she had been involved in plane-spotting in Westchester County during the Korean War as a member of the U.S. Air Force Air Defense Command, a civilian ground observer corps program. During World War II, with inadequate radar detection capacity available, 1.5 million civil defense volunteers worked in fourteen thousand observation posts, many of them small towers, to search the skies for enemy planes entering U.S. airspace. The work continued during the Korean War.[27] The plane-spotters, stationed in the towers and in tall buildings and working only with binoculars, gathered information to be analyzed for possible aerial bombing threats. Concentrated along the nation's coastlines, these posts would have been positioned in Westchester County for a view toward the Atlantic coast.[28] Would that maybe explain the eastern orientation of the stakes on the rock? Might the stakes have been used to anchor a small plane-spotting tower?

FIGURE 10.5 Plane-spotting in White Plains, New York. The tower stood on Partridge Road, now in a fully developed residential neighborhood. Travis Collection, Westchester County Historical Society. *(Courtesy of the Westchester County Historical Society. Photo by Boyce.)*

I have found two locations where the program built towers (about fifteen feet in height, big enough to accommodate two or three spotters) for this purpose on then-undeveloped, relatively high-elevation land in nearby White

Plains.[29] I also know my property was vacant during both World War II and the Korean War. The house near the rock built in the 1890s by Louis Block had been torn down in the 1920s, and the lot remained undeveloped for three decades, a perfect spot to utilize for such a noble cause. But unfortunately, I have been unable to confirm that the rock might have been used for plane-spotting.

ON LOCATION, LOCATION, LOCATION

With my elevation-based hypotheses leading to dead ends, I began to think in terms of the intersection of time period and geographic location, without considering the elevation/expansive view factor. Examining the property and its surroundings within the context of what could be learned about different eras led to a new set of possible explanations for the stakes. One night I had what at the time seemed like an epiphany—yes, I thought, maybe silent-film maker D. W. Griffith had made films there.

During the early 1920s, people referred to Mamaroneck as "Hollywood East," in large part because in 1919 the noted director had built a major film studio there, where for several years he filmed on location, both on his extensive studio lot on a fourteen-acre spit of land on Long Island Sound and in the surrounding neighborhoods. I knew that longtime residents had recorded their memories of the filming of at least three of the nine movies Griffith made in Mamaroneck. One man recalled, "I watched some of the picture *America* being shot [in 1924] at Gedney's Pond . . . where we used to ice skate."[30] Gedney Pond, part of the original Gedney property, is just twelve hundred feet from my house. He also remembered the shooting of scenes from the 1920 film *Way Down East* at houses not too far from mine.[31]

I imagined the Louis Block family giving over a part of their property, perhaps even the outcrop, for the filming of a movie scene, much as other Mamaroneck residents had done for the famous director. I hypothesized that Griffith might have used a tower for lights or cameras and set the stakes into the rock to anchor them. I actually found bits of information that suggest he used filming techniques requiring such supports. A location still photograph of *Way Down East*'s dramatic climax, set on an ice-clogged river with the unconscious heroine on a chunk of ice inching perilously close to a waterfall, shows the camera mounted on a long platform suspended over the waterfall and supported by guy wires anchored to rock. Another photograph shows Griffith's crew filming at night under large lights mounted on tall wooden towers. From what is apparent in the photographs, Griffith did not film these scenes—the latter one set on perfectly flat terrain—in what is now my yard. But the notion that Griffith used equipment to support his camera for challenging shots was supported by a finding in regard to yet another of the films he made in Mamaroneck. For *Orphans of the Storm*, a melodrama about two orphaned sisters separated and reunited during the French Revolution, Griffith built massive sets, recreating eighteenth-century streets of Paris and turning Mamaroneck into a "sightseer's mecca" throughout the summer and fall of 1921.[32] The liner notes for a DVD of the film mention that a reporter for a Midwestern newspaper had written about seeing Griffith perched atop a crane while shooting *Orphans*.[33]

Griffith's storyline in *Orphans* included big rocks in a couple of scenes. I found a photograph taken on the set in which Lillian Gish as the heroine, detained in the Prison for Fallen Women, appears with an inmate who is chained to a huge rock.[34] So why not my rock? Close inspection made possible by stopping the DVD revealed that the film's rock walls, caves, and fences appear to have been constructed of plaster "stones and mortar" or of rock piles that bear only a passing resemblance to my outcrop. Thus, I concluded that, although my research showed that Griffith did use devices to support and suspend cameras and light-

FIGURE 10.6 D. W. Griffith shooting under lights for *Way Down East* in Mamaroneck in 1921. *(Photograph courtesy of The Museum of Modern Art, Department of Film.)*

FIGURE 10.7 A production still from Griffith's *Orphans of the Storm*, 1921. Here Mamaroneck has been turned into a 1793 Paris street scene. *(Photograph courtesy of the Westchester County Historical Society.)*

ing equipment, and that rocks did come into play in one of the storylines, there was nothing to suggest he filmed on my property. Epiphany moments, even if exhilarating, do not always stand up to fact-checking.

Another location-based idea, albeit a less romantic one, developed from my efforts to confer with historic preservationists. I sent photographs, diagrams, and a property description to Richard Pieper, an architectural conservator specializing in the documentation of historical architectural technology and the conservation of masonry materials and metals. Based on his credentials, he seemed like just the kind of expert I should be consulting. He kindly responded to my query, concluding that the particular configuration of the metal stakes suggested they were placed there as part of some sort of derrick and boom hoisting system, the kind often used to move stone in quarries in the nineteenth and early twentieth centuries.[35] The most simple of these devices is the gin pole, a single, slightly leaning vertical mast, supported by fixed stays or guy ropes in the rear with a block and tackle pulley attached to the top for lifting. The deep crevice on the top of the outcrop might have provided a place to hold the mast, possibly made of timber. The stakes may have anchored the guys supporting it. One photograph I found of a Montana quarry excavated in 1929 shows guy wires supporting a derrick as well as a swivel base for it anchored to the ground with four large bolts arranged in a long rectangle similar in proportion to the broken iron stakes in the horizontal surface of my rock.[36] Since I have not been able to discern any evidence of a commercial deep excavation pit quarry on my property, my guess is such a device could have been used in a small surface ledge quarry, a place where in the eighteenth and nineteenth centuries builders quarried exposed bedrock, usually for local construction projects.[37] The boulders that make up the steps to the top of the outcrop might have been products of surface ledge quarrying in this spot. In fact, the one with the narrow cylindrical drill mark shows the telltale evidence of rock-splitting.

Another type of derrick and boom, possibly used at the site when the property was a working farm, might have been a hay derrick, a device to lift hay and form it into a

FIGURE 10.8 John Warner Barber (1798–1885). *Bolton Stone Quarry.* 1838. Ink on paper. 9 x 12 cm. *(Courtesy of The Connecticut Historical Society, Hartford, Connecticut.)*

FIGURE 10.9 *Rawlins Grey Sandstone Quarry, Kerr Marble & Stone Co.* 1890–1910. Miners posing with a slab of stone being hoisted by a stiff leg derrick. *(Courtesy of the Denver Public Library, Western History Collection, X-61323. Photograph by Ferris Studio, Rawlins, Wyoming.)*

haystack, shaped precisely so that it sheds rain and snow. An informative short film, available on-line at the Library of Congress, American Memory website, demonstrates, through narration and the making of a drawing, the technology involved in working with derricks and booms.[38]

Reading about developer Harry Rich Mooney's 1920s construction operation and his long-range plan for the property sparked an idea for another possible explanation related to quarrying. Perhaps the outcrop itself was once much larger. Richard Pieper, the architectural conservator, stated in an e-mail that if the outcrop had been the site of a quarry in the 1920s, then

> the evidence of quarrying (which would be of the stone surrounding the derrick) would be hidden beneath the soil. The developer would have been quarrying the stone to level the site for construction, and may have used the stone for the foundations of buildings built on site, or for . . . retaining walls [and] fill . . . nearby. The boom would have been used to transfer the removed stone to trucks or

FIGURE 10.10 Vermont Marble Quarry, Broadwater County, Montana. ca. 1937. Detail of the derrick swivel base at an abandoned mine site. *(Photograph courtesy of Library of Congress, Prints and Photographs Division, Historic American Engineering Record, HAER MONT,4-RADBU.V,1–3.)*

other conveyances. Such informal quarrying sometimes occurred when a rocky site required leveling. This was not a normal commercial quarrying venture per se, although the stone was often used for construction, and not just for fill. Boom bases or islands remain after the "quarry" is closed, because there is no way to boom the stone beneath it.[39]

If this were in fact the case, then Mooney apparently decided to build around the remaining boom base because his architectural drawing for a large apartment house shows a kind of "sawed-off" corner in the footprint of an otherwise rectilinear building. His architect designed it to accommodate the outcrop as it exists on the site today. (See fig. 7.6)

Known information about Mooney's operation supports this explanation. His sales director commented in the company's newsletter that installing the sewer lines "through eighteen feet of solid rock" was "an engineering feat . . . that . . . long will stand as an outstanding record to Mooney's credit."[40] Since Mooney promoted the fact that he did not use subcontractors and did most of the work on site, boasted about having to drill through deep bedrock in order to install sewers, and planned to eventually build a large apartment building right next to where the outcrop stands, it seems that he must have made provisions at least for the relocation of rock. It is evident today that some of that rock probably is a component of the foundations of the houses he built. Even if he did not do quarry work on the site, the height of the outcrop, with the bit of cement leveling added, and the as-yet-undeveloped area around it indeed would have made a perfect spot for storing, lifting, and loading materials to be conveyed to the construction sites nearby. Or maybe it was the construction of Louis Block's home in the mid-1890s that prompted the use of stone quarrying and lifting. Yet another couple of unconfirmed possibilities.

RECREATION

I moved on to consider more casual and recreational uses for the rock. One retired antiques dealer who thought he might be able to identify the origin of the stakes came to have a look at them. He speculated that some ambitious homeowner had simply put them there to suspend hanging flower pots. That idea was unpersuasive, considering the amount of work it would take to drill into rock and the fact that the placements of several of the stakes would not lend themselves to something hanging straight down. This was the one and only hypothesis I totally rejected.

Given that from 1896 to 1927 the house of a gentleman's estate was about fifty yards from the outcrop, perhaps owner Louis Block set the stakes into the rock to support some sort of recreational structure—a playhouse or a gazebo. My research on gazebos was fruitful. Gazebos and summerhouses, the latter term used almost exclusively by turn-of-the-century writers, are garden pavilions, modest in size, built for pleasure, and made to be attractive and often rustic. Offering a shaded rest spot and a place from which to view a garden, passersby, or a scenic vista, they date back to ancient Egypt and were popular from the sixteenth to the nineteenth centuries in England, where people built them in parks and on the grounds of private country estates. The term "gazebo" probably relates to the word "gaze" and specifically refers to its location in a spot commanding a view overlooking roads or countryside—a place to see or be seen. Gazebos sometimes include screens or glass and a door, depending on their purpose and location, but they are most often open and airy, described, sometimes, as being half made of air.

When a friend alerted me to a gazebo in the coastal Connecticut town of Rowayton, I thought I had found my answer. Standing proudly on a large chunk of bedrock by the beach, an octagon with corners tethered by guy wires and steel pins embedded into the rock, the gazebo had an uncanny similarity to the one I can imagine perched on my outcrop. The timing was right, too, the structure having been erected sometime between 1908 and 1923, years of the Block estate. I began looking for more evidence of historic gazebos in public and private places.

Other findings supported the idea that gazebos were popular and built upon rocks during the period of the Block family's residency in Mamaroneck. The influence of Andrew Jackson Downing's 1842 *Cottage Residences* is well-known. In it he discussed a "rustic pavilion or summer-

FIGURE 10.11 Early twentieth-century gazebo atop a rock at a beach club on the coast of Connecticut. *(Courtesy of the Roton Point Association. Photo by author.)*

FIGURE 10.12 Connecticut gazebo tethered to the rock with guy wires. *(Courtesy of the Roton Point Association. Photo by author.)*

house . . . on a knoll slightly elevated above the surrounding surface" as a key element in his recommendations for creating a tasteful country cottage.[41] In his earlier *A Treatise on the Theory and Practice of Landscape Gardening* he had discussed a summerhouse or prospect tower as a place to take in the view.[42] In his magazine, *The Horticulturalist*, Downing wrote in 1852 of summerhouses as structures that "afford more agreeable resting places, and, when erected in any fine point of view, they serve the double purpose of calling the attention to the best position for seeing it, and affording shade and rest while enjoying the out-stretched landscape." The article included two sketches of summerhouses, one situated atop a rocky knoll.[43] Frank J. Scott, who admired and studied with Downing, published in 1881 *The Art of Beautifying Suburban Home Grounds of Small Extent*, a book primarily devoted to plant material and planting schemes for the modest suburban home. Among its two hundred engravings, only one shows a summerhouse. Included without comment, it seemed to be taken for granted that summerhouses were an optional amenity for one's garden.[44]

By the turn of the twentieth century, interest in summerhouses was on the upswing. *Gardening*, a bi-weekly Chicago publication with a national readership, included in an 1895 issue an article titled, "A Rustic Summer House," stating that such structures were "within reach of everyone."[45] *House & Garden*, a popular monthly devoted to architecture, gardens, and home decoration, showed nearly a dozen gazebos in its pages between 1901 and 1903, one perched atop a rocky outcrop at the Fairmount Water Works in Philadelphia, a public works project combining beauty and utility.[46] *Country Life in America*, for homemakers, vacation-seekers, gardeners, farmers, and naturalists, began publication in 1901 and regularly included advertisements for "rustic work." Including outdoor seating, summerhouses, playhouses, cabins, and arbors made of logs and branches with the bark left on, these structures could be ordered in

FIGURE 10.13 Summerhouse from *The Horticulturist and Journal of Rural Art and Rural Taste. (Reprinted from* Horticulturist, *July, 1852, frontispiece. Photo by author.)*

sections, ready to assemble,[47] or made by the homeowner following instructions offered in the magazine.[48] A more specialized publication devoted to plant cultivation and grounds management, *The Garden Magazine*, included articles on garden amenities such as seats, sundials, flower boxes, fountains, pergolas, arbors, and summerhouses. Again, rustic work seemed to be the style of choice.[49]

And in examples of summerhouses close to home, a park in the adjacent town of Larchmont had two "pagodas" on rocks overlooking Long Island Sound as early as circa 1872. They were replaced in 1897 by Greek-style summerhouses and again in 1902 by rustic ones with posts of tree trunks.[50] A 1904 photograph shows a family posing in front of one of the summerhouses.[51] My rock surely would have afforded an expansive view of both a busy road with its carriage traffic as well as the countryside. It also would have been visible from the property's main residence as an attractive garden feature.

One other clue suggests a gazebo as a possible reason for the stakes in the rock. Downing had pointed to wisteria as a plant requiring a support, such as a summerhouse, to climb upon. And magazine articles around the turn of the century often recommended Chinese wisteria as the right plant for growing on summerhouses.[52] Right next to where a gazebo might have been on my property's outcrop is a very old Chinese wisteria vine. Today, in spring it blooms in fragrant, pendulous purple racemes that hang from the trees and shrubs where the tenacious vine manages to climb. By summer's end, with no architectural structure to climb upon, it has spread itself madly across the top of the rock, shooting out impossibly long vines, grabbing and twisting around chair legs, tree branches, whatever it can find.

So a gazebo or summerhouse seems like a good explanation for why stakes might have been embedded into the rock. The only problem with this explanation is the fact that the stakes are only on one side of the rock. One would expect them to be on all sides. Of course, maybe the additional stakes were once there, and then quarry workers removed them in the rock removal activity of the 1920s.

FIGURE 10.14 Members of the Fordyce family of Larchmont, New York, posing in 1904 in front of a gazebo on rocks overlooking Long Island Sound. *(Photograph courtesy of the Larchmont Historical Society, Larchmont, NY.)*

MONKEYS REDUX

Nothing was quite adding up, so I circled back to the monkey notion. Why had I abandoned this hypothesis? Through my odyssey of investigating all the possible explanations for the stakes-in-the-rock, I kept asking, where did Mrs. T——— get the idea about someone keeping monkeys "a long time ago"? I realized I needed to question my assumptions, which had been based on a twenty-first-century perspective reflected in the reactions of my peers, who uniformly expressed disbelief at the idea. Responding to the comments, I assumed it must have been exceedingly unusual to keep monkeys at home and therefore the practice would have warranted press coverage. But maybe one hundred years ago, people's attitudes toward such a diversion were different from what they are today. Or perhaps the press did not insert itself into people's domestic lives in the ways it does today. Or maybe keeping pet monkeys was common practice at the time. Where else would the idea have come from unless from the proverbial kernel of truth?

Louis Block, probably the person the former owner would have been referring to when she said "someone a long time ago," had died in 1926, his wife selling the property to developer Mooney in 1927. When Mrs. T——— and her husband bought the property, it was 1956, a mere twenty-nine years later. People in the town would have remembered things from just three decades earlier. So maybe the monkey story was not apocryphal after all. I set about investigating the idea once again.

Interest in exotic animals, including monkeys, has a long history in Western culture. In the fifteenth century BC, Queen Hatshepsut of Egypt sent hunters on a wild-animal-collecting expedition to bring back monkeys, leopards, birds, and even a giraffe, all from distant parts of the world. An Egyptian wall painting from 1300 BC shows exotic animals (including a monkey) being delivered to the pharaoh. Wealthy citizens in ancient Greece and Rome kept monkeys as a sign of high status; Holy Roman Emperor Frederick II had monkeys and other animals circa 1235 probably for the same reason. During the Renaissance, developing trade and exploration brought Europeans into contact with Africa, Asia, and the Americas, resulting in an increase in the importation of animals to Europe. By the early 1500s Pope Leo X even had a full menagerie that included monkeys at the Vatican. Throughout these periods, the keeping of exotic animals caged for human amusement was an expression of prestige and power, analogous to collecting rare art.[53]

In the eighteenth and nineteenth centuries, additional factors came into play. An interest in science and natural history emerged and offered another justification for keeping exotic animals. The expanding European empires made wildlife in faraway places more accessible; growing transportation and communication networks stimulated interest among naturalists, breeders, and entrepreneurs. And as society became increasingly urbanized, people's interest in the natural world and its wild animals increased.[54]

Transatlantic trade networks were the conduit for the appearance of exotic animals in port cities beginning in the colonial era. Responding to people's natural curiosity, ship captains would bring back an exotic animal or two from their worldwide voyages and exhibit them in order to make extra money. As early as 1720, a ship captain, returning from a voyage to Africa, brought back a lion to New York City.[55]

About the same time, small, itinerant animal shows for the display of a single species emerged. Entrepreneurs then found ways to expand the business of showing exotic animals. In 1797 one exhibited a large menagerie in New York. Traveling versions of the menagerie had appeared in America by 1813 and remained popular until the Civil War.[56] An inventory made at the end of the New York Menagerie's 1834 tour of New England shows that among the animals on display were an elephant, a rhinoceros, a zebra, a camel, a polar bear, tigers, and monkeys.[57]

Zoos emerged gradually in nineteenth-century Europe from the animal collections of royalty and the wealthy, becoming especially widespread in Germany. In 1868 a small zoo developed out of New York's Central Park menagerie, which had become a dumping ground for unwanted pets and carnival animals. The first real zoo in the United States opened in Philadelphia in 1874, incorporating a research arm, which established a new era in the developing zoological park concept.[58]

In the domestic realm, pet-keeping had come to North America with its European settlers, animals filling several roles: as hunters, guardians, workers, and companions. By the second half of the eighteenth century, it was routine to find birds, dogs, and cats in American homes. In the nineteenth century, pets also included small rodents, fish, and only occasionally the exotic animal, because unless they had the means to buy animals, people acquired pets from neighbors or captured them in the wild. The business of selling exotic animals in pet shops came with the development of international import specialists starting in the late nineteenth century.[59]

Had Louis Block wanted to acquire monkeys as pets in the late nineteenth century, a time when exotic animals were familiar to many Americans, he would have had ready access to them in New York City. Not only did ship captains and sailors show an occasional exotic animal, they also sold them informally at city wharfs throughout the nineteenth century. Two German brothers established the leading New York firm for importing and trading exotic animals and opened a shop in lower Manhattan not far from the harbor. One journalist reported in 1870 that in their store a visitor might find piles of cages housing monkeys for sale as pets.[60] In 1909, a British zoo official noted that near docks in port cities one could find "untidy and generally evil smelling little shops crowded with parrots and monkeys."[61]

One of Louis Block's neighbors on an estate just over the Mamaroneck border in Rye, Warner M. Van Norden, kept exotic animals around the turn of the century. He planned to crossbreed horses with zebras, which he purchased from the renowned animal importer Carl

Hagenbeck in 1906.[62] Hagenbeck, often considered the father of the modern zoo, was a fascinating character who in 1909 published a book telling the story of his work in the exotic animal business. His father, a fishmonger in Hamburg, Germany, had acquired a few seals and put them on display, eventually assembling a menagerie after purchasing a large collection of animals, including monkeys, from the Egyptian Sudan.[63] From this modest beginning, Hagenbeck grew the family business into a major exotic animal import and export company. From about 1865, the demand for wild and exotic animals in North America increased along with the development of menageries and circuses; one of Hagenbeck's early major customers was P. T. Barnum, who started his circus in 1871.

Hagenbeck's method for acquiring animals started with a collection of agents he called "travelers," who scoured Africa and Asia in search of various species and then led expeditions of as many as two hundred local hunters. Once caught, his animals would be referred to as "guests" and "emigrants." His agents paraded the larger animals and transported the small ones, such as monkeys (found in the Sudan, among other places), across the desert in cages on the backs of camels to a port on the Red Sea, where they continued their three-month journey by ship and railroad car to Hamburg. Hundreds of sheep and goats accompanied the caravans to provide milk for the young animals and meat for the carnivores.[64]

Hagenbeck supplied pet shops, menageries, circuses, and zoos across Europe and North America. He even opened his own menagerie at Manhattan Beach in Brooklyn in the summer of 1894. There were performances three times a day for a twenty-five-cent charge and a caged-animal exhibition called the "Monkey Paradise and Menagerie," open to visitors thirteen hours a day for a fee of ten cents.[65] "The great wild-beast firm of Carl Hagenbeck of Hamburg" produced just three months later yet another animal show at Madison Square Garden that included "ten ponies, one horse, thirty-three monkeys, one bear, one leopard, one young tiger, one young lion, one boarhound, and two small elephants."[66]

Imagining monkeys living on my rock, I had wondered about keeping them outdoors during cold New York winters. One of Hagenbeck's novel ideas was that, given fresh air and the space to roam in a natural environment, animals from tropical climates could acclimatize to a temperate zone such as that found in Europe and North America. He allowed his orangutans, chimpanzees, and baboons to roam at will. They would go outside even when the temperature fell below zero degrees Fahrenheit, retreating to a stove-warmed shelter when they chose.[67]

Hagenbeck's personal interest was in anthropoid apes, which include orangutans and chimpanzees. He set an example for how these animals could be kept as pets by treating them like children, training them to eat with a fork and spoon at a table, and feeding them the same breakfast food that he ate—fruits, bread, and milk. Another of his ideas, new at the time, was that company and stimulation helped keep animals healthy. Hagenbeck's book includes a photograph of him with two granddaughters posed with two baby tigers, a baby lion, and a monkey on their laps.[68] The same photograph appeared in the *New York Times* in a 1913 feature article about Hagenbeck.[69] As supplier, impresario, and model pet owner, Hagenbeck changed the exotic animal business around the world.

One well-known pet monkey owner was New York Governor-elect Alfred E. Smith, who at the start of his second administration in 1922 traveled with his family by train from New York City to the governor's mansion in Albany. A large throng was on hand at Grand Central Station to see them off. The *New York Times* reported that his children's menagerie, traveling with them, included several dogs, two ponies, a canary, an aquarium of gold fish, and Snooks, the monkey, who traveled comfortably, munching on chunks of ice, in a large parrot cage draped with burlap.[70]

From all this I conclude that Louis Block may well have had pet monkeys on his property. Born in Germany around 1850, he would have grown up in a culture enamored with wild animals and zoos; six major zoos opened in Germany between 1844 and 1871,[71] roughly the year he emigrated to America. Two of the zoos, in Hamburg and Hanover, were each just sixty miles from his home in Bremen. By the time he arrived in America, traveling menageries were everywhere, and the Central Park Menagerie in New York City had officially opened in 1864. During Block's time living in the city, Hagenbeck's exotic animal shows flourished. The New York Zoological Park (now the Bronx Zoo) would open in 1899, soon after the Block family moved to the suburbs. Louis Block would have had the opportunity for ample exposure to monkeys. When he arrived in Mamaroneck in 1896, his children were five, seven, and eleven, of just the age to enjoy such unusual pets on their new spacious country property. Finally, if Block did keep pet monkeys, he probably would have been just one of many who did so at the time.

IF ONLY A ROCK COULD TALK

So with about ten seemingly viable possible explanations, some more plausible than others, for how and why the stakes came to be embedded into the rock to consider, but not a single completely convincing one, I thought, "If only

FIGURE 10.15 Carl Hagenbeck with his grandchildren and pet monkey. This photograph also appeared in "How Hagenbeck Became the Wild Animal King," *New York Times*, April 20, 1913. *(Reprinted from* Hagenbeck, Beasts and Men, *1909, p. 116. Photo by author.)*

Reach Out

Traditional research can be a solitary endeavor. A good antidote to the isolation is to reach out and engage people—anyone and everyone who is interested—in conversations about the questions and mysteries concerning your property. And here I am not talking experts, just ordinary people who might say, "Maybe it was. . . ." You can often quickly get a real brainstorming session going. The process might lead to creative suggestions that you can then pursue through research. The old saying that "two heads are better than one" is true here.

After casual conversations about Sears, Roebuck and Co. mail-order houses (see chapter 1), three people tore out and gave me current newspaper real estate advertisements about Sears houses. This added to my store of information on Sears houses and broadened the context in which I was working. Even better was when a chat with a neighbor revealed that she had the collection of newsletters created by the developer of our neighborhood as a sales promotion piece in the 1920s (see chapter 7). She had forgotten how she had come upon the collection but was able to find it in her attic. It became a key resource in my investigation of one of the former owners of my property.

A guest at a party my husband and I hosted wanted to see the rock on our property after hearing me talk about it, so even though it was February and freezing cold, out and up we went to take a look. His comment, "I bet George Washington rode his horse up here during the Revolution," was based on nothing more than his casual knowledge of an important battle that had taken place nearby and the unusual topographical nature of the rock, near the edge of a hill, once-upon-a-time affording an expansive view. The point is not that this friend really knew for a fact that his supposition about Washington was true, but that it prompted me to look further into the history of the American Revolution in my area. That, in turn, led me to more discoveries about my property.

Many of my hypotheses about the origins of the stakes in the rock derived from conversations with various people. At another social gathering, I was describing "the strange stakes that surround the large rock on our property" when suddenly someone said, "Why, there is a gazebo atop a large rock at our beach club, and it is anchored to the rock with cables, so maybe there was a gazebo on your property"—another plausible hypothesis to pursue.

By engaging in conversation a neighbor who had grown up on our block in the 1940s, I confirmed what the former owner had told me about the enormous rock on the property. He said that as a child, he and his friends had always referred to it as "the monkey-zoo rock." I still did not really know what the rock had once been used for, but at least I then knew that the monkey story was generally accepted by the neighbors and not just the invention of a single person. And chatting about the monkey story prompted another person to tell me about a collection of archival material at a nearby historic house where I might find information about the late-nineteenth-century hobby of keeping exotic animals. My idea about the enslaved Africans and the rock emerged from a casual conversation, developed later through research, as did the one about the plane-spotting tower. All of these leads came about initially through informal dialogue, the spark that triggered in-depth research.

that rock could talk!" Oddly, as I go back to reconsider my hypotheses and review the evidence I have compiled to support them, I find myself saying, "Now that sounds like a good possibility," and then repeating the observation with the next one. The only problem is, I say it for all of them; it seems impossible to discount or reject any of them.

Maybe more than one of my ideas is correct. For example, though it sounds unlikely, think about it this way. Perhaps around the turn of the twentieth century, Louis Block had the stakes set into the rock to secure a gazebo, and then others later used them for guy wires to support either a gin pole mast for lifting stone or a plane-spotting tower. Or possibly workers put them there as part of a lifting device used in the construction of Block's house and later recycled them to anchor his gazebo or tether his monkeys. Or maybe smugglers inserted them into the rock to restrain enslaved Africans, and Block then later used them for the monkeys. The possibilities are many.

And consider this. Perhaps the term *monkey,* as it came down to Mrs. T———, originally referred to something other than an animal. *Monkey,* it turns out, is a term sometimes used in the quarry business. I ran across an entry for the word in a glossary written in the late 1930s by the staff of the Folklore Project of the Federal Writers' Project for the U.S. Works Progress Administration (WPA). A section on quarrying in Vermont defines *monkey* as slang for an automatic dumping mechanism on the carriages that ran on the cables extended from the gin pole to the banks of the quarry.[72] And the term has yet another meaning. One dictionary definition of *monkey* is "any of various machines, implements, or vessels; *esp*: the falling weight of a pile driver."[73] So maybe those meanings of the word explain the origins of whatever it was that Mrs. T——— heard about. From that hearsay, perhaps she concluded that there had been monkeys tied to the rock at one time.

Alas, there seems to be no way to know for sure who put the stakes into the rock or for what purpose, and there probably never will be. At least there is a shred of hope on the date question. Professor Lyman got back to me at the end of his sabbatical. In a preliminary examination of the specimens, he found relatively large slag inclusions, indicating the wrought iron was probably many decades old. Slag inclusions are nonmetallic, glasslike particles entrapped within the solidified metal. In wrought iron, these inclusions vary in composition and structure depending on the fabrication method used, and thus, hold the evidence about age. Just how old, he did not yet know.

As it came time for the lab course to begin, Professor Lyman needed a longer sample of the iron, so we cut off a second piece of stake—to be cut longitudinally and then sectioned transversely into small chunks, one for each lab team to work with—and mailed it to him. First, he sent a powdered sample to a lab in Cincinnati for powder x-ray diffraction analysis, which gave him some preliminary information. Then, with quite a team to guide them (a metallurgical technician, a graduate student teaching assistant, an undergraduate teaching assistant, and the professor), the thirty-one students in ten lab groups used various kinds of microscopy, spectrometry, and diffraction—light optical microscopy, scanning electron microscopy, transmission electron microscopy, energy-dispersive x-ray spectrometry, and selected area electron diffraction—to examine the microstructure of my wrought iron stakes. The students' primary task was to date the specimen by determining the process used to produce the raw pig iron later fashioned into wrought iron by the blacksmith. Their options were: 1660–1799 for the bloomery or finery processes, which used charcoal, produced from wood; 1800–1925 for the puddling process, which used coal; or 1926–1960 for the Aston process, which used a Bessemer converter to turn pig iron into a wrought iron precursor. Each iron-making process results in a slightly different slag microstructure and composition based on where the iron ore originated, what fuel was used, and the type of furnace employed.[74]

At the end of the course, the students' results varied widely and were inconclusive. However, student Alexander Hollenbach found phases present in the x-ray diffraction data that were consistent with the finery process, which would date the stakes before 1800. Alexander wanted to take the research further, so the next semester he and Dr. Lyman made a trip to Yale University (stopping by my property on the way to take a look at the stakes and the rock), where Dr. Robert Gordon, an expert in archaeometallurgy and early American wrought iron, examined my specimen and compared it with wrought irons in his extensive collection of dated specimens. He agreed the samples were likely to be pre-1926, but pointed out that a blacksmith's heating and beating tend to obliterate much of the evidence. He believes the date cannot be made more specific given the available evidence.

There is another problem that makes dating of metal processes difficult: older processes tend to continue after newer processes have been introduced. For example, the early eighteenth-century bloomery process continued until about 1900 at a few locations, but during the nineteenth century the furnace fuel may have changed from wood charcoal to mineral coal, which indeed complicates the dating of wrought iron.

But even if I am able to establish a date range, I may never know with certainty why and by whom the stakes were put into the rock. In the end, the unknown and the unknowable are things one has to accept. It does seem, though, that at the time the stakes were put there, and for some time afterward, the reason for their presence would have seemed perfectly obvious. It is only with the passage of time that a mystery develops, after the collective memory has forgotten the original purpose.

Epilogue

Kernels of Truth

"The reality is, no one owns the earth or what comes out of it. The earth owns us, and will have us back in its time."[1]

—Holland Cotter, *New York Times*, 2006.

The simple desire to find answers to questions about my property provided the motivation to do the research that resulted in this book, a genealogy of a piece of land. Solving the mysteries required separating fact from fiction. That called for work in multiple arenas: careful observing; conversing and consulting with others; researching in libraries, in archives, and on the Internet; and finally, putting everything into historical context.

In doing my research I came to appreciate the differences between undocumented and documented history. One day as I was wrapping up the book's final chapters, someone knocked at the front door. My daughter answered, and I heard her laugh and say, "I think my mom wants to talk to you." The reason for the man's visit? He was writing a novel about the Native Americans who inhabited our neighborhood four hundred years ago, and he had been drawn to the large rock on our property, having determined that it is the highest point in town. Certain that the early inhabitants would have used it as a lookout spot and thus would have gathered nearby, he wanted to know what I knew about the outcrop's history and if I had ever found any arrowheads.

Unfortunately, I had found neither arrowheads nor any other Native American artifacts, but I did have some information about the history of the area's earliest residents. We talked and thus began a mutually beneficial exchange of resources and ideas. He had been researching the early Native Americans of Mamaroneck for years, and his information and thoughts were helpful; however, his goals differed dramatically from mine. Our conversations made clear to me how much writing historical novels and writing history diverge from each other. I wanted to know what had happened on my property, not imagine or reconstruct what might have happened. I needed to document everything I discovered about the place and its former inhabitants.

CALICO: The Research Process

I like to think of the research process for investigating the history of a piece of land as falling into six broad categories. The word *calico* in North America means any inexpensive cotton material printed with a small, all-over pattern, often floral. In the eighteenth and nineteenth centuries it was the favored fabric for making patchwork quilts.[1] The term and its association with quilts, to me, are suggestive of the patchwork nature of the process of doing research—made up of many pieces, the result of a process sometimes deliberate and methodical, sometimes random, usually progressive, and always benefiting from a modicum of imagination. CALICO is a convenient acronym for the six key areas of the research methodology: context, archives, library, Internet, conversation, and observation.

Context is the framework for historical information. The meaning of any one discovery changes once it is put into a context. Sometimes the best we can do is to make a guess, but framing it in a historical context allows it to be an educated guess.

Archives house primary source material and unpublished documents that often cannot be found anywhere else.

Libraries contain a wealth of material for setting things into a context, for understanding the connections among the facts.

The Internet overlaps what may be found in libraries and archives and using it can save time and money. Increasingly, it is becoming a source for older published material where copyright is no longer an issue. The Internet also provides the speedy but contextual answer.

Conversation with experts and others will lead to additional sources and ideas to pursue through further research.

Observation is often a first step but is also an activity to return to again and again. Armed with more information, the observer sees things anew with each observation, leading to new conclusions. If we look at it long enough and carefully enough, the land will tell us its story.

The research needed to develop each chapter in this book, with a very few exceptions, required work in all six categories. There is no single, preferred order to follow. Each line of inquiry takes the researcher on a different path, but eventually the paths begin to intersect and overlap and can then be sewn together.

THE NEED FOR THE DEED

The key to uncovering the factual story of one small patch of land is the deed chain—finding all those owners. But think about it—the concept of land ownership is a peculiar one. Nature, the earth itself, eventually reclaims virtually every bit of land in spite of humankind's interventions and alterations. I was reminded of this recently when I came upon a wooded spot next to a pond on an island off the Maine coast where until a year ago there had been a dilapidated but imposing ice house. It had been there for more than one hundred years, a mainstay of the island for decades, an essential amenity in times before refrigeration. And now it is gone. Amazingly, there is not one trace of it left. No discernable evidence whatsoever. And that happened in a matter of months.

How can the land really be owned? It cannot be moved. The changes people make to it are limited and often temporary. Paradoxically, the character of a piece of land is both enduring and ephemeral, but in the end, out of the control of any of us and merely, in the words of George Washington's associate, Seneca Chief Tanacharison, "a Place of Residence for us."[2] In our culture land is, however, something we agree is "owned." Hence, the need for the deed.

Once the pieces of the deed puzzle were in place, I needed a frame or a context for them. The deeds provided some leads, but used as sources by themselves, they were rather skeletal. It is history that provides the context for the deed information to create a story. In my case there was no story of a so-called historical house, or even an old house, but the building and the land it occupies have histories nonetheless. They have stories to tell. Research, then, allowed me to put some flesh on the bones of the deed chain to find the stories.

The deeds laid the groundwork for chronicling the lives of selected owners and offered the starting point for using the journalist's basic five-W formula for story writing: finding the who, what, when, where, and why. After locating the deeds, other types of resources came into play: censuses, genealogies, maps, newspapers, wills, and more. The primary goal was to put the people into a historical context and answer key questions beyond the "who" and the "when" provided by the deed: what brought them to the property in the first place, where did they come from, what were their relationships to the land, how did attitudes regarding land change over time, what bearing did the owners' livelihoods have on their uses of the land, how did the property's proximity to a growing major city affect its development, and why did the residents leave or sell the land?

Careful consideration of deeds can uncover information leading in two directions—to big historical trends in land use and to the small story of an individual's use of a property. To cite just one example of how information in a deed pointed to a trend when put into historical context: I noticed in the deed chain that within a period of just over five years, from 1890 to 1895, the property changed hands five times. This was no anomaly at the time. Suburbanization was underway in the New York City metropolitan area, and real estate speculators knew that the trolley line in Mamaroneck would open in 1896, passing right by the property, ready to take a commuter to the railroad station where frequent trains headed for Grand Central Station. After the series of speculator-owners, it was surely with that knowledge that Louis Block bought the property, built a house, and by 1896 was commuting to the city. He stayed for over thirty years, the beneficiary of suburbanization.

The 1931 deed for the property contains an example of a small piece of information that led to a fuller understanding of a specific individual's story. This deed transferred six empty lots along with two large parcels, unsold due to the Great Depression, from developer Harry Rich

Mooney's company to another realty company. Why the large parcels? The 1927–28 *Mooney's Megaphone* newsletters that my neighbor had in her attic shed light on Mooney's plans. The large parcels were never subdivided, as they were being reserved for two apartment buildings, and though the apartment buildings never moved beyond the planning stages, had they been built, they would have been the crowning achievement in Mooney's concept of community—single-family houses and apartment buildings with shared recreational amenities.

The deeds, in addition to identifying the owners and providing the essential property descriptions and conveyance terms, offered other random, enticing details. For example, from deeds of the eighteenth century, I learned about occupations, familial relationships, locations of buildings and other alterations to the land, aspects of the social condition of women, and old customs such as earmarking farm animals. Deeds vary in the number and quality of the details they provide, but the small fragments of information can be keys to understanding the historical moment.

FACT AND FICTION

Fact and fiction sometimes intermingle, and what is shown to be uncertain or false—whether it is folklore, tradition, rumor, or pure fantasy—often contains a shred of truth. A professional storyteller once told me his listeners often ask, "Is that a true story?" His answer is always the same: "There is truth in every story." But sometimes a fiction develops from a kernel of truth, especially when the truth is unfamiliar or unpalatable.

One challenge that developed out of a fact/fiction conundrum was Mrs. T———'s "Sears house" comment. In that case, a vague recollection turned out to hold a grain of truth. The storyteller's idea applies here. Over the years, Mrs. T——— probably had heard little about the *McCall's* 1930s homes-of-the-month beyond what the first owner likely had told her. The magazine's homes-of-the-month feature was a relatively short-lived phenomenon two decades before Mrs. T——— and her husband entered the picture, and articles about it reached just a portion of the population. Sears, Roebuck mail-order houses, on the other hand, received broad media attention in the 1980s and 1990s. Mrs. T——— must have heard about them and then conflated the two kinds of houses.

If the monkeys-and-stakes riddle really did originate in the slave story, the kernel of truth was—something or someone had been tied to the stakes. Regardless of how the information came to Mrs. T———, if it were true, it would have been an uncomfortable truth in the mid-twentieth century, so it was perhaps easier for the transmitters of the story to believe that it had been monkeys chained to the rock rather than people. An apocryphal monkey story could have developed as a replacement for the no-longer-tolerable slave story. On the other hand, if the monkey story is true, there is ample circumstantial evidence to support it. And likewise, there is evidence for the various high elevation/tower ideas, the derrick-and-boom hypotheses, and the gazebo notion as well. Sorting out possibility from probability became one of the main challenges.

UNANSWERED QUESTIONS

A friend once took a job as a research assistant to a history scholar. New at the endeavor and mired in what seemed like endless searching, she asked, "How do you know when you are finished?" The scholar's response: "You are never finished." Even after my search moved on from the deeds and I had diligently researched a number of issues, there were still unanswered questions about my property's past.

The rock investigation as a whole is a perfect example of research never finished. The project was about opening up all the possibilities, an exercise in imaginative thinking. Research can be dry, tedious, and very narrowly focused, but a challenge like finding an explanation for the stakes allowed it to be creative and invigorating. (The process also happened to generate great fodder for dinner party conversation.) The rock-and-the-stakes mystery yielded many possible explanations, but the truth may never be known. Perhaps the failure to find the truth was a good thing. It certainly made the process more fun, if somewhat frustrating.

So in the end, as a result of this research, I have come to believe that the genealogy of a piece of land provides a corpus of cultural literacy, connecting individuals to each other, to our history, to our culture, and to the earth. With family genealogy many people encounter insurmountable barriers to completing the family tree—adoption, migration, displacement, slavery, illiteracy, and the loss or destruction of documentation. A genealogy of a piece of land, on the other hand, is democratic and offers a heritage available to everyone—everyone lives somewhere.

The land does, however, hold its secrets. Looking back in time, there is a certain point where our knowledge fades out and then there is darkness; one has to accept, at least temporarily, what cannot now be known. With history, though, the story is never finished. Certain facts of history exist, but our grasp of those facts changes constantly. Given the passage of time, heretofore unknown documents may surface, additional evidence may be uncovered, a new insight may surface, a new worldview or ideology may develop, or a new technology may emerge, challenging what we now accept as fact and allowing some of the remaining questions to be answered and the genealogy to be made more complete. As William Faulkner once wrote: "The past is never dead. It's not even past."[3]

Appendix
The Deed Chain of Owners

Name	Dates of ownership	Occupation/ Relationship	Land description	Price paid
Wappaquewam	? to 1661	Sakima	3 necks of land	
John Richbell	1661 to 1668	merchant and farmer	3 necks of land, and the right to "feed cattle or cutt Timber twenty miles Northward"	22 coats, 100 fathom of wampum, 12 shirts, 10 pairs of stockings, 20 hands of powder, 12 bars of lead, 2 firelocks, 15 hoes, 15 hatchets, 3 kettles
Margery Parsons	1668	mother-in-law of John Richbell	East neck	
Anne Richbell	1668 to 1697	wife of John Richbell	East neck	
Caleb Heathcote	1697 to 1716	merchant, judge, and mayor	East neck and "north into the woods . . . 20 miles"	600 pounds

Name	Dates of ownership	Occupation/ Relationship	Land description	Price paid
Eliezer Gidney	1716 to 1722	shipwright and farmer, Anne Richbell's son-in-law	80 acres	62 pounds
Isaac Gidney	1722 to 1771	farmer, son of Eliezer Gedney	80 acres; acreage increased through additional purchases	40 pounds
Isaac Gedney Jr.	1771 to 1784	farmer, son of Isaac Gedney	135 acres	by father's will
Absalom Gedney	1784 to 1793	farmer, cousin of Isaac Gedney	135 acres	1,048 pounds
William Gray	1793 to 1818	farmer	135 acres	1,145 pounds
James Gray	1818 to 1820	distiller in New York City, son of William Gray	135 acres	$5
David Lewis	1820 to 1826	grocer in New York City	201 acres	$6,500
Jacob Richee	1826 to ?	grocer in New York City	201 acres	$10,000
Benjamin Hadden	unknown	farmer	unknown	unknown
Margaret, Mary, & Deborah Hadden	by 1845 to 1853	daughters of Benjamin Hadden	6 acres	by father's will
John W. Mills of White Plains	1853 to 1861	investor/landlord	6 acres	$250 at auction

Name	Dates of ownership	Occupation/ Relationship	Land description	Price paid
Mary A. Dingee	1861	wife of Solomon Dingee, farmer	6 acres	$2,000
Helen Gambling	1861 to 1881	wife of William Gambling, town auditor	6 acres	$2,000
Mutual Life Insurance Co. of New York	1881 to 1883	mortgage foreclosure	7½ acres	$10,000 at auction
Erastus C. Benedict of Newark, NJ	1883 to 1890 1884 to 1890	bank organizer	7½ acres 4 acres	$12,000 $500
Richard B. Constantine of Orange, NJ	1890 to 1894	investor	7½ acres 4 acres combined the 2 plots	$15,000 $1,000
Herman Ottenberg of New York, NY	1894	investor	11½ acres	$1.00 & other unnamed "valuable considerations" plus an $8,000 mortgage
William W. Ladd Jr. of New York, NY	1894 to 1895	investor	11½ acres	$1.00 & other unnamed "valuable considerations" plus an $8,000 mortgage
George F. Brown & Mary D. Brown of New York, NY	1895	investor	11½ acres	$1.00 & other unnamed "valuable considerations" plus an $8,000 mortgage
Louis Block of New York, NY	1895 to 1896	refrigeration engineer and inventor	11½ acres	$16,000 plus an $8,000 mortgage

Name	Dates of ownership	Occupation/ Relationship	Land description	Price paid
Celia I. Block	1896 to 1927	wife of Louis Block	11½ acres	$10 & other unnamed "valuable considerations" plus an $8,000 mortgage
Mamaroneck Knolls, Inc. (Harry Rich Mooney)	1927 to 1931	real estate developer	11½ acres	$10 plus a $73,000 mortgage $1.00 & other unnamed "valuable considerations" plus a $17,000 mortgage
Romeria Realty	1931 to 1945	realty company	6 lots in the development & 2 large apartment plots	$250,000 mortgage
Village of Mamaroneck	1946	municipality	2 lots in the development & 2 large apartment plots	Tax lien foreclosure for unpaid taxes 1934 to 1945
Joseph DeMaria	1946 to 1956	real estate developer and plumbing business owner	one large apartment plot and 4 other lots elsewhere in the village	$5,000
Francis T——— and Marilyn T———	1956 to 2000	civil engineer	⅓ acre	

Notes

INTRODUCTION

1. "Home Ownership Showing Increase," *New York Times*, October 9, 1932; U.S. Census, "Housing Vacancies and Homeownership," http://www.census.gov.

2. "Harry Rich Mooney: Builder of Homes and Happiness," *Mooney's Megaphone*, November 12, 1927.

3. *Merriam-Webster's Collegiate Dictionary*, 10th ed., s.v. "palimpsest."

CHAPTER ONE

1. *Epigraph*. Sears, Roebuck and Co., *Sears, Roebuck Catalog of Houses, 1926: An Unabridged Reprint* (1926; repr., Philadelphia: Athenaeum/New York: Dover, 1991), 8–9.

2. Patricia Poore, "Pattern Book Architecture: Is Yours a Mail-Order House?" *Old-House Journal* 8, no. 12 (1980), 183, 190–93; Kay Halpin, "Sears, Roebuck's Best-kept Secret," *Historic Preservation* 33, no. 5 (1981): 25–29; Katherine Cole Stevenson and H. Ward Jandl, *Houses By Mail: A Guide to Houses from Sears, Roebuck and Company* (New York: Wiley/Preservation Press, 1986).

3. See Alan Murray, "Mail-Order Homes Sears Sold in 1909–37 Are Suddenly Chic," *Wall Street Journal*, February 11, 1985; David M. Schwartz, "When Home Sweet Home Was Just a Mailbox Away," *Smithsonian*, November 1985, 90–96, 98, 100–101; Betsy Brown, "Landmark Homes from Sears Catalogue," *New York Times*, December 21, 1986; Harriet Edleson, "Pages of History," *Washington Post*, December 26, 1991; Laura Gatland, "Humble, Huggable Mail-Order Homes," *Christian Science Monitor*, May 7, 1998; Denny Lee, "Mail-Order Homes: Insert House (A) Into Idyllic Landscape (B), *New York Times*, October 25, 2002; Mary Beth Breckenridge, "The Construction Side of Sears," *Journal News* (White Plains, NY), April 16–17, 2005; Cynthia Crossen, "Your Dream House: Delivered by Mail, Assembled by Number," *Wall Street Journal*, October 31, 2005; Elsa Brenner, "It Arrived in an Awfully Big Kit," *New York Times*, March 2,

2008. In addition, at least five of the original Sears mail-order house catalogues have been reprinted since 1990.

4. Advertisement of Peter J. Riolo Real Estate, *Rivertowns Enterprise* (Hastings-on-Hudson, NY), April 9, 2004.

5. Stevenson and Jandl, 253; Prudential Connecticut Realty newspaper advertisement for a house in Greenwich, Connecticut, source unknown, 2004.

6. Robert Schweitzer and Michael W. R. Davis, *America's Favorite Homes: Mail-Order Catalogues as a Guide to Popular Early 20th-Century Houses* (Detroit: Wayne State University Press, 1990), 57–61.

7. Ibid., 56.

8. Alfred Bruce and Harold Sandbank, *A History of Prefabrication* (1943; repr., New York: Arno, 1972), 56–57.

9. Schweitzer and Davis, 198; Advertisement, "Bennett Homes," *Fruit, Garden and Home* [later *Better Homes and Gardens*], February 1924, 51.

10. Stevenson and Jandl, 103, 106, 149–53, 221, 227–28. The 1940 catalogue is nearly the same as the 1939 version with no new house styles.

11. Rosemary Thornton, *The Houses That Sears Built: Everything You Ever Wanted to Know About Sears Catalog Homes* (Alton, IL: Gentle Beam, 2002), 87.

12. Dolores Hayden, *Building Suburbia: Green Fields and Urban Growth, 1820–2000* (New York: Pantheon, 2003), 105. Hayden says maybe 50,000 Sears homes were built and that Sears claims 110,000; most sources say about 100,000 of them were built.

13. Sears Archives Historic Homes, www.searsarchives.com.

14. The Homeland Co. advertisements, *Daily Times* (Mamaroneck, NY), September 9, 1937; *Standard Star* (New Rochelle, NY), September 16, 1937. These sister newspapers, for neighboring towns, contained the same real estate section each week.

15. J. Harold Hawkins, "The May Home of the Month Can Be Tailored to Order," *McCall's*, May 1937, 56. I was able to buy the May 1937 issue of *McCall's* on eBay for a modest sum.

16. "Cottage May Expand," *New York Times*, May 9, 1937. Evidence provided by a document in my town's tax assessor's office makes clear that one of the two second-floor bedrooms of my house was left unfinished until the early 1960s, the house expanding along with the family who lived there.

17. The original model house is no longer in its original location. Yet the site is identifiable by a stone wall still extant.

18. "Home Offered Which May Be Made Larger," *Washington Post*, May 2, 1937.

19. J. Harold Hawkins, *Cape Cod Colonial: McCall's Twelfth Home of the Month*, (Dayton, OH: McCall's Magazine, 1937), 1, 6, 9–10.

20. Information gleaned from "Home of the Month" series in *McCall's* issues from April 1936 through November 1938.

21. Land Developers and Home Builders Division of National Association of Real Estate Boards, *Home of the Month: Selected for its Livability in Cooperation with McCall's Magazine*, June 1937, http://www.realtor.org.

22. On the second page of some issues, next to the table of contents, *McCall's* editors would make reference to their readership, as in "a longtime favorite on McCall Street" (February 1934) or "Hollywood's loss is McCall Street's gain" (November 1935). See Frank Luther Mott, *A History of American Magazines, 1741–1930* (Cambridge, MA: Belknap of Harvard University Press, 1957), 4:580–86 for a discussion of *McCall's* use of this idea.

23. Mott, *History*, 4:585.

24. "Real Estate Notes," *New York Times*, June 28, 1936.

CHAPTER TWO

1. *Epigraph.* Harold E. Group, ed. *House-of-the-Month Book of Small Houses* (Garden City, NY: Garden City Publishing, 1946), 5.

2. Paul Byrne, staff photo, *Daily Times* (Mamaroneck, NY), September 10, 1956.

3. Ned Benton, "Did Larchmont Take the Wrong Path? Planning the Thruway 50 Years Ago," *Larchmont Gazette* (Larchmont, NY), May 13, 2004, http://www.larchmontgazette.com/2004/articles/20040513thruway.html.

4. Robert A. Caro, *The Power Broker: Robert Moses and the Fall of New York* (New York: Knopf, 1974), 19, 876.

5. Helen Leavitt, *Superhighway – Superhoax* (Garden City, NY: Doubleday, 1970), 53. The quote comes from a May 1964 speech before the National Highway Users Conference.

6. Caro, *Power Broker*, 19.

7. Leavitt, *Superhighway*, 22–23.

8. David J. St. Clair, *The Motorization of American Cities* (New York: Praeger, 1986), 20.

9. Caro, *Power Broker*, 144. Caro states that in 1919, there were fewer than seven million families with cars. By 1923, the number had more than tripled.

10. Phil Patton, *Open Road: A Celebration of the American Highway* (New York: Simon & Schuster, 1986), 67.

11. Ibid., 69.

12. Sadly, just three years after the centennial of the founding of the Bronx Parkway Commission, it seems that the river is still polluted in spite of recent efforts by government and community groups in the Bronx to clean it up. A New York State Supreme Court judge in February 2005 ordered the City of Yonkers to stop within fifteen months the flow of sewage that is emptying into storm sewers and then into the river. Lisa W. Foderaro, "In Yonkers, New Pressure to Clean up Bronx River," *New York Times*, March 14, 2005. (Hereafter in this chapter *New York Times* referred to as *NYT*.)

13. Marilyn E. Weigold, *Pioneering in Parks and Parkways: Westchester County, New York, 1895–1945*, Essays in Public Works History 9 (Chicago: Public Works Historical Society, 1980), 3–4. The author traces the history of Westchester's parkways and observes (p. 11) that public opinion regarding the building of highways was quite different in the 1920s than in 1980.

14. Bronx Parkway Commission, *Report to the Board of Estimate and Apportionment of the City of New York* (Bronxville, NY, April 15, 1912), 14.

15. Weigold, *Pioneering in Parks*, 6–7. Contemporary local newspaper coverage indicates that 370 homes were demolished to clear the way for the Bronx River Parkway. "Formal Opening of Bronx River Parkway Soon," *Daily Times*, November 8, 1925.

16. "Bronx Parkway Officially Opened," *NYT*, November 6, 1925.

17. Bronx Parkway Commission, *Final Report* (Bronxville, NY, 1925), 78.

18. Diana Rice, "A Magical Parkway Leads Out of City," *NYT*, August 16, 1925.

19. Georgia Fraser, "The Bronx River Parkway," *NYT*, July 30, 1925.

20. "The Way Westchester Does It," *House & Garden*, July 1926, 100.

21. Ibid., 100–101, 132. For a discussion of the history of the Bronx River Parkway, see the Westchester County Archives website, "Bronx River Parkway Reservation," http:// westchesterarchives.com/BRPR/BRPRHome.html.

22. Westchester County Park Commission, *Report to the Board of Supervisors of the County of Westchester* (April 30, 1923), 1. (Hereafter annual *Report* referred to as WCPC, *Report*.)

23. Westchester County Park Commission, *Report for the Acquisition of Parks, Parkways, or Boulevards* (May 17, 1923), 3–8.

24. WCPC, *Report* (April 30, 1924), 39.

25. Ibid., (April 30, 1925), 19. The commission minutes of December 18, 1924, cite a letter from the Mamaroneck Chamber of Commerce concerning the dreadful traffic conditions on the Boston Post Road. Westchester County Park Commission Minutes, December 18, 1924, item 9, 221, Westchester County Historical Society (hereafter referred to as WCPC Minutes).

26. "Westchester Asks Huge Park System," *NYT*, March 17, 1925.

27. Marilyn Weigold discusses two Westchester parkways, including the Pelham-Port Chester Parkway, in "Roads to No Where," *Westchester Historian* 55, no. 4 (1979): 87–89. See Jay Downer and James Owen, "Public Parks in Westchester County," in *History of Westchester County, New York*, ed. Alvah P. French (New York: Lewis Historical Publishing, 1925), 959–1012, for an overview of Westchester County park development by 1925, and Frank E. Sanchis, *American Architecture, Westchester County, New York: Colonial to Contemporary* (Harrison, NY: Harbor Hills, 1977), 444–57, for a more recent discussion of parks, parkways, and highways in the county.

28. WCPC, *Report* (April 30, 1925), 22.

29. WCPC Minutes, January 21, 1926, through December 8, 1927.

30. "Buys $800,000 Park Lands," *NYT*, January 22, 1926; "Buys Land for Parkways," *NYT*, February 10, 1926; "Tour Park Area in Westchester," *NYT*, November 13, 1926.

31. WCPC Minutes, February 9, May 3, July 31, and August 16, 1928.

32. Ibid., July 26, 1928.

33. WCPC, *Report* (April 30, 1930), 50.

34. "Holiday Traffic along Post Road Crowds Highway," *Daily Times*, July 3, 1926.

35. "New York Road Building Lags," *NYT*, October 24, 1937.

36. "Boston Post Road," *NYT*, March 6, 1950.

37. WCPC, *Report*, (April 30, 1930), 50.

38. Ibid., (April 30, 1925), 74, 79. The 1932 *Report* ([April 30], p. 9) states that total appropriations for 218 acres acquired to date for the Pelham-Port Chester Parkway were $5,212,403.70.

39. Ibid., (April 30, 1927), 19.

40. "Asks Park Economy for Westchester," *NYT*, October 17, 1932.

41. "Bronx River Road is Facing Closing," *NYT*, March 14, 1942.

42. "Railroads Protest Westchester Plans," *NYT*, January 26, 1926.

43. CPC, *Report* (April 30, 1927), 18.

44. WCPC Minutes, November 21, 1929, item 11, 642.

45. "Westchester to Push Post Road By-Pass," *NYT*, September 22, 1929.

46. Caro, *Power Broker*, 312.

47. "Park Council to Aid Westchester Plans," *NYT*, September 30, 1932.

48. C. Earl Morrow, "Regional Plan Advises Building," *NYT*, April 30, 1933; "Westchester to Act on Charter Thursday," *NYT*, March 10, 1936. See Weigold, "Roads to No Where," 87–89, for a brief summary of the parkway's progress from the 1920s to the 1950s.

49. Samuel J. T. Coe, "New York Road Building Lags," *NYT*, October 24, 1937.

50. "Westchester to Cut 1938 Fund for Parks," *NYT*, November 24, 1937.

51. "Truck Toll Route Favored by Moses," *NYT*, February 6, 1938.

52. "'Freeway' is Now Urged," *NYT*, December 13, 1936. The Regional Plan Association (RPA), a not-for-profit advocacy group founded in 1922, "prepares long range plans and policies to guide the growth and development of the New York-New Jersey-Connecticut metropolitan region." Regional Plan Association: Mission, http://www.rpa.org/mission.html.

53. "Truck Toll Route Favored by Moses." See also "High-Speed Bus and Truck Route Planned by Officials Over Abandoned W. & B. Road," *Daily Times*, February 7, 1938.

54. "Parkways Pushed for Westchester," *NYT*, April 24, 1938.

55. WCPC Minutes, December 11, 1941, item 18, 175.

56. Caro, *Power Broker*, 316.

57. "Building Shows Gain in Westchester," *NYT*, October 26, 1930.

58. "Model Home in New Rochelle Now Open for Inspection," *NYT*, July 28, 1935.

59. "Mamaroneck," *Mooney's Megaphone*, November 12, 1927.

60. Gosta Morner, "Harry Rich Mooney: Builder of Homes and Happiness," *Mooney's Megaphone*, November 12, 1927. The property Mooney sold to the Westchester County Park Commission was just under one-third of an acre and was located near where Saxon Woods Park adjoined the parkway's proposed highway; it had been scheduled for appropriation by the county for the park more than a year before Mooney bought it. Westchester County Park Commission, *Map of Lands to be Acquired for Saxon Woods Park, Westchester County, N.Y., December 30, 1925*, filed November 24, 1926.

61. "Defense Road Plan Irks Westchester," *NYT*, November 12, 1940.

62. "Westchester Supervisors Fight for Voice on Parkway Projects," *NYT*, November 26, 1940.

63. "Plans Protest on Parkway," *NYT*, December 1, 1940.

64. "Westchester Area Fights Road Bill," *NYT*, March 10, 1944.

65. "Woman Sues to Halt State Use of Land for 'Thruway' Project in Westchester," *NYT*, July 14, 1944.

66. "Highway Project under Sharp Fire," *NYT*, August 27, 1944.

67. Betty Moorsteen, "City Can Be Beautiful: Ask Lewis Mumford," *PM*, May 12, 1946.

68. Robert Moses, "New Highways for a Better New York," *NYT*, November 11, 1945.

69. WCPC Minutes, September 3, 1942, item 32, 11–12. "Westchester to Give State Right of Way," *NYT*, March 23, 1943.

70. "New Post Road Link Planned after War," *NYT*, September 11, 1942.

71. "Woman Sues."

72. St. Clair, *Motorization*, 149–50.

73. President George Bush signed legislation renaming the interstate system in 1990. "Landmarks in American Civil Engineering: Interstate Highway System," *Civil Engineering* 72, no. 11/12 (2002): 141.

74. "City Starts Work on 6-Lane Highway," *NYT*, September 21, 1949.

75. "Westchester Asks Its Thruway First," *NYT*, February 21, 1950. As the realization of the Thruway approached, nostalgia for the old Boston Post Road set in. Another article in the *New York Times* described it as approaching the end of a stage in its long career and as "an interesting alternative to the sanitary parkways. At least it lets one see the adjacent world rather than merely manicured shrubbery." Richard Cohen, "Where Paul Revere Was Once a Sunday Rider," *NYT*, June 11, 1959.

76. "Thruway Ground Broken," *NYT*, July 22, 1950.

77. "Westchester Gives Road Route to State," *NYT*, February 12, 1952.

78. Merrill Folsom, "Two Cities Mourn Thruway Invasion," *NYT*, April 11, 1953.

79. Folsom, "Thruway to Cut a Painful Gash Across Heart of New Rochelle," *NYT*, March 1, 1955. A photograph in the *Daily Times*, August 24, 1956, shows one of the cemeteries being carefully documented before the remains' removal to a nearby cemetery.

80. John Powell, "Old Indian Burial Tunnel May Ring Thruway Blasts," *Daily Times*, January 28, 1955; "Blasting in New Rochelle Beats a Red Man's Drum," *NYT*, January 29, 1955. Both articles are short and merely state that the caves, closed thirty years earlier, were suspected of amplifying the sound of the dynamite blasting and were an engineering safety concern.

81. Folsom, "Thruway."

82. "Mamaroneck School Board to Protest Thruway Exit," *Daily Times*, October 1, 1954.

83. "Village Board Joins Fight on Cloverleaf as Protests Mount," *Daily Times*, October 12, 1954.

84. Paul Byrne, staff photo caption, *Daily Times*, September 10, 1956.

85. Art Dunn, "Mild Thruway Blast Satisfies Officials," *Daily Times*, September 28, 1956.

86. Joseph C. Ingraham, "To Connecticut," *NYT*, October 5, 1958.

87. A number of authors have addressed the ways the federal government adopted road-building policies influenced by powerful special-interest groups and relied on general tax revenues rather than highway-user taxes to support highway building. These actions have influenced the broad public acceptance that highway building has enjoyed in the United States. See Leavitt, *Superhighway—Superhoax*; Kenneth T. Jackson, *Crabgrass Frontier: The Suburbanization of the United States* (New York: Oxford University Press, 1985); Dolores Hayden, *Building Suburbia: Green Fields and Urban Growth, 1820–2000* (New York: Pantheon Books, 2003); and Owen Gutfreund, *Twentieth-Century Sprawl: Highways and the Reshaping of the American Landscape* (New York: Oxford University Press, 2004).

88. Marshall Berman, *All That Is Solid Melts Into Air: The Experience of Modernity* (New York: Simon & Schuster, 1982), 313. Berman views Robert Moses as "the New York agent and incarnation" of the expressway world.

89. John H. Cox, "Don't Tear it Down . . . Move it Over!" *Westchester Life*, February 1952, 19, 23–24.

90. "The Cape Cod Cottage," pt. 2, *Architectural Forum* 90, no. 3 (1949): 105.

CHAPTER THREE

1. *Epigraph.* Samuel Chamberlain, "The Real Cape Cod," *House Beautiful*, August 1937, 15.

2. "The Cape Cod Cottage," pt. 1, *Architectural Forum* 90, no. 2 (1949): 89. Today Route 6 still traverses fourteen states and is the second longest U.S. route. Its designation, Grand Army of the Republic Highway, is in honor of Union veterans of the Civil War. Russ Lombard, "The Grand Army of the Republic (Memorial) Highway," U.S. Route 6 Tourist Association, http://www.route6tour.com.

3. "The One-Story Colonial House," *Architectural Forum* 59, no. 5 (1933): 373; "Cape Cod Cottage," *Architectural Forum* 90:101.

4. Richard Pratt, "Of Course We Want a Cape Cod Cottage," *Ladies Home Journal*, May 1940, 78.

5. Stanley Schuler, *The Cape Cod House: America's Most Popular Home* (Exton, PA: Schiffer, 1982).

6. Henry C. Kittredge, *Cape Cod: Its People and Their History* (Boston: Houghton Mifflin, 1930), 78.

7. Doris Doane, *A Book of Cape Cod Houses* (Old Greenwich, CT: Chatham, 1970), 11–26; Ernest Allen Connally, "The Cape Cod House: An Introductory Study," *Journal of the Society of Architectural Historians* 19, no. 2 (1960): 50–52; Schuler, *Cape Cod House*, 7–9.

8. Connally, "Cape Cod House," 47.

9. Timothy Dwight, *Travels in New-England and New-York* (New Haven, 1822), 3:79.

10. Henry D. Thoreau, *Cape Cod/Henry D. Thoreau*, ed. Joseph J. Moldenhauer (Princeton, NJ: Princeton University Press, 1988), 62–63, 249.

11. Schuler, *Cape Cod House*, 5.

12. Alan Gowans, *The Comfortable House: North American Suburban Architecture, 1890–1930* (Cambridge, MA: MIT Press, 1986), 104.

13. Robert Wendell, "Colonial Architecture," *House Beautiful*, March 1897, 53, 56.

14. R. Clipson Sturgis, "Two Old New England Houses," *House & Garden*, July 1903, 21, 27.

15. Aymar Embury II, *The Dutch Colonial House: Its Origin, Design, Modern Plan and Construction* (New York: McBride, Nast, 1913), i–ii. In 1929 this book was published under the title *Building the Dutch Colonial House: Its Origin, Design, Modern Plan and Construction*.

16. W. H. Cox, "Housing Development at Danielson, Conn." *American Architect* 113, no. 2213 (1918): 677–85. The article's author, a Boston architect, had drawn the plans. Today remnants of the development, including the apartment house and a number of the houses, stand adjacent to the town's abandoned textile mills.

17. "Bringing Colonial Architecture Up to Date: Illustrated by the Designs of Dwight James Baum," *Touchstone* 5, no. 1 (1919): 10, 16.

18. Dwight James Baum, "A Pilgrimage to Plymouth," pt. 1, *Architecture* 44, no. 3 (1921): 265; pt. 2, no. 4 (1921): 330.

19. Murray P. Corse, "Puritan Architecture," pt. 1, *Architecture* 45, no. 1 (1922): 1.

20. Charles Magruder, "The White Pine Monograph Series," *Journal of the Society of Architectural Historians* 22, no. 1 (1963): 39–41; *Survey of Early American Design*, Architectural Treasures of Early America (Pittstown, NJ: Main Street Press, 1987), 1:11. After 1924 the publication continued by subscription under different sponsorship until 1940. The entire twenty-six-year run of the *White Pine Series of Architectural Monographs* and its successor were reorganized along geographic lines and republished in ten volumes in 1987 to make the material available to preservationists and restorers.

21. Wallace Nutting, *Massachusetts Beautiful* (Framingham, MA: Old America Company, 1923).

22. Knowlton Mixer, *Old Houses of New England* (New York: Macmillan, 1927).

23. Alfred Easton Poor, *Colonial Architecture of Cape Cod, Nantucket and Martha's Vineyard* (New York: Helburn, 1932), foreword.

24. *Classic Houses of the Twenties: Loizeaux* (1927; repr., Philadelphia: Athenaeum/New York: Dover, 1992), 115.

25. Advertisement, Lowe Brothers, "Two Women Tell About Some Home-Making Things," *Good Housekeeping*, February 1922, 139.

26. Thomas Charles Devine, "A House in the Cape Cod Tradition," *International Studio* 97, no. 11 (1930): 53.

27. D. West Barber, "'Bungalows' in the Colonial Style," *Architectural Forum* 44, no. 3 (1926): 163.

28. Katherine Crosby, *The Cape Type of House*, The Library of Cape Cod History & Genealogy 10 (Yarmouthport, MA: Register Press, 1927), 1.

29. Ibid., 2, 6.

30. Mary Rogers Bangs, "Cape Cod: Where Houses Were Built to Suit the Land," *House Beautiful*, September 1926, 253.

31. "A Design for a Cape Cod House," *House Beautiful*, September 1926, 259.

32. William H. Schuchardt, "Impressions of Old Provincetown and Cape Cod," *American Architect* 136, no. 2576 (1929): 36.

33. Mary Kellogg, "Expanding a Cape Cod Cottage," *House Beautiful*, June 1923, 624–25, 660–63.

34. Kellogg, "The House That Harriet Built," *House Beautiful*, September 1923, 294.

35. Elspeth, "Cape Cod Cottage," *McCall's*, July 1930, 30.

36. D. Everett Waid, "Importance of Good Architecture in the Small House," *Architectural Forum* 44, no. 3 (1926): 137; Barber, "'Bungalows' in the Colonial Style," Ibid., 163–68.

37. "A New House Beautiful House," *House Beautiful*, January 1927, 38–39, 84.

38. Frank Waugh, "Picketed Gardens from Cape Cod," *House & Garden*, July 1929, 87, 104; "A Cottage After the Cape Cod Manner Set Down Among the Connecticut Hills," *House & Garden*, March 1930, 88–91; "After the Pattern of Cape Cod," *House & Garden*, August 1930, 78.

39. Henry Atherton Frost, "The Consistent Colonial House," *House Beautiful*, January 1930, 50–52, 93–95; "The Picturesque Cape Cod Type of Cottage," *Arts & Decoration*, June 1931, 38; Guy H. Lee, "A Collaborative Problem," *House Beautiful*, September 1931, 199–204, 260; "Cape Cod Architecture in Connecticut," *Arts & Decoration*, January 1932, 56–57; Charles S. Keefe, "Little Farm, New Canaan, Conn.—A Group which Reproduces the Intimate Vernacular of Cape Cod," *House & Garden*, February 1933, 40–41; "New England Furnishes the Inspiration for House & Garden's Third Little House," *House & Garden*, February 1933, 60–63.

40. "Provincetown," *Mooney's Megaphone*, April 15, 1928, 19.

41. Charles M. Willis, "Effective Economies in Building a House," *House Beautiful*, September 1931, 228–32, 254.

42. Leigh French Jr., "Three More Houses that Grow: Designed After Mediterranean, Cape Cod and Cotswold Styles," *House & Garden*, November 1931, 50; Grace E. Chaffee, "For Less Than Nine Thousand Dollars," *House Beautiful*, February 1932, 110–14, 144–45.

43. "Portfolio of 16 Small Colonial Houses," *American Home*, September 1938, 25–40, 57, 69, 72, 74.

44. "Better Homes in America Small House Competition," *Architectural Forum* 60, no. 3 (1934): 168.

45. Barbara M. Kelly, *Expanding the American Dream: Building and Rebuilding Levittown* (Albany: State University of New York Press, 1993), 18.

46. "Cape Cod Cottage," *Architectural Forum* 90:102.

47. Federal Housing Administration, "How to Own a Better Home," FHA form no. 702, Rev. May 15, 1936.

48. Federal Housing Administration, "How to Have the Home You Want," November 1, 1935.

49. "The Minimum Home," *Ladies Home Journal*, October 1937, 39.

50. Henry C. Kittredge, review of *Colonial Architecture of Cape Cod, Nantucket and Martha's Vineyard*, by Alfred Easton Poor, *New England Quarterly* 6, no. 2 (1933): 392.

51. Chamberlain, "Real Cape Cod," 15–16, 71.

52. Chamberlain, *A Small House in the Sun: The Visage of Rural New England* (New York: Hastings House, 1936); *Cape Cod in the Sun* (New York: Hastings House, 1937); and *Open House in New England* (New York: Hastings House, 1937).

53. Royal Barry Wills Associates, *Houses for Good Living* (Stamford, CT: Architectural Book Publishing, 1993), 7–11; "Royal Barry Wills Dead at 65; Noted for Small-Home Designs," *New York Times*, January 11, 1962; Schuler, *Cape Cod House*, 15–16.

54. "House of Charles G. Eichenberger, Egypt, Mass." *American Architect* 135, no. 2564 (1929): 341.

55. "Spirit of Old Cape Cod: Boston Architect Wins Medal For Design," *Boston American*, February 11, 1933; "Home-Design Medal Won By Boston Man," *New York Times*, February 8, 1933; Leon Keach, "The Architect and the House: Royal Barry Wills, Small Home Specialist," *Pencil Points* 18, no. 2 (1937): 77.

56. Samples of his newspaper plans, sketches and articles may be found in Royal Barry Wills, "Home Building Plans," *Boston Transcript*, March 16 and 23, 1935. The first of several books was *Houses for Good Living* (New York: Architectural Book Publishing, 1940).

57. "Cape Cod Cottage," *Architectural Forum* 90:103.

58. Kelly, *Expanding the American Dream*, 11–12.

59. Ibid., 54–55, 63.

60. "Cape Cod Cottage," *Architectural Forum* 90:103; Schuler, *Cape Cod House*, 16; Doane, *Cape Cod Houses*, 87–88.

61. Schuler, *Cape Cod House*, 16.

62. Sturgis, "Two Old New England Houses," 21.

63. "Cape Cod Cottage," *Architectural Forum* 90:89, 101.

64. "A Style That Never Grows Old," *Popular Mechanics*, November 1929, 879.

65. Ethel B. Power, "Variations on the Colonial," *House Beautiful*, July 1935, 66.

66. "A Style," *Popular Mechanics* 52:879.

67. "Cape Cod Cottage," *Architectural Forum* 90:103.

68. "A Style," *Popular Mechanics* 52:879.

69. Bangs, "Cape Cod," 253.

70. Power, "Variations on the Colonial," 66.

71. David Gebhard, "The American Colonial Revival in the 1930s," *Winterthur Portfolio* 22, no. 2/3 (1987):120.

72. Power, "Variations on the Colonial," 42, 66; *Popular Mechanics* 52:879.

73. Schweitzer and Davis, *America's Favorite Homes*, 86.

74. "House of the Year," *Country Living*, February 1989, 71–79, 150, 153.

75. David Maurer, "Cape Cod Updated," *Colonial Homes*, April 1995, 102–5; "Classic Cape Cod Cottage," *Colonial Homes*, November 1997, 90; "House Plans You Can Buy," *Country Living*, March 2005, 84; Penelope Rowlands, "The Maine Influence," *Architectural Digest*, June 2006, 168–75, 254.

CHAPTER FOUR

1. *Epigraph*. George Washington, *The Diaries of George Washington: 1748–65*, eds., Donald Jackson and Dorothy Twohig (Charlottesville: University Press of Virginia, 1976), 1:137, http://memory.loc.gov. A young George Washington recorded Tanacharison's words in his diary after a November 1753 meeting with the Native American leader. Tanacharison reported to Washington the content of a speech he had made to a French commander at a meeting two months earlier. Tanacharison played a key role in the French and Indian War, accompanying George Washington on a 1754 expedition to establish a fort at what would become Pittsburgh (ibid., 135–37).

2. Edward Floyd de Lancey, "The Origin and History of the Manors in New York, and in the County of Westchester," in *History of Westchester County, New York Including Morrisania, Kings Bridge, and West Farms, which have been Annexed to New York City*, ed. J. Thomas Scharf, 1:31–160*f* (Philadelphia, 1886), 1:144.

3. Ibid.

4. "Recorded for Mr. Richbell," September 23, 1661, New York State Department of State Deeds 2:192–93, Records Series # A0453, NYS Archives. (Here and elsewhere in quotations, I am using the original spelling and punctuation.)

5. The information supporting this statement is complex. Although a Dutch document of 1655 states that "the lands of *Vreedlandt* [Westchester County], [were] taken possession of during the time of the late Honble Director-General *Kieft* and bought from and paid for to the actual owners and proprietors, natives of this country, as the Book of Deeds and their signatures prove . . . ," the actual Dutch deed for this part of Westchester County has not been found. "Protest Against Thomas Pell for Settling on Lands Belonging to the Dutch with Notice to Quit," April 19, 1655, in B. Fernow, ed., *Documents Relating to the History and Settlements of the Towns Along the Hudson and Mohawk Rivers (with the exception of Albany) from 1630 to1684* (Albany, 1881), 38. There are a number of Dutch deeds from the 1630s and 1640s for many other parts of Westchester County (Fernow, 5, 10, 15, 20, 24), but I have been unable to find any documentation confirming that the part of the county that Wappaquewam sold to Richbell had previously been sold to Dutch settlers. I conclude, as does Blake Bell, who has researched the land directly south of Richbell's parcel, that the original Dutch record may have been destroyed in the 1911 New York State Library fire. Blake

Bell, "Where Is the Evidence of the 1640 Dutch Purchase from Native Americans of the Lands That Became Pelham?" Historic Pelham, December 5, 2006, http://historicpelham.blogspot.com/2006/12/where-is-evidence-of-1640-dutch.html.

6. Other proposed meanings include "He has stripes on his arms" and "a gathering where streams come together." Tina Kelley, "In Their Footsteps," *New York Times*, May 2, 2004.

7. De Lancey, "Mamaroneck," 1:846–88 in Scharf, *History of Westchester*, 1:846.

8. "Indian Signs," *Daily Times* (Mamaroneck, NY), September 18, 1961.

9. Alanson Skinner, *Exploration of Aboriginal Sites at Throgs Neck and Clasons Point, New York City*, vol. 5, *Contribution from the Museum of the American Indian, Heye Foundation* (New York: Museum of the American Indian Heye Foundation, 1919), 52; and Ives Goddard, "Delaware," in *Northeast*, vol. 15 of *Handbook of North American Indian*, ed. Bruce G. Trigger, 213–39 (Washington, DC: Smithsonian Institution, 1978), 214.

10. Jaap Jacobs, *New Netherland: A Dutch Colony in Seventeenth-Century America* (Leiden: Brill, 2005), 23; and Herbert C. Kraft, *The Lenape-Delaware Indian Heritage: 10,000 B.C.–A.D. 2000* (Lenape Books, 2001), 4, 9, note 2.

11. Eric Sanderson, *Mannahatta: A Natural History of New York City* (New York: Abrams, 2009), 119–123.

12. Kraft, *Lenape-Delaware Indian Heritage*, 257, 263, 267–68, 272, 276–78.

13. Adriaen van der Donck, *A Description of New Netherland*, eds. Charles T. Gehring and William A. Starna (Lincoln: University of Nebraska Press, 2008), 78–81; and Kraft, *Lenape-Delaware Indian Heritage*, 230–32, 239–40. The van der Donck source was first published in Dutch in 1655.

14. Peter Nabokov and Dean Snow, "Farmers of the Woodlands," in *America in 1492*, ed. Alvin M. Josephy, Jr., 119–45 (New York: Knopf, 1992), 126.

15. Bartlett Burleigh James and J. Franklin Jameson, eds., *Journal of Jasper Danckaerts, 1679–1680*, (New York: Scribner's, 1913), 55–56.

16. Kraft, "The Northern Lenape in Prehistoric and Early Colonial Times," in *The Lenape Indian: A Symposium*, ed. Herbert C. Kraft, 1–18 (South Orange, NJ: Archaeological Research Center, Seton Hall University, 1984), 6.

17. James Axtell, *Beyond 1492: Encounters in Colonial North America* (New York: Oxford University Press, 1992), 25–74.

18. David B. Quinn, ed., *New American World: A Documentary History of North America to 1612* (New York: Arno, 1979), 1:271–79.

19. Charles T. Gehring and William A. Starna, "Dutch and Indians in the Hudson Valley: The Early Period," *Hudson Valley Regional Review* 9, no. 2 (1992): 7.

20. Robert Juet, "Journal of Hudson's Voyage" [1609], in Quinn, *New American World*, 3:471–88; Evan Haefeli, "On First Contact and Apotheosis: Manitou and Men in North America," *Ethnohistory* 54, no. 3 (2007): 415–17, 432–33.

21. Kraft, *Lenape-Delaware Indian Heritage*, 366.

22. "Resolution of the States General on the Report of the Discovery of New Netherland," in *Documents Relative to the Colonial History of the State of New-York*, ed. E. B. O'Callaghan (Albany, 1856), 1:10; "Grant of Exclusive Trade to New Netherland," in ibid., 1:11; "Resolution of the States General on a Report of further Discoveries in New Netherland," in ibid., 1:12; Johan de Laet, "New World," 1625–1630, in *Narratives of New Netherland, 1609–1664*, ed. J. Franklin Jameson, 36–60 (1909; repr., New York: Barnes & Noble, 1967), 44, 50; and E. B. O'Callaghan, *History of New Netherland*, 2nd ed. (New York, 1855), 1:72–74.

23. "Effects of the West India Company, 1626," 35–37, in *Documents Relative*, 1:35.

24. Jonas Michaëlius to Adrianus Smoutius, August 11, 1628, New Netherland, 122–33, in Jameson, *Narratives of New Netherland*, 126–27.

25. Johan Prinz, "Report," [1644], in *Narratives of Early Pennsylvania, West New Jersey, and Delaware, 1630–1707*, ed. Albert Cook Myers, 95–116 (New York: Scribner's Sons, 1912), 103–4.

26. William Penn to the Committee of the Free Society of Traders, 1683, 224–44, in *Narratives of Early Pennsylvania*, 230.

27. Van der Donck, *Description*, 73–75, 96.

28. Russell Shorto, *The Island at the Center of the World: The Epic Story of Dutch Manhattan and the Forgotten Colony That Shaped America* (New York: Doubleday, 2004), 135–36.

29. Paul le Jeune, "Relation of What Occurred in New France in the Year 1634," 6:95–317 in *Travels and Explorations of the Jesuit Missionaries in New France, 1610–1791*, ed. Reuben Gold Thwaites, The Jesuit Relations and Allied Documents 6, (Cleveland, 1897), 299.

30. Kraft, *Lenape-Delaware Indian Heritage*, 367, 370, 375, 379; and Axtell, *Beyond 1492*, 135.

31. Kraft, *Lenape-Delaware Indian Heritage*, 382–84.

32. "A Proclamacon for a Post to goe monthly from this City to Boston & back againe," December 10, 1672, in *Minutes of the Executive Council of the Province of New York: Administration of Francis Lovelace, 1668–1673*, ed. Victor Hugo Paltsits (Albany: State of New York, 1910), 2:794.

33. Herman Moll, *A New and Exact Map of the Dominions of the King of Great Britain on ye Continent of North America, Containing Newfoundland, New Scotland, New England, New York, New Jersey, Pensilvania, Maryland, Virginia and Carolina. According to the Newest and most exact observations by Herman Moll Geographer*, [London]: T. Bowles, John Bowles, and J. King, 1715, viewed at Christie's auction house, New York, December 3, 2008. The "Beaver Map" designation derives from the map's sizeable and fanciful inset scene, depicting dozens of busy beavers standing erect in the guise of European tradesmen while building a dam.

34. Reginald Pelham Bolton, *Indian Paths in the Great Metropolis* (New York: Museum of the American Indian Heye Foundation, 1922), 15, 101, 121.

35. Sarah Kemble Knight, "The Journal of Madam Knight," 1704–05, in *The Puritans*, eds. Perry Miller and Thomas H. Johnson, (New York: American Book Company, 1938), 16, http://mith2.umd.edu/eada/html/display.php?docs=knight_journal.xml.

36. Van der Donck, *Description*, 100.

37. Kraft, *Lenape-Delaware Indian Heritage*, 256, note 30.

38. "Journal of New Netherland, 1647," in *Narratives of New Netherland*, 265–84; 271.

39. Power of Attorney to Cocko, in *The Second Book of Records of the Town of Southampton, Long Island, N.Y. with other Ancient Documents of Historic Value*, ed. William S. Pelletreau (Sag Harbor, NY, 1877), 16.

40. "Articles of Partnership," September 18, 1657, New York State Department of State Deeds 3:122–24, Records Series # A0453, NYS Archives.

41. "Mr. Richbell's Contract for Whales," April 24, 1659, New York State Department of State Deeds 2:67–68, Records Series # A0453, NYS Archives.

42. "Entered for Mr. John Richbell," October 3, 1665, New York State Department of State Deeds 2:107, Records Series # A0453, NYS Archives.

43. "Instructions for Mr. John Richbell," Barbados, September 10, 1657, New York State Department of State Deeds 3:126, Records Series # A0453, NYS Archives.

44. Ibid., 126–27.

45. With John Marshall as Chief Justice, the court ruled in *Johnson v. M'Intosh* that, though Native Americans had the right of occupancy, they were denied the right to sell land to private citizens by the fundamental principle, known as the discovery doctrine, derived from the practices of European colonization, that European nations acquired title to land they "discovered."

46. De Lancey, "Mamaroneck," in Scharf, *History of Westchester*, 1:848–49; and de Lancey, "Origin and History," ibid., 1:145.

47. John Finch, Edward Griffin, and Jacob Young deposed by Richard Lawes, March 11, 1661/62, New York State Department of State Deeds 2:198, Records Series # A0453, NYS Archives.

48. William Joanes deposed by Richard Lawes, April 5, 1662, New York State Department of State Deeds 2:196, Records Series # A0453, NYS Archives.

49. Peter Disbroe deposed by Richard Lawes and Francis Bell, March 12, 1661/62, New York State Department of State Deeds 2:194, Records Series # A0453, NYS Archives.

50. Ibid. Joanes deposition, Deeds 2:196, confirms this.

51. Undated Account, New York State Department of State Deeds 3:37, Records Series # A0453, NYS Archives.

52. "Recorded for Mr. John Richbell," June 6, 1666, New York State Department of State Deeds 2:128, Records Series # A0453, NYS Archives.

53. Thomas Revell v. John Richbell, in *Calendar of the Proceedings of the Court of Assizes, 1665–1672 (New York, N.Y.)*, 23, Manuscripts and Archives Division, New York Public Library.

54. "Mr. John Richbells Patent," October 16, 1668, New York State Department of State Letters Patent 4:68–69, Records Series # 12943, NYS Archives.

55. Ibid.

56. Berthold Fernow, ed., *The Records of New Amsterdam from 1653 to 1674 anno domini* (New York, 1897), 6:80, 259, 264–65, 270.

57. "Warrant for ye fetching Mr. John Richbell," 1671, Albany Assize Records, 391, in Robert Bolton, *The History of the Several Towns, Manors, and Patents of the County of Westchester from Its First Settlement to the Present Time* (New York, 1881), 1:471.

58. Thomas Revell v. John Richbell, *Calendar of the Proceedings*, 24.

59. Paltsits, *Minutes of the Executive Council*, February 23, 1669, 1:29.

60. Robert Bolton Jr., *A History of the County of Westchester from Its First Settlement to the Present Time* (New York, 1848), 524.

61. William Cronon, *Changes in the Land: Indians, Colonists, and the Ecology of New England* (New York: Hill & Wang, 1983), 55, 62–65.

62. Van der Donck, *Description*, 103.

63. John Heckewelder, *History, Manners, and Customs of the Indian Nations Who Once Inhabited Pennsylvania and the Neighboring States* (1876; repr., New York: Arno, 1971), 101.

64. Shorto, *Island*, 119.

65. Van der Donck, *Description*, 99.

66. Peter A. Thomas, "Cultural Change on the Southern New England Frontier, 1630–1665," in *Cultures in Contact: The Impact of European Contacts on Native American Cultural Institutions, A.D. 1000–1800*, ed. William W. Fitzhugh, 131–61 (Washington, DC: Smithsonian Institution, 1985), 144–49.

67. Cronon, *Changes in the Land*, 70.

68. Wood, "Indians of Westchester," 1:9–20 in Scharf, *History of Westchester*, 1:20.

69. Reginald Pelham Bolton, *Indian Life of Long Ago in the City of New York* (1934; repr., Port Washington, NY: Kennikat, 1971), 125–26.

70. Wood, "Indians of Westchester," in Scharf, *History of Westchester*, 1:18–20.

71. "The Eight Men to the Amsterdam Chamber of the West India Company," 1:209–13, in *Documents Relative*, 1:209–10.

72. Kraft, *Lenape-Delaware Indian Heritage*, 372, 374; Kraft, *Lenape: Archaeology, History, and Ethnography*, 200.

73. Prinz, "Report," in *Narratives of Early Pennsylvania*, 103.

74. Axtell, *Beyond 1492*, 108.

75. Van der Donck, *Description*, 69.

76. Dean R. Snow and Kim M. Lamphear, "European Contact and Indian Depopulation in the Northeast: The Timing of the First Epidemics," *Ethnohistory* 35, no. 1 (1988): 15–16, 23–24, 27–28; and Douglas H. Ubelaker, "North American Indian Population Size: Changing Perspectives," in *Disease and Demography in the Americas*, ed. John W. Verano and Douglas H. Ubelaker, 169–76 (Washington, DC: Smithsonian Institution, 1992), 174.

77. Daniel Denton, *A Brief Description of New York: Formerly called New-Netherlands with the Places thereunto Adjoyning* (1670; repr., New York, 1845), 6–7, http://books.google.com.

78. "The Indian Petition Read in Council," August 2, 1699, in Bolton, *History of the Several Towns*, 1:473.

79. Josiah S. Mitchell, "White Plains," 1:714–44 in Scharf, *History of Westchester*, 1:719.

80. Ibid., 476.

81. Skinner, "Exploration of Aboriginal Sites," 78.

82. George Muirson to the Secretary of the Society for the Propagation of the Gospel, Rye, New York, January 9, 1707/8, in E. B. O'Callaghan, ed., *The Documentary History of the State of New York*, 3:936–41 (Albany, 1850), 3:937.

83. Charles W. Baird, "Rye," 2:643–701 in Scharf, *History of Westchester*, 2:667–68.

84. "An Order Concerning Negros and Indian Slaves," October 4–6, 1682, in *New York Historical Manuscripts: English, Records of the Court of Assizes for the Colony of New York, 1665–1682,* Peter R. Christoph and Florence A. Christoph, eds. (Baltimore: Genealogical Publishing, 1983), 293.

85. "A List of the Indian Negro and Malatto Slaves Within and Belonging to the Township of Mamaroneck and Mannor of Scarsdale taken Aprill ye 5th 1755 by Joseph Sutton Capt.," in O'Callaghan, *Documentary History*, 3:511.

86. Bolton, *Indian Paths in the Great Metropolis*, 110–11.

87. "The Waldorf Mill and the Legend of the White Deer," *Westchester Historian* 32, no. 1 (1956): 10.

88. Ibid., 11–12.

89. Steve Chambers, "The Vanishing Voice of the Lenape," *Star-Ledger* (Newark, NJ), November 17, 2002, http://www.nj.com; Sanderson, 302. See http://www.delawarenation.com for information on the Delaware Nation today.

CHAPTER FIVE

1. *Epigraph.* Caleb Heathcote to the secretary of the Society for the Propagation of the Gospel, Manor of Scarsdale, November 9, 1705, in *Documentary History of The Protestant Episcopal Church in Connecticut, 1704–1789*, eds. Francis L. Hawks and William Stevens Perry, 1:8–12 (1863; repr., Hartford, CT: Historiographer, 1959), 9.

2. Lewis Morris to the Secretary of State, New York, February 9, 1707 [1708], 5:33–38, in *Documents Relative to the Colonial History of the State of New-York Procured in Holland, England and France*, ed. E. B. O'Callaghan (Albany, 1855), 5:38. Lewis Morris, Heathcote's friend and colleague, was the Lord of the Manor of Morrisania, a fellow Anglican, and, like Heathcote, a member of the Society for the Propagation of the Gospel in Foreign Parts. This quotation and the one by Heathcote above both appear in Fox's well-documented biography of Heathcote, on which I have drawn heavily in writing this chapter. Dixon Ryan Fox, *Caleb Heathcote, Gentleman Colonist: The Story of a Career in the Province of New York, 1692–1721* (New York: Charles Scribner's Sons, 1926).

3. Edward Floyd de Lancey, "The Origin and History of Manors in New York, and in the County of Westchester," in *History of Westchester County, New York Including Morrisania, Kings Bridge, and West Farms, which have been Annexed to New York City*, ed. J. Thomas Scharf, 1:31–160*f* (Philadelphia, 1886), 1:154.

4. Fox, *Caleb Heathcote*, 8–11.

5. Ibid., 14–18.

6. Joseph Barrett, "New Castle," 2:608–28, in Scharf, *History of Westchester,* 2:609.

7. Fox, *Caleb Heathcote*, 44–45, 50, 53; Herbert Alan Johnson, "The Prerogative Court of New York, 1686–1776," *American Journal of Legal History* 17, no. 2 (1973): 144.

8. Dixon Ryan Fox, ed., *The Minutes of the Court of Sessions (1657–1696), Westchester County, New York*, Publications of the Westchester County Historical Society 2 (White Plains, NY: Westchester County Historical Society, 1924), 71. Heathcote must have been among the first to take action in what would become a nationwide wolf eradication campaign lasting nearly two centuries, an effort beset by controversy that continues in some regions even in the twenty-first century. By the 1970s wolves were nearly extinct in the Northeast. Measures are now being taken to bring the wolf back to the Northeast by organizations such as the Wolf Conservation Center in Westchester County, one of the few such centers in the U.S. As its managing director has said, "Wolves are a symbol of our wildlife like lions are in Africa." Maggie Howell, in Diana Marszalek, "Bringing the Cry of the Wolf Back to the Northeastern Woods," *New York Times*, August 24, 2008.

9. Fox, *Caleb Heathcote*, 58–59.

10. Lloyd Ultan, *The Bronx In The Frontier Era* (Dubuque, IA: Kendall/Hunt, 1993), 169.

11. *Liber of Deeds*, A:238; B:371, Westchester County Clerk's Office, Land Records Division, White Plains, NY; Fox, *Caleb Heathcote*, 115.

12. De Lancey, "Origin and History of Manors," in Scharf, *History of Westchester*, 1:147, 152.

13. Barrett, "New Castle," in Scharf, *History of Westchester*, 2:609.

14. Robert Bolton, *The History of the Several Towns, Manors, and Patents of the County of Westchester from Its First Settlement to the Present Time* (New York, 1881), 1:475–76.

15. De Lancey, "Mamaroneck," 1:846–88 in Scharf, *History of Westchester*, 1:878–88.

16. Double dates such as this were used in the British Empire to clarify dates from January 1 to March 24 between 1582 and 1752. In the Julian or "old style" calendar, the year began with March 25, whereas in the Gregorian or "new style" calendar, adopted in much of Europe before 1750, the year began with January 1. The double dating custom developed as a way for historians to clear up confusion stemming from the 1752 change to the Gregorian calendar in England and its American colonies.

17. The other manors in Westchester and the years of their establishment included Fordham, 1671; Pelham, 1687; Philipsburgh, 1693; Cortlandt, 1697; and Morrisania, 1697.

18. The name Scarsdale derives from *scars,* a Saxon word for rocky crags, and *dale,* for valley. De Lancey, "Origin and History of Manors," in Scharf, *History of Westchester*, 1:141.

19. "Manor Grant of the Manor of Scarsdale," in Fox, *Caleb Heathcote*, 291.

20. Fox, *Caleb Heathcote*, 99–100, 107.

21. "The Waldorf Mill and the Legend of the White Deer," *Westchester Historian* 32, no. 1 (1956): 10.

22. De Lancey, "Origin and History of Manors," in Scharf, *History of Westchester*, 1:152.

23. Fox, *Caleb Heathcote*, 130–32, 135.

24. Governor Robert Hunter to the Lords of Trade, report, New York, June 23, 1712, 339–43, in O'Callaghan, *Documents Relative*, 5:341.

25. *Minutes of the Common Council of the City of New York, 1675–1776* (New York: Dodd, Mead, 1905), 3:27. A gibbet is the projecting arm of a gallows, from which criminals were hung, their bodies left suspended after execution as a warning to others.

26. Fox, *Caleb Heathcote*, 143–62.

27. Ibid., 164–71.

28. Caleb Heathcote to Governor Robert Hunter, Manor of Scarsdale, July 8, 1715, 5:430–31, in O'Callaghan, *Documents Relative*, 5:430.

29. Caleb Heathcote to Lord Charles Townshend, Manor of Scarsdale, July 16, 1715, 5:432–34, in O'Callaghan, *Documents Relative*, 5:433–34.

30. Fox, *Caleb Heathcote*, 142–43.

31. Lewis Morris to the Secretary of State, in O'Callaghan, *Documents Relative*, 5:38.

32. The mural, *Caleb Heathcote Taking the City of New York Mayoral Oath of Office in 1711*, installed in 1936, is by Warren Chase Merritt (1897–1968).

33. Fox, *Caleb Heathcote*, 243.

34. Charles W. Baird, "Civil Status of the Presbyterians in the Province of New York," *Magazine of American History* 3, no. 10 (1879): 595, 625.

35. Fox, *Caleb Heathcote*, 203.

36. Caleb Heathcote to Secretary of the S.P.G., April 10, 1704, ibid., 202.

37. Fox, *Minutes of the Court of Sessions*, 82–83.

38. Robert Bolton, *History of the Protestant Episcopal Church, in the County of Westchester, from its Foundation, A.D. 1693, to A.D. 1853* (New York, 1855), 152.

39. Fox, *Caleb Heathcote*, 254, 258.

40. The fifteen- by four-foot oil-on-canvas mural, *Caleb Heathcote Buys the Richbell Farm*, is by Gordon Samstag (1906–1990). Commissioned by the Section of Fine Arts, a public art program administered by the U.S. Treasury Department as part of the New Deal, it was installed in 1940.

41. Obituary of Caleb Heathcote, *American Weekly Mercury* (Philadelphia), March 9–16, 1721.

42. Caleb Heathcote, will dated February 29, 1719, proved April 19, 1721, no. 654, *Original Wills Filed in New York County Surrogate's Office, 1662–1829* [microform], New York Public Library.

43. Fox, *Caleb Heathcote*, 115–16.

44. Anne Richbell will dated April 1, 1700, proved May 19, 1700, no. 318, *Original Wills Filed in New York County Surrogate's Office, 1662–1829*, Liber 2:92, New York Public Library.

45. *Liber of Deeds*, E:385.

46. Fox, *Caleb Heathcote*, 280.

47. De Lancey, "Mamaroneck," in Scharf, *History of Westchester*, 1:866.

CHAPTER SIX

1. *Epigraph*. Hippolyte Taine (1828–1893), in J. Thomas Scharf, "Early Manners and Customs of the People of Westchester County," in *The History of Westchester County, New York Including Morrisania, Kings Bridge, and West Farms, which have been Annexed to New York City*, ed. J. Thomas Scharf, 1:457–72j, (Philadelphia, 1886), 1:457.

2. Eliezer Gedney was also spelled Eleazer Gidney. The spelling of the family's surname seems to have shifted between the two spellings throughout the 1700s, becoming more often Gedney with time. In town records of the 1700s, the name is spelled both Gedney and Gidney, sometimes both ways in the same document, in reference to the same person. Mary O'Connor English, ed., *Early Town Records of Mamaroneck* (Mamaroneck, NY: Town of Mamaroneck, 1979), 51–52. In deeds of 1716, 1721 and 1722 involving Isaac Jr.'s father, grandfather, and uncles, the surname is spelled Gidney. In deeds dated 1738, 1784, and 1785 involving Isaac Jr., his wife, mother, father and uncle, it is spelled Gedney. *Liber of Deeds*, E:385, 414, 415; L:204, Westchester County Clerk's Office, Land Records Division, White Plains, NY.

3. English, *Early Town Records*, 187–88.

4. Henry B. Dawson, "Westchester-County, New-York, During the American Revolution," 1:177–457 in Scharf, *History of Westchester*, 1:177. According to Dawson, in the fall of 1769 it was stated in the New York Assembly that the Manors of Cortlandt and Philipsburgh alone contained one-third of the residents of Westchester County. These farmers rented their land through long-term leases with landlords who often sold the land whenever tenants could purchase it. The tenants of Philipsburgh, Westchester's largest manor, were relatively content and secure compared to tenant farmers elsewhere in New York, where there were landlord/tenant clashes between 1740 and 1757 and a revolt in 1766. Robert McCluer Calhoon, *The Loyalists in Revolutionary America, 1760–1781* (New York: Harcourt Brace Jovanovich, 1973), 416–18.

5. E. Marie Becker, "The 801 Westchester County Freeholders of 1763 and the Cortlandt Manor Land-Case Which Occasioned Their Listing," *New York Historical Society Quarterly* 35, no. 3 (1951): 296.

6. Enslaved people made up roughly 13–16 percent of the population in Westchester County from 1698 to 1771. Evarts B. Greene and Virginia D. Harrington, *American Population Before the Federal Census of 1790* (New York: Columbia University Press, 1932), 92, 102. In 1698, four out of a total of sixteen families in Mamaroneck owned one enslaved worker each. "Census of 1698 for Mamaroneck, Morrisania and New-Rochelle," *New York Genealogical and Biographical Society Record* 59, no. 2 (1928): 103–4. A 1755 census shows a total of forty-eight enslaved people in Mamaroneck and Scarsdale, two owned by Isaac Jr.'s uncle, John, in Scarsdale. Most of the twenty-four slave owners listed owned one or two. "A List of the Indian Negro and Malatto Slaves Within and Belonging to the Township of Mamaroneck and Mannor of Scarsdale taken Aprill ye 5th 1755 by Joseph Sutton Capt." in E. B. O'Callaghan, ed., *The Documentary History of the State of New York* (Albany, 1850), 3:511. By 1790, Isaac Jr. owned one enslaved worker, his son owned none, and his cousin Absalom, who eventually bought the Harbor Heights property and owned it in 1790, owned four. *Heads of Families at the First Census of the United States Taken in the Year, 1790, New York* (Washington, DC: U.S. Government Printing Office, 1908), 199.

7. Dawson, "Westchester-County," 178.

8. Journal of the Committee of Safety, Die Sabbati, 10 ho. a.m., January 20, 1776, in *Journals of the Provincial Congress, Provincial Convention, Committee of Safety and Council of Safety of the State of New-York, 1775–1776–1777* (Albany, 1842), 1:258 (hereafter referred to as *JPC*).

9. For general information on farming in the Hudson Valley in the nineteenth century, see Martin Bruegel, *Farm, Shop, Landing: The Rise of a Market Society in the Hudson Valley, 1780–1860* (Durham, NC: Duke University Press, 2002).

10. Becker, "801 Westchester County Freeholders," 310, 315–17.

11. According to Dawson, Reverend Thomas Stannard wrote to the Venerable Society, November 5, 1729, in regard to Westchester County: "'Their employment is husbandry, even Innkeepers, Shopkeepers, Smiths, and Shoemakers not excepted; so that we pray, pay, and wait too, for everything done in this Country.'" Dawson, writing in 1886, commented, "Within the period of our own recollection, this primitive combination of occupations was widely continued; and every one who is acquainted with the County, now, can readily call to mind more than one instance still existing." Dawson, "Westchester-County," 178.

12. Greene and Harrington, *American Population*, 92, 105.

13. "Census of 1698,"103–4.

14. *Heads of Families at the First Census*, 199–200.

15. English, *Early Town Records*, 186–87.

16. Dixon Ryan Fox, *Caleb Heathcote, Gentleman Colonist: The Story of a Career in the Province of New York, 1692–1721* (New York: Charles Scribner's Sons, 1926), 231.

17. Robert Bolton, *History of the Protestant Episcopal Church in the County of Westchester, from its Foundation, A.D. 1693, to A.D. 1853* (New York, 1855), 130, 633.

18. Otto Hufeland, *Westchester County During the American Revolution, 1775–1783* (White Plains, NY: Westchester County Historical Society, 1926), 98.

19. Janice Potter, *The Liberty We Seek: Loyalist Ideology in Colonial New York and Massachusetts* (Cambridge, MA: Harvard University Press, 1983), 108.

20. In a letter to the governor of Connecticut, the clerk of the Greenwich Committee of Inspection reported in regard to the state of affairs in neighboring Westchester County: "For three and four miles round [a certain property in Mamaroneck], there are not more than eight or ten Whigs to one hundred and twenty Tories." Amos Mead, Clerk, Committee of Inspection to Governor Trumbull, Greenwich, Connecticut, December 26, 1775, in Peter Force, *American Archives: Fourth Series, Containing a Documentary History of the English Colonies in North America, from the King's Message to Parliament, of March 7, 1774, to the Declaration of Independence of the United States*, American Archives 4 (Washington, DC, 1843), 4:591.

21. Harold Drimmer, "The Westchester Militia in the American Revolution," *Westchester Historian* 73, no. 1 (1997): 9–10.

22. Dawson, "Westchester-County," 195–96, 204–5.

23. Cadwallader Colden to the Earl of Dartmouth, New York, July 6, 1774, in E. B. O'Callaghan, *Documents Relative to the Colonial History of the State of New-York Procured in Holland, England and France* (Albany, 1858), 8:470.

24. Calhoon, *Loyalists*, 371.

25. Unknown author to Mr. Rivington, Rye, September 24, 1774, in *Rivington's New-York Gazetteer; or the Connecticut, Hudson's River, New-Jersey, and Quebec Weekly Advertiser*, October 13, 1774.

26. At least two dozen other similar signed Loyalist declarations, resolves, letters, proclamations, protests, addresses, and resolutions were published from late 1773 to 1775 in New York and Massachusetts. Potter, *Liberty*, 219–20.

27. Hufeland in *Westchester County* (11) refers to a Paul Revere ride that took place on May 7, 1774. David Hackett Fischer lists all the specifics of Revere's "Revolutionary Rides," which included five to New York City between December 1773 and November 1775 and thirteen others to various locations in New England and along the Atlantic coast as far south as Philadelphia. Boston's Town Meeting asked Revere to travel to New York with the news of the Intolerable Acts, and he left Boston on May 14, 1774, for that purpose, according to Fischer. David Hackett Fischer, *Paul Revere's Ride* (New York: Oxford University Press, 1994), 26, 299–300.

28. Calhoon, *Loyalists*, 408.

29. Ibid., 245. Calhoon (205) states that Seabury's four tracts were among the more than 400 published in regard to the pre-Revolutionary controversy.

30. [Samuel Seabury], *Free Thoughts on the Proceedings of the Continental Congress . . . in a Letter to the Farmers . . .* (New York, [November 16,] 1774), 4, 14–15. Taken prisoner on November 22, 1775, by a group of Patriots, Seabury was held in Connecticut until December, when the local committee failed to prove he was the author of the Westchester Farmer pamphlets. For some time afterward he was subjected to harassment by Patriot troops until finally in 1776 he took refuge

behind British lines, where he stayed until 1783. After the war, Seabury was named the first bishop of the American Episcopal Church. Bruce E. Steiner, *Samuel Seabury, 1729–1796: A Study in the High Church Tradition* (Athens: Ohio University Press, 1971), 159–67, 216.

31. Steiner, *Samuel Seabury,* 145, 149.

32. Potter, *Liberty*, 7, 55, 59, 179–80.

33. Poplicola to Mr. Rivington, in *Rivington's New-York Gazetteer*, November 18, 1773.

34. Potter, *Liberty*, 29.

35. Ibid., 107–31.

36. [Seabury], *A View of the Controversy Between Great Britain and her Colonies . . . in a Letter To the Author of a Full Vindication of the Measures of the Congress . . .* (New York, [December 24,] 1774), 9.

37. Potter, *Liberty*, 121–25.

38. Moses Coit Tyler, *The Literary History of the American Revolution, 1763–1783* (New York: Frederick Ungar, 1957), 1:20.

39. Potter, *Liberty*, 7–9.

40. Steiner, *Samuel Seabury*, 131. Though historians state that many farmers of the time were illiterate, Isaac Gedney Jr., it seems, could at least sign his name. *Liber of Deeds*, I:249. On Westchester County deeds of this era, many women and some men signed with their mark. On a deed dated 1721 Eleazer Gidney Sr., Isaac Gedney Jr.'s grandfather, signed his name, whereas his wife, Anna Gidney, made her mark. *Liber of Deeds*, E:414.

41. Bolton, *History of the Protestant*, 288. Timothy Wetmore and his brother, James Jr., emigrated to Canada after the Revolution. Potter in *Liberty* (188, note 39) refers to Timothy Wetmore as an Anglican cleric, which he apparently was not.

42. Lewis Morris, Appointment of Delegates to the Provincial Convention from Westchester County, White Plains, April 11, 1775, in *Calendar of Historical Manuscripts Relating to the War of the Revolution, in the Office of the Secretary of State, Albany, New York* (Albany, 1868), 1:20.

43. Calhoon, *Loyalists*, 251.

44. Unknown author to Mr. Rivington, County of Westchester, April 13, 1775, in *Rivington's New-York Gazetteer*, April 20, 1775.

45. Philip Davidson, *Propaganda and the American Revolution, 1763–1783* (Chapel Hill: University of North Carolina Press, 1941), 299.

46. One of the signatures was that of Captain Absalom Gedney, who purchased the original Gedney family farm from Isaac Gedney Jr. in 1784. Another signature was William Grey's, the William Gray who subsequently bought the farm from Absalom Gedney in 1793.

47. Dawson, "Westchester-County," 248–49, 257.

48. The general association was a document to be signed in association or solidarity to defend the colony of New York: "We, the . . . inhabitants of New-York, do voluntarily and solemnly engage and associate, under all the ties held sacred amongst mankind, at the risk of our lives and fortunes, to defend by arms the United American Colonies against the hostile attempts of the British fleets and armies. . . ." Journal of the Committee of Safety, Die Mercurii, 4 ho. p.m., March 27, 1776, in *JPC*, 1:389.

49. Journal of the Committee of Safety, Die Sabbati, 9 ho. a.m., September 16, 1775, in *JPC*, 1:149–50.

50. Frederic Shonnard and W. W. Spooner, *History of Westchester County, New York, from its Earliest Settlement to the Year 1900* (New York: New York History, 1900), 313.

51. Sub-Committee of the Committee of Westchester-County to the Provincial Congress, White Plains, November 1, 1775, in Journal of the Provincial Congress, Die Veneris, 10 ho. a.m., November 3, 1775, in *JPC*, 1:192; Dawson, "Westchester-County," 296. Job Haddon's property bordered the north side of Isaac Gedney Jr.'s farm. *Liber of Deeds*, I:248 and M:500.

52. *Liber of Deeds*, H:85.

53. Shonnard and Spooner, *History of Westchester County,* 313–14.

54. Eunice Purdy, testimony before the Westchester County Committee of Safety, White Plains, September 28, 1775, in Correspondence of the Provincial Congress, &c., in *JPC*, 2:84.

55. Dawson, "Westchester-County," 293–95.

56. Colonel Gilbert Budd, testimony, New York, November 3, 1775, Journal of the Provincial Congress, Die Veneris, 5 ho. p.m., November 3, 1775, in *JPC*, 1:194. Budd was lieutenant colonel of the Second Regiment of the Westchester County

militia. His property was the southern border of Isaac Gedney Jr.'s and was separated from Gedney's by a stone wall described in various deeds. *Liber of Deeds*, I:248, M:500.

57. Sub-Committee of the Committee of Westchester-County to the Provincial Congress, White Plains, November 1, 1775, in Journal of the Provincial Congress, Die Veneris, 10 ho. a.m., November 3, 1775, in *JPC*, 1:192.

58. Colonel Gilbert Budd, testimony, New-York, November 3, 1775, in Journal of the Provincial Congress, Die Veneris, 5 ho. p.m., November 3, 1775, in *JPC*, 1:193–94.

59. Provincial Congress to Gilbert Drake, Chairman of the Committee of Westchester County, New York, November 3, 1775, in ibid., 194.

60. Journal of the Committee of Safety, Die Sabbati, 10 ho. a.m., January 20, 1776, in *JPC*, 1:256–58, 263; Dawson, "Westchester-County," 295.

61. Sorting out the two Isaac Gedneys, who were first cousins, and Isaac Jr.'s father, Isaac Sr. of Mamaroneck, presented a formidable challenge in researching this chapter.

62. Journal of the Committee of Safety, Die Sabbati, 10 ho. a.m., January 20, 1776, through Die Veneris, 10 ho. a.m., February 2, 1776, in *JPC*, 1:256–80; Journal of the Provincial Congress, Die Mercurii, 4 ho. p.m., March 6, 1776, in *JPC*, 2:341–42.

63. Journal of the Committee of Safety, Die Mercurii, 4 ho. p.m., March 27, 1776, in *JPC*, 1:388.

64. Isaac Gedney to Chairman of the Provincial Congress, White Plains Jail, April 20, 1776, in Correspondence of the Provincial Congress, in *JPC*, 2:115. There is no way to know if Isaac Gedney wrote this letter himself, however, the denial of the use of pen, ink, and paper indicates the Committee thought or knew he could write.

65. William Sutton, testimony before the Westchester Committee of Safety, White Plains, July 23, 1776, in *Calendar of Historical Manuscripts*, 1:428.

66. Governor William Tryon to the Earl of Dartmouth, On Board the Ship *Duchess of Gordon*, New York Harbour, November 11, 1775, in O'Callaghan, *Documents Relative*, 8:643.

67. Journal of the Provincial Congress, Die Mercurii, 9 ho. a.m., June 5, 1776, in *JPC*, 1:476–77.

68. Beginning July 10, 1776, the governing body was no longer called "the Provincial Congress of the Colony of New-York." It became "the Convention of Representatives of the State of New-York." Journal of the Provincial Convention, White Plains, Wednesday Morning, July 10, 1776, in *JPC*, 1:519.

69. Ibid., Die Sabbati, 4 ho. p.m., September 21, 1776, in *JPC*, 1:638.

70. Hufeland, *Westchester County*, 148.

71. "General Sir William Howe, Orders, Head Quarters, White Plains, November 4, 1776," in Stephen Kemble and others, *The Kemble Papers*, New-York Historical Society Collections, Publications Fund Series, 250585 (New York, 1884), 16:402–3.

72. Hufeland, *Westchester County*, 330–31.

73. "Howe, Orders," in *Kemble Papers*, 399.

74. "Journals of Lieut.-Col. Stephen Kemble, Saturday, November 2, 1776," 1–247 in *Kemble Papers*, 96.

75. Hufeland, *Westchester County*, 269–70.

76. General George Washington, General Orders, Head Quarters, White-Plains, October 31, 1776, in *The Writings of George Washington from the Original Manuscript Sources, 1745–1799*, John C. Fitzpatrick, ed. (Washington, DC: U.S. Government Printing Office, 1932), 6:234.

77. Ibid., 238.

78. Miles Oakley to General George Washington, November 9, 1776, in Force, *American Archives: Fifth Series, Containing a Documentary History of the United States of America, from the Declaration of Independence, July 4, 1776, to the Definitive Treaty of Peace with Great Britain, September 3, 1783*, American Archives 5 (Washington, DC, 1853), 3:620. This incident was part of the burning of the village of White Plains by the Massachusetts regiment of Major John W. Austin, who was court-martialed and discharged from the army. Hufeland, *Westchester County*, 156–60.

79. Governor William Tryon to Lord George Germain, On Board the Ship *Duchess of Gordon*, New York Harbour, November 28, 1776, in O'Callaghan, *Documents Relative*, 8:92.

80. Journal of the Committee of Safety, Monday Morning, October 14, 1776, in *JPC*, 1:673–74.

81. Samuel Townsend to Governor George Clinton, Bedford, June 7, 1779, in State of New York, *Public Papers of*

George Clinton, First Governor of New York (Albany, NY, 1901), 5:47.

82. Johann Carl Philipp von Krafft, *Journal of Lieutenant John Charles Philip von Krafft of the Regiment von Bose, 1776–1784*, Collections of the New-York Historical Society for the Year 1882 (New York, 1883), 60–61, 64–65.

83. John Thomas Jr. to the Convention of the State of New York, Westchester County, December 23, 1776, in Correspondence of the Provincial Congress, in *JPC*, 2:260.

84. Lieutenant Colonel James Millen to General Robert Howe, Phillips Mannor, March 9, 1780, in *Public Papers of George Clinton*, 5:552–53.

85. General William Heath to Governor George Clinton, Head quarters, West Point, November 1, 1780, in *Public Papers of George Clinton* (1902), 6:366.

86. See the discussion of Cowboys and others in Catherine S. Crary, "Guerrilla Activities of James DeLancey's Cowboys in Westchester County: Conventional Warfare or Self-Interested Freebooting?" in Robert A. East and Jacob Judd, eds., *The Loyalist Americans: A Focus on Greater New York* (Tarrytown, NY: Sleepy Hollow Restorations, 1975), 14–24.

87. Journal of the Council of Safety, Sunday, January 4, 1778, in *JPC*, 1:1107.

88. Hufeland, *Westchester County*, 318.

89. Journal of the Committee of Safety, Thursday Morning, December 12, 1776, in *JPC*, 1:750; Journal of the Provincial Convention, Monday Morning, April 7, 1777, in *JPC*, 1:869.

90. Journal of the Provincial Convention, Die Mercurii, 4 ho. p.m., March 26, 1777, in *JPC*, 1:851.

91. Philip Pell Jr. to Colonel Robert Benson, Fishkill, December 22, 1780, in *Public Papers of George Clinton*, 6:515.

92. Timothy Dwight, *Travels in New-England and New-York* (New Haven, 1822), 3:491–92. The Bible quotation is from Judges v, 6–7, (492).

93. William G. Fulcher, "Recorded Action Taken by Freeholders and Inhabitants of the Town of Mamaroneck as Found in the Town Record," *Quarterly Bulletin of the Westchester County Historical Society* 13, no. 1 (1937): 39.

94. Lieutenant Colonel Aaron Burr to General Alexander McDougall, White Plains, January 13, 1779, in Matthew L. Davis, *Memoirs of Aaron Burr with Miscellaneous Selections from his Correspondence* (New York, 1838), 1:142–43.

95. Josiah S. Mitchell, "White Plains," 1:714–44 in Scharf, *History of Westchester*, 1:728.

96. Prince Gedney, interview by John MacLean McDonald, October 23, 1850, in McDonald Papers (1850), 7:1048–49, collection of Westchester County Historical Society, Elmsford, NY.

97. *Revolutionary Services and Civil Life of General William Hull, Prepared from his Manuscripts, by his daughter, Mrs. Maria Campbell* (New York, 1848), 148.

98. Hufeland, *Westchester County*, 419–21, 423, 431, 436.

99. Ibid., 448.

100. *Liber of Deeds*, I:248. Captain Absalom Gedney, the cousin to whom Isaac Gedney Jr. sold his property in 1784, was among a group of eleven Westchester County men who were summoned before a committee of the Provincial Congress in June 1776 for being "disaffected to the American cause." Journal of the Provincial Congress, Die Mercurii, 9 ho. a.m., June 5, 1776, in *JPC*, 1:476. He was subsequently listed as one to be arrested. His summons ordered him to appear on July 6, 1776. Minutes of the Committee to Detect Conspiracies, Thursday, a.m., June 27, 1776, in *Calendar of Historical Manuscripts*, 1:341, 369. The disposition of his case is unknown because there are no more minutes for the committee until 1777.

101. *Calendar of Historical Manuscripts*, 1:618–19.

102. Sabine, 1:519. This Gidney was a New Rochelle innkeeper involved in the cannon-spiking episode with blacksmith Isaac.

103. Joseph Gedney emigrated to Nova Scotia after the war. Lorenzo Sabine, *Biographical Sketches of Loyalists of the American Revolution with an Historical Essay*, 2nd ed. (Boston, 1864; repr., Baltimore: Genealogical Publishing, 1979), 1:468. His notoriety as a Tory stemmed from, among other things, his volunteering as a guide for Hessian troops at the Battle of White Plains. John A. Todd, "Greenburgh," 2:172–283 in Scharf, *History of Westchester*, 2:279.

104. *Liber of Deeds*, I:267–68.

105. *Liber of Deeds*, L:204.

106. "Vital Records of Christ's Church at Rye, Westchester County, New York," *New York Genealogical and Biographical Society Record* 37, no. 4 (1906): 259.

CHAPTER SEVEN

1. *Epigraph*. "Future of New Wards," *New York Times*, May 17, 1896.

2. Robert A. East and Jacob Judd, eds., *The Loyalist Americans: A Focus on Greater New York* (Tarrytown, NY: Sleepy Hollow Restorations, 1975), 107, 119. Absalom Gedney is listed as having been on the rent role of the Frederick Philipse manor from 1768 to 1784.

3. Mary O'Connor English, ed., *Early Town Records of Mamaroneck* (Mamaroneck, NY: Town of Mamaroneck, 1979), 184–88.

4. Map of Mamaroneck, Drawn from Manuscript Map found in State Records at Albany, made in 1797, in Edward Floyd de Lancey, "Mamaroneck," in *History of Westchester County, New York Including Morrisania, Kings Bridge, and West Farms, which have been Annexed to New York City*, ed. J. Thomas Scharf, 1:846–88 (Philadelphia, 1886), 1:846; Richard M. Lederer Jr., "Population Tables for Westchester County: 1698–1980," *Westchester Historian*, 64, no. 3 (1988): 83. At the time the population was about 500.

5. Richard Maass, "'We Think He Deserves To Suffer': Keeping an Eye on Westchester," *Westchester Historian* 66, no. 2 (1990), 40; Unknown author to Mr. Rivington, County of Westchester, April 13, 1775, in *Rivington's New-York Gazetteer*, April 20, 1775; Henry B. Dawson, "Westchester-County, New-York, During the American Revolution," 1:177–457 in Scharf, *History of Westchester*, 1:329.

6. Journal of the Committee of Safety, Die Lunae, A. M., March 3, 1777, in *Journals of the Provincial Congress, Provincial Convention, Committee of Safety and Council of Safety of the State of New-York, 1775–1776–1777* (Albany, 1842), 1:821.

7. *Longworth's American Almanac, New-York Register, and City Directory* (New York, 1813–1821), s.v. "James Gray, distiller."

8. English, *Early Town Records*, 101.

9. *Longworth's*, 1806–1822, s.v. "David Lewis, grocer"; and English, *Early Town Records*, 215.

10. *Longworth's*, 1827, s.v. "Jacob Richee, grocer." This is the last year that he is listed. Property transactions are found in *Liber of Deeds*, I:248; M:500; T:97; U:323; 26:280, Westchester County Clerk's Office, Land Records Division, White Plains, NY.

11. Roger Panetta, "Westchester, the American Suburb: A New Narrative," in *Westchester, the American Suburb*, ed. Roger Panetta, 5–75 (New York: Fordham University Press; Yonkers, NY: Hudson River Museum, 2006), 8.

12. Solon Robinson, "A Day in Westchester County," *The American Agriculturist* 10 January 1851, 31.

13. Panetta, "Westchester," 13, 70; Geoffrey Crayon [Washington Irving], "Sleepy Hollow," in *The Works of Washington Irving*, (New York, 1885), 3:605.

14. Hans Huth, *Nature and the American: Three Centuries of Changing Attitudes* (Lincoln: University of Nebraska Press, 1957), 122–23.

15. John R. Stilgoe, *Borderland: Origins of the American Suburb, 1820–1939* (New Haven: Yale University Press, 1988), 65, 68–73.

16. Dolores Hayden, *Building Suburbia: Green Fields and Urban Growth, 1820–2000* (New York: Pantheon, 2003), 22.

17. Panetta, "Westchester," 9.

18. Kenneth T. Jackson, *Crabgrass Frontier: The Suburbanization of the United States* (New York: Oxford University Press, 1985), 94.

19. Lederer, "Population Tables," 81–92.

20. *Liber of Deeds*, 455:70; 461:167; 463:28; 999:279; 1024:417; 1040:274; 1199:323,327; 1356:125; 1373:472; 1402:52; 1411:30.

21. Asa Greene, *A Glance at New York* (New York, 1837), 15.

22. Huth, *Nature and the American*, 122.

23. Andrew Jackson Downing, *A Treatise on the Theory and Practice of Landscape Gardening, Adapted to North America; with a View to the Improvement of Country Residences*, 6th ed. (1859; repr., New York: Funk & Wagnalls, 1967), viii, x, 19–21, 26–39.

24. A. J. Downing, *Cottage Residences, Rural Architecture & Landscape Gardening* (1842; repr., Watkins Glen, NY: American Life Foundation, 1967).

25. George B. Tatum, Introduction, in A. J. Downing, *The Architecture of Country Houses* (1850; repr., New York: Da Capo, 1968), v.

26. Susan Fenimore Cooper, "Small Family Memories," 1883, in *Correspondence of James Fenimore Cooper*, ed. James Fenimore Cooper [grandson], 7–72 (New Haven: Yale University Press, 1922), 48, http://external.oneonta.edu.

27. John Richardson, *The Annals of London: A Year-by-Year Record of a Thousand Years of History* (Berkeley: University of California Press, 2000), 254.

28. Greene, *A Glance*, 4, 260–62.

29. Jackson, *Crabgrass Frontier*, 34.

30. Herbert H. Harwood, Jr., *The New York, Westchester & Boston Railway: J. P. Morgan's Magnificent Mistake* (Bloomington: Indiana University Press, 2008), 7–8.

31. "Future of New Wards," *New York Times*, May 17, 1896.

32. Harwood, *New York, Westchester & Boston*, 81, 97; Hayden, *Building Suburbia*, 23, 97; Suzannah Lessard, "Reflections, The Suburban Landscape: Oyster Bay, Long Island," *New Yorker*, October 11, 1976, 68.

33. "Ice Made While They Waited," *New York Times*, January 20, 1893; *The American Society of Mechanical Engineers Yearbook*, 1919, http://www.archive.org.

34. Block, Louis, 1902, Apparatus for the Manufacture of Ice, US Patent 726,852, filed February 15, 1902, and issued May 5, 1903; Block, Louis, 1909, Means for Drying Air, US Patent 961,710, filed September 20, 1909, and issued June 14, 1910, htttp://www.google.com/patents?id=DlVbAAAAEBAJ&pg=PA2&lpg=PA2&dq=%22louis+block%22+mamaroneck&source=bl&ots=jV0_N9bQXL&sig=Vyw93POcDPp7LibeTjOCUbfUxAk&hl=en&ei=uQ-XSdnKMoGCtwfarpGpCw&sa=X&oi=book_result&resnum=10&ct=result - PPA2,M1.

35. "Cities of Westchester and Her County Seat," *New York Times*, May 3, 1903.

36. United States of America, Bureau of the Census (Washington, DC: National Archives and Records Administration), New York, Richmond (Staten Island), 1880; New York, Mamaroneck, 1900, 1910, 1920, Ancestry Library Edition, 1790–1930, Provo, Utah, U.S.A.: The Generations Network, Inc., 2004, http://ancestrylibrary.proquest.com. This is the library version of Ancestry.com.

37. Jackson, *Crabgrass Frontier*, 101.

38. Harwood, *New York, Westchester & Boston*, 90. The New York, Westchester & Boston line went to 180th Street in the Bronx and on to the Harlem River; the New York, New Haven & Hartford went to Grand Central Station.

39. Sanborn Library, *Map of Mamaroneck, N.Y.*, 1919.

40. Jackson, *Crabgrass Frontier*, 157–62.

41. *Catalogue of Officers and Graduates of Columbia University* (New York: Columbia University, 1906), 175, 729.

42. Christopher Gray, "A Walk on the Sunnyside Street," *New York Times*, March 13, 2005.

43. "Recreation Spaces for Home Centres," *New York Times*, April 26, 1931.

44. "Harry Rich Mooney's Crowning Achievement," *Larchmont Fables*, 1926, 5, 7, 13.

45. Display Ad, *New York Times*, September 3 and 10, 1926. (The ad says, "I live in the Gables myself and oversee every detail of its operation.")

46. "The Beginning and End of Your Search," *Mooney's Megaphone*, April 15, 1928, cover.

47. "Mamaroneck," *Mooney's Megaphone*, November 12, 1927, unpaginated.

48. Mary P. LoGiudice, ed., *Celebration: Village of Mamaroneck Centennial, 1895–1995*, (Mamaroneck, NY: Village of Mamaroneck, 1995), 77.

49. "Transportation Facilities," *Mooney's Megaphone*, April 15, 1928, 7.

50. "Messages from Mamaroneck Knolls," "Crown Court," and "Mamaroneck Gables," *Mooney's Megaphone*, November 12, 1927.

51. *Mooney's Megaphone*, November 12, 1927; April 15, 1928, 15–18, 21, repr. *National Real Estate Journal*, March 19, 1928.

52. Display Ad, *New York Times*, November 27, 1927; *Mooney's Megaphone*, April 15, 1928, 14, 16. The ad notes that five and six thousand people respectively had visited the house during the first two Sundays it was open to the public. Such crowds would have been truly extraordinary given the single-egress, cul-de-sac character of the development.

53. "Built with the Pride of the True Craftsman," *Mooney's Megaphone*, April 15, 1928, 11–12.

54. "Say It With a Home," *Mooney's Megaphone*, April 15, 1928, 6.

55. "Boy Camp Leader Tells of Wreck," *New York Times*, September 3, 1913.

56. "Mrs. Mooney's Mother Killed in Florida," *Larchmont Times* (Larchmont, NY), February 16, 1928.

57. "Larchmont Knolls Residents Seek Aid," *Daily Times* (Mamaroneck, NY), November 19, 1925.

58. *Liber of Deeds*, 3204:388; "Business Records: Judgments," *New York Times*, December 24, 1938, January 12, 1939.

59. "Fair Temple Held Sign City Has Soul," *New York Times*, January 24, 1939; "Defends 'Trailer Town,'" *New York Times*, April 16, 1939; "La Guardia Favors Trailer Camp Plan," *New York Times*, August 2, 1939.

60. "Harry Rich Mooney, Realty Developer," *New York Times*, May 24, 1957; "Pistol Mishap Kills Boy," *New York Times*, April 27, 1946. Mooney's fifteen-year-old son accidentally shot and killed a friend.

61. Jackson, *Crabgrass Frontier*, 187.

62. *Liber of Deeds*, 4476:223; 5606:46.

CHAPTER EIGHT

1. *Epigraph.* State of New York, Senate, *Report of the Commissioners Appointed to Ascertain the Boundary Line Between the States of New-York and Connecticut, appointed April 9, 1856*, Doc. 165, 37, Albany, NY, [1857].

2. Ibid.

3. For overviews of the controversy see Charles W. Baird, *Chronicle of a Border Town: History of Rye, Westchester County, New York, 1660–1870, Including Harrison and the White Plains till 1788* (1871; repr., Harrison, NY: Harbor Hills Books, 1974), 105 127, and J. Thomas Scharf, "The Boundary, Topography and Geology of Westchester County," in *History of Westchester County, New York Including Morrisania, Kings Bridge, and West Farms, which have been Annexed to New York City*, ed. J. Thomas Scharf, 1:1–9 (Philadelphia, 1886), 1:2–5. Daniel J. Pratt, *Report of the Regents of the University on the Boundaries of the State of New York*, 2, (Albany, 1884) contains all of the documents pertaining to the controversy from the seventeenth through the nineteenth century.

4. "West India Company to the States General," May 5, 1632, in O'Callaghan, *Documents Relative*, 1:50–52.

5. "Answer to the Remonstrance of the Dutch Ambassadors," May 23, 1632, 1:57–59, in O'Callaghan, *Documents Relative*, 1:58.

6. Russell Shorto, *The Island at the Center of the World: The Epic Story of Dutch Manhattan and the Forgotten Colony That Shaped America* (New York: Doubleday, 2004), 236–38.

7. Ronald D. Cohen, "The Hartford Treaty of 1650: Anglo-Dutch Cooperation in the Seventeenth Century," *New-York Historical Society Quarterly* 53, no. 4 (1969): 320, 332.

8. Scharf, "Boundary," in Scharf, *History of Westchester*, 1:3; Shorto, *Island*, 289–300.

9. Pratt, *Report of the Regents*, 228–29.

10. Ibid., 230.

11. Subsequent letters between various authorities indicate that the English continued to believe that the line ran twenty miles east of the Hudson River. Duke of York to Governor Edmund Andros, Whitehall, April 6, 1675, and January 28, 1675/6; John Werden to Governor Andros, St. James, May 7, 1677; Governor Thomas Dongan to Secretary Allyn, New York, October 9, 1683; Governor Dongan to Governor Robert Treat, New York, November 5, 1683, in Pratt, *Report of the Regents*, 232–34, 239, 241.

12. "John Richbell Patent from Governor Lovelace," October 16, 1668, New York State Department of State Letters Patent 4:68, Records Series # 12943, New York State Archives.

13. Scharf, "Boundary," in Scharf, *History of Westchester*, 1:4.

14. Dixon Ryan Fox, *Caleb Heathcote, Gentleman Colonist: The Story of a Career in the Province of New York, 1692–1721* (New York: Charles Scribner's Sons, 1926), 190.

15. *Report of the Commissioners*, 8.

16. Scharf, "Boundary," in Scharf, *History of Westchester*, 1:4–5.

CHAPTER NINE

1. *Epigraph.* Edward Steichen, *A Life in Photography* (Garden City, NY: Doubleday/Museum of Modern Art, 1963), ch. 1, unpaginated.

2. *Moonrise—Mamaroneck, New York* is in the collection of the Museum of Modern Art; *The Pond—Moonrise* is in the collection of the Metropolitan Museum of Art; and *The Pond—Moonlight*, formerly of the Gillman Paper Company Collection and the Metropolitan Museum of Art, is, as of 2006, owned by a private collector.

3. Steichen, *A Life in Photography*, ch. 1.

4. "$2.9 Million Photo Sets a World Record," *New York Times*, February 15, 2006.

5. Randy Kennedy, "A Big Sale Spurs Talk of a Photography Gold Rush," *New York Times*, February 17, 2006.

6. Elizabeth Lesure, "Record-setting 'Pond' Photo Taken in Mamaroneck," *Journal News* (White Plains, NY), February 16, 2006; Liz Sadler, "$2.9M Photo's Origins a Mystery," *Journal News*, February 17, 2006; Sadler, "Expert Resets Sights on $3M Photograph," *Journal News*, February 18, 2006.

7. Steichen, *A Life in Photography*, ch. 1.

8. Ibid.

9. Charles H. Caffin, "Philadelphia Photographic Salon," *Harper's Weekly*, 42 (November 5, 1898): 1087.

10. Steichen, *A Life in Photography*, ch. 1.

11. Joel Smith, *Edward Steichen: The Early Years* (Princeton, NJ: Princeton University Press/Metropolitan Museum of Art, 1999), 12.

12. William B. Dyer, "The Chicago Salon," *Camera Notes* 4 (July 1900): 70.

13. Weston J. Naef, *The Collection of Alfred Stieglitz: Fifty Pioneers of Modern Photography* (New York: Viking/Metropolitan Museum of Art, 1978), 468. *Camera Notes* 4 (January 1901) included five of Steichen's photographs (135, 139, 145, 147, 153) and his review, "British Photography from an American Point of View," (175–81).

14. Sidney Allan [Sadakichi Hartmann], "Eduard J. Steichen, Painter-Photographer," *Camera Notes* 6 (July 1902): 15. The circumstances referred to were probably those that led Stieglitz to resign as editor of *Camera Notes* with that issue, citing conflict with the sponsoring and conservative Camera Club of New York, and shortly thereafter to found a new journal, *Camera Work*, where he could more independently pursue his agenda of encouraging experimental photography.

15. Penelope Niven, *Steichen: A Biography* (New York: Clarkson Potter, 1997), 119, 147–48, 193. The Caffins' house and barn still stand, now surrounded by newer suburban homes.

16. Caffin, *Photography as a Fine Art: The Achievements and Possibilities of Photographic Art in America* (1901; repr., New York: American Photographic Book Publishing, 1972), 155.

17. Edward Steichen to Alfred Stieglitz, undated, YCAL MSS 85, box 46, folder 1092, Alfred Stieglitz/Georgia O'Keeffe Archive, Yale Collection of American Literature, Beinecke Rare Book and Manuscript Library, Yale University.

18. Niven, *Steichen*, 449, 458–60, 599, 611–12.

19. "Corrections: For the Record," *New York Times*, February 18, 2006.

20. Benjamin Genocchio, "Hey Mamaroneck, Recognize This Pond?" *New York Times*, February 26, 2006.

21. Steichen, *A Life in Photography*, ch. 1.

22. Edward Steichen to Alfred Stieglitz, March 1909, box 46, folder 1095, Stieglitz/O'Keeffe Archive. Steichen, in a handwritten catalogue in this letter, lists a dozen photographs with the times they were taken from 11:00 p.m., hourly through the night, to just before dawn.

23. "In the Real Estate Field," *New York Times*, April 14, 1901; *Liber of Deeds*, 1574:379, Westchester County Clerk's Office, Land Records Division, White Plains, NY; *Atlas of Westchester County, N.Y.*, (New York: G. W. Bromley, 1914).

24. Genocchio, "Hey Mamaroneck."

25. Westchester County Park Commission, *Map of Lands to be Acquired for Saxon Woods Park, Westchester County, N.Y.*, map no. 2739, November 24, 1926; and Sanborn Library, *Map of Mamaroneck, N.Y.*, 1919.

26. Gosta Morner, "Harry Rich Mooney: Builder of Homes and Happiness," *Mooney's Megaphone*, November 12, 1927, unpaginated. In reality, the price Mooney sold it for was not nominal, but rather at a higher rate than what he had paid for the rest of his property.

27. Niven, *Steichen*, 192–93, 198–99.

28. Carl Sandburg, *Steichen the Photographer* (New York: Harcourt, Brace, 1929), 62.

29. Smith, *Edward Steichen*, 25. It was reproduced in F. Matthies-Masuren, *Die Photographische Kunst im Jahr 1904* (Halle: W. Knapp, 1904), 47, and exhibited in *Catalogue of the Ninth Annual Exhibition of the Art Association of Richmond, Indiana, 1905* (Richmond, 1905), no. 845, as *Solitude*.

30. Charles H. Caffin, "The Art of Edward J. Steichen," *Camera Work* 30 (April 1910): 34.

31. Charles Isaacs quoted in Sadler, "But Mamaroneck Historian Says."

32. Sarah Hermanson Meister, curator, Department of Photography, Museum of Modern Art, conversation with author, November 4, 2009.

CHAPTER TEN

1. *Epigraph*. S. D. Smith, *Slavery, Family, and Gentry Capitalism in the British Atlantic: The World of the Lascelles, 1648–1834* (Cambridge: Cambridge University Press, 2006), 108.

2. Smith, "Gedney Clarke of Salem and Barbados: Transatlantic Super-Merchant," *New England Quarterly* 76, no. 4 (2003): 502–5.

3. Ibid., 506–8.

4. Ibid., 509–12.

5. Smith, "Gedney Clarke of Salem," 513; *Letter Book of John Watts: Merchant and Councillor of New York, January 1, 1762–December 22, 1765*, ed. Dorothy C. Barck, Collections of the New-York Historical Society, vol. 61 (New York: New-York Historical Society, 1928), 31–32. In one of the 1762 letters to Clarke in Barbados, Watts explained the nature of the slave business in New York: "For this market they must be young the younger the better if not quite Children, those advanced in years will never do I should imagine a Cargo of them none exceeding thirty might turn out at fifty pounds a head gross Sales. Males are best. Such a Number as you mention we cannot easily vend from fifty to a hundred would run high enough, but Virginia could take off a great many. Our Duty is four pound a head from the West Indies forty shillings from Africa. New Jersey pays none at all for which reason the Master might lay a mile or two below the Town & send up word."

6. *Letter Book of John Watts*, 31–32.

7. James G. Lydon, "New York and the Slave Trade, 1700–1774," *William and Mary Quarterly*, 3rd ser., 35, no. 2 (1978): 380–81, 384, 387.

8. Ibid., 378.

9. Edgar J. McManus, *A History of Negro Slavery in New York* (Syracuse: Syracuse University Press, 1966), 38–39; Lydon, "New York," 385–86.

10. "A List of the Indian Negro and Malatto Slaves Within and Belonging to the Township of Mamaroneck and Mannor of Scarsdale taken Aprill ye 5th 1755 by Joseph Sutton Capt." in O'Callaghan, *Documentary History*, 3:511.

11. *Heads of Families at the First Census of the United States Taken in the Year, 1790, New York* (Washington, DC: U.S. Government Printing Office, 1908), 199.

12. *Letter Book of John Watts*, 9–12, 47, 159, 360–61, 363–64, 380.

13. Smith, "Gedney Clarke of Salem," 523–26.

14. Sarah Kemble Knight, "The Journal of Madam Knight," 1704–05, in *The Puritans*, eds. Perry Miller and Thomas H. Johnson, (New York: American Book Company, 1938), 51, http://mith2.umd.edu. In her journal she wrote, "we travailed through Merrinak, a neet, though little place, wth a navigable River before it, one of the pleasantest I ever see. . . ."

15. Simon Smith, e-mail message to author, February 11, 2004.

16. Professor Simon D. Smith is currently a member of the faculty of the Wilberforce Institute for the Study of Slavery and Emancipation (WISE) at the University of Hull, Yorkshire, U.K.

17. Smith, *Slavery, Family, and Gentry*, 108.

18. Alice Morse Earle, "The Revival of the Sun Dial," *House & Garden*, May 1904, 223–28.

19. Walter A. Dyer, "Sun-Dials in Modern Gardens," *Country Life in America*, March 1906, 538–41, 616–20.

20. Mary Gage and James Gage, *The Art of Splitting Stone: Early Rock Quarrying Methods in Pre-Industrial New England, 1630–1825*, 2nd ed. (Amesbury, MA: privately printed, 2005), 3.

21. Andrea C. Cook, John R, Southon, and Jeffrey Wadsworth, "Using Radiocarbon Dating to Establish the Age of Iron-Based Artifacts," *JOM* 55, no. 5 (2003), http://www.tms.org/pubs/journals/JOM/0305/Cook-0305.html. Specifically, only iron-based materials that were made with fuels of wood and charcoal, not coal, can be dated using radiocarbon technology, and that effectively eliminates most modern steel made after 1800.

22. "Indian Signs," *Daily Times* (Mamaroneck, NY), September 18, 1961.

23. Edward Floyd de Lancey, "Mamaroneck," in *History of Westchester County, New York Including Morrisania, Kings Bridge, and West Farms, which have been Annexed to New York City*, ed. J. Thomas Scharf, 1:846–888 160*f* (Philadelphia, 1886), 1:870.

24. Advertisement, "Caldwell Tanks and Towers," W. E. Caldwell Co., *Country Life in America*, July 1902, lxiv.

25. "Where We Get Our Water," *Facts, Figures and Photographs of Interest to the Residents of the Town of Mamaroneck* (Mamaroneck, NY: Town of Mamaroneck, 1955), 16; *Mamaroneck 1661–1961: A Panorama of Her First Three Centuries*, (Mamaroneck, NY: Town of Mamaroneck, March 1961), 28.

26. See, for example, Historic American Engineering Record, "Windmill at Water Mill, Suffolk County NY," Library of Congress, American Memory, http://memory.loc.gov.

27. Online Air Defense Radar Museum, "The Ground Observer Corps," http://www.radomes.org/museum/documents/GOC/GOC.html.

28. "Bombers' Approach Darkens Big Area in 3-State Practice," *New York Times*, June 9, 1943.

29. Arthur T. Broes, "White Plains Goes to War, 1941–1942," *Westchester Historian* 72, no. 2 (1996): 39.

30. Gloria Pritts, "D. W. Griffith Studio in Mamaroneck," *Conversations About Mamaroneck & Old Rye Neck*, Fall 1998, 13–15.

31. Ibid.

32. Robert M. Henderson, *D. W. Griffith: His Life and Work* (New York: Oxford University Press, 1972), 233.

33. Russell Merritt, Liner Notes, *Orphans of the Storm*, DVD, directed by D. W. Griffith (1921; Chatsworth, CA: Image Entertainment, 1996).

34. Mamaroneck, D. W. Griffith Studio, 1921, G-73, Photograph Collection, Westchester County Historical Society.

35. Richard Pieper, e-mails to author, February 24 and March 4, 2005.

36. Historic American Engineering Record, "Vermont Marble Quarry, Abandoned Mine Site, Broadwater County, MT," Library of Congress, American Memory, http://memory.loc.gov.

37. Gage, *Art of Splitting Stone*, 9, 13.

38. Leslie J. Stewart, "The Hay Derrick," Historic American Engineering Record, Library of Congress, American Memory http://memory.loc.gov.

39. Richard Pieper, e-mail to author, March 4, 2005.

40. Gosta Morner, "Harry Rich Mooney: Builder of Homes and Happiness," *Mooney's Megaphone*, November 12, 1927, unpaginated.

41. A. J. Downing, *Cottage Residences, Rural Architecture & Landscape Gardening* (1842; repr., Watkins Glen, NY: American Life Foundation, 1967), 162.

42. Andrew Jackson Downing, *A Treatise on the Theory and Practice of Landscape Gardening, Adapted to North America; with a View to the Improvement of Country Residences*, 6th ed. (1859; repr., New York: Funk & Wagnalls, 1967), 282.

43. "Domestic Notices: Kiosques or Summer Houses," *The Horticulturalist and Journal of Rural Art and Rural Taste* 7, no. 7 (1852): 339.

44. Frank J. Scott, *The Art of Beautifying Suburban Home Grounds of Small Extent* (New York, 1881).

45. "A Rustic Summer House," *Gardening*, March 1, 1895, 179–80.

46. "The Fairmount Water-Works, Philadelphia," *House & Garden*, June 1901, 15.

47. Advertisement, "Rustic Work for the Country Grounds," Dunne & Co., *Country Life in America*, August 1902, lxxv, and October 1902, cxxviii; "The Rustic Summer House of Red Cedar and Laurel," D. P. Van Gorden, *Country Life in America*, June 1902, xliib.

48. W. C. Egan, "Points on Rustic Work," *Country Life in America*, April 1903, cxciv–cxcvi.

49. Henry H. Saylor, "Garden Furniture," *The Garden Magazine*, June 1907, 278–81; Richard Ferris, "Practical Suggestions for Rustic Work," ibid., January 1909, 276.

50. Judith Doolin Spikes, *Larchmont, N.Y.: People and Places* (Larchmont, NY: Fountain Square Books, 1991), 70.

51. Ibid., *Images of America: Larchmont* (Portsmouth, NH: Arcadia, 2003), 92.

52. Downing, *A Treatise*, 397; "A Rustic Summer House," *Gardening* 3, no. 60 (1895): 179–80.

53. R. J. Hoage, Anne Roskell, and Jane Mansour, "Menageries and Zoos to 1900," in *New Worlds, New Animals: From Menagerie to Zoological Park in the Nineteenth Century*, eds. R. J. Hoage and William A. Deiss, 8–18 (Baltimore: Johns Hopkins University Press, 1996), 9–14.

54. Sally Gregory Kohlstedt, "Reflections on Zoo History," 3–7, in *New Worlds*, 3–4.

55. Vernon N. Kisling Jr., "The Origin and Development of American Zoological Parks to 1899," 109–125, in *New Worlds*, 110.

56. Ibid., 109, 112.

57. Richard W. Flint, "American Showmen and European Dealers: Commerce in Wild Animals in Nineteenth-Century America," 97–108, in *New Worlds*, 98.

58. Kisling, "Origin and Development," 116.

59. Katherine C. Grier, *Pets in America: A History* (Chapel Hill: University of North Carolina Press, 2006), 20–24, 231–32, 242.

60. Flint, "American Showmen," 97, 101–2.

61. P. Chalmers Mitchell, introduction, in Carl Hagenbeck, *Beasts and Men: Being Carl Hagenbeck's Experiences for Half a Century among Wild Animals*, trans. Hugh S. R. Elliot and A. G. Thacker (London: Longmans, Green, 1909), vi.

62. "To Raise Zebroids," *New York Daily Tribune*, November 18, 1906.

63. Hagenbeck, *Beasts and Men*, 2, 7.

64. Ibid., 11, 47, 61, 65–66, 69.

65. "Hagenbeck's Trained Animals," *New York Times*, June 24, 1894; Advertisement, "New Hagenbeck Arena," *New York Times*, June 17, 1894.

66. "Animals for Hagenbeck's," *New York Times*, September 2, 1894.

67. Hagenbeck, *Beasts and Men*, 40, 202.

68. Hagenbeck, *Beasts and Men*, 116, 273, 283–84, 287.

69. "How Hagenbeck Became the Wild Animal King," *New York Times*, April 20, 1913.

70. "Smith Will Start for Albany Today," *New York Times*, December 28, 1922; "Cheering Throngs in Albany Welcome 'Al' Smith in Storm," *New York Times*, December 29, 1922.

71. Hoage, Roskell, and Mansour, "Menageries and Zoos," 17.

72. C. F. Derven, "Glossary of Terms Used in Slate Quarries Around Poultney, Vermont," November 22, 1938, Document 86, 5–6 (Washington, DC: Library of Congress, 1936–40), http://lcweb2.loc.gov.

73. *Merriam-Webster's Collegiate Dictionary*, 10th ed., s.v. "monkey."

74. Alexander Hollenbach, "Analysis of Wrought Iron Sample from Mamaroneck, New York" (executive summary for project in course MAT 203, Materials Structure at the Nanoscale, with Dr. Charles E. Lyman, Lehigh University, Bethlehem, PA, April 30, 2010), 4.

EPILOGUE

1. *Epigraph*. Holland Cotter, "Who Owns Art?" *New York Times*, March 29, 2006.

2. *The Diaries of George Washington*, Donald Jackson and Dorothy Twohig, eds. (Charlottesville: University Press of Virginia, 1976), 1:137, http://memory.loc.gov.

3. William Faulkner, *Requiem for a Nun* (1950; repr., New York: Vintage Books, 1975), 80.

Sidebar Notes

THE INTERNET AND THE WEB

1. "The Cape Cod Cottage," pt. 1, *Architectural Forum* 90, no. 2 (1949): 89.

THINK LOCAL

1. "Indian Signs," *Daily Times* (Mamaroneck, N.Y,), September 18, 1961.

MAGAZINES

1. Frank Luther Mott, *A History of American Magazines, 1885–1905* (Cambridge, MA: Belknap of Harvard University Press, 1957), 4:2, 11–12.

CHANGING LANGUAGE, CHANGING ATTITUDES

1. Jonas Michaëlius to Adrianus Smoutius, August 11, 1628, New Netherland, 122, in Jameson, *Narratives of New Netherland,* 126.

2. "The Waldorf Mill and the Legend of the White Deer," *Westchester Historian* 32, no. 1 (1956): 10.

3. Charles C. Mann, *1491: New Revelations of the Americas Before Columbus* (New York: Knopf, 2006), xi, 340.

THE DEED CHAIN

1. *Liber of Deeds*, C:287; E:414 G:327, 26, 280, Westchester County Clerk's Office, Land Records Division, White Plains, NY.

2. Deed, Wampus to Caleb Heathcote, 19 October 1696, in Bartlett, "New Castle," in Scharf, *History of Westchester* 2:608.

3. William Cronon, *Changes in the Land: Indians, Colonists, and the Ecology of New England* (New York: Hill & Wang, 1983), 66.

4. *Liber of Deeds*, M:500.

5. *Liber of Deeds*, I:248.

6. *Liber of Deeds*, F:16.

METES AND BOUNDS

1. *Liber of Deeds*, B:371, Westchester County Clerk's Office, Land Records Division, White Plains, NY.

2. *Liber of Deeds*, B:385.

PRIMARY SOURCES

1. Harry Hansen, *Scarsdale: From Colonial Manor to Modern Community* (New York: Harper & Brothers, 1954), 16.

2. *Minutes of the Common Council of the City of New York, 1675–1776* (New York: Dodd, Mead, 1905), 3:27. A gibbet is the

projecting arm of a gallows, from which criminals were hung, their bodies left suspended after execution as a warning to others.

3. Dixon Ryan Fox, *Caleb Heathcote, Gentleman Colonist: The Story of a Career in the Province of New York, 1692–1721* (New York: Charles Scribner's Sons, 1926), 132–33.

4. Governor Robert Hunter to the Lords of Trade, report, New York, 23 June 1712, 339–43, in O'Callaghan, *Documents Relative*, 5:341.

WILLS AND PROBATE: A CAUTIONARY TALE

1. *Liber of Deeds*, A:85–87, Westchester County Clerk's Office, Land Records Division, White Plains, NY.

2. Harry Macy Jr., "New York Probate Records Before 1787," Spring 1991, updated March 2001, www.newyorkfamilyhistory.org.

3. The abstracts were in William S. Pelletreau, *Early Wills of Westchester County, New York from 1664 to 1784* (New York, 1898), 9; and Anne Richbell, page 366, *New York City Wills, 1665–1707*, http://search.ancestrylibrary.com. The extract was in Robert Bolton Jr., *A History of the County of Westchester from Its First Settlement to the Present Time* (New York, 1848), 292. The copied will is in Thomas C. Cornell, *Adam and Anne Mott: Their Ancestors and Their Descendants* (Poughkeepsie, NY, 1890), 317–19; the original will is in Ann Richbell will dated April 1, 1700, proved May 19, 1700, no. 318, *Original Wills Filed in New York County Surrogate's Office, 1662–1829*, Liber 2:92, New York Public Library.

STONEWALLS: WHAT THEY TELL US

1. *Liber of Deeds*, I:248, M:500, U:323, 26:280, Westchester County Clerk's Office, Land Records Division, White Plains, NY.

2. "Statistics of Fences in the United States," in *Report of the Commissioner of Agriculture for the Year 1871* (Washington, DC, 1872), 501, 510.

3. Budd testimony, *JPC*, 1:194.

4. Hufeland, *Westchester County*, 72, 100, 111, 113.

5. Hufeland, *Westchester County*, 113, 121, 134, 136, 137, 171, 197, 235, 255, 308, 309, 377, 420.

EYEWITNESS ACCOUNTS

1. Johann Carl Philipp von Krafft, *Journal of Lieutenant John Charles Philip von Krafft of the Regiment von Bose, 1776–1784*, Collections of the New-York Historical Society for the Year 1882 (New York, 1883), 60–61, 64–65.

2. Sarah Kemble Knight, "The Journal of Madam Knight," 1704–05, in *The Puritans*, eds. Perry Miller and Thomas H. Johnson, (New York: American Book Company, 1938), 16, http://mith2.umd.edu/eada/html/display.php?docs=knight_journal.xml.

3. Prince Gedney, interview by John MacLean McDonald, October 23, 1850, in McDonald Papers (1850), 7:1048–49, collection of Westchester County Historical Society, Elmsford, NY.

4. Adriaen van der Donck, *A Description of New Netherland*, eds. Charles T. Gehring and William A. Starna (Lincoln: University of Nebraska Press, 2008), 73.

5. Colonel Gilbert Budd, testimony, New-York, November 3, 1775, in Journal of the Provincial Congress, Die Veneris, 5 ho. p.m., November 3, 1775, in *JPC*, 1:193. 6. Complaint of Phoebe Oakley, *Calendar of Revolutionary MMS.*, I:541, quoted in Hufeland, *Westchester County*, 161–62.

6. Complaint of Phoebe Oakley, *Calendar of Revolutionary MMS.*, I:541, quoted in Hufeland, *Westchester County*, 161–62.

MAPS

1. Richard M. Lederer Jr., *The Place-Names of Westchester County, New York* (Harrison, NY: Harbor Hills Books, 1978), 8, 11, 10, 28, 100, 106, 117, 129.

2. William Cronon, *Changes in the Land: Indians, Colonists, and the Ecology of New England* (New York: Hill & Wang, 1983), 65.

LIBRARIES

1. Paul LeClerc quoted in Patricia Cohen, "Library Leader In Era of Change To Step Down," *New York Times*, November 19, 2009.

ASSUME NOTHING

1. "'White Hat' M'Carty's Suit," *New York Times*, January 4, 1881.

2. "Big Suburban Realty Deal," *New York Times*, February 14, 1900.

3. "In the Real Estate Field," *New York Times*, June 24, 1904; "At Auction," *New York Times*, July 10, 1904.

CALICO: THE RESEARCH PROCESS

1. Richmond Huntley, "American Patchwork Quilts," *American Collector*, http://www.collectorsweekly.com.

Selected Bibliography

I list here the writings I have used in the preparation of this book with the exception of most of the many articles in magazines and newspapers that I consulted to provide a time-period context, as well as the advertisements therein. Also excluded is bibliographic information for maps, deeds, censuses, and FHA brochures. This information, however, may be found in the notes.

ARCHIVES AND SPECIAL COLLECTIONS

Bronx Parkway Commission Collection. Deeds. Maps and Plans Collection. Westchester County Archives, Elmsford, NY.

Maps Collection. Mamaroneck Village Archives, Mamaroneck, NY.

McDonald Papers. Photographs Collection. Westchester County Historical Society, Elmsford, NY.

New York State Department of State Deeds. New York State Department of State Letters Patent. New York State Archives, Albany.

Proceedings of the Court of Assizes. Manuscripts and Archives Division, New York Public Library.

Steichen, Edward, Collection. Erna and Victor Hasselblad Photography Study Center. Museum of Modern Art, New York.

Stieglitz, Alfred, Collection. Joyce F. Menschel Photography Library. Metropolitan Museum of Art, New York.

Stieglitz, Alfred/Georgia O'Keeffe Archive, Yale Collection of American Literature, Beinecke Rare Book and Manuscript Library. Yale University.

Van Norden, Warner, Album. Jay Heritage Center Archives, Rye, NY.

SOURCES

Allan, Sidney [Sadakichi Hartmann]. "Eduard J. Steichen, Painter-Photographer." *Camera Notes* 6, no. 1 (1902): 15–16.

Andrews, Edna. "Cultural Sensitivity and Political Correctness: The Linguistic Problem of Naming Author(s)." *American Speech* 71, no. 4 (1996): 389–404. http://www.jstor.org/stable/455713.

Axtell, James. *Beyond 1492: Encounters in Colonial North America*. New York: Oxford University Press, 1992.

Baird, Charles W. "Civil Status of the Presbyterians in the Province of New York." *Magazine of American History* 3, no. 10 (1879): 593–628.

———. *Chronicle of a Border Town: History of Rye, Westchester County, New York, 1660–1870, Including Harrison and the White Plains till 1788*. 1871. Reprint, Harrison, NY: Harbor Hills Books, 1974.

Ballon, Hilary, and Kenneth T. Jackson. *Robert Moses and the Modern City: The Transformation of New York*. New York: Norton, 2007.

Barck, Dorothy C., ed. *Letter Book of John Watts: Merchant and Councillor of New York, January 1, 1762–December 22, 1765*. Collections of the New-York Historical Society 61. New York: New-York Historical Society, 1928.

Becker, E. Marie. "The 801 Westchester County Freeholders of 1763 and the Cortlandt Manor Land-Case Which Occasioned Their Listing." *New-York Historical Society Quarterly* 35, no. 3 (1951): 283–321.

Berman, Marshall. *All That Is Solid Melts Into Air: The Experience of Modernity*. New York: Simon & Schuster, 1982.

Bolton, Reginald Pelham. *Indian Life of Long Ago in the City of New York*. 1934. Reprint, Port Washington, NY: Kennikat, 1971.

———. *Indian Paths in the Great Metropolis*. New York: Museum of the American Indian Heye Foundation, 1922.

Bolton, Robert, Jr. *A History of the County of Westchester from Its First Settlement to the Present Time*. New York, 1848.

———. *History of the Protestant Episcopal Church, in the County of Westchester, from its Foundation, A.D. 1693 to A.D. 1853*. New York, 1855.

———. *The History of the Several Towns, Manors, and Patents of the County of Westchester from Its First Settlement to the Present Time*. New York, 1881.

Broes, Arthur T. "White Plains Goes to War, 1941–1942." *Westchester Historian* 72, no. 2 (1996): 37–46.

Bruce, Alfred, and Harold Sandbank. *A History of Prefabrication*. 1943. Reprint, New York: Arno, 1972.

Bruegel, Martin. *Farm, Shop, Landing: The Rise of a Market Society in the Hudson Valley, 1780–1860*. Durham, NC: Duke University Press, 2002.

Caffin, Charles H. "The Art of Edward J. Steichen." *Camera Work*, no. 30 (April 1910): 33–36.

———. *Photography as a Fine Art: The Achievements and Possibilities of Photographic Art in America*. 1901. Reprint, New York: American Photographic Book Publishing, 1972.

Calhoon, Robert McCluer. *The Loyalists in Revolutionary America, 1760–1781*. New York: Harcourt Brace Jovanovich, 1973.

Caro, Robert A. *The Power Broker: Robert Moses and the Fall of New York*. New York: Knopf, 1974.

Catalogue of Officers and Graduates of Columbia University. New York: Columbia University, 1906.

Chamberlain, Samuel. *Cape Cod in the Sun*. New York: Hastings House, 1937.

———. *Open House in New England*. New York: Hastings House, 1937.

———. *A Small House in the Sun: The Visage of Rural New England*. New York: Hastings House, 1936.

Christoph, Peter R., and Florence A. Christoph, eds. *Records of the Court of Assizes for the Colony of New York, 1665–1682*. Vol. 5, *New York Historical Manuscripts: English*. Baltimore: Genealogical Publishing, 1983.

Classic Houses of the Twenties: Loizeaux. 1927. Reprint. Philadelphia: Athenaeum/New York: Dover, 1992.

Cohen, Ronald D. "The Hartford Treaty of 1650: Anglo-Dutch Cooperation in the Seventeenth Century." *New-York Historical Society Quarterly* 53, no. 4 (1969): 311–32.

Connally, Ernest Allen. "The Cape Cod House: An Introductory Study." *Journal of the Society of Architectural Historians* 19, no. 2 (1960): 47–56.

Cook, Andrea C., John R. Southon, and Jeffrey Wadsworth. "Using Radiocarbon Dating to Establish the Age of Iron-Based Artifacts." *JOM* 55, no. 5 (2003). http://www.tms.org/pubs/journals/JOM/0305/Cook-0305.html.

Cooper, Susan Fenimore. "Small Family Memories." 1883. In *Correspondence of James Fenimore Cooper*, edited by James Fenimore Cooper, 7–72. New Haven, CT: Yale University Press, 1922. http://external.oneonta.edu.

Cox, W. H. "Housing Development at Danielson, Conn." *American Architect* 113, no. 2213 (1918): 677–85.

Crayon, Geoffrey [Washington Irving]. "Sleepy Hollow." In *The Works of Washington Irving*. New York, 1885.

Cronon, William. *Changes in the Land: Indians, Colonists, and the Ecology of New England*. New York: Hill & Wang, 1983.

Crosby, Katherine. *The Cape Type of House*. Library of Cape Cod History & Genealogy 10. Yarmouthport, MA: Register Press, 1927.

Davidson, Philip. *Propaganda and the American Revolution, 1763–1783*. Chapel Hill: University of North Carolina Press, 1941.

Davis, Matthew L. *Memoirs of Aaron Burr with Miscellaneous Selections from his Correspondence*. Vol. 1. New York, 1838.

Denton, Daniel. *A Brief Description of New York: Formerly called New-Netherlands with the Places thereunto Adjoyning*. 1670. Reprint, New York, 1845. http://books.google.com.

Derven, C. F. "Glossary of Terms Used in Slate Quarries Around Poultney, Vermont." 1938. In Document 86. Washington, DC: Library of Congress, 1936–40, http://lcweb2.loc.gov

Doane, Doris. *A Book of Cape Cod Houses*. Old Greenwich, CT: Chatham, 1970.

Downer, Jay, and James Owen. "Public Parks in Westchester County." In *History of Westchester County, New York*, edited by Alvah P. French, 959–1012. New York: Lewis Historical Publishing, 1925.

Downing, A. J. *The Architecture of Country Houses*. 1850. Reprint, New York: Da Capo, 1968.

———. *Cottage Residences, Rural Architecture & Landscape Gardening*. 1842. Reprint, Watkins Glen, NY: American Life Foundation, 1967.

Downing, Andrew Jackson. *A Treatise on the Theory and Practice of Landscape Gardening, Adapted to North America; with a View to the Improvement of Country Residences*. 6th edition. 1859. Reprint, New York: Funk & Wagnalls, 1967.

Drimmer, Harold. "The Westchester Militia in the American Revolution." *Westchester Historian* 73, no. 1 (1997): 3–11.

Dwight, Timothy. *Travels in New-England and New-York*. 4 vols. New Haven, 1822.

Dyer, William B. "The Chicago Salon." *Camera Notes* 4, no. 1 (1900): 69–72.

East, Robert A., and Jacob Judd, eds. *The Loyalist Americans: A Focus on Greater New York*. Tarrytown, NY: Sleepy Hollow Restorations, 1975.

Embury, Aymar II. *The Dutch Colonial House: Its Origin, Design, Modern Plan and Construction*. New York: McBride, Nast, 1913.

English, Mary O'Connor, ed. *Early Town Records of Mamaroneck*. Mamaroneck, NY: Town of Mamaroneck, 1979.

Fernow, B., ed. *Documents Relating to the History and Settlements of the Towns Along the Hudson and Mohawk Rivers (with the exception of Albany) from 1630 to 1684*. Albany, 1881.

Fischer, David Hackett. *Paul Revere's Ride*. New York: Oxford University Press, 1994.

Force, Peter, comp. *American Archives: Fifth Series, Containing a Documentary History of the United States of America, from the Declaration of Independence, July 4, 1776, to the Definitive Treaty of Peace with Great Britain, September 3, 1783*. American Archives 5. Vol. 3. Washington, DC, 1853.

———. *American Archives: Fourth Series, Containing a Documentary History of the English Colonies in North America, from the King's Message to Parliament, of March 7, 1774, to the Declaration of Independence of the United States*. American Archives 4. Vol. 4. Washington, DC, 1843.

Fox, Dixon Ryan. *Caleb Heathcote, Gentleman Colonist: The Story of a Career in the Province of New York, 1692–1721*. New York: Charles Scribner's Sons, 1926.

Fox, Dixon Ryan, ed. *The Minutes of the Court of Sessions (1657–1696), Westchester County, New York*. Publications of the Westchester County Historical Society 2. White Plains, NY: Westchester County Historical Society, 1924.

French, Alvah, ed. *History of Westchester County, New York*. New York: Lewis Historical Publishing, 1925.

Fulcher, William G. "Recorded Action Taken by Freeholders and Inhabitants of the Town of Mamaroneck as Found in the Town Record." *Quarterly Bulletin of the Westchester County Historical Society* 13, no. 1 (1937): 39–48.

Gage, Mary, and James Gage. *The Art of Splitting Stone: Early Rock Quarrying Methods in Pre-Industrial New England, 1630–1825*. 2nd ed. Amesbury, MA: privately printed, 2005.

Galassi, Peter. *American Photography, 1890–1965, from The Museum of Modern Art, New York*. With essay by Luc Sante. New York: Museum of Modern Art, 1995.

Gebhard, David. "The American Colonial Revival in the 1930s." *Winterthur Portfolio* 22, no. 2/3 (1987): 109–48.

Gehring, Charles T., and Robert S. Grumet. "Observations of the Indians from Jasper Danckaerts's Journal, 1679–1680." *William and Mary Quarterly*, 3rd ser., 44, no. 1 (1987): 104–20.

Gehring, Charles T., and William A. Starna. "Dutch and Indians in the Hudson Valley: The Early Period." *Hudson Valley Regional Review* 9, no. 2 (1992): 1–25.

Goddard, Ives. "Delaware." In *Northeast*, vol. 15 of *Handbook of North American Indian*, edited by Bruce G. Trigger, 213–39. Washington, DC: Smithsonian Institution, 1978.

Gowans, Alan. *The Comfortable House: North American Suburban Architecture, 1890–1930*. Cambridge, MA: MIT Press, 1986.

Greene, Asa. *A Glance at New York*. New York, 1837.

Greene, Evarts B., and Virginia D. Harrington. *American Population Before the Federal Census of 1790*. New York: Columbia University Press, 1932.

Grier, Katherine C. *Pets in America: A History*. Chapel Hill: University of North Carolina Press, 2006.

Group, Harold E., ed. *House-of-the-Month Book of Small Houses*. Garden City, NY: Garden City Publishing, 1946.

Gutfreund, Owen. *Twentieth-Century Sprawl: Highways and the Reshaping of the American Landscape*. New York: Oxford University Press, 2004.

Haefeli, Evan. "On First Contact and Apotheosis: Manitou and Men in North America." *Ethnohistory* 54, no. 3 (2007): 407–43.

Hagenbeck, Carl. *Beasts and Men: Being Carl Hagenbeck's Experiences for Half a Century among Wild Animals*. Translated by Hugh S. R. Elliot and A. G. Thacker. London: Longmans, Green, 1909.

Halpin, Kay. "Sears, Roebuck's Best-kept Secret." *Historic Preservation* 33, no. 5 (1981): 25–29.

Harwood, Herbert H. Jr. *The New York, Westchester & Boston Railway: J. P. Morgan's Magnificent Mistake*. Bloomington: Indiana University Press, 2008.

Hawkins, J. Harold. *Cape Cod Colonial: McCall's Twelfth Home of the Month*. Dayton, OH: McCall's Magazine, 1937.

Hayden, Dolores. *Building Suburbia: Green Fields and Urban Growth, 1820–2000*. New York: Pantheon Books, 2003.

Heckewelder, John. *History, Manners, and Customs of the Indian Nations Who Once Inhabited Pennsylvania and the Neighboring States*. 1876. Reprint, New York: Arno, 1971.

Henderson, Robert M. *D. W. Griffith: His Life and Work*. New York: Oxford University Press, 1972.

Historic Pelham. www.historicpelham.com.

Hoage, R. J., and William A. Deiss, eds. *New Worlds, New Animals: From Menagerie to Zoological Park in the Nineteenth Century*. Baltimore: Johns Hopkins University Press, 1996.

Horwitz, Tony. *A Voyage Long and Strange: Rediscovering the New World*. New York: Holt, 2008.

Hufeland, Otto. *Westchester County During the American Revolution, 1775–1783*. White Plains, NY: Westchester County Historical Society, 1926.

Huth, Hans. *Nature and the American: Three Centuries of Changing Attitudes*. Lincoln: University of Nebraska Press, 1957.

Jackson, Donald, and Dorothy Twohig, eds. *The Diaries of George Washington*. Vol 1. Charlottesville: University Press of Virginia, 1976. http://memory.loc.gov/ammem/gwhome.html.

Jackson, Kenneth T. *Crabgrass Frontier: The Suburbanization of the United States*. New York: Oxford University Press, 1985.

Jacobs, Jaap. *New Netherland: A Dutch Colony in Seventeenth-Century America*. Leiden: Brill, 2005.

James, Bartlett Burleigh, and J. Franklin Jameson, eds. *Journal of Jasper Danckaerts, 1679–1680*. New York: Scribner's, 1913.

Jameson, J. Franklin, ed., *Narratives of New Netherland, 1609–1664.* 1909. Reprint, New York: Barnes & Noble, 1967.

Jenkins, Stephen. *The Old Boston Post Road.* New York: Putnam's Sons, 1913.

Johnson, Herbert Alan. "The Prerogative Court of New York, 1686–1776." *American Journal of Legal History* 17, no. 2 (1973): 95–144.

Josephy, Alvin M. Jr. *America in 1492: The World of the Indian Peoples Before the Arrival of Columbus.* New York: Knopf, 1992.

Journals of the Provincial Congress, Provincial Convention, Committee of Safety and Council of Safety of the State of New-York, 1775–1776–1777. Albany, 1842.

Juet, Robert. "Journal of Hudson's Voyage." [1609]. In *New American World: A Documentary History of North America to 1612.* Vol. 3, edited by David B. Quinn, 471–88. New York: Arno, 1979.

Kelly, Barbara M. *Expanding the American Dream: Building and Rebuilding Levittown.* Albany: State University of New York Press, 1993.

Kemble, Stephen. William Howe, Henry Clinton, and Daniel Jones. *The Kemble Papers.* Vol. 16, New-York Historical Society: Collections, Publications Fund Series. New York, 1884.

Ketchum, Richard. *Divided Loyalties: How the American Revolution Came to New York.* New York: Holt, 2002.

Kim, Sung Bok. "The Limits of Politicization in the American Revolution: The Experience of Westchester County, New York." *Journal of American History* 80, no. 3 (1993): 868–89.

Kittredge, Henry C. *Cape Cod: Its People and Their History.* Boston: Houghton Mifflin, 1930.

Knight, Sarah Kemble. "The Journal of Madam Knight." 1704–05. In *The Puritans*, edited by Perry Miller and Thomas H. Johnson. New York: American Book Company, 1938. http://mith2.umd.edu/eada/html/display.php?docs=knight_journal.xml.

Krafft, Johann Carl Philipp von. *Journal of Lieutenant John Charles Philip von Krafft of the Regiment von Bose, 1776–1784.* Collections of the New-York Historical Society for the Year 1882. New York, 1883.

Kraft, Herbert C. *The Lenape-Delaware Indian Heritage: 10,000 B.C.–A.D. 2000.* Lenape Books, 2001.

———. "The Northern Lenape in Prehistoric and Early Colonial Times." In *The Lenape Indian: A Symposium*, edited by Herbert C. Kraft, 1–18. South Orange, NJ: Archaeological Research Center, Seton Hall University, 1984.

Land Developers and Home Builders Division of National Association of Real Estate Boards. *Home of the Month: Selected for its Livability in Cooperation with McCall's Magazine, June 1937*, www.realtor.org.

"Landmarks in American Civil Engineering: Interstate Highway System." *Civil Engineering* 72, no. 11/12 (2002): 141.

Leavitt, Helen. *Superhighway – Superhoax.* Garden City, NY: Doubleday, 1970.

Lederer, Richard M. Jr. "Population Tables for Westchester County: 1698–1980." *Westchester Historian* 64, no. 3 (1988): 81–92.

Lessard, Suzannah. "Reflections—The Suburban Landscape: Oyster Bay, Long Island." *New Yorker*, October 11, 1976, 44–79.

Lippsett, Paula B. *Mamaroneck Town: A History of "The Gathering Place," 1661–1997.* Mamaroneck, NY: Town of Mamaroneck, 1997.

LoGiudice, Mary P., ed. *Celebration: Village of Mamaroneck Centennial, 1895–1995.* Mamaroneck, NY: Village of Mamaroneck, 1995.

Longwell, Dennis. *Steichen: The Master Prints, 1895–1914, The Symbolist Period.* New York: Museum of Modern Art, 1978.

Longworth's American Almanac, New-York Register, and City Directory. New York, 1813–21.

Lydon, James G. "New York and the Slave Trade, 1700–1774." *William and Mary Quarterly*, 3rd ser., 35, no. 2 (1978): 375–94.

Maass, Richard. "'We Think He Deserves To Suffer': Keeping an Eye on Westchester." *Westchester Historian* 66, no. 2 (1990), 35–41.

Magruder, Charles. "The White Pine Monograph Series." *Journal of the Society of Architectural Historians* 22, no. 1 (1963): 39–41.

Mamaroneck 1661–1961: A Panorama of Her First Three Centuries. Mamaroneck, NY: Town of Mamaroneck, 1961.

McManus, Edgar J. *A History of Negro Slavery in New York.* Syracuse, NY: Syracuse University Press, 1966.

Minutes of the Common Council of the City of New York, 1675–1776. Vol. 3. New York: Dodd, Mead, 1905.

Mixer, Knowlton. *Old Houses of New England.* New York: Macmillan, 1927.

Mooney's Megaphone. 1927–28.

Mott, Frank Luther. *A History of American Magazines, 1741–1930.* 5 vols. Cambridge, MA: Belknap of Harvard University Press, 1957.

Myers, Albert Cook, ed. *Narratives of Early Pennsylvania, West New Jersey, and Delaware, 1630–1707.* New York: Scribner's Sons, 1912.

Nabokov, Peter, and Dean Snow. "Farmers of the Woodlands." In *America in 1492*, edited by Alvin M. Josephy Jr., 119–45. New York: Knopf, 1992.

Naef, Weston J. *The Collection of Alfred Stieglitz: Fifty Pioneers of Modern Photography.* New York: Viking/Metropolitan Museum of Art, 1978.

Niven, Penelope. *Steichen: A Biography.* New York: Clarkson Potter, 1997.

Nutting, Wallace. *Massachusetts Beautiful.* Framingham, MA: Old America, 1923.

Oatman, Russell Swinton. *The Cape Cod Collection of House Designs.* Princeton, MA: R. S. Oatman, 1985.

O'Callaghan, E. B., ed. *The Documentary History of the State of New York.* Vol. 3. Albany, 1850.

———. *Documents Relative to the Colonial History of the State of New-York Procured in Holland, England and France.* 15 vols. Albany, 1853–87.

———. *History of New Netherland.* 2nd edition. 2 vols. New York, 1855.

Paltsits, Victor Hugo, ed. *Minutes of the Executive Council of the Province of New York: Administration of Francis Lovelace, 1668–1673.* 2 vols. Albany: State of New York, 1910.

Panetta, Roger. "Westchester, the American Suburb: A New Narrative." In *Westchester, the American Suburb*, edited by Roger Panetta, 5–75. New York: Fordham University Press/Yonkers, NY: Hudson River Museum, 2006.

Patton, Phil. *Open Road: A Celebration of the American Highway.* New York: Simon & Schuster, 1986.

Pelletreau, William S., ed. *The Second Book of Records of the Town of Southampton, Long Island, N.Y. with other Ancient Documents of Historic Value.* Sag Harbor, NY, 1877.

Poor, Alfred Easton. *Colonial Architecture of Cape Cod, Nantucket and Martha's Vineyard.* New York: Helburn, 1932.

Potter, Janice. *The Liberty We Seek: Loyalist Ideology in Colonial New York and Massachusetts.* Cambridge, MA: Harvard University Press, 1983.

Pratt, Daniel J. *Report of the Regents of the University on the Boundaries of the State of New York.* Vol. 2. Albany, 1884.

Pritts, Gloria. "D. W. Griffith Studio in Mamaroneck." *Conversations About Mamaroneck & Old Rye Neck.* (Fall 1998): 13–15.

Revolutionary Services and Civil Life of General William Hull, Prepared from his Manuscripts, by his daughter, Mrs. Maria Campbell. New York, 1848.

Richardson, John. *The Annals of London: A Year-by-Year Record of a Thousand Years of History.* Berkeley: University of California Press, 2000.

Sabine, Lorenzo. *Biographical Sketches of Loyalists of the American Revolution with an Historical Essay*, 2nd ed. 1864. Reprint, Baltimore: Genealogical Publishing, 1979.

Salisbury, Neal. "The Indians' Old World: Native Americans and the Coming of Europeans." *William and Mary Quarterly*, 3rd ser., 53, no. 3 (1996): 435–58.

Sanchis, Frank E. *American Architecture, Westchester County, New York: Colonial to Contemporary.* Harrison, NY: Harbor Hills, 1977.

Sandburg, Carl. *Steichen the Photographer.* New York: Harcourt, Brace, 1929.

Sanderson, Eric. *Mannahatta: A Natural History of New York City.* New York: Abrams, 2009.

Scharf, J. Thomas. *History of Westchester County, New York Including Morrisania, Kings Bridge, and West Farms, which have been Annexed to New York City.* 2 vols. Philadelphia, 1886.

Schuler, Stanley. *The Cape Cod House: America's Most Popular Home*. Exton, PA: Schiffer, 1982.

Schweitzer, Robert, and Michael W. R. Davis. *America's Favorite Homes: Mail-Order Catalogues as a Guide to Popular Early 20th-Century Houses*. Detroit: Wayne State University Press, 1990.

[Seabury, Samuel]. *Free Thoughts on the Proceedings of the Continental Congress . . . in a Letter to the Farmers. . . .* New York, [November 16,] 1774.

———. *A View of the Controversy Between Great Britain and her Colonies . . . in a Letter To the Author of a Full Vindication of the Measures of the Congress. . . .* New York, [December 24,] 1774.

Sears Archives Historic Homes, www.searsarchives.com.

Sears, Roebuck and Co. *Sears, Roebuck Catalog of Houses, 1926: An Unabridged Reprint*. 1926. Reprint, Philadelphia: Athenaeum/New York: Dover, 1991.

Shonnard, Frederic, and W. W. Spooner. *History of Westchester County, New York, from its Earliest Settlement to the Year 1900*. New York: New York History, 1900.

Shorto, Russell. *The Island at the Center of the World: The Epic Story of Dutch Manhattan and the Forgotten Colony That Shaped America*. New York: Doubleday, 2004.

Skinner, Alanson. *Exploration of Aboriginal Sites at Throgs Neck and Clasons Point, New York City*. Vol. 5, *Contribution from the Museum of the American Indian, Heye Foundation*. New York: Museum of the American Indian Heye Foundation, 1919.

Smith, Joel. *Edward Steichen: The Early Years*. Princeton, NJ: Princeton University Press/New York: Metropolitan Museum of Art, 1999.

Smith, S. D. *Slavery, Family, and Gentry Capitalism in the British Atlantic: The World of the Lascelles, 1648–1834*. Cambridge: Cambridge University Press, 2006.

Snow, Dean R., and Kim M. Lamphear. "European Contact and Indian Depopulation in the Northeast: The Timing of the First Epidemics." *Ethnohistory* 35, no. 1 (1988): 15–33.

Spikes, Judith Doolin. *Larchmont, N.Y.: People and Places*. Larchmont, NY: Fountain Square Books, 1991.

State of New York, Commissioners Appointed to Settle the Disputed Boundary Lines with the State of Connecticut. *Report of the Regents of the University, on the Boundaries of the State of New York*. 2 vols. Albany, 1874–78.

State of New York. *Public Papers of George Clinton, First Governor of New York*. Vol. 5. Albany, NY, 1901.

———. *Report of the Regents of the University on the Boundaries of the State of New York*. 2 vols. Albany, 1884.

State of New York, Senate. *Report of the Commissioners Appointed to Ascertain the Boundary Line Between the States of New-York and Connecticut, appointed April 9, 1856*. Albany, NY, [1857].

"Statistics of Fences in the United States." In *Report of the Commissioner of Agriculture for the Year 1871*, 497–512. Washington, DC, 1872.

St. Clair, David J. *The Motorization of American Cities*. New York: Praeger, 1986.

Steichen, Edward. *A Life in Photography*. Garden City, NY: Doubleday/New York: Museum of Modern Art, 1963.

Steichen, Joanna. *Steichen's Legacy: Photographs, 1895–1973*. New York: Knopf, 2000.

Steiner, Bruce E. *Samuel Seabury, 1729–1796: A Study in the High Church Tradition*. Athens: Ohio University Press, 1971.

Stevenson, Katherine Cole, and H. Ward Jandl. *Houses By Mail: A Guide to Houses from Sears, Roebuck and Company*. New York: Wiley/Preservation Press, 1986.

Stilgoe, John R. *Borderland: Origins of the American Suburb, 1820–1939*. New Haven, CT: Yale University Press, 1988.

Thomas, Peter A. "Cultural Change on the Southern New England Frontier, 1630–1665." In *Cultures in Contact: The Impact of European Contacts on Native American Cultural Institutions, A.D. 1000–1800*, edited by William W. Fitzhugh, 131–61. Washington, DC: Smithsonian Institution, 1985.

Thoreau, Henry D. *Cape Cod/Henry D. Thoreau*. Edited by Joseph J. Moldenhauer. Princeton, NJ: Princeton University Press, 1988.

Thornton, Rosemary. *The Houses That Sears Built: Everything You Ever Wanted to Know About Sears Catalog Homes*. Alton, IL: Gentle Beam, 2002.

Thorson, Robert M. *Exploring Stone Walls: A Field Guide to New England's Stone Walls*. New York: Walker, 2005.

Thwaites, Reuben Gold. *Travels and Explorations of the Jesuit Missionaries in New France, 1610–1791*. Vol. 6, *The Jesuit Relations and Allied Documents*. Cleveland, 1897.

Trigger, Bruce. "Early Native North American Responses to European Contact: Romantic versus Rationalistic Interpretations." *Journal of American History* 77, no. 4 (1991): 1195–215.

Tyler, Moses Coit. *The Literary History of the American Revolution, 1763–1783*. 2 vols. New York: Ungar, 1957.

Ubelaker, Douglas H. "North American Indian Population Size: Changing Perspectives." In *Disease and Demography in the Americas*, edited by John W. Verano and Douglas H. Ubelaker, 169–76. Washington, DC: Smithsonian Institution, 1992.

Ultan, Lloyd. *The Bronx In The Frontier Era*. Dubuque, Iowa: Kendall/Hunt, 1993.

Van der Donck, Adriaen. *A Description of New Netherland*. Edited by Charles T. Gehring and William A. Starna. Lincoln: University of Nebraska Press, 2008.

"Vital Records of Christ's Church at Rye, Westchester County, New York." *New York Genealogical and Biographical Society Record* 37, no. 4 (1906): 259.

"The Waldorf Mill and the Legend of the White Deer." *Westchester Historian* 32, no. 1 (1956): 10.

Washington, George. *The Writings of George Washington from the Original Manuscript Sources, 1745–1799*. Edited by John C. Fitzpatrick. Vol. 6. Washington, DC: US Government Printing Office, 1932.

Weigold, Marilyn E. *Pioneering in Parks and Parkways: Westchester County, New York, 1895–1945*. Essays in Public Works History 9. Chicago: Public Works Historical Society, 1980.

———. "Roads to No Where." *Westchester Historian* 55, no. 4 (1979): 87–89.

"Where We Get Our Water." In *Facts, Figures and Photographs of Interest to the Residents of the Town of Mamaroneck*. Mamaroneck, NY: Town of Mamaroneck, 1955.

Wills, Royal Barry, Associates. *Houses for Good Living*. Stamford, CT: Architectural Book, 1993.

Index